Microsoft® SQL Server® 2008 Analysis Services Step by Step

Scott Cameron,
Hitachi Consulting

PUBLISHED BY
Microsoft Press
A Division of Microsoft Corporation
One Microsoft Way
Redmond, Washington 98052-6399

Copyright © 2009 by Hitachi Consulting

Library of Congress Control Number: 2009920805

Printed and bound in the United States of America.

1 2 3 4 5 6 7 8 9   QWT   4 3 2 1 0 9

Distributed in Canada by H.B. Fenn and Company Ltd.

A CIP catalogue record for this book is available from the British Library.

Microsoft Press books are available through booksellers and distributors worldwide. For further information about international editions, contact your local Microsoft Corporation office or contact Microsoft Press International directly at fax (425) 936-7329. Visit our Web site at www.microsoft.com/mspress. Send comments to mspinput@microsoft.com.

Microsoft, Microsoft Press, Access, Excel, Internet Explorer, PerformancePoint, PivotChart, PivotTable, SharePoint, SQL Server, Visio, Visual Studio, Windows, Windows Server, and Windows Vista are either registered trademarks or trademarks of the Microsoft group of companies. Other product and company names mentioned herein may be the trademarks of their respective owners.

The example companies, organizations, products, domain names, e-mail addresses, logos, people, places, and events depicted herein are fictitious. No association with any real company, organization, product, domain name, e-mail address, logo, person, place, or event is intended or should be inferred.

This book expresses the author's views and opinions. The information contair
express, statutory, or implied warranties. Neither the authors, Microsoft Corp
will be held liable for any damages caused or alleged to be caused either direc

Acquisitions Editor: Ken Jones
Developmental Editor: Sally Stickney
Project Editor: Lynn Finnel
Editorial Production: Custom Editorial Productions, Inc.
Technical Reviewer: John Welch. Technical Review services provided by Cor
member of CM Group, Ltd.
Cover: Tom Draper Design

Body Part No. X14-72193

Contents at a Glance

Table of Contents

Part I **Understanding Business Intelligence and Analysis Services**

What do you think of this book? We want to hear from you!

Microsoft is interested in hearing your feedback so we can continually improve our books and learning resources for you. To participate in a brief online survey, please visit:

www.microsoft.com/learning/booksurvey/

What do you think of this book? We want to hear from you!

Microsoft is interested in hearing your feedback so we can continually improve our books and learning resources for you. To participate in a brief online survey, please visit:

www.microsoft.com/learning/booksurvey/

Acknowledgments

I am very grateful for the assistance and support I received from Hitachi Consulting while writing SQL Server 2008 Analysis Services Step by Step. Kevin Davis managed the project, provided daily motivation, and did a masterful job of juggling the schedule, coordinating the efforts of the co-authors and contributing authors, and communicating with Microsoft Press. Co-authors Dave DuVarney, Joe Kasprzak, and Bryan Smith; and contributing authors Harlan Smith, Phillip Duong, Shay Jones, Robert Brawn, and Renee De Voursney generously contri-buted their personal time and eased my workload. Reed Jacobsen, my long-time mentor, and Stacia Misner, Paul Turley, Richard Osbourn, and Ryan Clay contributed their technical expertise. Hilary Feier gave encouragement and, along with Carr Krueger, Drew Naukum, and Lance Baldwin, arranged the support from Hitachi Consulting that granted to me the time to write this book. David Han and Mary Gianopoulos performed additional project management.

I appreciate the opportunity to write this book given to me by Microsoft Press and the guidance I received from the team of editors. Thanks to Ken Jones, program manager, and Sally Stickney, developmental editor, who sponsored and initiated the project; and to Lynn Finnel, project editor, who showed great patience and assembled a great team of editors. Thanks also to technical editors John Welch, Matthew Roche, and Phillippe Freddi, who helped ensure that the explanations and procedures are correct and understandable, and editors Megan Smith-Creed, Becka McKay, Julie Hotchkiss, and Tom Lewis.

Finally, thanks to my wife Tarya, who patiently endured the many days when the alarm clock went off very early in the morning.

My apologies to anyone I may have overlooked. To all who have contributed to the creation of this book, my most sincere thanks.

Scott Cameron
March 2009

Introduction

Microsoft SQL Server 2008 Analysis Services is the multidimensional online analytical processing (OLAP) component of Microsoft SQL Server 2008 that integrates relational and OLAP data for business intelligence (BI) analytical solutions. The goal of this book is to show you how to use the tools and features of Analysis Services so you can easily create, manage, and share OLAP cubes within your organization. Step-by-step exercises are included to prepare you for developing your own BI solutions.

To help you learn the many features of Analysis Services, this book is organized into four parts. Part I, "Understanding Business Intelligence and Analysis Services," introduces BI, multidimensional analysis, and OLAP and explains how Analysis Services implements the benefits of OLAP. Part II, "Design Fundamentals," teaches you how to design data sources, data source views, dimensions, and cubes. Part III, "Advanced Design," shows you how to use Multidimensional Expressions (MDX) and aggregate functions to perform complex calculations and summarizations, and to create key performance indicators (KPIs). In addition, this part covers special Analysis Services features for advanced dimension design, financial analysis, globalization, and a variety of interactions that extend the analytical capabilities of cubes. You will also learn how to create analytical reports using Microsoft Office Excel and SQL Server 2008 Reporting Services. Part IV, "Production Management," explains how to use security to control access to cubes and to restrict the data that a particular user can see, how to design partitions to manage database scalability, and how to manage and monitor Analysis Services databases.

Finding Your Best Starting Point in This Book

This book covers the full life cycle of an Analysis Services solution from development to deployment. If you're responsible only for certain activities, you can choose to read the chapters that apply to your situation and skip the remaining chapters. Use the following table to find your best starting point.

If you are	Follow these steps
An information consumer who uses OLAP to make decisions	1. Install the practice files as described in the section, "Installing and Using the Practice Files." 2. Work through Parts I and II to become familiar with the basic capabilities of Analysis Services. 3. Skim chapters of interest to you in Part III to understand how additional features might meet your analytical requirements.
A BI analyst who develops OLAP models and proto- types for business analysis	1. Install the practice files as described in the section, "Installing and Using the Practice Files." 2. Skim Part I to review BI concepts and learn how Analysis Services implements OLAP. 3. Work through Part II to develop the necessary skills to create a prototype cube. 4. Review the chapters that interest you in Parts III and IV to learn about advanced features of Analysis Services, to understand how cubes are accessed by users, and learn how cubes are managed after they are put into production.
An administrator who maintains server resources or production migration processes	1. Install the practice files as described in the section, "Installing and Using the Practice Files." 2. Skim Parts I, II, and III to understand the functionality that is included in Analysis Services. 3. Work through Part IV to learn how to manage and secure cube access and content on the server as well as how to configure, monitor, and manage server components and performance.
A BI architect who designs and develops analytical solutions	1. Install the practice files as described in the section, "Installing and Using the Practice Files." 2. Complete Part I to become familiar with the benefits of Analysis Services. 3. Work through Parts II and III to learn how to create dimensions and cubes and how to implement advanced design techniques. 4. Complete Part IV to understand how to design cubes that imple- ment the security, performance, and processing features of Analysis Services.

Conventions and Features in This Book

This book presents information using conventions designed to make the information read- able and easy to follow. Before you start, read the following list, which explains conventions you'll see throughout the book and points out helpful features that you might want to use.

Conventions

- Each exercise is a series of tasks. Each task is presented as a series of numbered steps (1, 2, and so on).

- Notes labeled "tip" provide additional information or alternative methods for completing a step successfully.

- Notes labeled "important" alert you to information you need to check before continuing.

- Text that you type appears in **bold**.

- A plus sign (+) between two key names means that you must press those keys at the same time. For example, "Press Alt+Tab" means that you hold down the Alt key while you press the Tab key.

Hardware and Software Requirements

You'll need the following hardware and software to complete the practice exercises in this book:

- A 32-bit or 64-bit version of SQL Server 2008 Enterprise edition or SQL Server 2008 Developer edition. You need to install the Database Engine, Analysis Services, and Reporting Services components of SQL Server 2008. During installation add your Windows login ID to the list of SQL Server and Analysis Services system administrators.

> **Tip** You can download a fully functional 180-day trial version of SQL Server 2008 Enterprise Edition from *http://www.microsoft.com/sqlserver/2008/en/us/trial-software.aspx*.

- SQL Server 2008 Enterprise Edition requires Microsoft Windows Server 2008 or Windows Server 2003 SP2. SQL Server 2008 Developer Edition requires Microsoft Windows Server 2008, Windows Server 2003 SP2, Windows Vista, or Windows XP SP2.

- 1.0 GHz Pentium III+ processor (2.0 Ghz or faster recommended) for 32-bit SQL Server 2008.

- 1.4 Ghz (2.0 Ghz or faster recommended) AMD Opteron, AMD Athlon 64, Intel Xeon with Intel EM64T support, Intel Pentium IV with EM64T support processor, or 1.0 Ghz or faster Itanium processor for 64-bit SQL Server 2008.

- 512 MB (2 GB or more recommended) of available physical RAM.

- Video with VGA or higher resolution with at least 1,024 x 768 pixel resolution.

- CD-ROM or DVD-ROM drive.

- Microsoft mouse or compatible pointing device.

Detailed requirements for installing SQL Server 2008 can be found in the SQL Server Books Online article "Hardware and Software Requirements for Installing SQL Server 2008" (*http://msdn.microsoft.com/en-us/library/ms143506.aspx*).

The step-by-step exercises in this book and the accompanying practice files were tested using Windows Vista Enterprise Service Pack 1 and Microsoft SQL Server 2008 Developer Edition. If you're using another version of the operating system or SQL Server 2008, you might notice some slight differences.

Practice Files and SQL Server 2008 Configuration

The companion CD inside this book contains the practice files that you'll use as you perform the exercises. The practice files and the step-by-step instructions in the lessons let you learn by doing, which is an easy and effective way to acquire and remember new skills. The companion CD also contains a SQL Server 2008 database that is the data source for the analytical solutions that you will create and use throughout this book.

Installing the Practice Files

Follow these steps to install the practice files on your computer so that you can use them with the exercises.

1. Remove the companion CD from the package inside this book and insert it into your CD-ROM drive.

 Note An end user license agreement should open automatically. If this agreement does not appear, open Computer on the desktop or Start menu, double-click the icon for your CD-ROM drive, and then double-click StartCD.exe.

2. Review the end user license agreement. If you accept the terms, select the accept option and then click Next.

   A menu will appear with options related to the book.

3. Click Install Practice files.

4. Follow the instructions that appear.

   The practice files will be copied from the CD to your hard drive. The default installation folder is C:\Microsoft Press\Analysis Services 2008 SBS. If you install the practice files in a different location, you'll need to reference the new location when working through the exercises. Each chapter in this book explains when and how to use any practice files for that chapter. When it's time to use a practice file, the book will list the instructions for how to open the file.

Tip In the C:\Microsoft Press\Analysis Services 2008 SBS\Answers folder, you'll find a separate folder for each chapter in which you make changes to the practice files. The files in these folders are copies of these sample files when you complete a chapter. You can refer to these files if you want to preview the results of completing all exercises in a chapter.

5. Remove the CD from your CD-ROM drive.

Configuring SQL Server 2008

The exercises in this book will have you create an Analysis Services database and populate that database using data contained in a SQL Server database. The exercises assume that SQL Server 2008 is installed on your computer. The following steps will guide you through the process of configuring SQL Server and Analysis Services so that you can complete the exercises. To complete these steps you must first install the practice files; you will also need to be a member of the Administrators group on your computer.

Analysis Services will need to connect to SQL Server, so you must first discover the Windows login user name for Analysis Services and then grant SQL Server permissions to that user name.

1. On the Microsoft Windows task bar, click Start. In the Search box, type **services** and then in the Programs group select Services. If a User Account Control dialog box appears, click Continue. (If you are using Windows XP or Windows Server 2003, click Start, select Control Panel, select Administrative Tools, and then select Services.)

2. In the Services window, find SQL Server Analysis Services in the Name column and make a note of the value in the Log On As column.

Important The Analysis Services login user name will be a two-part name with the format *DomainName\Username* or *.\Username* or it may be *Network Service* or *Local Service*. You will use this user name in step 5.

3. Close the Services window.

4. On the Microsoft Windows task bar, click the Start button and then click Computer. In Windows Explorer, browse to C:\Microsoft Press\Analysis Services 2008 SBS\Setup. Right-click SSAS_Login.sql and select Open. In the Connect To Database Engine dialog box, click Cancel.

   Microsoft SQL Server Management Studio opens and displays the SSAS_Login.sql file in edit mode. This SQL script file creates a SQL Server login for Analysis Services (unless it already exists) and then grants permissions to that login. You will need to edit the script and enter the Analysis Services login user name that you discovered in step 2.

Chapter 1
Business Intelligence: A Data Analysis Foundation

In this chapter, you will learn how to:

- Understand the purpose and structure of a business intelligence system.
- Understand multidimensional data analysis concepts.
- Learn how a data warehouse implements a dimensional data model.
- Learn how Analysis Services implements a dimensional data model.

Introducing Business Intelligence

Business intelligence (BI) is information that has been derived from the data contained in your organization's operational systems or external sources. Business intelligence should help you make better decisions faster. Suppose you are the president of a small, new company, Adventure Works Cycles, that manufactures and sells bicycles, bicycle components, clothing, and accessories for North American, European, and Asian markets. Adventure Works needs to grow, but has limited resources to support expansion. You have decisions to make, and to make those decisions you must have particular information. You keep up with general business trends by reading the *Wall Street Journal*, and you keep a bookmark in your browser pointed at *www.bloomberg.com*. This information, along with your experience, enables you to make subjective, "gut-feeling" decisions. But you want to start making objective, by-the-numbers decisions. The numbers you need are in your company's order-processing, accounting, human resources, and other business systems. You also need to get third-party-provided market forecasts and exchange rates. You need a tool that will bring together all of this information and put it at your fingertips. That tool is a BI system. A BI system is the solution for gathering data from multiple sources, transforming that data so that it is consistent and stored in a single location, and presenting the information to you for analysis and decision making.

A BI system can have up to five layers:

1. A data source layer
2. A data transformation layer
3. A data storage and retrieval layer
4. An analytical layer
5. A presentation layer

The data source layer is composed of the data in the systems your organization uses to conduct its day-to-day operations; data in text files, Microsoft Office Excel spreadsheets, or Microsoft Office Access databases; and data you acquire from external sources. Because this data is in many different sources, it is extremely difficult to use it to create reports and perform analysis. The data transformation layer is used to extract the data from the multiple sources, modify the data so that it is internally consistent, and load it into a data storage system.

The data storage and retrieval layer is a data warehouse that has been created in a relational database management system. The data warehouse is the system of record. It contains authoritative numbers for your organization. A mature enterprise data warehouse contains data related to all aspects of your organization. Your data warehouse is a busy and complex place. Data loads occur monthly, weekly, daily, or even more frequently. Reports and analytical queries run day and night. To reduce the burden on the data warehouse and to simplify user access, data about individual subject areas is extracted from your data warehouse, summarized, and loaded into data marts. The data marts can be relational databases or they can be multidimensional OLAP (online analytical processing) databases. Analysis Services is one example of a multidimensional OLAP database.

The purpose of the analytical layer of your BI system is to turn data into information and to provide quick and easy access to that information for decision makers. Multidimensional OLAP databases form the analytical layer of your BI system. When detailed data from the data warehouse is loaded into a multidimensional OLAP database, summarized values are precalculated. Because summary values are stored in the database, reports and analytical queries execute quickly. When data is loaded into a multidimensional OLAP database, metadata is added to the data. Metadata is data about the data. The metadata in an OLAP database includes information about relationships and hierarchies in the data, how the data should be sorted and summarized, and how it should be formatted for presentation. The metadata in the OLAP database is what turns data into information. Complex calculations can be created and then stored in the OLAP database. This makes information access easier, because report and query writers don't have to repeatedly create calculations, and everyone in your organization will be able to use the exact same calculation formulas.

Reporting and visualization tools form the presentation layer of your BI system. Applications in the presentation layer of your BI system can query your data warehouse, data marts, or multidimensional OLAP databases and present it in a variety of formats. Your BI system can send reports to your outside sales force and delivery workers' mobile phones to direct their daily activities. Analytic workflow diagrams illustrate complex business processes and at each node show the information decision makers need to make high-valued choices. Interactive analytical reports with slice-and-dice, pivot, and drilldown capabilities and multidimensional data visualizations help managers and analysts troubleshoot issues and find information to help your organization operate more efficiently and take advantage of new opportunities. Dashboard reports with key performance indicators enable executives to quickly determine whether the organization is meeting its strategic objectives.

You shouldn't be dogmatic about what constitutes your BI system. A BI system can have all the layers mentioned earlier or only a few. For example, if you're using Analysis Services in a near-real-time monitoring system, you can load data directly from a manufacturing systems-control database into your multidimensional OLAP database every few minutes. The presentation layer of your BI system then reads data from Analysis Services and displays a diagram showing each machine on the production line and how well it is currently performing compared to its long-term average. This BI system has no data warehouse and the data transformation and analytical layers are combined. The complexity of your BI system isn't important. What is important is that your BI system provides information that is relevant to the decisions you need to make, understandable and persuasive, reliable, quick and easy to access and manipulate, and available when you need it.

Multidimensional Data Analysis

You use your BI system to perform multidimensional data analysis. Don't let this term intimidate you. You most likely have already been performing multidimensional data analysis for some time. If you've ever read a report that shows numerical data by various attributes—for example, completed surveys by customer segment by month—you have performed multidimensional data analysis. In this case, customer segment and month are the dimensions you are using to analyze survey data.

In this section, you will learn about multidimensional data analysis concepts such as attributes, hierarchies, and dimensions. This will prepare you for Chapter 2, "Understanding OLAP and Analysis Services," in which you will learn about multidimensional OLAP databases and the particular advantages of Analysis Services.

Attributes in Data Analysis

To help you understand attributes and hierarchies, consider the scenario in which, as president of Adventure Works Cycles, you would like to know more about how your company is performing. You ask your business analyst for a report and the answer he gives you is shown in Table 1-1.

TABLE 1-1 Adventure Works Performance

42

You're dumbfounded. You know this is the answer to something, but what? This report is meaningless. *Numbers without context may be data, but they are not information.* In business intelligence, a summarizable numerical value that you use to monitor your organization is called a *measure*. When looking for numerical information, one of the first things you do is determine what measure you want to see. A measure could represent Sales Dollars, Shipment Units, Defects Per Hour, or Ad Campaign Responses. You ask to see a report of Adventure Works units sold. The report you get is shown in Table 1-2.

TABLE 1-2 Adventure Works Sales

Units Sold
70

Adding a label to your number has turned data into information. You can tell that the number 70 represents the value of Units Sold. The label is *metadata*—data about data. One of the ways your BI application turns data into information is by adding metadata. Looking at a single value doesn't tell you much. You want to break it out into something more informative. For example, how has your company done over time? You ask for a monthly analysis, and Table 1-3 shows the new report.

TABLE 1-3 Adventure Works Units Sold by Month

Jan 2011	Feb 2011	Mar 2011	Apr 2011
4	14	27	25

You now have more information because you can see more metadata. One attribute of each Units Sold value is the month it was sold. Your company has been operating for four months, so across the top of the report you find a list of four attribute labels for the months. Also note that the month labels are sorted chronologically instead of being sorted alphabetically or randomly. The order in which the attribute labels appear on the report is also metadata, and it is critical for your understanding of how your company has performed over time.

You're still not satisfied with the monthly report. Your company sells more than one product. How did each of those products do over time? You ask for a new report of Units Sold by product and by month as shown in Table 1-4.

TABLE 1-4 Adventure Works Units Sold by Product and Month

	Jan 2011	Feb 2011	Mar 2011	Apr 2011
Mountain-500 Black, 40	1	3	1	2
Mountain-500 Black, 44		2		1
Mountain-500 Black, 48		1	2	1
Mountain-500 Silver, 40		1	2	1
Mountain-500 Silver, 44		1	1	1
Mountain-500 Silver, 48	2			
Road-750 Black, 44			10	7
Road-750 Black, 48			5	9
Hitch Rack	1	6	6	3

You now have even more information because you can see even more metadata. Each Units Sold value now has two attributes: the particular month and the particular product that was sold. Your company produces three product models in a variety of sizes and colors for a total of nine unique products. So nine attribute labels appear along the left side of your report: one for each product.

Because Adventure Works is a small company, it is easy to understand the business by looking at a report like Table 1-4 that shows detailed numbers. However, as Adventure Works grows and begins to produce a large number of products, a report like this will grow to many pages. The many lines of detail in the report will make it hard to understand the trends in your company's performance. The notion that too much detail can make it more difficult to understand your company's performance is supported by psychological studies that indicate that most people can comprehend about seven items or seven groups of items. These studies show that grouping—*aggregating*—is the way humans deal with too much detail. As Adventure Works grows, you will want to group the increasing number of individual products into model, subcategory, and category groups. Optimally, each group would contain about seven items.

You can begin to create groups of products by looking for common attributes. Table 1-5 shows how you can separate a product name into model name, color, and size attributes.

TABLE 1-5 Product Attributes

Product	Model	Color	Size
Mountain-500 Black, 40	Mountain-500	Black	40
Mountain-500 Black, 44	Mountain-500	Black	44
Mountain-500 Black, 48	Mountain-500	Black	48
Mountain-500 Silver, 40	Mountain-500	Silver	40
Mountain-500 Silver, 44	Mountain-500	Silver	44
Mountain-500 Silver, 48	Mountain-500	Silver	48
Road-750 Black, 44	Road-750	Black	44
Road-750 Black, 48	Road-750	Black	48
Hitch Rack	Hitch Rack		

So now you have three additional lists of product attribute labels that you could use to create groups on a report. Because *list of attribute labels* is wordy, BI practitioners just call each list an *attribute*. Because the labels in each list are related to each other and belong in the same attribute, the labels are called *members*. So, for example, the Model attribute has three members: Hitch Rack, Mountain-500, and Road-750. The Color attribute has two members: Black and Silver.

The Product attribute is the *key attribute*. The key attribute uniquely identifies the members of all the other attributes. If you're looking at a member of the Product attribute, you know the members of all the other attributes for that Product. For example, you know that the Mountain-500 Silver, 42 product is a size 42, silver-colored Mountain-500 model bicycle. Another way to identify a key attribute is that when you create a list of related attributes such as Table 1-5, the members of the key attribute are unique. Model is not a key attribute. If you're looking at the Mountain-500 member of the Model attribute, you don't know whether the Color is Black or Silver and you don't know the Size. You can also see that the members of the Model attribute are repeated in Table 1-5.

You can now request that your analyst create a report that groups products by model as shown in Table 1-6.

TABLE 1-6 **Adventure Works Units Sold by Model, Product, and Month**

	Jan 2011	Feb 2011	Mar 2011	Apr 2011
Mountain-500	3	8	6	6
Mountain-500 Black, 40	1	3	1	2
Mountain-500 Black, 44		2		1
Mountain-500 Black, 48		1	2	1
Mountain-500 Silver, 40		1	2	1
Mountain-500 Silver, 44		1	1	1
Mountain-500 Silver, 48	2			
Road-750			15	16
Road-750 Black, 44			10	7
Road-750 Black, 48			5	9
Hitch Rack	1	6	6	3
Hitch Rack	1	6	6	3

Your report now has summary information. The value of Units Sold for each Model is the sum, or *aggregation*, of the value of Units Sold of the related Products. The Model and Product attribute members are arranged in a *hierarchy*, with members of the Model attribute forming the top level of the hierarchy and members of the Product attribute forming the bottom level of the hierarchy. The ability to arrange products and models into a hierarchy and to aggregate product values into the value for a model provides additional metadata that increases the ability of your data to convey information.

The report in Table 1-6 is getting closer to something you can use when Adventure Works produces many products. When you have a hierarchy, you don't have to display all the levels. In this case, you only want to see the Model level, so you ask your analyst to exclude the Product level from the report. Table 1-7 shows the summary report that gives you a more comprehensible view of your company's performance.

TABLE 1-7 **Adventure Works Units Sold by Model and Month**

	Jan 2011	Feb 2011	Mar 2011	Apr 2011
Mountain-500	3	8	6	6
Road-750			15	16
Hitch Rack	1	6	6	3

So far, you have seen how the detail level product attribute can be separated into a collection of related attributes. When you perform multidimensional data analysis, you will work with many other attributes. For example, you will often create reports with date, employee, geography, customer, and other attributes. You have also learned how the product and model attributes can be organized into a simple hierarchy and then used to create a report that groups and summarizes detail data. In the next section, you will learn more about creating hierarchies.

Hierarchies in Data Analysis

You create a hierarchy by arranging related attributes into levels. The Product by Model hierarchy displayed only two levels, but a hierarchy can have many levels. For example, you could create a Date hierarchy with many levels by using the Month attribute as the lowest level and then adding *intermediate levels* made of members of the Quarter and Year attributes. You could then add one more level to the top of the Date hierarchy called the *All level*. The All level contains a single member—All Dates—that is the aggregation of all the members of the Year level. Figure 1-1 shows some of the members of the Date hierarchy arranged in All, Year, Quarter, and Month levels.

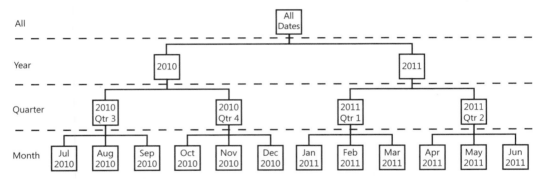

FIGURE 1-1 Date hierarchy

You can think of the members of a hierarchy as participating in parent-child relationships. A member of a level is the parent of the related members of the next-lowest level. A member of a level is a child of the related members of the next-highest level. Figure 1-1 shows that 2011 is the parent of 2011 Qtr 1 and 2011 Qtr 2. You can also see that Feb 2011 is the child of 2011 Qtr 1. The Date hierarchy is a *natural hierarchy*. In a natural hierarchy, every child member has only one parent. The Size by Color hierarchy is not a natural hierarchy. The 40 member of the Size level has two parents: the Black and Silver members of the Color level.

Figure 1-1 also shows that a hierarchy can have many branches. When you come to the end of the branches of a tree you find a leaf. At the end of the branches of a hierarchy you find *leaf members*. A hierarchy may or may not have an All member, but every hierarchy must have leaf members.

You can turn every attribute into an *attribute hierarchy* that has only two levels by using the attribute as the leaf level and then adding an All level. You could create a Color hierarchy that has the All-level member All Products and leaf-level members Black and Silver.

Some hierarchies, such as the Date hierarchy, are *balanced*. As Figure 1-1 shows, no matter what path you follow along the branches, you find a member at every level, and each path has the same number of levels. In a balanced hierarchy, it's easy to give names to the levels.

Some hierarchies are *unbalanced*. An organization chart is often unbalanced. For example, many companies might have many more employees—and thus many more levels of management—in the manufacturing organization than in human resources. Work breakdown structures and charts of account are additional examples of unbalanced hierarchies. In an unbalanced hierarchy, it's often difficult to give names to specific levels, but leaf members are always the ones that have no children below them. Figure 1-2 shows that in an unbalanced hierarchy, no matter what path you follow along the branches, you find a member at every level. Some paths, however, might have more levels than others. In other words, the leaf members may belong to different levels.

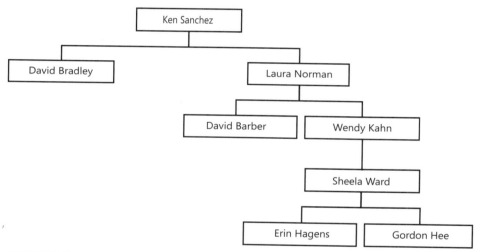

FIGURE 1-2 Organization chart

Some hierarchies appear to blur the distinction between balanced and unbalanced. For example, in a geographic hierarchy, you might have easily named levels—All, Country, State/Province, and City—but some countries may not have states or provinces. These are *ragged* hierarchies. Figure 1-3 shows that no matter what path you follow, each path has the same number of levels. However, some paths may not have a member at every level. In a ragged hierarchy, leaf members always belong to the same level.

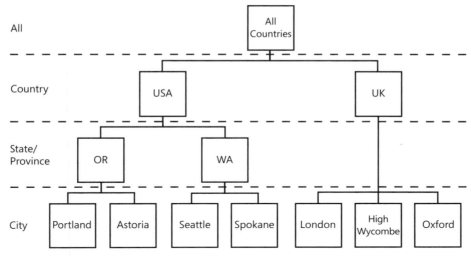

FIGURE 1-3 Ragged hierarchy

Hierarchies are created by arranging related attributes in levels. A hierarchy may have as few as two levels or may contain many levels. A hierarchy has a lowest level, called the *leaf level*, then several intermediate levels, and finally the top level. In most hierarchies, the top level will be the All level and will contain a single All member. You may think of the members of a hierarchy as having parent-child relationships. If a child member has only one parent member, then the hierarchy is a natural hierarchy. If a hierarchy is a balanced hierarchy, then every path in the hierarchy has the same number of levels and every level has a member. In an unbalanced hierarchy, different paths in the hierarchy may have different numbers of levels, and in a ragged hierarchy, every path has the same number of levels, but not all levels have a member.

Dimensions in Data Analysis

To help you learn about dimensions, let's review a couple of the reports that you've already seen in the preceding section. Table 1-8 shows the Adventure Works Units Sold by Month report that you first saw in Table 1-3. In this report, total Units Sold is subdivided by the members of the Month attribute. The number of months—four—determines the number of values in this report. This is analogous to calculating linear distances in the physical world: the length of a line is simply its length.

TABLE 1-8 Adventure Works Units Sold by Month

Jan 2011	Feb 2011	Mar 2011	Apr 2011
4	14	27	25

Table 1-9 shows the Adventure Works Units Sold by Model and Month report that first appeared in Table 1-7. In this report, monthly Units Sold values are further subdivided by the members of the Model attribute. The potential number of values in the report equals the number of models multiplied by the number of months, so you now have up to 12 values to consider. This is analogous to calculating the area of a rectangle in the physical world: the area of a rectangle is equal to its length times its width. The report even looks like a rectangle.

TABLE 1-9 Adventure Works Units Sold by Model and Month

	Jan 2011	Feb 2011	Mar 2011	Apr 2011
Mountain-500	3	8	6	6
Road-750			15	16
Hitch Rack	1	6	6	3

The comparison to a rectangle, however, applies only to the arithmetic involved in calculating the number of values, not to the shape of the report. You could just as easily rearrange your report by placing the Month attribute on rows so that the report would look like Table 1-10.

TABLE 1-10 Adventure Works Units Sold by Model and Month

Hitch Rack	Jan 2011	1
Hitch Rack	Feb 2011	6
Hitch Rack	Mar 2011	6
Hitch Rack	Apr 2011	3
Mountain-500	Jan 2011	3
Mountain-500	Feb 2011	8
Mountain-500	Mar 2011	6
Mountain-500	Apr 2011	6
Road-750	Jan 2011	
Road-750	Feb 2011	
Road-750	Mar 2011	15
Road-750	Apr 2011	16

Whether the values in your report form a rectangle as in Table 1-9 or they form a line as in Table 1-10, you still have the potential for 12 values if you have four members of the Month attribute and three members of the Model attribute. Your report has 12 potential values because the members of the Model attribute and the members of the Month attribute are independent. Each model gets its own sales value—even if that value is zero—for each month.

Consider a new report. Suppose that Adventure Works sells products in two different states and you'd like to know the number of units of each model sold in each state. Also, in addition to seeing these numbers by month, you would also like a total for all months. To generate this report, your analyst adds the State attribute to the rows of the report and replaces the Month attribute with the Month attribute hierarchy. The new report is shown in Table 1-11.

TABLE 1-11 **Adventure Works Units Sold by State, Model, and Month**

		All Months	Jan 2011	Feb 2011	Mar 2011	Apr 2011
WA	Hitch Rack	9		4	3	2
	Mountain-500	18	2	6	5	5
	Road-750	19			9	10
OR	Hitch Rack	7	1	2	3	1
	Mountain-500	5	1	2	1	1
	Road-750	12			6	6

The report now has two members of the State attribute, three members of the Model attribute, and five members of the Month attribute hierarchy. The number of potential values, 30, equals the number of states multiplied by the number of models multiplied by the number of months. This is analogous to calculating the volume of a cube in the physical world: the volume of a cube is its length multiplied by its width multiplied by its height.

It's clear that for this report the comparison to a cube applies to the arithmetic used to calculate the number of values in the report and doesn't apply to the report's physical shape. The values in Table 1-11 are arranged in a rectangle. Table 1-12 shows the first few rows of the same report, except the Month hierarchy has been placed on rows. This report shows the same information as Table 1-11, but the values are now arranged in a line.

TABLE 1-12 **Adventure Works Units Sold by State, Model, and Month**

WA	Hitch Rack	All Months	9
WA	Mountain-500	All Months	18
WA	Road-750	All Months	19
OR	Hitch Rack	All Months	7
OR	Mountain-500	All Months	5
OR	Road-750	All Months	12
WA	Hitch Rack	Jan 2011	
WA	Mountain-500	Jan 2011	2
WA	Road-750	Jan 2011	
OR	Hitch Rack	Jan 2011	1
OR	Mountain-500	Jan 2011	1
OR	Road-750	Jan 2011	
WA	Hitch Rack	Feb 2011	4
WA	Mountain-500	Feb 2011	6
WA	Road-750	Feb 2011	

But whichever way you lay out your report, State, Model, and Month are independent attributes and hierarchies, and the total number of potential values in the report equals the number of members in the first independent attribute (two States) multiplied by the number of members in the second independent attribute (three Models) multiplied by the number of members in the independent attribute hierarchy (five Months).

To calculate length, area, and volume, you multiply the lengths of an object's dimensions. To calculate the potential values in a report, you multiply the number of members in the report's independent attributes and hierarchies. *The independent attributes and hierarchies are the dimensions of the report*, so BI practitioners have borrowed the term *dimension* from mathematics. Dimensions contain attributes and hierarchies. For example, the report in Table 1-11 displays the State attribute that belongs to the Geography dimension, the Model attribute that belongs to the Product dimension, and the Month attribute hierarchy that belongs to the Date dimension. Although the term *dimension* is borrowed from mathematics, it is important to remember that a data analysis dimension is very different from a physical dimension. Using the term *dimension* doesn't imply anything about how attributes and hierarchies should be physically arranged on a report or even about how multidimensional data should be stored in a database.

A dimension may contain more than one attribute, but every dimension has one and only one key attribute. Any other attributes that are related to the key attribute belong in the same dimension. Because attributes belong to dimensions, attribute members are also dimension members. So, for example, Product is the key attribute of the Product dimension. If you know the value of a Product attribute, you also know the value of the Model, Color, and Size attributes, so these attributes also belong in the Product dimension. Silver is a member of the Color attribute and 48 is a member of the Size attribute, so Silver and 48 are also members of the Product dimension.

Dimensions also contain hierarchies. In the preceding section titled "Hierarchies in Data Analysis," you learned that hierarchies are created by organizing attributes into levels. The attributes used to create a hierarchy must be in the same dimension and the hierarchy will also belong to that dimension. For example, the Product by Model hierarchy is composed of attributes contained in the Product dimension, so the Product by Model hierarchy also belongs in the Product dimension.

The dimension that contains measures is structured differently than all other dimensions. There is no Measures attribute and no hierarchies are created from measures. Instead, there is only a Measures dimension that contains the list of attribute labels that identify measures. Table 1-13 shows a report in which the Units Sold and Sales Dollars members of the Measures dimension are displayed on columns.

TABLE 1-13 **Adventure Works Sales by State, Model, and Month**

		Jan 2011		Feb 2011		Mar 2011		Apr 2011	
		Units	$	Units	$	Units	$	Units	$
WA	Hitch Rack			4	$480	3	$360	2	$240
	Mountain-500	2	$1,105	6	$3,265	5	$2,775	5	$2,750
	Road-750					9	$4,860	10	$5,400
OR	Hitch Rack	1	$120	2	$240	3	$360	1	$120
	Mountain-500	1	$565	2	$1,105	1	$540	1	$540
	Road-750					6	$3,240	6	$3,240

Units = Units Sold, $ = Sales Dollars

The report now contains a fourth dimension. The number of values in the report still equals the product of the number of members in each dimension: 2 × 3 × 4 × 2, which equals 48. But there is not—and there does not need to be—any kind of physical world analogue. Remember that dimensions are simply a convenient way of grouping related attributes and hierarchies, and having four (or 20 or 60) dimensions is just as realistic as having three. Adding dimensions just increases the number of values displayed on a report or stored in a database.

In the physical world, the object you are measuring changes depending on how many dimensions there are. For example, a one-dimensional inch is a linear inch, but a two-dimensional inch is a square inch, and a three-dimensional inch is a cubic inch. A cubic inch is a completely different object from a square inch or a linear inch. In your report, however, the object that you measure as you add attributes and hierarchies from multiple dimensions is always the same: a numerical value—and a numerical value in a "four-dimensional" report and a numerical value in a "one-dimensional" report are the same. In the reporting world, an additional dimension simply creates a new, independent way to subdivide a measure.

Table 1-13 shows that adding a fourth dimension does not transform a rectangular report into a hyper-cube, but that's not to say that adding a new dimension is trivial. Suppose that you start with a report with two dimensions: 30 products and 12 months, or 360 possible values. Adding three new members to the product dimension increases the number of values in the report to 396, a 10 percent increase. Adding a third dimension with three new members, however, increases the number of values in the report to 1,080, a 300 percent increase. Consider this extreme example: With 128 members in a single dimension, a report has 128 possible values, but with those same 128 total members split up into 64 dimensions—with two members in each dimension—a report has 18,446,744,073,709,551,616 possible values!

This section has introduced multidimensional data analysis. A dimensional data model has measures, numerical values that can be aggregated, and related attributes and hierarchies organized into dimensions. The dimensions provide metadata that turns the numerical data into information and makes analysis possible. The dimensions provide the descriptive labels for the numbers and let you know how the data should be grouped, sorted, formatted, and aggregated.

A dimensional data model can be implemented in a relational database management system (RDBMS) or in a multidimensional OLAP database. In fact, it is very common for a BI system to have both. Data from source systems is extracted, transformed, and loaded into a data warehouse stored in a RDBMS. Then the data is extracted from the data warehouse and loaded into a multidimensional OLAP database. In the next two sections, you will learn how a dimension model is implemented in each type of database.

Understanding a Dimensional Data Warehouse

Many BI systems have a dimensional data warehouse as their data storage and retrieval layer. The data warehouse is stored in a relational database management system (RDBMS). At a very simple level, you can think of a relational database as a set of tables. Each table has rows and columns, like an Excel spreadsheet. In a dimensional data warehouse, dimensions are stored in dimension tables. Measures are called *facts* and are stored in *fact tables*.

A Fact Table

In a dimensional data warehouse, a table that stores the detailed values for measures, or facts, is called a fact table. Table 1-14 gives a conceptual view of the first few rows of the FactSales fact table. It stores Units Sold and Sales Dollars by State, Product, and Month.

TABLE 1-14 FactSales Fact Table

State	Product	Month	UnitsSold	SalesDollars
OR	Hitch Rack	Jan 2011	1	$120.00
OR	Mountain-500 Silver, 40	Jan 2011	1	$565.00
OR	Mountain-500 Silver, 48	Jan 2011	1	$552.50
WA	Mountain-500 Silver, 48	Jan 2011	1	$552.50
OR	Hitch Rack	Feb 2011	2	$240.00
WA	Hitch Rack	Feb 2011	4	$480.00

In these sample rows from a fact table, the first three columns—State, Product, and Month—are key columns. The values in the key columns relate the facts in the fact table row to a row in each dimension table. The remaining two columns—UnitsSold and SalesDollars—contain the numerical facts. Each column in a fact table is typically either a key column or a fact column, but it is also possible to have other columns for reference purposes—for example, purchase order numbers or invoice numbers.

A fact table contains a column for each measure. Different fact tables have different measures. A Sales fact table might contain two measure columns—one for Dollars and one for Units. A shop-floor fact table might contain three measure columns—one for Units, one for Minutes, and one for Defects.

The rows of a fact table all must be at the same level of detail and must be related to the same set of dimensions. In the FactSales table shown in Table 1-14, every row must contain monthly data and must have a value for state and product. If your organization sets quarterly sales quotas for each product subcategory, that data must be stored in a different fact table. The level of detail stored in a fact table is called the *granularity* of the fact table. The dimensions that a fact table is related to are referred to as the *dimensionality* of the fact table. Facts that have different granularity or different dimensionality must be stored in separate fact tables. It is very common for a data warehouse to have many fact tables.

The sample rows in Table 1-14 illustrate the conceptual layout of a fact table. Actually, a fact table almost always uses an integer, called a *dimension key*, for each dimension member, rather than a descriptive name. For example, Table 1-15 shows a fact table in which the State column has been replaced by the StateKey column and the values for OR and WA have been replaced by 1 and 2. In a similar fashion, the Product and Month columns have been replaced by dimension key columns and the text values in these columns have been replaced by dimension key values. Because a fact table tends to contain a very large number of rows—in a reasonably large data warehouse, the fact table might easily have hundreds of millions of rows—using an integer dimension key can substantially reduce the size of the fact table.

TABLE 1-15 FactSales Table

StateKey	ProductKey	MonthKey	UnitsSold	SalesDollars
1	483	201101	1	120.00
1	591	201101	1	565.00
1	594	201101	1	552.50
2	594	201101	1	552.50
1	483	201102	2	240.00
2	483	201102	4	480.00

When you put integer dimension keys into the fact table, the labels for the dimension members have to be put into a different table—a dimension table. You must have a dimension table for each dimension key in a fact table.

Dimension Tables

A dimension table contains one row for each member of the key attribute of the dimension. The key attribute has two columns: one column contains the integer dimension key and another column contains the attribute label. Table 1-16 shows a simple version of the product dimension table.

TABLE 1-16 DimProduct Dimension Table

ProductKey	Product
483	Hitch Rack
596	Mountain-500 Black, 40
598	Mountain-500 Black, 44
599	Mountain-500 Black, 48
591	Mountain-500 Silver, 40
593	Mountain-500 Silver, 44
594	Mountain-500 Silver, 48
604	Road-750 Black, 44
605	Road-750 Black, 48

In the data warehouse, the key attribute in a dimension table must contain a unique value for each member of the dimension. In relational database terms, this key attribute is called a *primary key column*. Each dimension key column in a fact table corresponds to the primary key column of one of the dimension tables. Each key value that appears once in the dimension table may appear multiple times in the fact table. For example, the Product Key 483, for Hitch Rack, should appear in only one dimension table row, but it may appear in many fact table rows. This is called a *one-to-many relationship*. In the fact table, a dimension key column (which is on the many side of the one-to-many relationship) is called a *foreign key column*. The relational database uses the matching values from the primary key column (in the dimension table) and the foreign key column (in the fact table) to join the records in a fact table to the corresponding records in the dimension table.

The dimension table will typically have additional columns that contain the members of the other attributes in the dimension. Table 1-17 shows the product dimension table with Product, Subcategory, Category, Color, Size, and List Price attributes.

TABLE 1-17 DimProduct Dimension Table

ProductKey	Product	Subcategory	Category	Color	Size	ListPrice
483	Hitch Rack	Bike Racks	Accessories			120.00
596	Mountain-500 Black, 40	Mountain Bikes	Bikes	Black	40	539.99
598	Mountain-500 Black, 44	Mountain Bikes	Bikes	Black	44	537.99
599	Mountain-500 Black, 48	Mountain Bikes	Bikes	Black	48	534.99
591	Mountain-500 Silver, 40	Mountain Bikes	Bikes	Silver	40	565.00
593	Mountain-500 Silver, 44	Mountain Bikes	Bikes	Silver	44	561.00
594	Mountain-500 Silver, 48	Mountain Bikes	Bikes	Silver	48	552.50
604	Road-750 Black, 44	Road Bikes	Bikes	Black	44	540.00
605	Road-750 Black, 48	Road Bikes	Bikes	Black	48	540.00

Many dimension attributes can be used to create groups of dimension records, and then the related facts can be summarized for each group. For example, Product dimension records can be grouped into Bikes and Accessories categories, and then the number of Units Sold for each category can be calculated. Attributes that can be used to create groups are called *aggregatable*, and the summary value is called an *aggregate*. Aggregate is a more general term than *summary value*. Summary value implies that the value is derived by summing individual values. When you calculate an aggregate, you may sum the individual values, but you could also count, find the minimum or maximum, average, or apply some other calculation to the individual values.

Not all attributes are aggregatable. For example, it would not be useful to create groups using the List Price attribute and then sum the number of Units Sold for each list price, because List Price has many distinct values. A customer dimension often contains many non-aggregatable attributes: street address, telephone number, e-mail address, and so on. These non-aggregatable attributes are referred to as *member properties*. Member properties are added to reports to provide additional information on a report that already contains an aggregatable attribute. For example, a report could display sales by the aggregatable Customer attribute and then list the Telephone Number and E-Mail Address member properties.

Surrogate Keys and Slowly Changing Dimensions

One reason for using an integer key for dimension members is to reduce the size of the fact table. Also, an integer key allows seemingly duplicate members to exist in a dimension table. In a Customer dimension, for example, you might have two different customers named John Smith, but each one is assigned a unique Customer Key, guaranteeing that each member key appears only once in the dimension table.

Of course, because the data warehouse is generated by extracting data from an operational system, the two John Smiths will undoubtedly have unique keys already. One may be C125423A and the other F234654B. These are called *application keys* or *business keys* because they came from the applications you use to operate your business. If you already have unique keys for each customer (or product or region), does the data warehouse really need to generate new keys for its own purposes, or can it just use the application keys to guarantee uniqueness?

Most successful data warehouses do generate their own unique keys. These extra, redundant unique keys are called *surrogate keys*. Sometimes people who are accustomed to working with production databases have a hard time understanding why a data warehouse should create new surrogate keys when unique application keys are already available. There are three reasons for creating unique surrogate keys in a data warehouse: surrogate keys can be integers, surrogate keys enable you to integrate data from multiple systems, and surrogate keys allow you to have slowly changing dimensions.

Surrogate keys can be integers even if the application key is not. This can make the data warehouse fact table consume less space. It takes less space in the fact table to store an integer such as 54352 rather than a string such as C125423A. This is the least important reason for creating surrogate keys.

A data warehouse integrates data from multiple source systems. It is common for source systems to have different application keys for the same dimension member or, conversely, the same application key for different dimension members. If you generate a surrogate key for each dimension member, you don't have to rely on the application keys. For example, in the Sales system, the product application key A543 might refer to a Mountain-100 bike, while in the manufacturing system (which was created by a completely different group of people), the product application key A543 might refer to a Road-650 bike. A more common example is one that happens when two companies merge. In the parent company's sales system, customer C125423A may refer to John Smith, but in the subsidiary's sales system, C125423A might coincidentally refer to Abigail Torres. Even such supposedly unique values as an American social security number can be granted to a new person when the government believes that the person who was assigned the number originally is deceased. Using surrogate keys in the data warehouse prepares the warehouse for such eventualities.

One of the most compelling reasons for using surrogate keys in a data warehouse is to handle occasions when the value of an attribute changes over time. Dimensions where attribute values can change are called *slowly changing dimensions*. For example, last year the list price of the Hitch Rack was $110, but this year the list price is $120. In the order-processing system, the price was simply changed from $110 to $120 in the master product list and new orders use the new price. In a data warehouse, you have history to consider. Do you want to pretend that the Hitch Rack has always sold for $120 or do you want the data warehouse to reflect the fact that last year the price was $110? If you simply use the application key to represent the rack, you don't have a lot of choice. If, on the other hand, you had the foresight to create surrogate keys for the product, when the list price changed, you simply created a new record with a new surrogate key for the more expensive version of the exact same Hitch Rack, and kept the application key as just another attribute. The ability to create multiple instances of a single product, customer, or any other dimension member is an extremely important benefit of surrogate keys, and it is particularly important in a data warehouse where you are maintaining historical information.

Surrogate keys are a critical part of the design of most data warehouses. The foreign key in the fact table and the primary key in the dimension table are then completely under the control of the data warehouse.

Alternative Table Structures

In an operational database, it is critical for data to be consistent across the entire application: If you change a customer's address in one part of the system, you want the changed address to be immediately visible in all parts of the system. Because of this need for consistency, operational databases tend to be broken up into many tables so that any value is stored only once in a single table. Any time the value is needed, a join to the table containing the value can be created. Ensuring that a value is stored in only one place is one element of a process called *normalization*, and it is very important in operational database systems.

In a data warehouse dimension, you may have multiple attributes that form a natural hierarchy. A database designer who is familiar with creating operational databases will want to normalize the dimension so that each level of the hierarchy has a separate table. For example, the operational database designer might want to normalize the Product dimension by creating a Subcategory table in which each subcategory appears only once, and a separate Category table in which each category appears only once. This, of course, would require foreign keys in the Product and Subcategory tables that join to unique primary keys in the Subcategory and Category tables respectively.

If you execute a report using data from the data warehouse, however, many joins can make the query slow. For example, suppose you want to see Sales Amount for the Bikes category for the year 2011. To aggregate by Bikes, you have to join each row in the fact table to the Product table, and then to the Subcategory table, and then to the Category table. To aggregate by the year 2011, you also have to join the fact table to the Month table, to the Quarter table, and finally to the Year table. And you have to do all those joins for all the rows in the fact table, discard the rows that are not related to the Bikes category and the year 2011, and then sum Sales Amount in the remaining rows. Joining all of the Product dimension and Date dimension tables to the fact table makes the query for this report much slower than if all the Product attributes were in a single table and all the Date attributes were in a single table.

Consequently, in many data warehouses, all the attributes for a single dimension are stored in a single dimension table—even if that means that attribute members such as categories and years are stored redundantly. Storing redundant values in a single table is called *denormalizing* the data. Performing a single join to find the Year and a single join to find the Category can be much faster than performing many joins to get the same data, so denormalizing the dimension tables in a data warehouse is often worthwhile.

Creating a single denormalized table for each dimension results in a *star schema*. When you diagram a star schema, each fact table is surrounded by a single table for each dimension, and the result looks a bit like a star. Normalizing each of the dimension tables so that each dimension has several tables results in a *snowflake schema*, because the "points" of the star are broken up into little branches that look like a snowflake. In reality, it isn't the data warehouse that is the star or snowflake schema, because one dimension might be a fully normalized snowflake schema dimension while another dimension in the same data warehouse might be a fully denormalized star schema dimension.

If you are creating a data warehouse for the purpose of creating reports directly from a relational database, then you should carefully consider whether each dimension should be stored in a star schema dimension table or in multiple snowflake dimension tables. If, however, you use the warehouse primarily as a data source for Analysis Services, the difference between star or snowflake dimension tables is much less significant and you can use other reasons, such as which database structure is easier to create and update, as the basis for a design decision.

A dimension with an unbalanced hierarchy, such as an Employee dimension, requires a slight variation of the snowflake schema dimension table design. In an Employee dimension, the key attribute members are all employees. Each employee's manager, however, is also an employee. Unlike a standard snowflake dimension, where the parent member is in a new level and gets a new table, in an Employee dimension, the parent member simply points back to a different member of the key attribute in the original dimension table. This is called a *parent-child* dimension because both the parent member and the child member are in the same table. In relational database terms, this pointing back from one attribute to the key attribute of the same table is called a *self-referential join*. A parent-child dimension provides a great deal of flexibility in how a hierarchy is organized, but querying a table with a self-referential join can be difficult.

In this section you have learned how a dimensional data model is implemented in a relational database data warehouse. The data warehouse has fact tables that contain measures, also called *facts*, and dimension tables containing attributes. The data warehouse designer can choose to store a natural hierarchy in a set of snowflake schema dimension tables, but it can also store all the attributes of a dimension in a star schema table. A dimension with an unbalanced hierarchy can be stored in a table with a self-referential join.

You can't use a relational database data warehouse to implement all aspects of a dimensional model because the amount of metadata that can be stored in a relational database is limited. In a dimension table, the names of the attributes (the column names) are metadata, but the names of the attribute members are data in the rows of the table. A star schema dimensional table contains no metadata about how attributes should be organized into hierarchies. For example, if the Product dimension is stored in a single star schema dimension table, there is no information in the table that shows that products aggregate into subcategories that aggregate into categories. Of course, you can organize natural hierarchies into a set of snowflake schema tables, but you don't have a way to designate the levels of hierarchies that are not natural hierarchies. There is no metadata about how attribute members should be sorted and no designation of which attributes are aggregatable and which are not aggregatable. Each fact table contains data at a single level of detail, so there are no summary or aggregate values, and no metadata about the appropriate type of aggregation to apply to a fact. Finally, in a data warehouse, the dimension and fact data are stored in separate tables. When you query the data warehouse, you must include in your query instructions how you want to join the dimension tables to the fact table.

Because a relational database data warehouse doesn't fully implement all aspects of a dimensional model, report and query writers must use their personal knowledge of the metadata that is not stored in the data warehouse to make up for this deficiency. Because the metadata is not in the data warehouse, individuals must embed the metadata in each query and report, leading to human-induced errors and reports and queries that display inconsistent data. A multidimensional OLAP database has a much greater capability to store metadata and so can be used to implement a dimensional model.

Multidimensional OLAP

In a BI system, the multidimensional OLAP database resides between the data storage and retrieval layer and the presentation layer. It converts the relational data warehouse data into a fully implemented dimensional model that makes it fast and flexible for creating analytical reports and data visualizations. Because different OLAP databases vary in the features they provide and their physical implementation, in this section I will introduce how Analysis Services implements a dimensional data model.

The columns containing numerical data in a fact table correspond to measures in a dimensional model, so each fact table is a group of measures. Analysis Services organizes information in a logical construct called a *measure group* that corresponds to a single fact table and its related dimensions. Conceptually, a measure group is similar to a fact table but with a few significant differences. Like a fact table, a measure group contains one column for each dimension and one column for each measure. Also like a fact table, a measure group contains a row for each possible combination of members from each dimension. Unlike a fact table, however, which contains data only for a single level of detail, a measure group contains data for the single level of detail and aggregated data for all higher levels of detail. For a measure group with State, Product, and Date dimensions, a few sample rows can be conceptualized as shown in Table 1-18.

TABLE 1-18 **Sales Measure Group**

State	Product	Date	Units Sold	Sales Amount
All	All	All	70	31,305
WA	All	All	46	21,235
WA	Bikes	All	37	20,155
WA	Road Bikes	All	19	10,260
WA	Road-750 Black, 48	All	13	7,020
WA	Road-750 Black, 48	2011	13	7,020
WA	Road-750 Black, 48	Mar 2011	4	2,160

The bottom row of Table 1-18 corresponds to a row that would be in the fact table—it contains the same level of detail as the fact table. None of the other rows would appear in the fact table—each has at least one member from a higher level of a dimension hierarchy. In every row that has a higher-level member, the fact data has been aggregated by summing a lower level of detail data. These few rows illustrate only a tiny sample of the possible values in even this small measure group.

You may have noticed that in Table 1-18 both the column headers and dimension data are bold and only the numeric data is in plain text. This is intentional and is meant to show that both the dimension names and the dimension member names are metadata. You can also see that the dimension data is organized into hierarchies. Because this is a simple example, it doesn't show all of the ways in which Analysis Services implements a dimensional data model. In Chapter 4, "Creating Dimensions," you will see that you can apply a sort order to dimension members and designate attributes as aggregatable or non-aggregatable.

Analysis Services can combine several related measure groups and a set of dimensions into a *cube*. Not every measure group contains data from every dimension, but if a measure group is in a cube, it cannot contain data from a dimension that is not in the cube. Like the term *dimension*, the term *cube* is borrowed from mathematics. The number of possible values in a measure group is the product of the number of members in every dimension in the measure group, just as the number of units in a cube is the product of the units on each edge of the cube. So the product of the number of members in all the dimensions in a cube gives the largest possible size of any measure group in the cube. In the physical world, the term *cube* refers to an object with three dimensions. In Analysis Services, a cube is simply fact and dimension data stored on a disk, with no implication about the number of dimensions the cube contains. A cube can have as few as one dimension or as many dimensions as you may need.

In this chapter you learned the purpose and structure of a business intelligence system. A BI system is used to perform multidimensional data analysis. A dimensional model turns numeric data into information by adding metadata to the numbers. The metadata is contained in dimensions composed of attributes and hierarchies that are associated with the numerical data, also called *measures*. A data warehouse can be used to partially implement a dimensional model in a relational database, but to get all the analytical benefits, the dimensional model must be implemented in a multidimensional OLAP database such as Analysis Services.

In Chapter 2, you will learn more about the benefits of OLAP databases and the particular advantages of Analysis Services.

Chapter 2
Understanding OLAP and Analysis Services

In this chapter, you will learn how to:

- Understand the definition of OLAP and the benefits a multidimensional OLAP database can add to a business intelligence system.

- Understand the advantages of Microsoft SQL Server 2008 Analysis Services.

- Understand the role Analysis Services plays in the Microsoft business intelligence platform.

- Understand the tools for developing and managing Analysis Services databases.

Business intelligence (BI) is a way of thinking. A data warehouse is a general structure for storing the data needed for good BI. But data in a warehouse is of little use until it is converted into the information that decision makers need. In this chapter, you will first learn the general benefits of online analytical processing (OLAP)—one of the best technologies for converting data into information—and then you will learn how Microsoft Analysis Services implements the benefits of OLAP.

Understanding OLAP

The first version of Analysis Services was named OLAP Services. Even though the name now reflects the purpose of the product rather than the technology, the technology is still important. Understanding the history of the term *OLAP* can help you understand its meaning.

In 1985, E. F. Codd coined the term *online transaction processing* (OLTP) and proposed 12 rules that define an OLTP database. His terminology and criteria became widely accepted as the standard for databases used to manage the day-to-day operations (transactions) of a company. In 1993, Codd came up with the term *online analytical processing* (OLAP) and again proposed 12 criteria to define an OLAP database. This time, his criteria did not gain wide acceptance, but the term *OLAP* did—many people thought it was the perfect term to describe databases designed to facilitate performing analysis.

Some people use OLAP simply as a synonym for dimensional data warehousing. Usually, however, the term *OLAP* describes specialized tools that make warehouse data easily accessible. One term that is almost always associated with OLAP—but never associated with relational databases—is *cube*. Different OLAP tools define, store, and manage cubes differently, but when you hear the word *cube* you're in the OLAP world.

What is the benefit of an OLAP cube over a relational database? Typically, OLAP tools add the following three benefits to a relational database:

- Consistently fast response
- Metadata-based queries
- Spreadsheet-style formulas

Before looking specifically at Analysis Services, let's consider how OLAP in general provides these benefits.

Consistently Fast Response

One way that OLAP provides a consistently fast response is by calculating and storing aggregate values and the results of formulas when a cube is loaded. Basically, the idea is that you either pay for the time of the calculation at query time or you pay for it in advance. OLAP allows you to pay for the calculation time in advance, so queries run faster. In terms of how data is physically stored, OLAP tools fall into two basic types: a spreadsheet model and a database model. Analysis Services storage is basically the database model, but it's useful for you to understand some of the issues and benefits of spreadsheet model OLAP.

In a spreadsheet, you can insert a value or a formula into any cell. Spreadsheets are very useful for complex formulas because they give you a great deal of control. However, the data a spreadsheet can contain is restricted to a limited number of rows and columns, and is essentially a two-dimensional structure. An OLAP cube can contain much more data than a spreadsheet and provides for multiple dimensions. With spreadsheet model OLAP, the database physically stores aggregate values and formula results in the cube. That is both a good thing and a bad thing. It's a good thing because you can precalculate very complex formulas and store the resulting values in any cell in the cube. Because the results of the complex formulas are already calculated, queries execute very quickly. On the other hand, it's a bad thing because storing all aggregate values and storing the results of all the formulas in a cube uses a tremendous amount of storage space. It limits the size of the OLAP cube because of a problem called *data explosion*.

The story of the man who invented chess can help illustrate the problem of data explosion. The man lived in India, and according to legend his name was Sessa. The king of India was very impressed with the game of chess and asked Sessa to name his reward. Sessa's request was so modest that it offended the king: He asked simply for one grain of rice for the first square of his chess board, two grains for the second square, four grains for the third, and so forth, doubling the number of grains of rice for each of the 64 squares of the board. Of course, by the time the king's magicians calculated the total amount of rice needed to pay the reward, they realized that it would require a warehouse 3 meters by 5 meters by twice the distance to the sun to pay the reward (had they known the metric system and the distance to the sun). In one version of the legend, the king simply solved the problem by cutting off Sessa's head. In another version, the king was more noble and also more clever. He gave Sessa a sack, pointed him to the warehouse and told him to go count out his reward—no rush. The problem Sessa gave the king was the result of a geometric progression: When numbers increase geometrically, they get very large very quickly.

The size of a cube increases geometrically with the number of dimensions. That is the problem with OLAP stored using a spreadsheet model. Because data could potentially be stored in any cell in the cube space, data explosion becomes a very real problem that must be managed. The more dimensions you include in the cube, and the more members in each dimension (granularity), the greater the data explosion potential. Spreadsheet-based OLAP tools typically have elaborate and complicated techniques for managing data explosion; even so, they are still very limited in size.

Spreadsheet-based OLAP tools are typically associated with financial applications. Most financial applications involve relatively small databases coupled with complex, non-additive calculations.

OLAP tools that store cube data using a database model behave very differently. They don't store the results of formulas and don't store all of the aggregate values. Instead, they take advantage of the fact that most reporting requires addition, and addition is an associative operation. For example, when adding the numbers 3, 5, and 7, it doesn't matter whether you add 3 and 5 to get 8 before adding the 7, or whether you add 5 and 7 to get 12 before adding 3. In either case, the final answer is 15. In a purely relational database, you can get fast query results by creating aggregate tables. In an aggregate table, you pre-summarize values that will be needed in a report. For example, a fact table that includes thousands of products, five years of daily data, and perhaps several other dimensions may contain millions of rows. A report of sales by product subcategory by quarter may require several minutes to run, even if you have only 50 subcategories and 20 quarters. But if you pre-summarize the data into an aggregate table that includes only subcategories and quarters, the aggregate table will have at most 1,000 rows (50 subcategories times 20 quarters gives a maximum of 1,000 possible rows), and a report requesting totals by subcategory and by quarter will not take very long to execute. In fact, because of the associative nature of addition, a report requesting totals by category and by year can use the same aggregate table, again producing results very quickly.

Perhaps the biggest benefit of OLAP stored using the database model is the ability to avoid data explosion. Because you need relatively few aggregate tables to provide fast query results, you can have much larger cubes with many more dimensions and attributes than by using a spreadsheet model. Perhaps the biggest disadvantage of OLAP stored using a database model is that there is no inherent way to physically store a value that is the result of a formula. All formulas must be calculated when a query is executed.

Even OLAP cubes that are stored using the database model can calculate some non-associative values very quickly. For example, Average Selling Price is not an additive value—you can't simply add prices together. But to calculate Average Selling Price by Product Category, you simply sum Sales Amount and Sales Quantity for each category and then divide Sales Amount by Sales Quantity. Because you are calculating a simple ratio of two additive values, the result is essentially just as fast as retrieving a simple additive value.

One of the major benefits of OLAP is the ability to precalculate and store values so that reports can be rendered very quickly. Different OLAP technologies use different storage techniques that have different strengths and weaknesses, but a good OLAP database will provide a much faster query response than a relational database whenever highly summarized values or complex formulas are involved.

Metadata-Based Queries

When you query a relational data warehouse, you use Structured Query Language (SQL). SQL is an excellent language, but it was developed primarily for transaction systems, not for reporting applications. One of the problems with SQL is not the language itself, but the fact that relational databases provide relatively little information about how the data is stored and structured, and perhaps more important, what the data means. In other words, relational databases contain only a small amount of metadata. Most of the information about the database has to come from you—the person writing the SQL query.

An OLAP database, on the other hand, contains a great deal of metadata. For example, when you create an OLAP cube, you define not only what the measures are, but also how they should be aggregated, what each measure's label should be, and even how the number should be formatted. Likewise, in an OLAP database, when you create a dimension with many attributes, you define which attributes are aggregatable, and whether any of the attributes should be used to form the levels of a hierarchy. Unfortunately, SQL does not provide the ability for you to write a query that takes advantage of the additional metadata contained in an OLAP database. Consequently, when you use an OLAP data source, you use a different query language: multidimensional expressions, or MDX.

You may be concerned about having to learn a new query language that can be used only with Analysis Services. Fortunately, MDX has been adopted by many OLAP vendors. In 2001, Microsoft, Hyperion, and SAS formed the XML for Analysis (XMLA) council to formulate a common specification for communicating with OLAP data sources. The query language chosen for the XMLA specification is MDX. Most major OLAP vendors have joined the XMLA council and now have XMLA providers. (For more information about XMLA, see the council's Web site at *www.xmla.org*.) So everything you learn about MDX queries in this book applies to Analysis Services and also applies to other OLAP databases.

One of the key benefits of a standardized metadata-based OLAP query language is that you can use a general-purpose OLAP browser to query any of the OLAP databases. For example, with a Microsoft Analysis Services cube, you can choose to use Microsoft client tools such as those included in Microsoft Office, or you can choose query tools from many other vendors. Any client tool that uses MDX or XMLA can understand your cube and generate meaningful reports without the need for you to create custom queries. In other words, because MDX query statements are based on the metadata stored in an OLAP cube, you can probably use a tool that generates the query for you, and you won't have to write any MDX query statements at all.

If you do have a reason for writing custom MDX queries, the metadata makes it much easier than writing SQL queries. For example, if you create a query in SQL that calculates the total Sales Units for each customer's City, you still need to add a clause to make sure that the cities are sorted properly. In an MDX query, you simply state that you want the members of the City attribute and you automatically get the default sort order as defined in the metadata. As another example, in a relational database table that contains both Country and City columns, nothing suggests that cities belong to countries instead of countries belonging to cities. If you want to show all the cities in Germany, you must query for cities and then explicitly include in your query a clause that filters for Germany. In an OLAP cube, where Country is defined as the parent of City, you can just query for the children of Germany.

This is just a small sample of the types of powerful queries you can write using MDX. Many other kinds of queries that are difficult to write in SQL—such as a cross-tabulation that shows the best-selling products as column headings and the best-selling regions as row headings—are relatively simple to write using MDX. Some reports that are simply impossible to create using SQL—such as nesting multiple layers of attributes as column headings—are very simple to create using MDX.

Spreadsheet-Style Formulas

Arguably half the world's businesses are managed using spreadsheets. Spreadsheets are notoriously decentralized, error-prone, difficult to consolidate, and impossible to manage. So why are they such a key component of business management? Because spreadsheet formulas are intuitive to create. To calculate a product's percent of total sales, you point at the product cell, add a division sign (/), point at the total cell, press Enter, and you're done. Fiddle with the formula a little and you can copy it to calculate the percentage for any product. When you're creating the percentage formula, you don't need to worry about how the total got calculated; you solved that with a different formula, so now you can simply use the result. The same is true for other formulas such as month-to-month growth, growth from the same month of the prior year, and many other useful analytical formulas. Many very useful formulas that would be difficult to create using a SQL query are easy to create in a spreadsheet.

But even from a spreadsheet user's perspective, formulas have inherent problems. A spreadsheet formula is inherently two-dimensional: You have numbers for rows and letters for columns. If you need to replicate the same spreadsheet for a different time period—particularly one that has different products or different dates—it is cumbersome to modify the formulas. And it is easy to make mistakes: Nothing about the reference C12 reassures you that you are indeed getting the value for March and not for April. As formulas become long and complex, even the original creator can have difficulty figuring out what the formula really means. In addition, you can easily replace a formula in the middle of a range with an "adjusted" formula, or a constant value, and then forget that you made the change.

From a management perspective, spreadsheet formulas have even bigger problems. The formulas in a spreadsheet are critical business logic, and yet they are spread out all over the organization. The growth calculation created by one person may have some subtle differences from the one created by someone else, even though they ostensibly (and apparently) use the same logic.

Formulas in OLAP cubes have many of the same benefits as spreadsheet formulas. For example, when creating an MDX formula, you can reference any cell in the entire cube without concern for how the value in that cell was calculated.

Most OLAP databases have their own proprietary formula languages. Even databases that support MDX queries as part of the XMLA specification may not support the full potential of MDX formulas. Microsoft Analysis Services has a very rich implementation of MDX formulas. Here are a few examples of ways that MDX formulas are even easier than spreadsheet formulas:

- **MDX formulas use named references.**   References in a spreadsheet formula to other cells in the spreadsheet display only the row and column of the cell. In MDX, formulas reference other cells in the cube using meaningful names. Thus, instead of =C14/D14, the formula might be [Actual]/[Budget].

- **MDX formulas are easy to manage.**   In a spreadsheet, a formula must be explicitly copied to each cell that needs it. If you change your spreadsheet so that it contains 500 products instead of 50 products, you must copy your formula into the new rows. In Analysis Services, an MDX formula is defined generically. A formula that is defined to apply to products applies to however many products are displayed on the report. Likewise, if you create a new worksheet—say, for a new region—you must make sure that the formulas on the new worksheet point to the proper cells. In Analysis Services, switching to a new region automatically uses the same generic MDX formula.

- **MDX formulas are multidimensional.**   The nature of a spreadsheet reference is two-dimensional, with a letter for the column and a number for the row. This inherently limits the number of dimensions you can easily incorporate into a formula. MDX references use a structure (similar to the structure used for geometric coordinates) that is not tied to a two-dimensional physical location, and, if necessary, can explicitly include dozens of dimensions. In addition, an MDX reference simplifies the use of multiple dimensions by taking advantage of the concept of a *current member*. For example, in the same way that copying the formula =C14/D14 to multiple sheets in a single workbook automatically uses the values from cells on the current sheet, using the MDX formula [Actual]/[Budget] automatically uses the current time period, or the current department, or the current product.

- **MDX formulas take advantage of metadata.**   A spreadsheet formula has no knowledge of the relationships between the cells on the sheet. That is, it has no metadata. MDX formulas, on the other hand, can take advantage of a cube's metadata and use dimension member relationships to perform calculations that are difficult to perform in a spreadsheet. For example, in a spreadsheet, it is easy to calculate the percentage each product contributes to the grand total, but it is very difficult to calculate the percentage each product contributes to its product category. In MDX, because the metadata can include information about hierarchical relationships, calculating the Percent of Parent within a product hierarchy is very easy.

This is just a sampling of the ways that an MDX formula can be more powerful than a simple spreadsheet formula. In addition, MDX formulas are stored on the server, putting business logic into a centralized, manageable location rather than spreading the business logic across hundreds of independent spreadsheets.

An OLAP database provides consistently fast query response, allows you to take advantage of the metadata stored in the database to create simple queries that perform complex analysis, and provides formula functionality that is similar to that of spreadsheet-style formulas but is easier to create and manage.

Understanding Analysis Services

You don't need Analysis Services as part of your BI system. You could create a BI system with a data warehouse and a couple of reporting applications. Even if you want to have the benefits of OLAP in your BI system, you can choose any of several OLAP vendors. So what makes Microsoft SQL Server 2008 Analysis Services a good choice? In the first section of this chapter, you learned three major benefits of OLAP technology. Now you will learn how Analysis Services provides those benefits.

Analysis Services and Speed

Speed comes from storing precalculated values. Querying a 100-million-row table for a grand total is going to take much more time than querying a 100-row summary table. Because most queries can be satisfied using aggregates based on associative operators (sum, minimum, maximum, count, and so on), Analysis Services uses database model storage with the equivalent of summary tables for aggregations. Of course, it can store the data in a special format that is particularly efficient for storage and retrieval, but conceptually, creating aggregations in Analysis Services is the same as creating summary tables in a relational database. Because the aggregation rules are associative, you don't need to create a cell for every possible value. Rather, you create strategic aggregations so that relatively few aggregations can support queries for many different levels of summary data.

The biggest problem with creating summary tables in a relational data warehouse is the incredible amount of administrative work involved:

- First, you must decide which of the potentially thousands or millions of possible aggregate tables you will actually create.

- Second, you must create, populate, and update the aggregate tables.

- Third, you must change your reports and queries to use the appropriate aggregate tables.

Each one of these steps is a major undertaking. Analysis Services basically takes care of all of them for you. (You can do some tuning, but the process is essentially automatic.) Analysis Services has sophisticated tools to simplify the process of designing, creating, maintaining, and querying aggregate tables, which it then stores in its extremely efficient proprietary structures. Managing aggregations has always been an extremely strong feature of Analysis Services.

Because of its ability to create strategic aggregations and thus avoid data-explosion issues, Analysis Services can handle extremely large, multi-terabyte data warehouses.

Analysis Services and Metadata

Analysis Services stores much more metadata than a relational data warehouse. Metadata is associated with both dimensions and cubes.

Dimension Metadata

Consider a Customer dimension. In a relational data warehouse, you could have a Customer dimension table with a primary key column that contains values that uniquely identify each customer. The Customer table would also contain a several columns containing customer attributes. For example, you might have Street Address, City, Country, Region, Age, Age Group, Gender, and potentially many other attributes. In Analysis Services, you define the dimension and create the key attribute from the primary key column. You then have additional attributes created from the other columns in the dimension table.

Some attributes, such as Street Address, are never used for aggregating or selecting customers, so you flag them as non-aggregatable in the dimension's metadata.

Some attributes, such as Gender, can be used for displaying aggregate values on a report, but at other times you will want to ignore Gender and aggregate by some other attribute. You may want to view totals by Age Group for All Genders. For each attribute in a dimension, Analysis Services automatically creates a hierarchy with two levels. The top level contains a single All member, which is the aggregation of all the members of the attribute. Selecting the All member of the attribute hierarchy is equivalent to ignoring the attribute.

Some attributes form a natural hierarchy. For example, each customer has an age, and each age belongs to an age group. Analysis Services allows you to create a multilevel, user-defined hierarchy of attributes that reflects this relationship. A customer might belong to multiple hierarchies. For example, in your organization, you might have each customer belong to a city, which belongs to a country, which then belongs to a region. In Analysis Services, you can define multiple, multilevel, user-defined hierarchies from attributes in a single dimension.

Analysis Services gracefully handles hierarchies in which the levels do not form a natural hierarchy. Consider a Product dimension that contains Product and Size attributes. There are various types of sizes. Some clothing items, such as shirts, come in S, M, L, and XL sizes, whereas shoes and dresses have numeric sizes, and men's trousers have two sizes—waist and inseam. A hierarchy that has a Product level and a Size level is very useful, but is not a natural hierarchy. There is also potential for data explosion. Most of the possible combinations of Product and Size do not actually exist and will have no related numeric data. Fortunately, Analysis Services recognizes the combinations that actually exist and ignores all the other combinations. You can create a user-defined hierarchy with Product and Size levels. Even if you don't create this hierarchy, you can nest Product and Size on the rows or columns of a report. Because Analysis Services uses a feature called *auto-exists* to automatically recognize the combinations of attribute members that actually exist, it allows an incredible amount of reporting flexibility while maintaining excellent query performance.

Cube Metadata

In Analysis Services, a cube is a collection of measure groups that contain numeric data, called *measures*. The measures in a measure group are all related to the same set of dimensions and are at the same level of detail. For example, you could have Sales Amount and Sales Units by Product, Customer, and Date. You might also have Target Amount and Target Units by Product Category and Quarter. Because the target data has different dimensionality and granularity than the actual data, it must be stored in a separate measure group. When you query a relational data warehouse, you must specify how to join the dimension tables to the fact table. In Analysis Services, dimension data and measures are already joined in the measure group. When you query Analysis Services, you only need to request which dimensions and measures you want to view.

Analysis Services will summarize measures based on dimension hierarchies. Different measures need to have different summary rules applied. You may want to sum dollar amounts and units; count orders; get a distinct count of customers; find minimum or maximum error rates; and get inventory levels on the last work day of the month, quarter, or year. When you query a relational data warehouse, you must include in your query instructions on how to summarize measures. When you query Analysis Services, you just request measures that are already summarized.

Thus an Analysis Services cube is the combination of all the measure groups. This means that a single cube can contain measures with different dimensionality. This pushes the meaning of cube even further from its geometrical origins. Perhaps you can visualize a cube as a cluster of crystals of varying sizes and shapes, many of which share common sides. In this new way of thinking, a single cube can contain all the metadata for all the data in your data warehouse. Because of this, a cube is now sometimes called a Unified Dimensional Model, or UDM. Frequently a cube contains more information than any single person would want to view. For example, a sales director will want to view target and actual sales, a purchasing manager will want to see target sales and inventory, and a warehouse manager will only want to see inventory. In Analysis Services, you can create a perspective for each of these individuals that lets them see only the data in the cube that is relevant to their needs.

Cubes and measure groups are both logical and physical structures, but when you design a cube, you can deal with these two aspects of a cube independently. This means that when you develop a cube, you can first concentrate on defining metadata so that client tools can access data. You don't have to worry about how the data is stored. As soon as you have the cube's metadata defined, you can configure how the cube stores its data. Conceptually, each measure group contains all the detail values stored in the fact table, but that doesn't mean that the measure group must physically copy and store all of that data. If you choose, you can make the measure group dynamically retrieve values as needed from the fact table. In this case, you're using the measure group only to define metadata. This is called *relational OLAP*, or ROLAP. For faster query performance, you can have Analysis Services load the detail values into its own proprietary storage structure and precalculate aggregate values. This will provide improved query performance. This is called *multidimensional OLAP*, or MOLAP. Analysis Services allows you, the cube designer, to decide to use MOLAP or ROLAP. Aside from performance differences, where the detail values are physically stored is completely invisible to a user of a cube. Whether you use MOLAP or ROLAP, when you execute a query the results are stored in memory, on a space-available basis, to make subsequent queries faster. You can think of MOLAP storage as a disk-based cache that allows the Analysis Server to load the memory cache much faster than if it had to retrieve data from a relational data warehouse.

Analysis Services Formulas

Even without any explicit formulas, an Analysis Services cube contains many calculations—the totals that aggregate up the hierarchies in each dimension are calculations, and they happen automatically. If you create a cube that consists primarily of additive measures—for example, a cube that summarizes sales or other transactions—the basic cube engine does most of the calculation work. When you create MOLAP aggregations, Analysis Services physically stores the values needed to query sum, count, minimum, and maximum calculations extremely quickly. In addition, you can create calculated members that perform calculations on aggregated values. Calculated members make it easy to create values such as average prices, weighted averages, ratios, growth calculations, and other key performance indicators (KPIs) to analyze your data. In addition to including sophisticated built-in tools for creating calculated members using MDX functions, Analysis Services allows you to access Microsoft Visual Studio function libraries. You can even write your own external functions.

Because a cube contains multiple measure groups, it is easy to create calculations that include measures from different fact tables. For example, you could calculate a percentage by dividing Sales Amount by Sales Target even though the two measures are in different measure groups.

Finance Formulas

Financial applications typically require much more sophisticated formulas than simple addition. This is one of the reasons spreadsheets are very popular for financial analysis. Analysis Services uses the following special features to support financial analysis:

- **Unary operators**   Most financial analysts expect expenses (which are really negative) to show up as positive numbers. Some accounts—such as the number of employees—are called *memo accounts* and should not be added or subtracted. Analysis Services provides a mechanism for properly managing these types of accounts.

- **Semi-additive calculations**   Some measures are actually snapshots at a point in time. Typical examples include inventory quantities and bank account balances. These measures should be added up over all dimensions except time. Analysis Services supports semi-additive calculations.

- **By-account aggregations**   Sometimes a single measure should behave differently depending on what type of account it is. For example, a Revenues account should add up over time, but an Inventory account should not. The *By Account* aggregation function allows you to have different aggregation definitions for different account types within a single measure.

- **Script assignments**   For certain complex financial calculations, you need to change a value that would otherwise be calculated in the cube and then allow that value to be re-aggregated within the normal dimension aggregation rules. You can think of it as changing a specific formula in a spreadsheet, even when other formulas depend on it.

Analysis Services is able to quickly respond to queries, even when the source data contains hundreds of millions of detail rows. An Analysis Services cube is a metadata-rich environment that turns data into information and makes it possible for you to create powerful analytical queries using MDX. Analysis Services is like a spreadsheet on steroids, enabling you to create complex formulas that can be applied across the enterprise to very large amounts of data. Because of these benefits, Analysis Services has become a very important component of Microsoft's business intelligence platform.

Analysis Services and the Microsoft Business Intelligence Platform

Microsoft provides a comprehensive set of BI applications that enable you to create an enterprise-scale, fully functional BI system. This section briefly describes these applications but doesn't go into a lot of detail. The purpose of this section is to show you the important role Analysis Services plays and how it interacts with the other applications in the Microsoft BI platform.

The Microsoft BI platform is based on SQL Server 2008 and the 2007 Microsoft Office System. SQL Server 2008 is actually a suite of the following products:

- **SQL Server Database Engine**   Often referred to simply as SQL Server, the SQL Server Database Engine is a relational database management system that meets the needs of the data source layer. Many operational systems—for example, enterprise resource planning, finance and accounting, human resources, and point of sale—use SQL Server as their database engine. SQL Server also acts as your BI system's data storage and retrieval layer. Enhancements to SQL Server 2008 have increased its enterprise data-warehouse and data-mart capabilities.

  Analysis Services interacts with SQL Server in several ways. The most common way is for Analysis Services to query your SQL Server data warehouse and data marts and load the data into its own multidimensional data storage. If extremely large amounts of data are frequently added to your enterprise data warehouse, the amount of time Analysis Services can take to load the data into its own storage and the cost of storing your data in both SQL Server and Analysis Services can become prohibitive. In this case, Analysis Services can respond to analytical queries using data stored in SQL Server. If you need real-time BI, Analysis Services can access data stored in operational systems. Analysis Services and SQL Server can work together so that when new data is loaded into your SQL Server data warehouse or data marts, SQL Server notifies Analysis Services and then Analysis Services can update its own multidimensional data storage.

- **Integration Services**   A data integration application that can serve as the data transformation layer. You can use Integration Services to extract data from a variety of data sources, transform the data, and then load the data into your enterprise data warehouse, data marts, or directly into Analysis Services. You can also use Integration Services to programmatically create, modify, and delete Analysis Services database objects.

- **Analysis Services**   Provides both multidimensional OLAP and data mining functionality. It provides the capabilities needed in the analytical layer. This book concentrates on multidimensional OLAP, which provides both precalculated aggregation of business measures for improved query performance and complex calculation capabilities. You can learn more about Analysis Services data mining functionality at the SQL Server 2008 Data Mining home page at *http://www.microsoft.com/sqlserver/2008/en/us /data-mining.aspx*.

- **Reporting Services**   Enables enterprise reporting functionality in the presentation layer. You can use Reporting Services to design reports, schedule report execution, and deliver reports in a variety of formats. Analysis Services is often used as a data source for Reporting Services reports.

The following Microsoft Office System 2007 products are also part of the Microsoft BI platform:

- **Microsoft Office Excel 2007**   A presentation-layer desktop application that enables ad hoc analysis. Excel can access Analysis Services data and create PivotTables and PivotCharts. The integration between Excel 2007 and Analysis Services 2008 has been greatly enhanced compared to prior versions of the products. Excel 2007 is able to take advantage of Analysis Services features such as KPIs, drillthrough, translations, and server actions.

- **Microsoft Office Visio 2007**   Another presentation-layer desktop application used to create powerful data visualizations. You can use Visio to create drawings and diagrams. You can then create a connection between Visio and Analysis Services, retrieve data, and associate the data with the individual shapes in your diagram.

- **Microsoft Office PerformancePoint Server**   The newest member of the Office System suite of products. PerformancePoint Server (PPS) is an integrated BI performance-management solution. PerformancePoint is composed of two servers: PerformancePoint Planning Server (PPS Planning) and PerformancePoint Monitoring and Analytics Server (PPS M&A). PPS M&A provides the presentation layer with Web-based analytics. You can use it to create dashboard pages that contain analytical reports and charts and KPIs. You can use Analysis Services as the data source for PPS M&A dashboards. PPS Planning is an operational application used for planning and budgeting. It uses Analysis Services as its reporting, consolidation, and business rule calculation engine.

- **Microsoft Office SharePoint Server**   A presentation-layer integrated Web site that enables collaboration so that you can share all your BI content. It provides a single location for users to access Reporting Services reports, Excel workbooks, and Visio diagrams. A new feature in Microsoft Office SharePoint Server, Excel Services, allows you to centrally manage and publish Excel workbooks. You can use Microsoft Office SharePoint Server to create dashboards containing KPIs and analytical reports and views.

You can learn more about Microsoft BI at *http://www.microsoft.com/bi*.

Analysis Services Tools

Two additional applications are part of the SQL Server 2008 suite of products. These are the tools that you use to work with Analysis Services. When you are responsible for an Analysis Services cube, or UDM, you perform two basic roles. On the one hand, you act as a developer, designing and creating the dimensions and cubes. On the other hand, you act as an administrator, keeping deployed cubes up to date and performing properly. In a large-scale implementation, it is common for these two roles to be performed by different people, or even for multiple people to be involved in each role. Analysis Services recognizes that these are completely different roles and gives you two completely different tools for performing them.

For the developer, Analysis Services provides Business Intelligence Development Studio (BIDS). This is actually a version of Visual Studio 2008 with business intelligence designers installed instead of designers for C# or VB.NET. If you use Visual Studio to write .NET applications, BIDS integrates smoothly with your existing installation. If you do not use Visual Studio for any other purpose, the Visual Studio environment, along with the business intelligence designers, is included with SQL Server 2008. Within BIDS, you can have multiple developers working on different parts of a single project, deploying the Analysis Services application to development, test, or production servers as appropriate. You can even integrate BIDS with Microsoft Visual Studio Team System 2008 or Microsoft Visual Source Safe 2005 so that you can safely manage your Analysis Services database source code. If you want to automate either development or production tasks, you can use the .NET libraries in Analysis Management Objects (AMO), or you can use XMLA scripts.

For the administrator, Analysis Services provides SQL Server Management Studio (SSMS). This is another version of the Visual Studio environment configured to enable you to administer SQL Server, Analysis Services, Reporting Services, and Integration Services. SSMS enables you to control access to Analysis Services databases and load data into cubes. In SSMS you can modify a limited set of database properties, but you can't make design changes. You can create and execute MDX queries and XMLA command scripts.

Analysis Services is very effective at implementing the three benefits of OLAP. It uses a database model—with automatic management of aggregations—to handle extremely large databases with little or no data explosion. It allows you to create a metadata model that accurately represents the true nature of both dimensions and cubes. And it supports a powerful implementation of the MDX formula language with capabilities that range from simple calculated ratios to complex financial calculations with sophisticated ripple-up effects. In essence, Analysis Services is simple enough for small, uncomplicated organizations and powerful enough for large or complex organizations, allowing all types of organizations to add analytical power to their BI solutions.

Chapter 3
Accessing Source Data

In this chapter, you will learn how to:

- Use Business Intelligence Development Studio to create a business intelligence solution and an Analysis Services project.

- Create a data source using the Data Source Wizard.

- Develop a data source view using the Data Source View Wizard.

- Create data source view diagrams.

- Add logical primary keys and entity relationships to a data source view.

- Create named calculations and named queries.

In this chapter, you will take the first steps toward creating an Analysis Services database, beginning by creating an Analysis Services project within a business intelligence solution. An Analysis Services project contains all of the code needed for one Analysis Services database. You will then add a data source to your project. A data source contains the information Analysis Services needs to connect to a source database. Finally, you will add a data source view that contains information about the tables and views in the source database. The data source view also allows you to provide supplemental metadata.

Creating a Business Intelligence Solution

Throughout this book, you will be using SQL Server Business Intelligence Development Studio (BIDS) to design and deploy a sample Analysis Services business intelligence solution. BIDS serves as the development environment for all of the SQL Server business intelligence tools, including Integration Services and Reporting Services, in addition to Analysis Services. If you are familiar with the Microsoft Visual Studio application development environment, you will notice that BIDS is Visual Studio with additional project templates specifically designed for SQL Server business intelligence. BIDS contains four main windows that you will use to develop BI applications: Designer Window, Solution Explorer, Properties Window, and Toolbox. With the exception of the Toolbox window, which is not used for developing Analysis Services projects, you will work with each of these BIDS components extensively as you work through the procedures in this book.

To get started, you will create a business intelligence solution that contains a single Analysis Services project. Then in the following sections of this chapter, you will add a data source and a data source view to the project and add additional functionality in each of the remaining chapters of this book. The Analysis Services database that you will create is the analytical layer of a full-featured business intelligence solution. Most business intelligence solutions will also have a data transformation layer that extracts data from business systems, transforms the data, and then loads it into a data mart or data warehouse. Business intelligence solutions also have a presentation layer that provides reporting and data visualization. The code for the data layer and presentation layer can be contained in additional projects within a business intelligence solution. These other layers of a business intelligence solution are beyond the scope of this book, but they can be developed using the functionality of SQL Server 2008 Database Engine, Integration Services, Reporting Services, and Office 2007.

Create a new Analysis Services project

1. On the Microsoft Windows task bar, click Start, point to All Programs, expand the Microsoft SQL Server 2008 folder, and then select SQL Server Business Intelligence Development Studio.

2. On the File menu, point to New and then select Project.

> **Note** In BIDS, you create a solution that may contain multiple projects. However, the File menu doesn't have an item that allows you to create a solution. Instead, you choose to create a new project and BIDS will automatically create a solution for you.

3. Select the Business Intelligence Projects project type and select the Analysis Services Project template. The New Project dialog box also contains templates for Integration Services and Reporting Services projects.

4. Name your project **Adventure Works SSAS**. The text in the Solution Name box changes automatically to match the project name. When you create a solution that might have multiple projects, you can rename the solution so that the name is more representative of the entire solution.

5. Select Create Directory for Solution and change the solution name to **Adventure Works BI**.

6. Confirm that the solution location is C:\Users\<*YourUserName*>\Documents \Visual Studio 2008\Projects.

   This folder is the default location for any solution you create using Visual Studio 2008. If you have previously created a Visual Studio project, the solution location will display the location of the last project you created.

> **Note** If you are using Windows XP or Windows Server 2003, the default location for Visual Studio 2008 solutions is C:\Documents and Settings\<*YourUserName*> \My Documents\Visual Studio 2008\Projects.

The New Project dialog box should look similar to the following:

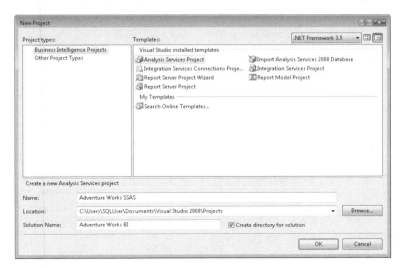

7. Click OK to create the project. BIDS will create the Adventure Works SSAS project and display it in Solution Explorer.

You may not see the Adventure Works BI solution. With the default BIDS settings, if a solution contains only one project, BIDS will not display the solution. The solution will be displayed when you add another project. If you would like to display the solution even when there is only one project, select Options from the Tools menu and then select Always Show Solution on the Projects And Solutions tab of the Options dialog box.

Creating a Data Source

The first task in creating an Analysis Services project is to create a data source. The data source contains the information that Analysis Services uses to connect to the source database. It contains the data provider name, the server and database name, and the authentication credentials that Analysis Services will use.

The source data must be contained in a relational database. Analysis Services can read data contained in SQL Server 2008, Microsoft Access, Teradata, Oracle, IBM DB2, and other relational databases for which you have an OLE DB or ODBC driver, but it cannot read data from a Microsoft Office Excel file, a text file, or other nonrelational data sources. Analysis Services connects to a relational database using a .NET or OLE DB data provider. When you create a data source, BIDS will default to the SQL Server Native Client data provider. BIDS also includes data providers for other databases such as Microsoft Access and Oracle. If BIDS doesn't include a data provider for the database that contains your source data, you will need to install that database's client connectivity components.

> **Note** The approved list of data providers can be found in the SQL Server 2008 Books Online article "Defining Data Sources," located at *http://msdn.microsoft.com/en-us/library/ms175608.aspx*.

Create a data source

1. In BIDS in Solution Explorer, right-click the Data Sources folder and select New Data Source. The Data Source Wizard appears.

2. On the Welcome page, click Next.

3. On the Select How To Define The Connection page, click the New button. The Connection Manager dialog box appears.

4. Type a server name: **localhost**.

5. In the Select Or Enter A Database Name list box, select SSAS2008SBS. The Connection Manager dialog box should now look like this:

6. Click Test Connection. A dialog box opens with the message "Test connection succeeded." Click OK.

   Now is a good time to ensure that BIDS can connect to the source database—you will not be able to successfully create a data source view unless BIDS has database connectivity. If you receive an error message, verify that you have permission to read from the source database and that you have properly specified the data source provider, server name, and database name.

7. Click OK to close the Connection Manager dialog box.

8. In the Data Source Wizard, on the Select How To Define The Connection page, click Next.

   The Impersonation Information page appears. On this page, you configure the Windows security credentials that Analysis Services will use when it connects to the data source you defined in steps 4 through 7.

   - The Use A Specific Windows User Name And Password option lets you enter the user name and password of a Windows user account.

   - The Use The Service Account option will have Analysis Services use its service logon user ID to connect to the data source.

   - The Use The Credentials Of The Current User option is only used for some very specialized circumstances. It is important to note that when you use this option, Analysis Services will not use the Windows user name and password of the current user for most processing and query tasks.

   - The Inherit option causes this data source to use the impersonation information contained in the Analysis Services DataSourceImpersonationInfo database property.

   The most commonly selected options are Use The Service Account or Use A Specific Windows User Name and Password.

9. On the Impersonation Information page, select Use The Service Account and click Next.

10. Leave SSAS2008SBS as the data source name and click Finish to complete the wizard.

> **Tip** The name of a data source defaults to the name of the database that it references. In general, this name works well and helps you remember which database each data source points to. However, if the name of the source database in your development environment is different than the name of the source database in your test or production environments, you want to give the data source a more generic name that is meaningful in all three environments.

   Notice that the Data Sources folder now contains the file SSAS2008SBS.ds. This XML file contains the data source information that you just created using the Data Source Wizard.

Now that you have created a data source, you are ready to create a data source view.

Creating a Data Source View

A data source view is a logical data model that exists between your physical source database and Analysis Services dimensions and cubes. When you create a data source view, you designate the tables and views in the source database that contain data that you want to use to build dimensions and cubes. BIDS connects to the source database and reads the table and view definitions and stores that metadata in the data source view. Metadata is "data about the data": the names of the tables and views, the column names, data types, primary key columns, and foreign key relationships.

The data source view allows you to provide additional metadata. If you need to transform data, you can add a named calculation that contains a SQL expression to a table. If you need to filter, group, or join data from multiple tables, you can create a logical table called a *named query* that contains a SQL select statement. Although it is common for source data to be stored in a single data warehouse or data mart, sometimes the business data you need to access is stored in multiple databases. You can create a data source for each database and then add tables from the databases into a single data source view. You can then add logical foreign key relationships to the data source view to show how the data from different databases should be joined together.

When you create dimensions and cubes, you will start with the basic metadata stored in the data source view and enhance it with information about hierarchical relationships, sort order, proper formatting, and so forth, so that your Analysis Services database becomes a metadata-rich data analysis environment.

Create a data source view

1. In Solution Explorer, right-click the Data Source Views folder and select New Data Source View. The Data Source View Wizard appears.

2. On the Welcome page, click Next.

3. On the Select a Data Source page, select the SSAS2008SBS relational data source and click Next.

    The Select Tables And Views page appears. The Available Objects list shows all of the tables and views contained in the source database. The Included Objects list displays the tables and views that will appear in your data source view.

4. Double-click DimAccount to add it to the Included Objects list. Alternatively, you can select a table or multi-select several tables and then click the Add button (>) to add the table or tables to the Included Objects list.

    The Select Tables and Views page should look like the following:

5. Select the DimAccount table and then click Add Related Tables.

   The Data Source Wizard analyzes the foreign key relationships in the source database and adds the FactFinance table to the Included Objects list. The FactFinance table is the only table related to DimAccount.

6. In the Filter box, type **dim** and click the Filter button.

   You can filter the Available Objects list in order to make it easier to find the tables and views that you want to include in your data source view. In the SSAS2008SBS database, all dimension table names begin with "Dim", so the Available Objects list now shows all of the dimension tables in SSAS2008SBS.

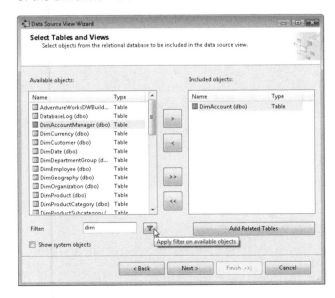

7. Click the Add All button (>>) to add the dimension tables to the Included Objects list.

8. In the Filter box, delete dim, type **fact**, and click the Filter button. Click the Add All button (>>) to add the fact tables to the Included Objects list.

9. Clear the Filter box and click the Filter button. The tables and views that remain in the Available Objects list are in the SSAS2008SBS database, but they will not be included in your data source view. The Select Tables and Views page should look similar to this:

10. Click Next. On the Completing The Wizard page, accept the default name SSAS2008SBS and click Finish. The Data Source View designer appears, displaying the tables you selected.

    Notice that the Data Source Views folder in Solution Explorer contains the file SSAS2008SBS.dsv. This XML file contains the data source view information that you just created using the Data Source View Wizard.

> **Tip** If the source database changes, you want your data source view to change as well. Select Refresh from the Data Source View menu, and BIDS compares the source database tables and the data source view metadata, shows you the differences, and allows you to accept or ignore changes.

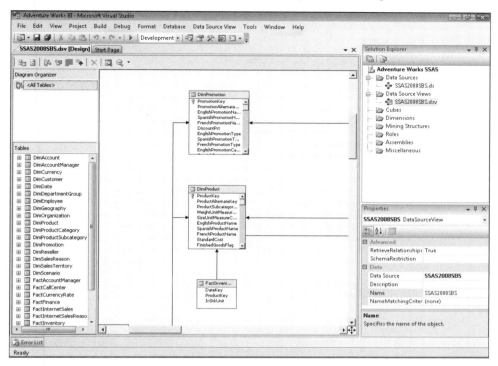

Browse a data source view

If your data source view contains many tables, you won't be able to see all of the tables in the diagram pane. The following procedure shows you how to browse the contents of a data source view.

1. Click and hold the four-headed arrow button at the lower-right corner of the data source view diagram pane. The table locator looks like the following image.

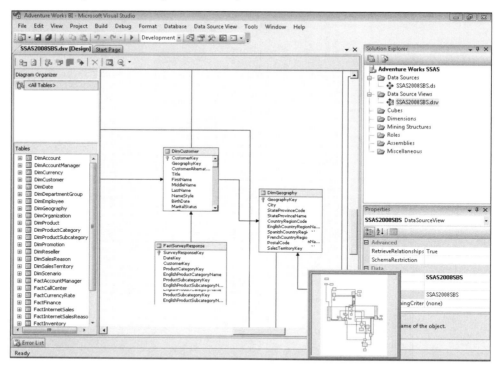

2. Drag your mouse around the table locator. The diagram pane scrolls to match your movements.

3. Click a table name in the Tables pane. The diagram pane scrolls so that it is centered on the table you selected.

Modifying a Data Source View

The data source view you have created contains metadata that was read from the source database. You can now enhance the data source view by adding additional metadata. You can add logical primary keys and relationships. You can also add a SQL expression to a table or add a logical table based on a SQL query. A data source view diagram may contain a large number of tables and relationships. This makes it hard to understand the structure of the source data. To get a more understandable view of the data, you can create additional data source view diagrams that display a subset of related tables.

Create a subject area diagram

You can create a diagram that contains a subset of the tables in your data source view. I like to create a diagram for each fact table and all of its related dimension tables.

1. On the Data Source View menu, select New Diagram. A new diagram appears in the Diagram Organizer pane. The diagram pane is empty.

2. In the Diagram Organizer, change the name of the diagram to **Internet Sales**. The Diagram Organizer and diagram pane should look like this:

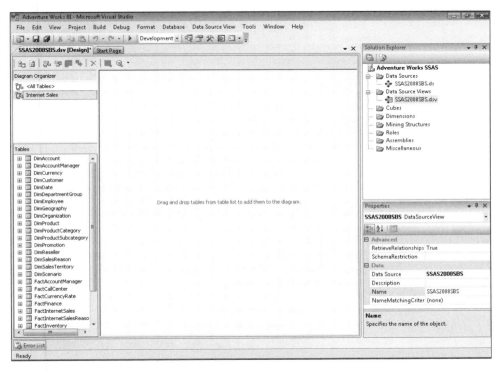

3. Right-click in the diagram pane and select Show Tables.

> **Important** In a diagram, you can choose to show or hide tables without affecting other diagrams in the data source view. Any other changes you make to one diagram are applied to all diagrams in the data source view.

4. In the Show Tables dialog box, select FactInternetSales. The Show Tables dialog box should look like the following image.

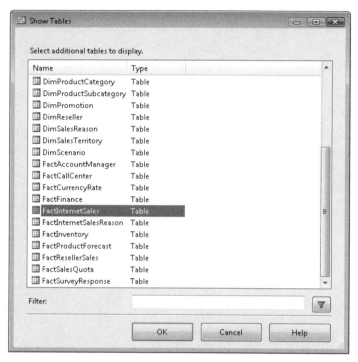

5. Click OK. Right-click the header of the FactInternetSales table and select Show Related Tables.

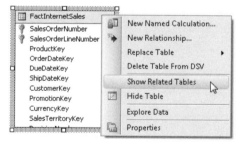

All of the tables related to FactInternetSales appear in the diagram.

6. Right-click a blank area of the diagram pane and select Switch To Diagonal Layout.

You can arrange tables in the data source view using rectangular layout or diagonal layout. With rectangular layout, the relationship lines are drawn between the tables. I prefer diagonal layout where the relationship lines are drawn between the columns that are related.

> **Tip** When you switch between rectangular layout and diagonal layout, BIDS will rearrange the tables in your diagram. You should select rectangular or diagonal layout before you manually arrange the tables in your diagram.

7. Right-click a blank area of the diagram pane, point to Zoom, and select 75%. You may wish to further organize your diagram by selecting each table and moving or resizing it. With a little practice, you can get your data source view diagram pane to look like this:

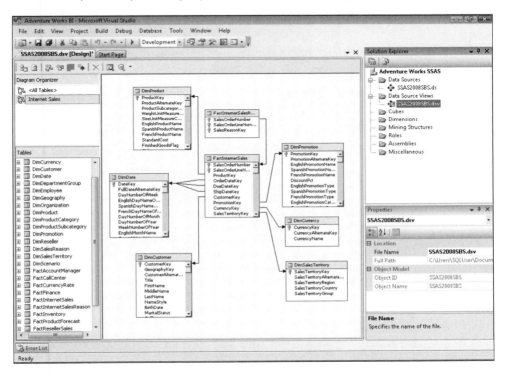

Add primary keys and relationships

The SSAS2008SBS database contains tables with product category and subcategory informa-tion that you will want to include in your data source view. The metadata for these two tables is incomplete. No primary keys or relationships have been defined. In this procedure, you will show these tables in the Internet Sales diagram and add logical primary keys and relation-ships. A database primary key designates the column(s) that uniquely identify the rows in a table and does not allow any rows to have duplicate values in the primary key columns. A logical primary key in the data source view also designates the columns that uniquely identify the rows in a table, but it doesn't enforce uniqueness. You must have some other mechanism to guarantee that there is a unique value for each row in the table or Analysis Services will generate errors when you try to process a dimension.

1. In the Tables list, select DimProductSubcategory, drag it onto the diagram pane, and drop it near DimProduct.

2. In the DimProductSubcategory table, right-click the ProductSubcategoryKey column and select Set Logical Primary Key. BIDS creates a logical primary key on the DimProductSubcategory table and displays a key icon next to ProductSubcategoryKey.

> **Note** A table can have a primary key with more than one column. Just select the primary key columns and then right-click and select Set Logical Primary Key.

3. Click ProductSubcategoryKey in the DimProduct table and drop it on ProductSubcategoryKey in the DimProductSubcategory table.

   BIDS creates a relationship between the DimProduct and DimProductSubcategory tables and displays a relationship line showing that the tables are joined on ProductSubcategoryKey. Your diagram pane should look similar to this:

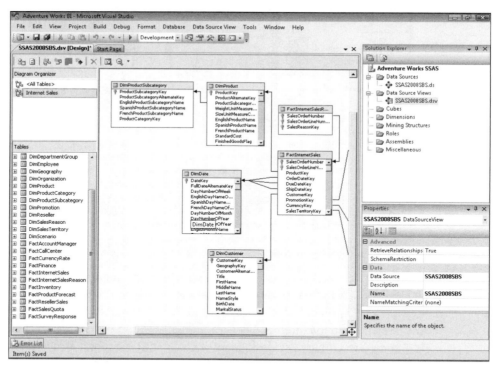

4. In the Tables list, select DimProductCategory, drag it onto the diagram pane, and drop it near DimProductSubcategory.

5. In the DimProductCategory table, right-click the ProductCategoryKey column and select Set Logical Primary Key.

6. Click ProductCategoryKey in the DimProductCategory table and drop it on ProductCategoryKey in the DimProductSubcategory table. The Specify Relationship dialog box appears, warning you that you have reversed the typical foreign key–primary key relationship.

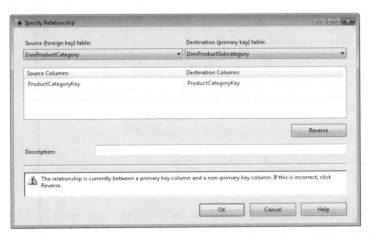

7. Click Reverse to correct the logical foreign key relationship and then click OK. You may want to rearrange the tables in your diagram so that the data source view now looks like the following image.

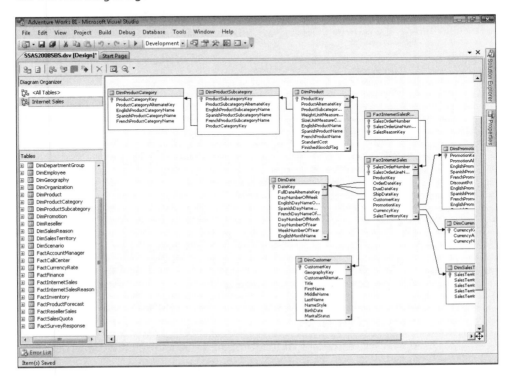

Add a named calculation

You may need to apply transformations to your source data. It is common to append columns, parse data from a column, or perform calculations. For example, you may want to append customers' first and last names or you may want to add sales amount, tax amount, and shipping to get the total amount. In the next procedure, you add the characters FY to the fiscal year so that users can easily distinguish fiscal and calendar dates.

1. Right-click the header of the DimDate table and select New Named Calculation. The Create Named Calculation dialog box appears.

2. In the Column Name box, type **FiscalYearName**.

3. In the Expression box, type this SQL expression:

   ```
   'FY ' + CONVERT(CHAR(4),FiscalYear)
   ```

 Important The SQL expression that you enter is passed through to the source database. It must use valid SQL syntax for the relational database management system (RDBMS) that is hosting your data. I often use SQL Server Management Studio to write a SQL query that contains the SQL expression, execute the query to make sure the expression is correct, and then copy the expression and paste it into the named calculation.

The Create Named Calculation text box now looks like this:

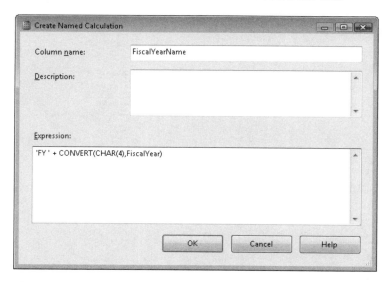

4. Click OK. The new named calculation FiscalYearName now appears as the last column in the DimDate table.

5. Right-click the header of the DimDate table and select Explore Data. Scroll to the far right to see the values in the FiscalYearName column.

The Explore Data screen should look similar to this:

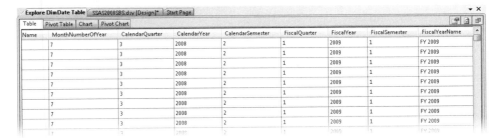

Name	MonthNumberOfYear	CalendarQuarter	CalendarYear	CalendarSemester	FiscalQuarter	FiscalYear	FiscalSemester	FiscalYearName
	7	3	2008	2	1	2009	1	FY 2009
	7	3	2008	2	1	2009	1	FY 2009
	7	3	2008	2	1	2009	1	FY 2009
	7	3	2008	2	1	2009	1	FY 2009
	7	3	2008	2	1	2009	1	FY 2009
	7	3	2008	2	1	2009	1	FY 2009
	7	3	2008	2	1	2009	1	FY 2009
	7	3	2008	2	1	2009	1	FY 2009

6. Close the Explore DimDate Table window.

Create a named query

Sometimes you may need to apply transformations to your data that are more complicated than just applying a SQL expression. You may want to filter, group, or join data from multiple tables. You can do this by creating a SQL SELECT statement and then putting the statement into a named query.

In the next procedure, you will replace the DimCustomer table with a named query. The SQL SELECT statement will join DimCustomer and DimGeography so that you can identify a customer's city, state, and country.

1. Right-click the header of the DimCustomer table, point to Replace Table, and select With New Named Query.

The Create Named Query dialog box appears. The diagram pane shows the DimCustomer table with each column selected, the grid pane shows each column from DimCustomer, and the SQL pane shows the corresponding SQL select statement. These three panes are alternative displays of the same information.

2. Click the Add Table button.

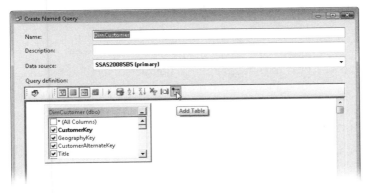

3. In the Add Table dialog box, select DimGeography, click Add, and then click Close.

4. In the DimGeography table, select City, StateProvinceName, and EnglishCountryRegionName. The Create Named Query dialog box now looks like the following image.

> **Important** The SQL query that you enter is passed through to the source database. It must use valid SQL syntax for the RDBMS that is hosting your data. I often use SQL Server Management Studio to write and execute a SQL query and then copy the query and paste it into the Create Named Query SQL pane.
>
> BIDS attempts to validate your SQL query when you close the Create Named Calculation dialog box. Sometimes BIDS is unable to parse valid SQL and raises an error. If you know that your SQL query is valid, you can click the Switch To Generic Query Builder button. Then BIDS will not attempt to validate your SQL query.

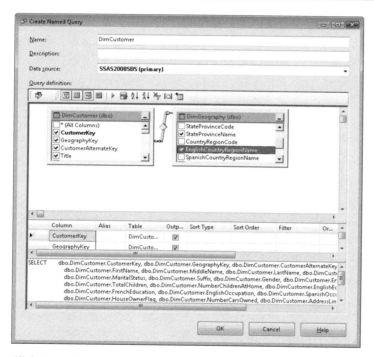

5. Click OK. The icon next to DimCustomer in the table header has changed from a single table to multiple tables, indicating that DimCustomer is now a named query.

6. In the Diagram Organizer pane, select the <All Tables> diagram and then in the Tables pane, select DimCustomer.

The changes you made in the Internet Sales diagram have also been made in the <All Tables> diagram. DimCustomer is a named query everywhere it appears in your data source view.

The fields you selected in your Named Query can be found when you scroll within the DimCustomer table:

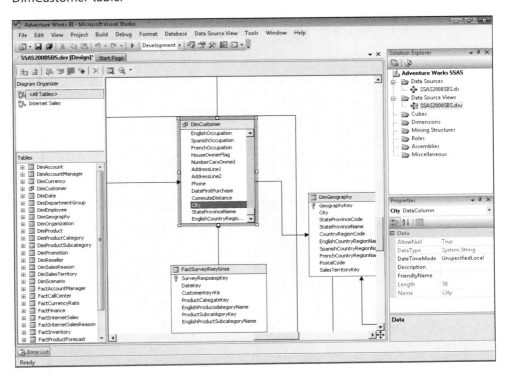

7. Click the Save All button and close BIDS.

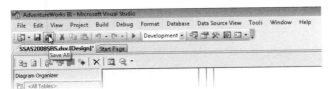

In this chapter, you learned how to create a business intelligence solution and an Analysis Services project using SQL Server Business Intelligence Development Studio. You created a data source that contains the information Analysis Services uses to connect to a database. You then created a data source view that contains the definitions of the tables and views in a source database. Because a data source view that contains many tables can be hard to comprehend, you created a diagram that displayed a subset of the tables in the data source view. The source database was missing some primary keys and foreign key relationships, so you added logical primary keys and relationships to the data source view. Finally, in order to transform the source data, you added a named calculation containing a SQL expression and a named query containing a SQL query to the data source view.

In Chapter 4, "Creating Dimensions," and in Chapter 5, "Creating a Cube," you will create dimensions and cubes based on the metadata contained in the data source view. When you process these dimensions and cubes, Analysis Services will use the information in the data source to connect to the source database.

Chapter 4
Creating Dimensions

In this chapter, you will learn how to:

- Analyze source data using the Data Source View Designer.

- Create standard, time, and parent-child dimensions using the Dimension Wizard.

- Deploy a dimension and browse its members.

- Modify a dimension using the Dimension Designer.

- View and respond to Design Warnings.

- Create attribute relationships and user-defined hierarchies.

- Configure dimension and attribute properties.

In Chapter 1, "Business Intelligence: A Data Analysis Foundation," you learned that you turn data into information by adding dimensions that contain attributes and hierarchies to numerical values. The dimensions add context and meaning to numbers. This is one of the major benefits provided by a dimensional database. In Chapter 2, "Understanding OLAP and Analysis Services," you learned that you can create a dimensional database in SQL Server and then use that data to create a multidimensional OLAP database in Analysis Services. Chapter 3, "Accessing Source Data," explained how you establish a connection between a relational database and Analysis Services. It also showed how to designate the relational database tables that contain the data you want to load into Analysis Services dimensions and cubes.

In this chapter, you have been provided with an Analysis Services project that already contains a data source and data source view. The data source view references some of the dimension tables in the SSAS2008SBS data mart. In this chapter, you will create Analysis Services dimensions based on the SSAS2008SBS data mart dimension tables. You will use the Dimension Wizard to create dimensions and work with the Dimension Designer to review a dimension's structure, modify its properties, and browse its data. You will create three different kinds of dimensions—standard, time, and parent-child—to become familiar with some of the options available to you when designing dimensions. But before you begin creating Analysis Services dimensions, you should become familiar with the data that those dimensions will contain.

Previewing Dimension Data

One of the most important steps to take before designing a dimension in Analysis Services is to thoroughly understand the source data. View the data to become familiar with it and try to understand how the data relates to the functioning of your organization. Find the erroneous or missing data—don't believe those who tell you that their data is clean. Some data may be less dirty than other data, but you will always find data issues. Discover the hierarchical relationships that exist in the data. You should learn how the data in one table may be related to data in other tables and whether the relationships are enforced by foreign keys. You will also need to determine whether any of the data needs to be transformed before it is loaded into a dimension.

You can use the Data Source View Designer to explore dimension data. The Data Source View Designer lets you use a grid, chart, pivot table, or pivot chart to view the data in a table. But first you'll need to open the AdventureWorks BI solution.

Open the AdventureWorks BI solution

1. On the Microsoft Windows task bar, click Start, point to All Programs, expand the Microsoft SQL Server 2008 folder, and then select SQL Server Business Intelligence Development Studio.

2. On the File menu, point to Open and select Project/Solution.

3. In the Open Project dialog box, browse to the C:\Microsoft Press\Analysis Services 2008 SBS\Analysis Services 2008 SBS\Chapter 04\AdventureWorks BI folder.

4. Select the AdventureWorks BI.sln file and click Open.

Now that you have opened the AdventureWorks BI solution, you are ready to explore some of the dimension tables in the AS2008SBS data mart.

Explore dimension data

1. In Solution Explorer, expand the Data Source Views folder, right-click SSAS2008SBS.dsv, and select View Designer.

2. In the Diagram Organizer pane, select the First Dimensions diagram.

   The First Dimensions data source view diagram displays the data source tables for the Product, Date, and Employee dimensions.

   The Product dimension is a snowflake dimension: the DimProduct table has a foreign key relationship to the DimProductSubcategory table, which has a foreign key relationship to the DimProductCategory table.

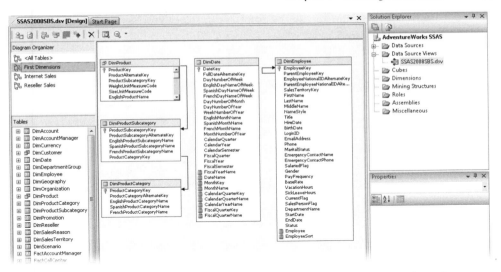

DimDate is a standard dimension table, but several calculated members have been created so that the data will be transformed as it is loaded into Analysis Services.

The DimEmployee table has a foreign key relationship between the ParentEmployeeKey column and the EmployeeKey column. This self-referencing relationship indicates that Employee is a parent-child dimension.

3. In the Diagram pane, right-click the header of the DimProduct table.

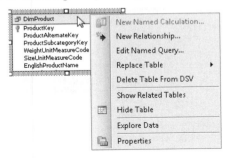

4. Select Explore Data. You can see that many of the rows have a null value in the ProductSubcategoryKey column.

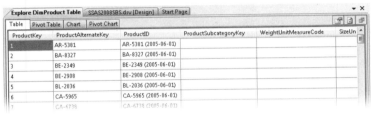

This example of missing data means that the subcategory of many products is unknown. You can determine how severe this problem is by creating a chart.

5. Click the Chart tab. In the column list, select ProductSubcategoryKey and clear all the other column check boxes. Press ENTER.

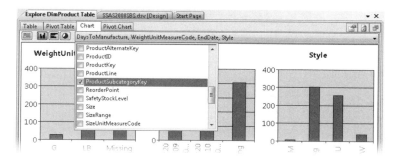

The chart shows that more than 200 rows in the table have a missing value for ProductSubcategoryKey. In the procedure titled "Use the Dimension Wizard to Create the Product Dimension" in the following section, you will create a Subcategory attribute in the Product dimension. When you browse the Subcategory attribute, you will see an Unknown member. Because you have taken the time to become familiar with the data in the DimProduct table, when you see the Unknown member in the Subcategory attribute, you will be able to understand that it represents the rows in the DimProduct table where the ProductSubcategoryKey contains null values.

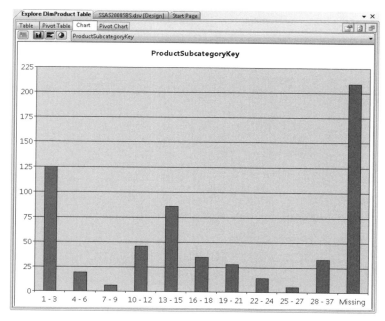

6. Close the Explore DimProduct Table viewer.

In the First Dimensions diagram, you can see that several of the columns in the DimDate table have been marked with a calculator icon. In Chapter 3, you learned that these are calculated members. If someone else created the data source view and you are unfamiliar with the calculated members, you should understand the SQL expression they contain and view the results of the transformation that they apply to the source data.

7. In the DimDate table, right-click the FiscalYearName calculated member and select Edit Named Calculation.

   The FiscalYearName calculated member contains the following SQL Expression.

   ```
   'FY ' + CONVERT(CHAR(4), FiscalYear)
   ```

   This expression appends FY to the value in the FiscalYear column.

8. Click OK. In the First Dimensions diagram, right-click the header of the DimDate table and select Explore Data.

9. In the Explore DimDate Table dialog box, scroll to the right until you can see the FiscalYear column and the FiscalYearName calculated member.

   You can see that the FiscalYearName calculated member appends FY to the value in FiscalYear column. This will make it very easy for report readers to determine whether a year is a fiscal year or a calendar year.

10. Continue scrolling to the right and notice the values of the other calculated members.

    Many of the calculated members in this table have been designed to help you create Fiscal Date and Calendar Date hierarchies in the Date dimension.

11. Close the Explore DimDate Table viewer.

    Take a moment to explore the data in the other tables. In particular, you may want to explore the Employee and EmployeeSort calculated members in the DimEmployee table. These calculated members were included to help you create an Employee attribute that displays employees' first and last names, but sorts their names by last name and then by first name. The Employee calculated member combines an employee's first and last names into a single value for display and the EmployeeSort calculated member combines the employee's last and first name into a single value that you can use for sorting purposes.

Now that you have become familiar with the dimension data in the source database, you are ready to begin creating Analysis Services dimensions.

Creating a Standard Dimension

You must use the Dimension Wizard to create the initial structure of a dimension. As you work through the steps of the wizard, you will select the data source tables, the key attribute, and other attributes that you want to include in the dimension. You will also use the wizard to configure some of the more important attribute properties. However, in most cases the dimension design will not be complete. After you have completed the initial dimension design using the wizard, you will frequently use the Dimension Designer to further enhance your dimension. The following procedure will introduce you to the process of creating a dimension with the Dimension Wizard; you will learn more about using the Dimension Designer in the section titled "Modifying a Dimension" later in this chapter.

Use the Dimension Wizard to create the Product dimension

1. In Solution Explorer, right-click the Dimensions folder and select New Dimension. On the Welcome to the Dimension Wizard page, click Next.

   The Select Creation Method page shows four methods you can use to create a dimension. By default, the wizard selects the most common method: Use An Existing Table.

   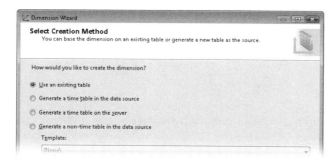

2. Verify that Use An Existing Table is selected and click Next.

   The Specify Source Information page will appear. You will use this page to designate the main dimension table and to select the columns in that table used to create the dimension's key attribute.

   Before you can designate a dimension table, you must first indicate the data source view that contains that table. The AdventureWorks SSAS project has only one data source view, so on the Specify Source Information page, the SSAS2008 data source view has already been selected.

3. Verify that SSAS2008SBS has been selected from the Data Source View list.

   When you select a data source view, the Dimension Wizard retrieves the names of all the tables in the data source view and displays them in the Main Table list. The main table of your dimension must contain the column(s) you will use to create the key attribute of your dimension.

4. Select DimProduct from the Main Table list.

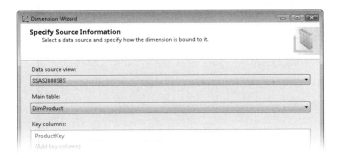

The Dimension Wizard assumes that the primary key of the main table will be the key attribute and selects this column in the Key Column and Name Column lists. The primary key of the DimProduct table is the ProductKey column.

5. Verify that ProductKey has been selected from the Key Columns list.

Every attribute has a member name. The member name is the text that appears in a report or a browser, so you want these names to be meaningful and descriptive. Many times, however, a source table for a dimension has one column that contains a descriptive name and another column that has an integer key that uniquely identifies each member. This is particularly true for key attributes. Every attribute has two properties: KeyColumns references the column (or columns, in the case of a composite key) that uniquely identifies an attribute member and NameColumn references the column that contains the descriptive labels. For many key attributes, the integer key will be used as the KeyColumns and another descriptive column will be used as the NameColumn. By default, Analysis Services uses the same column for the member key and for the member name. You can, however, specify a member name that's different than the key. Since the ProductKey column is just a unique integer that doesn't convey any information about the product to a report viewer, you will choose the ProductID column that contains the product's catalog number and date the product was introduced to be the attribute name as the name of the attribute.

6. Select ProductID from the Name Column list and then click Next.

The Dimension Wizard examines the foreign key relationships in the data source view and looks for any other tables that might also be included in this dimension. The tables are then displayed on the Select Related Tables page. The DimProduct table is part of the snowflake Product dimension that also contains the DimProductSubcategory and

DimProductCategory tables. Because DimProduct has a foreign key relationship to DimProductSubcategory, which has a foreign key relationship to DimProductCategory, these tables are displayed and selected by default. You will want to use data from these tables to create Category and Subcategory attributes.

7. Verify that the DimProductSubcategory and DimProductCategory tables are selected. Click Next.

On the Select Dimension Attributes page, the Dimension Wizard lists all of the columns from the tables you have selected. The wizard assumes that you want to create an attribute for the primary key of each table, so Product Key, Product Subcategory Key, and Product Category Key are already selected. You can then choose additional columns you want to include as attributes in your dimension.

8. From the Available Attributes list, select English Product Name, Color, List Price, Size, and Status.

    The name of an attribute may appear in a report or browser, so you want the attributes to have friendly names. To rename an attribute, click the Attribute Name text box to put it into edit mode and then rename the attribute.

9. Rename the following attributes.

Attribute	New Name
Product Key	Product ID
English Product Name	Product
Product Subcategory Key	Subcategory
Product Category Key	Category

When users browse a cube, they select an attribute to see measures aggregated by the members of the attribute. This is useful for some attributes, but not all. For example, in the Product dimension, users will want to browse the cube by Category, Subcategory, and Product. However, because very few products have the same price, users probably won't want to browse the cube by the List Price attribute. Instead, users will most likely want to browse the cube by Product and then display each product's List Price. Attributes such as List Price, which are additional information about another attribute, are called *member properties*. They are used for filtering and detailed reporting.

In the wizard, you disable browsing and prevent Analysis Services from creating aggregates by clearing the Enable Browsing check box. You can also disable browsing in the Dimension Designer by setting the value of an attribute's *AttributeHierarchyEnabled* property to *False*.

10. In the List Price row of the Available Attributes list, clear the Enable Browsing check box.

The list of Available Attributes page should look like this:

11. Click Next. On the Completing The Wizard page, change the name of the dimension to Product and click Finish. The Dimension Designer appears, displaying the structure of the Product dimension.

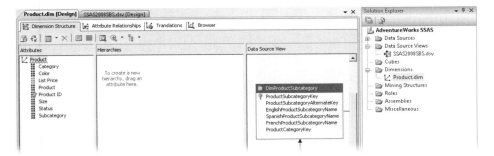

Deploying an Analysis Services Database

You should view the members of a dimension early in the development cycle to ensure that you have not made any errors, to determine whether any data issues might affect the dimension design, and to make sure that the dimension members appear as anticipated. You may find that you need to add or modify data source view calculated members to change the format of dimension member names, or you may find that the sort order of an attribute needs to be changed.

Before you can browse the members of a dimension, you must first deploy your design to the Analysis Services server. As you progressed through the pages of the Dimension Wizard, an XML file containing the dimension design was created. You can see that file, Product.dim, in the Dimensions folder of the AdventureWorks SSAS project in Solution Explorer. When you deploy the AdventureWorks SSAS database, the contents of all the XML files in the database, including Product.dim, are copied to the Analysis Services server, the dimension structure is created, and source data is then processed into the dimension.

Deploy and browse a dimension

1. On the Build menu, select Deploy AdventureWorks SSAS. If the AdventureWorks SSAS database already exists on the server, this dialog box may appear:

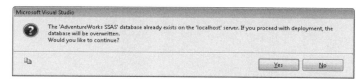

   Click Yes to delete the prior version of the database and continue with the current deployment.

   When the Product dimension has been deployed and processed successfully, the message Deployment Completed Successfully appears in the Deployment Progress window, which by default is located in the lower-right corner of BIDS.

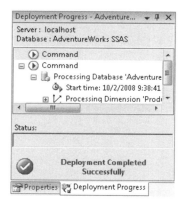

   Now that the dimension design has been deployed to the server and source data processed into the dimension, you can browse the data contained in the Analysis Services dimension.

2. Click the Browser tab of the Dimension Designer.

The Browser tab contains a list of all the hierarchies in the dimension and a Level and Members pane that you can use to browse the dimension. The Current Level indicator displays the level of the selected member. The indicator shows that the All member of the Category hierarchy belongs to the hierarchy's (All) level.

Hierarchy List

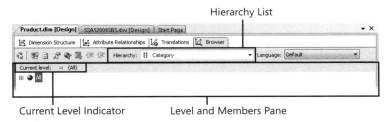

Current Level Indicator   Level and Members Pane

3. In the Level and Members pane, expand the All member and select the first Category member. The current level indicator shows that the member belongs to the Category level.

The members of the Category attribute are being displayed as integers because the attribute is based on the ProductCategoryKey column of the DimProductCategory table. In the procedure titled "Set the *NameColumn* Property" in the following section, you will modify the attribute so that it displays descriptive category names.

The Category attribute also includes the Unknown member. In the procedure titled "Explore Dimension Data" earlier in the chapter, you saw that some of the records in the DimProduct table had a null *ProductSubCategoryKey* value. These records have been assigned to the Unknown member in both the Category and Subcategory attributes.

The Unknown Member

Often when you are dealing with relational databases, data integrity issues are a problem, especially when you are in a prototyping stage of development or when you are building a cube from a source that is not a standard data warehouse. In these situations, a fact table record may have a dimension key that does not exist in the dimension table.

Normally, if you try to process a cube from a fact table that contains a dimension key that is not yet found in the dimension, the processing operation will fail. However, when you are building a prototype or when your solution requires near-real-time information, you may want to ignore this type of error and allow processing to continue.

By enabling the *UnknownMember* property of a dimension and by setting the value of the *KeyErrorAction* property of a cube to ConvertToUnknown, you can avoid processing errors when a fact table contains a missing or invalid key for that dimension. In this situation, values from the fact table will be assigned to the Unknown dimension member. This results in the total value of each measure in the cube equaling the total value of each fact in the fact table.

The *UnknownMember* property has three possible values: *Visible*, *Hidden*, and *None*. The default setting for the *UnknownMember* property is *Visible*, so you'll notice a member named Unknown in each attribute hierarchy of a new dimension, even though you don't have a record with that name in your dimension table. If you set the value of the property to *Hidden*, the dimension will contain an Unknown member, but it will not be visible. If you set the property to *None*, the dimension will not contain an Unknown member, and processing a fact table that contains a dimension key not contained in the dimension will cause an error. If you prefer, you can use the use the dimension *UnknownMemberName* property to assign a different name to the unknown member.

4. Expand the Hierarchy list. The List Price attribute does not appear in the list because its *AttributeHierarchyEnabled* property has been set to *False*.

Even though you can't browse the List Price attribute, you can see its members when you display it as a member property of the Product ID attribute.

5. Select Product ID from the Hierarchy list and expand the All member. Click the Member Properties button and select List Price.

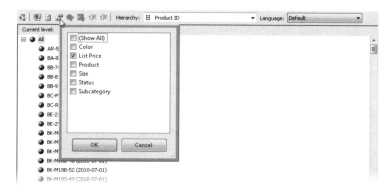

6. Click OK. The Members and Levels pane shows each Product ID and its List Price member property.

7. From the Hierarchy list, select each of the other attribute hierarchies. For each hierarchy, expand All to view the attribute members.

Except for Category and Subcategory, every attribute has members that display text names. The Category and Subcategory attributes have integer names because they were created from the integer primary key columns in the DimCategory and DimSubcategory tables. In the next procedure, you will modify these attributes so that they display descriptive textual names.

Modifying a Dimension

You can use the Dimension Designer to enhance the dimension design. On the Dimension Structure tab, you can create additional attributes; create user-defined hierarchies; and modify dimension, attribute, and hierarchy properties. On the Attribute Relationships tab, you can create the natural hierarchies that Analysis Services uses to aggregate numeric values. On the Translations tab, you can configure the dimension so that it displays dimension, attribute, hierarchy, and member names in multiple languages. You will learn more about translations in Chapter 9, "Currency Conversion and Multiple Languages."

The Dimension Wizard only lets you set the *NameColumn* property for the key attribute. If you want to set the *NameColumn* property for any other attribute, you must use the Dimension Designer. When you browsed the Product dimension, you saw that the Category and Subcategory attribute members display integers. In the following procedure, you will use the Dimension Designer to modify the *NameColumn* property so that these two attributes display descriptive names.

Set the *NameColumn* property

1. In the Dimension Designer, click the Dimension Structure tab.

2. In the Attributes pane, right-click the Category attribute and select Properties.

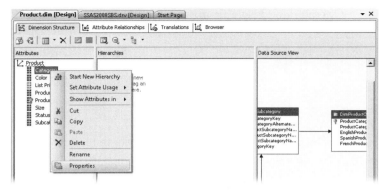

The Properties window appears. Its default location is the lower-right corner of BIDS.

3. In the Properties window, select the *NameColumn* property. An ellipsis (...) button appears on the right.

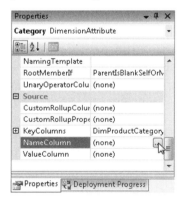

4. Click the NameColumn ellipsis button. In the Name Column dialog box, select EnglishProductCategoryName. Click OK.

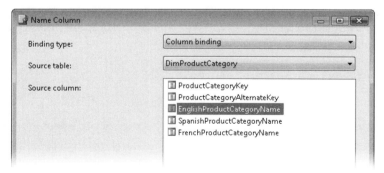

5. Repeat steps 2 through 4 to set the value of the Subcategory attribute *NameColumn* property to EnglishProductSubcategoryName.

In the Attributes pane, you can see a blue wavy line underneath the name of the Product dimension. This wavy line indicates that BIDS has raised a Design Warning. Design Warnings, also sometimes called AMO Warnings, are based on a set of rules that can be found in the SQL Server Books Online article "Design Warning Rules." These rules are designed to help developers implement best practices leading to reduced processing time, faster query response, and improved user experience.

If you're like me, when you write a document in Microsoft Word, you see many red and green wavy lines indicating Word has detected spelling and grammar errors. In most cases, I need to make a change, but Word is not always correct. For example, in this book I've written database table names that Word flagged as spelling errors. And sometimes, Word and I just have to agree to disagree about grammar. In this same spirit, you will have to evaluate each Design Warning raised by BIDS and decide if you will change your design or ignore the warning.

View Design Warnings

There are two methods you can use to view Design Warnings. You can point at an object that is marked with a blue wavy line or you can view the list of all Design Warnings.

1. Point to the Product dimension in the Attributes pane. A tooltip with the message Create Hierarchies In Non-Parent Child Dimensions appears.

2. On the View menu, select Error List. A warning with the same message appears in the Error List. This list is refreshed whenever you build or deploy a solution, so it may not always reflect all the latest errors and warnings.

Note You can learn more about a Design Warning by searching on the message in SQL Server 2008 Books Online. You'll find articles describing the best practice that is the basis for each Design Warning.

The Design Warning raised on the Product dimension indicates that you need to create hierarchies in the Product dimension. This design warning is vague because there are three ways you can create hierarchies in an Analysis Services dimension: attribute hierarchies, user-defined hierarchies, and natural hierarchies you identify when you create attribute relationships.

By default, an attribute hierarchy has two levels. The top level contains the All member. The bottom, or leaf, level contains the members of the attribute. When you create an attribute, an attribute hierarchy is also automatically created. So the warning can't be about attribute hierarchies.

You create attribute relationships to identify the natural hierarchies that exist in the dimension. Remember, in a natural hierarchy, each child must have only one parent. A natural hierarchy may contain more than two levels. Creating attribute relationships speeds up database processing by reducing the amount of memory needed for dimension processing, increases query performance by providing for faster data access and improved query execution plans, and results in more effective aggregation design if user-defined hierarchies based on the natural hierarchies in the dimension are also created. You will create attribute relationships later in this chapter in the procedure titled "Create Attribute Relationships."

User-defined hierarchies can also have multiple levels, but they do not have to be natural hierarchies. They are used to help users browse or query a dimension, but they do not affect a cube's storage structure. When a user browses or queries a cube using a user-defined hierarchy, behind the scenes Analysis Services maps the user-defined hierarchies to the attribute hierarchies and attribute relationship hierarchies and then retrieves data from the cube.

In the next two procedures, you will respond to the Design Warning by creating two user-defined hierarchies. The first user-defined hierarchy has levels composed of the members of the Category, Subcategory, and Product attributes. This is a natural hierarchy, because each product has only one parent subcategory, which has only one parent category. It is very common for users to want to drill down and drill up using a natural hierarchy. The second user-defined hierarchy that you create has levels composed of the members of the Color and Size attributes. This hierarchy helps users see what sizes are available for a particular color. In this hierarchy, a single size may have multiple parent colors, so it is not a natural hierarchy.

Create the Product Category user-defined hierarchy

1. In the Attributes pane, right-click Category and select Start New Hierarchy. A new user-defined hierarchy with Category as the top level is created in the Hierarchies pane.

   You now need to add Subcategory as an intermediate level and Product as the leaf level.

2. Drag the Subcategory attribute from the Attributes pane and drop it on <new level>.

3. Drag the Product attribute from the Attributes pane and drop it on <new level>.

You want to give the user-defined hierarchy a descriptive name. Every hierarchy name must be unique, so you cannot give a user-defined hierarchy the same name as an attribute hierarchy.

4. In the Hierarchies pane, right-click the new hierarchy header and select Rename.

5. In the hierarchy header, type in **Product by Category** and press <Enter>. Your new user-defined hierarchy should look like this:

Create the Size Color By user-defined hierarchy

1. In the Attributes pane, right-click Color and select Start New Hierarchy. A second user-defined hierarchy with Color as the top level is created.

2. Drag the Size attribute from the Attributes pane to the new hierarchy and drop it on <new level>.

3. In the Hierarchy pane, right-click the new hierarchy header and select Rename. Type in **Size by Color**. The Hierarchies pane now displays two user-defined hierarchies.

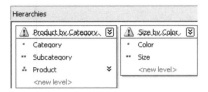

Note If the attribute hierarchy displayed at the top of a user-defined hierarchy has an All level, the user-defined hierarchy will also have an All level. Changing the attribute property *IsAggregatable* to *False* for the attribute displayed at the top of the user-defined hierarchy will remove the All level from the attribute hierarchy and the user-defined hierarchy.

You have modified the dimension based on the Design Warning that appeared earlier, yet a wavy line remains underneath the Product dimension in the Attributes pane, plus there are more wavy lines underneath the names of both of the user-defined hierarchies. In the next few procedures, you will view all the Design Warnings, modify your design based on some of the alerts, and ignore the remainder. BIDS even lets you dismiss the Design Warnings you want to ignore so that they no longer appear in the designer.

View the Product dimension Design Warning

1. Point at the Product dimension in the Attributes pane. A tooltip with the message Avoid Visible Attribute Hierarchies For Attributes Used As Levels In User-Defined Hierarchies appears.

Because you created user-defined hierarchies, several of the attributes in the Product dimension now appear in both an attribute hierarchy and a user-defined hierarchy. This may confuse some users when they browse a cube. They may not know which hierarchy they should use, or interactions between the hierarchies might lead to confusion. For example, the Category attribute is in both the Category attribute hierarchy and the Product by Category user-defined hierarchy. If a user ends up with the Category attribute on both rows and columns, all of the numeric values will be blank except on the diagonal of the grid where the Category on rows is the same as the Category on columns.

> **Important** You can hide an attribute hierarchy so that it will not appear in a browser. But it is important for you to understand that the attribute hierarchy still exists. A user who is aware of the hierarchy can write an MDX query and retrieve the members of the hierarchy.

In the next procedure, you will hide several attribute hierarchies.

Hide attribute hierarchies

1. In the Attributes pane, right-click Category and select Properties.

2. In the Properties window, scroll up to the Advanced group and select the *AttributeHierarchyVisible* property. Change the property value to *False*.

3. Repeat steps 1 and 2 for the Subcategory and Product attributes.

Create attribute relationships

If you point to either of the user-defined hierarchies, you will see the following Design Warning: Attribute Relationships Do Not Exist Between One Or More Levels Of This Hierarchy. This May Result In Decreased Query Performance. In this procedure, you will respond to this warning by modifying the attribute relationships in the Product dimension. When you modify the attribute relationships, you create multilevel hierarchies that Analysis Services uses to aggregate numerical values. These aggregated values enable Analysis Services to provide fast query performance.

1. Click the Attribute Relationships tab. You can see in the attributes diagram that some attribute relationships already exist. Every attribute must be related to the key attribute, Product ID. Category is *indirectly related* to Product ID while the rest of the attributes are *directly related* to Product ID. The Dimension Wizard was able to create the indirect relationship between Product ID and Category based on the foreign key relationships of dimension tables.

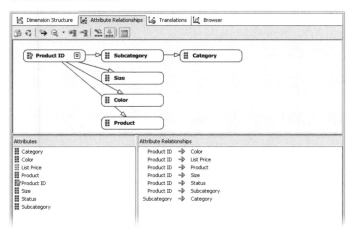

The diagram shows that Analysis Services can derive a *Category* value by aggregating the values of all its related *Subcategory* values. But Analysis Services isn't able to derive a *Subcategory* value from Product because Product and Subcategory have no relationship. You will now create this relationship.

2. On the Dimension menu, select New Attribute Relationship.

3. From the Source Attribute Name list, select Product, and in the Related Attribute Name list, select Subcategory.

4. Click OK. The diagram pane now shows the natural hierarchy of Category, Subcategory, Product, and Product ID.

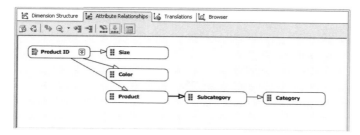

5. Click the Dimension Structure tab. The Product Category Hierarchy no longer displays a Design Warning. A few Design Warnings still appear. Later in this chapter, in the procedure titled "Dismiss Design Warnings," you will dismiss the Avoid Visible Attribute Hierarchies For Attributes Used As Levels In User-Defined Hierarchies warning.

In the preceding procedures, you modified the Category and Subcategory attributes so that they would display descriptive names instead of integers; created two user-defined hierarchies; and hid the Category, Subcategory, and Product attributes. As a best practice, you should frequently check your work. You should now deploy the dimension to send the modifications you have made to the Analysis Services server and reprocess the dimension. You will then be able to browse the dimension and verify your work.

Deploy and browse the Product dimension

1. On the Build menu, select Deploy AdventureWorks SSAS. When the Product dimension has been deployed and processed successfully, the message Deployment Completed Successfully appears in the Deployment Progress window.

2. In the Dimension Designer, click the Browser tab. A warning appears at the bottom of the Level And Members pane.

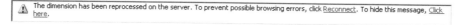

Because the dimension has been modified, deployed, and processed, you need to reconnect the browser to the Analysis Services server to view the most recent version of the dimension.

3. Click the Reconnect button.

4. Expand the Hierarchy list. Because you set the *AttributeHierarchyVisible* property to *False*, the Category, Subcategory, and Product attribute hierarchies do not appear in the list.

5. From the Hierarchy list, select the Product by Category hierarchy. Expand the All member, Bikes, and Mountain Bikes.

   The Category and Subcategory attributes display descriptive member names instead of integers. If you wish, you can continue to browse this hierarchy and confirm that it is a natural hierarchy.

6. Expand the Hierarchy list and select Size By Color. Expand the All member, Black, and Blue. You can see that many sizes appear as children of both Black and Blue. Size by Color is not a natural hierarchy.

The Design Warning Avoid Visible Attribute Hierarchies For Attributes Used As Levels In User-Defined Hierarchies related to the Color and Size attributes remains. In this case, you are going to leave the attribute hierarchies visible, so you can dismiss the warning. However, you should always be very careful about dismissing a Design Warning, because the warning may be identifying a best practice that needs to be implemented to improve Analysis Services performance.

Dismiss Design Warnings

1. On the View menu, select Error List.

   The Error List appears at the bottom of your screen.

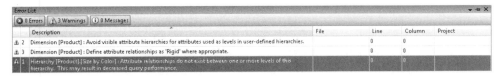

2. Right-click the warning Hierarchy [Product].[Size by Color] : Attribute Relationships Do Not Exist Between One Or More Levels Of This Hierarchy. This May Result In Decreased Query Performance, and select Dismiss.

3. In the Comments field, type **Not a natural hierarchy.**

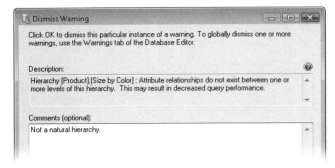

4. Click OK.

5. Repeat steps 2 and 4 to dismiss the two remaining warnings. You can leave the Comments field blank. The Error list is now empty.

In a real-world design scenario, it may not always be advisable to dismiss design warnings, as they can serve as useful reminders of best practices and might assist in troubleshooting efforts. You can simply choose to ignore the warnings and proceed with deployment without dismissing them if desired. If you do decide to dismiss warnings, you may occasionally want to review the list of Design Warnings that you have previously dismissed. You may find that you have dismissed a Design Warning that needs to be heeded. It is also useful to read the list of Design Warning Rules that are used to generate warnings. The next procedure shows you how to view these two lists and how to re-enable a dismissed warning.

View Design Warning Rules and re-enable a dismissed Design Warning

1. In Solution Explorer, right-click AdventureWorks SSAS and select Edit Database.

2. In the Database Designer, click the Warnings tab.

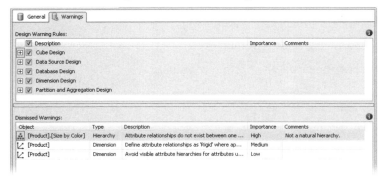

3. In the Design Warning Rules pane, expand Dimension Design.

You can see the list of best practices that are selected before the Dimension Designer raises a Design Warning. After you become more familiar with Analysis Services and these best practices, you may want to clear the check box next to a rule to prevent that rule from being applied.

4. In the Dismissed Warnings pane, select the error Define Attribute Relationships As "Rigid" Where Appropriate.

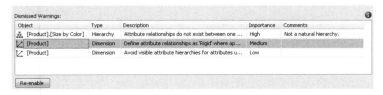

5. Click the Re-enable button at the bottom of the pane.

   The warning disappears from the Dismissed Warnings list. You will apply the best practice of creating rigid attribute relationships in Chapter 14, "Managing Partitions and
   Database Processing."

 Note Re-enabled warnings will not appear in the Error List until you once again build or
deploy your Analysis Services project.

Creating a Time Dimension

There's practically no such thing as an OLAP database without a Time dimension. Often, a
Time dimension contains months as the lowest level of detail—aggregated into quarters
and years. Sometimes, a Time dimension contains days as the lowest level of detail. On
occasion—particularly if you're monitoring a manufacturing operation or Internet activity—
you might create a dimension with minutes or even seconds as the lowest level of detail.
Whatever the level of detail, a Time dimension has certain unique qualities.

For example, time typically occurs in regular intervals. Each hour contains 60 minutes, each
day contains 24 hours, each quarter contains three months, and each year contains four
quarters. This repetitive nature of time encourages certain questions, such as, "How does
this month compare to the same month of last year?" The multidimensional expressions
language (MDX), which you'll learn about in Chapter 6, "Creating Advanced Measures and
Calculations," has functions that make it easy to answer this type of question. By flagging a
dimension as a Time dimension, and flagging certain attributes within a dimension as specific
units of time, you can make those functions easy to use.

The Time dimension contains natural hierarchies. January 1 belongs to January, which belongs to the first quarter of a given year. You can use these relationships to create a user-defined calendar year hierarchy. But many organizations use a fiscal year. Their starting day of the year is not January 1 and the first quarter of the fiscal year is not the same as the first quarter of the calendar year. Fortunately, you can also create a user-defined fiscal year hierarchy.

Of course, time isn't completely uniform because the 365 days in a year aren't evenly divisible by the 7 days in a week or the 12 months in a year. Some months have 30 days; some have 31, 28, or occasionally 29. Months begin on different days of the week. Different countries have different national holidays and organizations may or may not observe each holiday. You may want to flag weekdays versus weekend days and which days are paydays. Irregularities are a fact of life in Time dimensions, and when working with time, you need to be prepared for both the regularities and the irregularities.

Analysis Services provides three ways to create a Time dimension:

- You can create a Time dimension from an existing table, similar to the way you created the Product dimension from existing tables.

- You can provide the Dimension Wizard with a start and end date and other time-related details, and the wizard will generate the Time dimension for you. The wizard can create and populate a relational database table for you and then build the time dimension from that table.

- You can provide the Dimension Wizard with a start and end date and other time-related details, and the wizard will build a Time dimension that exists only in the Analysis Services database.

You should consider several factors before you have the Dimension Wizard generate the Time dimension for you. One best practice is to use the Integer data type for the key attribute of a dimension. Integers use less storage space and can be queried faster than string or date data types. However, the key attribute of the Time dimension generated by the Dimension Wizard will have the Date data type. This means that your fact tables must also use dates as the Time dimension foreign key. The key attribute of the wizard-generated Time dimension must be Date, and no attribute representing a shorter interval of time is allowed. Finally, the wizard does not allow you to create special date attributes such as Holiday or Payday.

The most common way to create a Time dimension is to use an existing database table. The following procedures will show you how.

Create a Time dimension

1. In Solution Explorer, right-click the Dimensions folder and select New Dimension. On the Welcome To The Dimension Wizard page, click Next.

   The Select Creation Method page shows four methods you can use to create a dimension. By default, the wizard has selected the most common method: Use An Existing Table.

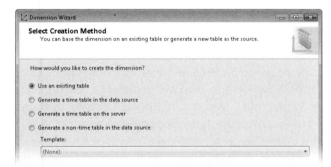

2. Verify that Use An Existing Table is selected and click Next. The AdventureWorks SSAS project has only one data source view, so on the Specify Source Information page, the SSAS2008 data source view has already been selected.

3. Verify that SSAS2008SBS has been selected from the Data Source View list. The Dimension Wizard has retrieved the list of all the tables in the SSAS2008SBS data source view.

4. Select DimDate from the Main Table list.

   The main table of your dimension must contain the columns used to create the key attribute of your dimension. The Dimension Wizard assumes that the primary key of the main table will be the key attribute and selects this column to be the Key Column and Name Column of the key attribute of the dimension. The primary key of the DimDate table is the DateKey column.

5. Verify that DateKey has been selected from the Key Columns list.

6. Select DateName from the Name Column list. The Specify Source Information page should now look like the following image. Click Next.

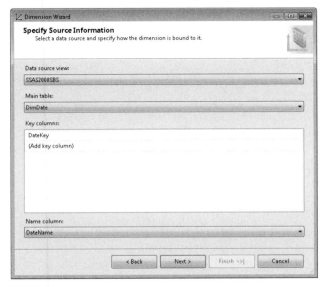

7. On the Select Dimension Attributes page, click Date Key and rename the attribute to **Date**.

Each attribute has an *AttributeType* property that Analysis Services and some client applications may be able to use to provide advanced functionality. In a Time dimension, you can use the Attribute Type property to designate what unit of time each attribute represents. Analysis Services then uses this information to help perform complex time calculations. There are also Attribute Type properties for accounting, currency conversion, geography, and other uses. Analysis Services can take advantage of the accounting and currency conversion attribute types. All other attribute types are provided as a way to convey additional information about an attribute to a client application.

8. In the list of Attribute Types, expand Date, expand Calendar, and select Date.

9. Click OK. Repeat steps 8 and 9 to rename the following attributes and modify their Attribute Type properties as shown in the following table.

Select Attribute	Rename To	Attribute Type
English Month Name	Month Name	Month of Year
Month Number Of Year	Month Number Of Year	Regular
Calendar Year	Calendar Year	Year
Fiscal Year	Fiscal Year	Fiscal Year
Month Key	Month	Month
Calendar Quarter Key	Calendar Quarter	Quarter
Fiscal Quarter Key	Fiscal Quarter	Fiscal Quarter

The Select Dimension Attributes now looks like the following image. Click Next.

10. On the Completing The Wizard page, change the name of the dimension to Date and click Finish.

> **Important** Because you selected time-related values for Attribute Type properties, the Dimension Wizard set the Date dimension's *Type* property to *Time*. You can view this property by selecting the Date dimension in the Attributes pane of the Dimension Structure tab and then finding the Type property in the Properties window.

The Dimension Wizard only lets you set the *NameColumn* property for Date, the key attribute. You must use the Dimension Designer to set the *NameColumn* property for all the other attributes in the Date dimension.

Set the *NameColumn* property

1. In the Attributes pane, right-click the Calendar Quarter attribute and select Properties.

2. In the Properties window, scroll down to the Source group and select the *NameColumn* property. An ellipsis button appears on the right.

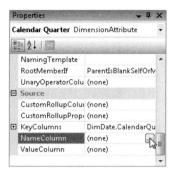

3. Click the NameColumn ellipsis button. In the Name Column dialog box, select CalendarQuarterName.

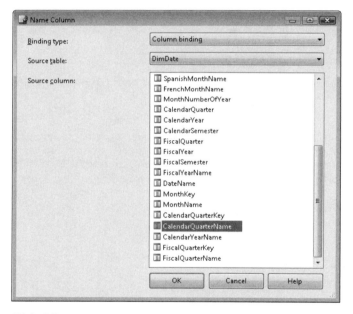

4. Click OK.

5. Repeat steps 1 through 4 to set the *NameColumn* property for each attribute as shown in the following table.

Attribute	NameColumn
Calendar Year	CalendarYearName
Fiscal Quarter	FiscalQuarterName
Fiscal Year	FiscalYearName
Month	MonthName

Notice that BIDS has raised a Design Warning. If you point to the Date dimension, the following message appears: Create Hierarchies In Non-Parent Child Dimensions.

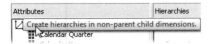

You will respond to this warning by creating two user-defined hierarchies in the following procedures.

Create the Calendar Date user-defined hierarchy

1. In the Attributes pane, right-click the Calendar Year attribute and select Start New Hierarchy.

2. Drag the Calendar Quarter attribute from the Attributes pane and drop it on <new level>.

3. Repeat step 2 to add the Month and Date attributes to the hierarchy.

4. Right-click the hierarchy header and select Rename. Type in **Calendar Date**.

5. Right-click the Month level and select Rename. Type in **Calendar Month**. You have now created a new user-defined hierarchy, Calendar Date, with Calendar Year, Calendar Quarter, Calendar Month, and Date levels.

Create the Fiscal Date user-defined hierarchy

1. In the Attributes pane, right-click the Fiscal Year attribute and select Start New Hierarchy.

2. Drag the Fiscal Quarter attribute from the Attributes pane to the new hierarchy and drop it on <new level>.

3. Repeat step 2 to add the Month and Date attributes to the new hierarchy.

4. Right-click the new hierarchy header and select Rename. Type in **Fiscal Date**.

5. Right-click the Month level and select Rename. Type in **Fiscal Month**. The two new user-defined hierarchies should look like the following image.

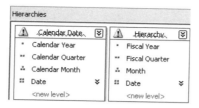

Now that you have created the two user-defined hierarchies, you can see that each has a Design Warning. If you point to one of the hierarchies, you see the following message: Attribute Relationships Do Not Exist Between One Or More Levels Of This Hierarchy. This May Result In Decreased Query Performance.

In the next procedure, you will respond to the Design Warnings by modifying the attribute relationships in the Date dimension.

Modify attribute relationships

1. In the Dimension Designer, click the Attribute Relationships tab.

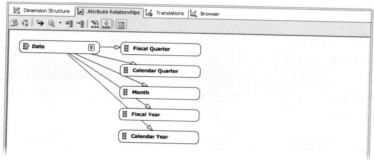

2. In the Attribute Relationships diagram, drag the Month node to the Calendar Quarter node.

3. Drag the Calendar Quarter node to the Calendar Year node. You have now created an attribute relationship hierarchy with Calendar Year, Calendar Quarter, Month, and Date levels as shown in the Attribute Relationships Diagram pane.

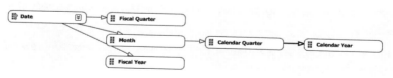

Now create an attribute relationship hierarchy for the fiscal calendar.

4. In the Attribute Relationships diagram, drag the Month node to the Fiscal Quarter node.

5. Drag the Fiscal Quarter node to the Fiscal Year node.

You have now created an attribute relationship hierarchy with Fiscal Year, Fiscal Quarter, Month, and Date levels as shown in the Attribute Relationships Diagram pane.

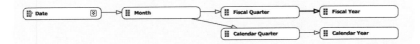

6. Click the Dimension Structure tab. The Calendar and Fiscal user-defined hierarchies no longer display a Design Warning.

In the preceding procedures, you created the Date dimension and modified its attributes to display formatted values instead of keys. You also created Calendar and Fiscal hierarchies. Now is a good time to deploy and browse the dimension to validate your design.

Deploy and browse the Date dimension

1. In Solutions Explorer, right-click AdventureWorks SSAS and select Deploy. It should only take a few moments for the project to deploy and process the database.

2. In the Dimension Designer, click the Browser tab. The Calendar hierarchy is displayed.

3. Expand the All, CY 2008, CY 2008 Qtr 3, and July 2008 members.

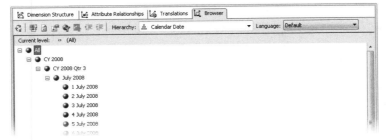

Take a moment to select other hierarchies from the Hierarchy list and browse their members.

4. Select Month Name from the Hierarchy list. Expand the All member.

The two month attributes are Month and Month Name. The Month attribute includes both the month name and the year. You can use it to display a historical time series. The Month Name attribute includes only the month name. You can use it to create a crosstab with Years on rows and Month Name on columns. This type of crosstab report enables you to spot seasonal trends easily.

You can now see that the members of the Month Name attribute are sorted alphabetically, not chronologically.

By default, attribute members are ordered by the values of the attribute key. The sort order depends on whether the key column data type is numeric, date, or string. You can modify the attribute so that it will be alphabetically sorted by the value of its name column or so that it will be ordered by the values of a related attribute key or name column.

Modify Month Name to sort chronologically

The Month Number Of Year attribute contains the integer value for each month. It naturally sorts in the correct chronological order. You will modify the Month Name attribute so that it is ordered by the values of the Month Number Of Year attribute.

1. On the Browser tab, select Month Number Of Year from the Hierarchy list. Expand the All member. You can see that the Month Number Of Year has the correct sort order that you want to apply to the Month Name attribute.

You now need to establish a relationship between Month Name and Month Number Of Year.

2. Click the Attribute Relationships tab.

3. In the Attribute Relationships pane, right-click the Date -> Month Number of Year relationship and select Edit Attribute Relationship.

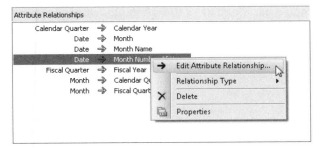

4. In the Edit Attribute Relationship dialog box, select Month Name from the Source Attribute Name list.

5. Click OK. A new node in the Attribute Relationships Diagram now represents the relationship you just modified.

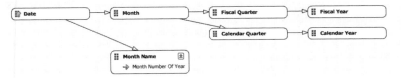

Now that you have created this relationship, you can modify the Month Name attribute properties so that it will be ordered by Month Number Of Year.

6. Click the Dimension Structure tab. In the Attributes pane, right-click Month Name and select Properties.

7. In the Properties window, scroll up to the Advanced group. Set the value of the *OrderBy* property to *AttributeKey* and the value of the *OrderByAttribute* property to *Month Number of Year*.

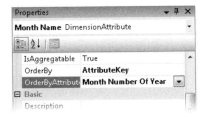

Because the Month Number of Year attribute is only used to sort the Month Name attribute, you do not need to use it to browse a cube or create aggregates.

8. In the Attributes pane, right-click Month Number Of Year and select Properties.

9. In the Properties window, set the value of the *AttributeHierarchyEnabled* property to *False* and set the value of the *AttributeHierarchyVisible* property to *False*.

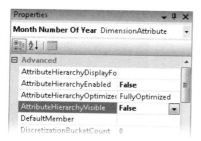

Now that you have applied a chronological sort order to the Month Name attribute, you should deploy and browse the Date dimension to verify your work.

Deploy and browse the Date dimension

1. In Solutions Explorer, right-click AdventureWorks SSAS and select Deploy. After a few moments, the database will be successfully deployed and processed.

2. In the Dimension Designer, click the Browser tab. Because the dimension has been modified, deployed, and processed, you need to reconnect the browser to the Analysis Services server to view the most recent version of the dimension.

3. Click the Reconnect button.

4. Select Month Name from the Hierarchy list and expand the All member. The members of the Month Name hierarchy are now ordered chronologically.

You have now created the Product and Date dimensions. Both are standard dimensions. A standard dimension may contain standard or ragged hierarchies, but may not have an unbalanced hierarchy. If you need an unbalanced hierarchy, you have to create a parent-child dimension.

Creating a Parent-Child Dimension

A parent-child dimension is distinguished by the fact that it contains a hierarchy based on a *recursive relationship*. The hierarchical relationship between superior and subordinate employees is a common example of a recursive relationship. An employee who is a frontline worker will have a supervisor who is also an employee. The supervisor will have a manager who is an employee and the manager will have a director who is an employee. The director has an executive assistant who has no subordinates.

The recursive employee relationships of an organization can be modeled using an Employee dimension table that has one record for each employee. The primary key of the table is the EmployeeKey column, which contains a unique ID for each employee. The unique ID of the employee's superior is contained in a ParentEmployeeKey column. That is, the ParentEmployee column has a foreign key relationship to the EmployeeKey column. This self-join between two columns of the Employee table identifies it as a parent-child dimension. For any employee in the organization, the Employee dimension table stores only the employee's superior. However, you can *recursively* (repeatedly) query the table to find any of the employee's superiors or subordinates.

Notice that the branches of the organization do not have the same number of levels. The relationship between the director and the frontline employee has four levels, while the relationship between the director and executive assistant only has two levels. This is an unbalanced hierarchy. You can create only unbalanced hierarchies from dimension tables that contain a recursive relationship between two columns.

Create an Employee dimension

1. In Solution Explorer, right-click the Dimensions folder and select New Dimension. On the Welcome To The Dimension Wizard page, click Next.

2. On the Select Creation Method page, verify that Use An Existing Table is selected and click Next.

3. On the Specify Source Information page, verify that SSAS2008SBS has been selected from the Data Source View list.

4. Select DimEmployee from the Main Table list.

5. Verify that EmployeeKey has been selected from the Key Columns list.

6. Select Employee from the Name Column list.

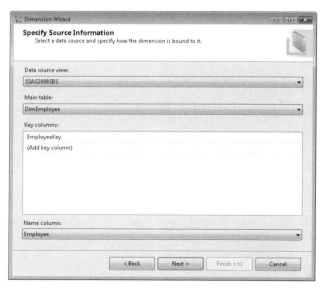

7. Click Next. The Dimension Wizard examines the foreign key relationships in the data source view and determines that you might want to include data from the DimSalesTerritory table in the Employee dimension. To keep the dimension simple, you exclude the DimSalesTerritory table.

8. On the Select Related Tables page, clear the DimSalesTerritory check box and then click Next.

   On the Select Dimension Attributes page, the Dimension Wizard lists all of the columns in the DimEmployee table. You can then select the columns you want to include in the dimension. The wizard has identified the primary key and foreign key columns and assumes that you want to use them to create attributes, so Employee Key, Parent Employee Key, and Sales Territory Key are already selected. You want to exclude Sales Territory Key.

9. On the Select Dimension Attributes page, click Employee Key and rename the attribute **Employee**.

10. Click Parent Employee Key and rename the attribute **Employees**.

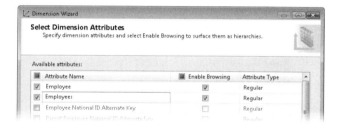

You want to order the employee names by the values in the EmployeeSort column.

11. Select Employee Sort.

12. Clear the Sales Territory check box and then click Next.

13. On the Completing The Wizard page, change the name of the dimension to **Employee** and click Finish.

When you created the Employee dimension, the wizard identified the self-join between the EmployeeKey and ParentEmployeeKey columns in the DimEmployee table and used these columns to create a parent-child hierarchy. In the next procedure, you will take a moment to view the attribute properties used to configure a parent-child hierarchy.

View parent-child attribute properties

1. On the Dimension Structure tab in the Attributes pane, right-click the Employee attribute and select Properties.

The Employee attribute is used to create the child level of the parent-child hierarchy. You can see that its *Usage* property is set to *Key*. The child level of the parent-child hierarchy must be the key attribute of the dimension. You can also see that the wizard set the *AttributeHierarchyVisible* property to *False*. Setting this property is optional and not required to enable the parent-child hierarchy.

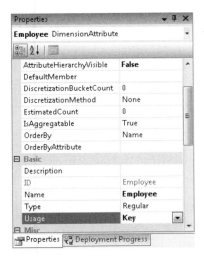

2. In the Attributes pane, right-click the Employees attribute and select Properties. The Employees attribute is used to create the parent level of the parent-child hierarchy. You can see that its *Usage* property is set to *Parent*.

 Note Each dimension has one and only one attribute with the value of the *Usage* property set to *Key*. If you have a parent-child dimension, one and only one attribute has the value of the *Usage* property set to *Parent*. All other attributes have the value of the *Usage* property set to *Regular*.

When you explored the data in the DimEmployee table, you saw that the Employee column contained the employees' first and last names. You want to have the names sorted by last name and then by first name, the way the employee names are stored in the EmployeeSort column.

Modify Employee attribute to sort by last name and first name

1. Click the Attribute Relationships tab. In the Attributes Relationships pane, you can see that the relationship between Employee and Employee Sort already exists.

2. Click the Dimension Structure tab. In the Attributes pane, right-click the Employee attribute (not Employees) and select Properties.

3. In the Properties window, set the value of the *OrderBy* property to *AttributeName* and set the value of the *OrderByAttribute* property to *Employee Sort*.

   Because the Employee Sort attribute is used only to sort the Employee attribute, you do not need to use it to browse a cube or create aggregates.

4. In the Attributes pane, right-click Employee Sort and select Properties.

5. In the Properties window, set the value of the *AttributeHierarchyEnabled* property to *False* and set the value of the *AttributeHierarchyVisible* to *False*.

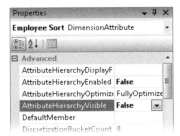

In many organizations, managers have their own individual performance measures and also have measures based on the performance of the team. In these circumstances, you need the manager's name to appear twice in the Employees dimension. You also need to be able to determine which instance of the manager's name represents his or her individual performance and which instance represents his or her team's performance.

Figure 4-1 shows a small portion of the Employee dimension representing David Bradley's team. The instance of David Bradley where he is a parent member will be associated with measures that represent his team's performance. Usually this will be a sum or average of his team members. The instance of David Bradley that is a child member will be associated with his individual measures. The child member is also called the *data member*. You can flag data members to make them easier to recognize. In Figure 4-1, (Direct) has been added as a suffix to the name of David Bradley's data member.

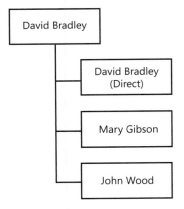

FIGURE 4-1 Employee hierarchy

Modify Employees attribute to flag members with data

To flag data members, you must modify the parent attribute's *MembersWithDataCaption* property.

1. In the Attributes pane, right-click the Employees attribute and select Properties.

2. In the Properties window, scroll to the Parent-Child group and select the *MembersWithDataCaption* property. Type in *** (Direct)**.

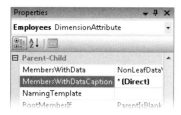

When you browse a parent-child hierarchy, the first asterisk (*) in the *MembersWithDataCaption* property will be replaced by member names.

Now that you have created the Employee dimension, modified it so that employee names will sort by last name and then first name, and flagged members with data, you should deploy and browse the dimension to ensure that your work is correct.

Deploy and browse the Employee dimension

1. In Solutions Explorer, right-click AdventureWorks SSAS and select Deploy. When the Employee dimension has been deployed and processed successfully, the message Deployment Completed Successfully appears in the Deployment Progress window.

2. In the Dimension Designer, click the Browser tab.

3. Expand the Hierarchies list. Because the value of the *AttributeHierarchyVisible* property is *False* for the Employee and Employee Sort attributes, Employees is the only hierarchy in the Hierarchies list.

4. Select the Employees hierarchy.

5. In the Level And Members pane, expand the All member, Ken Sánchez, and David Bradley. Select Wanida Benshoof.

   The current level indicator shows that Wanida Benshoof is a member of the Level 04 level. You can also see that the employee names are sorted by last name and then by first name, and that David Bradley has a data member.

6. Expand Terri Duffy, Roberto Tamburello, and Ovidiu Cracium. Select Thierry D'Hers. Notice that each parent has a child data member. The child data member has the same name as the parent member plus the suffix (Direct).

Thierry D'Hers is a member of the Level 06 level. Employees is an unbalanced hierarchy, in which some branches of the hierarchy have more levels than other branches.

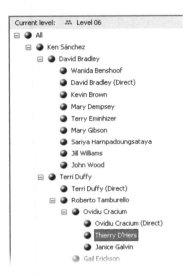

In a user-defined hierarchy, the level names default to the name of the attribute used to create the level. You can rename the levels if you wish. In a parent-child hierarchy, many levels are created from a single attribute. The default names of the levels are Level 01, Level 02, and so on. You can also rename the levels in a parent-child hierarchy by creating a level naming template.

Create a level naming template for a parent-child hierarchy

1. Click the Dimension Structure tab. In the Attributes pane, right-click the Employees attribute and select Properties.

2. In the Properties window, scroll to the Parent-Child group, select the *NamingTemplate* property, and then click the ellipsis button that appears on the right.

3. In the Level Naming Template dialog box, type **CEO** in the field next to the asterisk.

4. Repeat step 3 to add three more levels: **Manager**, **Supervisor**, and **Employee**. The Level Naming Template dialog box should look similar to this.

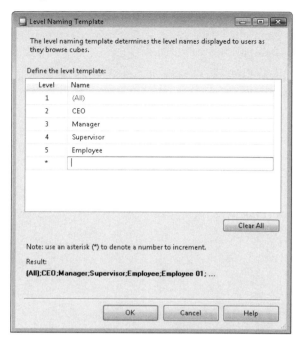

5. Click OK.

In the Employee dimension, all of the members aggregate into a single member, Ken Sánchez, who then aggregates into the All member. The All member is redundant and can be removed.

Remove the All level

1. Click the Dimension Structure tab. In the Attributes pane, right-click the Employees attribute and select Properties.

2. In the Properties window, scroll to the Advanced group. Set the value of the *IsAggregatable* property to *False*.

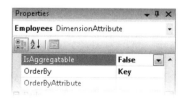

  Tip *IsAggregatable* means that the individual members of an attribute can be summarized into a single All member. Setting the property to *False* removes the All member from the attribute hierarchy. You will not see the effect of changing this property until the dimension is deployed and processed.

In the Attributes pane, you can see that removing the All member has caused a Design Warning for the Employees attribute to appear. If you point to the warning, the following message appears: Define The Default Member For Non-Aggregatable Attributes In Either The *DefaultMember* Property Or The Cubes' MDX Script.

When you first create an attribute, it has an All member that Analysis Services also uses as the default member. When you remove the All member, you also remove the default member. You can specify a new default member using the *DefaultMember* property.

Set the default member

1. In the Attributes pane, right-click the Employees attribute and select Properties.

2. In the Properties window, scroll to the Advanced group, select the *DefaultMember* property, and then click the ellipsis button that appears on the right.

3. In the Set Default Member dialog box, select Choose A Member To Be The Default.

4. Expand the All member and select Ken Sánchez.

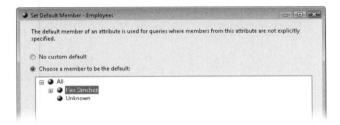

5. Click OK. The Employees attribute Design Warning will disappear.

Deploy and browse the Employee dimension

1. In Solutions Explorer, right-click AdventureWorks SSAS and select Deploy.

2. When the database is successfully processed, click the Browser tab in the Dimension Designer. You need to reconnect the browser to the Analysis Services server to view the most recent version of the dimension.

3. Click the Reconnect button. You can see that the Employees hierarchy does not have an All member.

4. Select Ken Sánchez. The current level indicator now shows that Ken Sánchez is a member of the CEO level.

In this chapter you learned how to explore dimension data using the Data Source View Designer. You created standard, time, and parent-child dimensions using the Dimension Wizard. You then used the Dimension Designer to further enhance these dimensions. To improve Analysis Services query performance, you created attribute relationships. To make it more convenient for users to browse a cube, you added user-defined hierarchies. You modified attribute properties so that they would display descriptive names, hide attribute hierarchies, change the attribute sort order, remove the All level, provide a parent-child hierarchy with level names, and so on. In Chapter 5, "Creating a Cube," you will use these dimensions and data from a fact table to create a cube.

Chapter 5
Creating a Cube

In this chapter, you will learn how to:

- Create a cube using the Cube Wizard.

- Modify a cube using the Cube Designer.

- Combine data with different dimensionality and granularity in a single cube.

- Rename and format measure groups and measures.

- Add measure groups, measures, and calculated members to an existing cube.

- Browse a cube using the Cube Designer browser.

In Chapter 4, "Creating Dimensions," you learned how to create standard, time, and parent-child dimensions. In this chapter, you use the Cube Wizard to combine these dimensions with numeric data in a cube. You then use the Cube Designer to modify the cube to make it more user-friendly, add measures and calculations, and enhance its functionality. You also use a browser to view the data in the cube.

Previewing Cube Data

Before you design a cube, you should familiarize yourself with the data contained in the fact tables that will be loaded into the cube's measure groups. View the fact data and try to understand how the data is generated by your organization's business processes. You need to know which columns in each fact table you want to use to create measures in your cube. Relational database table and column names are often cryptic, and the columns contain no information on how the data should be formatted. You may want to give your measure groups and measures more user-friendly names and apply formats to the data. Determine how each fact should be aggregated. For example, does the fact represent a flow, like sales, that should be summed over time? Or does it represent a balance, like inventory, that should be summed at each point in time?

In Chapter 4, you explored the data contained in the dimension tables. Now, before you create a cube, you should determine how the fact tables are related to the dimension tables. You may find that some fact rows contain dimension keys that are null or do not exist in the dimension table. The level of detail for a dimension in the fact table may be different than the level of detail of the dimension. For example, the fact table may have rows with monthly data, whereas the date dimension contains daily data.

You can explore the fact table data using the Data Source View Designer, but first you need to open this chapter's version of the AdventureWorks BI Solution.

Open the AdventureWorks BI solution

1. On the Microsoft Windows task bar, click Start, point to All Programs, expand the Microsoft SQL Server 2008 folder, and then select SQL Server Business Intelligence Development Studio.

2. On the File menu, point to Open and select Project/Solution.

3. In the Open Project dialog box, browse to the C:\Microsoft Press\Analysis Services 2008 SBS\Chapter 05\AdventureWorks BI folder.

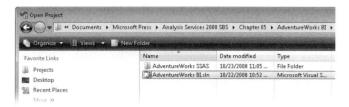

4. Select the AdventureWorks BI.sln file and click Open.

Explore the cube's fact and dimension tables

1. In Solution Explorer, expand the Data Source Views folder, right-click SSAS2008SBS.dsv, and select View Designer.

   By default, the <All Tables> diagram is displayed. Making sense of this diagram is difficult, because it shows all of the tables and relationships in the data source view. Other diagrams have been created in the data source view that are easier to understand, because they only contain a single fact table and its related dimension tables. Each of these diagrams corresponds to one of the measure groups you will create in your cube.

2. In the Diagram pane, select the Internet Sales diagram.

   This diagram shows that the Internet sales data is related to the product and date dimensions. The FactInternetSales table is related to the DimProduct table by the ProductKey column, which is contained in both of the tables. There are three individual relationships between the FactInternetSales and DimDate tables based on the OrderDateKey, DueDateKey, and ShipDateKey columns contained in the fact table. The cube needs to be able to display these three different dates.

   The FactInternetSales table also contains OrderQuantity, SalesAmount, and TotalProductCost columns that will become measures in your cube.

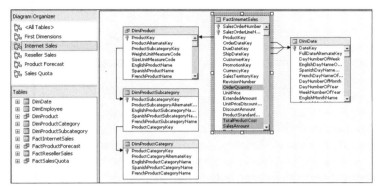

3. In the Diagram pane, select the Reseller Sales diagram.

   The Reseller Sales diagram shows that sales made to resellers are related to the product and date dimensions in the same way that Internet sales are related to these two dimensions. But the reseller sales data has different dimensionality than the Internet sales data. The reseller sales data also shows which employee is responsible for each sale as indicated by the relationship between the EmployeeKey columns in the FactResellerSales and DimEmployee tables.

   Similar to FactInternetSales, the FactResellerSales table also contains OrderQuantity, SalesAmount, and TotalProductCost columns that will become measures in your cube. Because these three columns are named the same in both fact tables, you need to name your measures carefully so you can distinguish between Internet and reseller sales data.

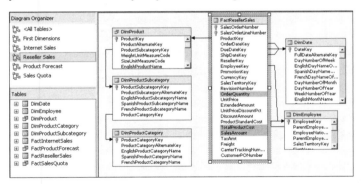

4. In the Diagram pane, select the Product Forecast diagram.

   The Product Forecast diagram shows that forecast data has both different dimensionality and granularity than the Internet and reseller sales data. The dimensionality is different because there is only a single relationship between the forecast data and the date dimension. The granularity is different because product sales are forecasted at the product subcategory and month level of detail. You can see this by noting that the relationship between the FactProductForecast and DimProductSubcategory tables is based on the ProductSubcategoryKey column and the relationship between the FactProductForecast and DimDate tables is based on the MonthKey column.

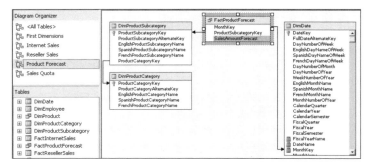

5. In the Diagram pane, select the Sales Quota diagram.

   The Sales Quota diagram shows that the sales quota data has different dimensionality and granularity than any of the other fact tables. Similar to the forecast data, the sales quota data is related to the date dimension at the month level. But instead of having a forecast for each product category, the quota data shows sales targets for each employee.

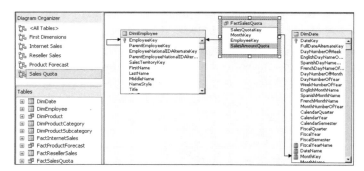

Now that you have become familiar with the fact and dimension tables, you are ready to create a cube.

Using the Wizard to Create a Cube

The Cube Wizard guides you through the process of selecting the fact table data and the dimensions that you bring together into a cube. In the Cube Wizard, you select a data source view. All of the fact and dimension tables for the cube must be in that data source view. You then identify the fact table columns that will be used to create measures in the cube. For each fact table, the wizard will create a measure group that contains the measures created from the columns in the table. In each measure group, you can also create a measure that counts the number of rows in the fact table. A cube requires at least one measure group that must contain at least one measure, but you most likely will choose to have several measure groups in your cube. Multiple measure groups in the same cube are most meaningful when they have at least one dimension in common. After you have selected the measures that will be in the cube, you then select the dimensions. The dimensions you include in the cube must be based on dimension tables that are related to the fact tables in the cube. Finally, you give the cube a name and the wizard will create the cube.

Create a cube

1. In Solution Explorer, right-click the Cubes folder and select New Cube. On the Welcome To The Cube Wizard page, click Next.

   The Select Creation Method page shows four methods you can use to create a cube. By default, the wizard has selected the most common method: Use Existing Tables.

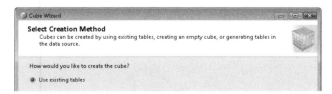

2. Verify that Use Existing Tables is selected and click Next.

   You use the Select Measure Group Tables page to select the fact tables that store the data you want to include in the measure groups contained in the new cube.

   Before you can select any fact tables, you must first indicate the data source view that contains the tables. The AdventureWorks SSAS project has only one data source view, so the SSAS2008SBS data source view has already been selected from the Data Source View list.

3. Verify that SSAS2008SBS has been selected from the Data Source View list.

   When you select a data source view, the Cube Wizard retrieves the names of all the tables in the data source view and displays them in the Measure Group Tables list. You need to select the tables that contain the data you want loaded into measure groups.

4. In the Measure Group Tables list, select the FactResellerSales, FactInternetSales, and FactProductForecast tables.

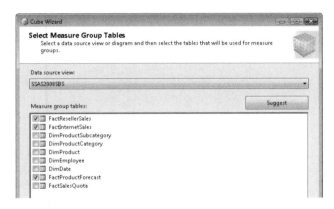

5. Click Next. The Select Measures page lists the measure groups and measures that the wizard will create. The wizard will create one measure group for each fact table that you selected on the previous page and will create a measure for every numeric column in those fact tables that is not a dimension key. By default, the wizard selects all the measures. This is many more measures than you need in your cube, so in the next step you will clear most of them.

6. Clear the Measure check box at the top of the list of measures.

Clearing the Measure check box clears all of the measures in the list. Because a cube must contain at least one measure group and one measure, an error message "At least one measure group must be selected" appears at the bottom of the page.

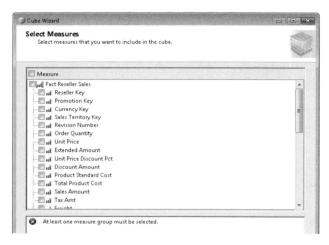

7. In the Fact Reseller Sales measure group, select the Order Quantity and Sales Amount measures. As soon as you select one measure, the error message disappears.

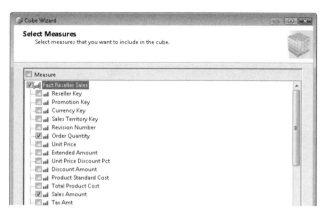

8. In the Fact Internet Sales measure group, select the Order Quantity – Fact Internet Sales and Sales Amount – Fact Internet Sales measures.

The names of the measures are derived from the names of the columns in the fact tables. Because measure names in a cube must be unique, if a column name appears in more than one fact table, the Cube Wizard appends the name of the fact table to the column name.

9. In the Fact Product Forecast measure group, select the Sales Amount Forecast measure.

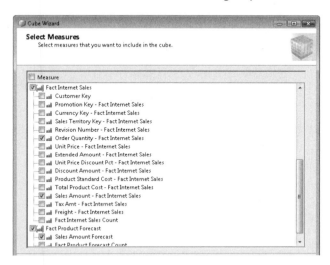

10. Click Next.

    The Cube Wizard finds all of the dimensions that are related to the measure groups you selected in prior steps and displays them in a list on the Select Existing Dimensions page. The wizard identifies that the Product, Date, and Employee dimensions are related to the measure groups in your cube, because in the SSAS2008SBS data source view, the measure group fact tables are related to the product, date, and employee dimension tables.

11. On the Select Existing Dimensions page, verify that the Product, Date, and Employee dimensions are selected.

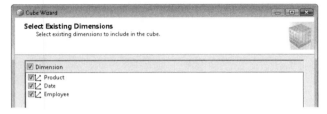

12. Click Next. The Select New Dimensions page lists additional dimensions that the Cube Wizard can create. To keep your first cube simple, you won't create any new dimensions.

13. Clear the Dimension check box at the top of the list of dimensions.

Note Clearing the Dimension check box clears all of the tables in the list.

14. Click Next. On the Completing The Wizard page, change the name of the cube to **AdventureWorks**.

15. Click Finish. The Cube Designer appears, displaying the structure of the AdventureWorks cube.

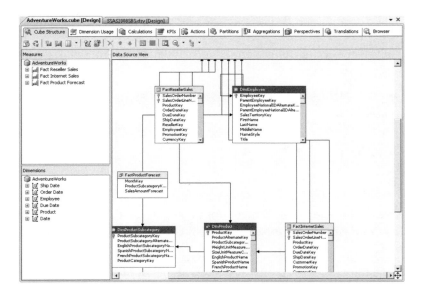

Role-Playing Dimensions

In the procedure "Explore the cube's fact and dimension tables," you saw that the Internet and reseller fact tables contain three date columns. To show this information, your cube needs the date dimension to play three different roles. The Cube Wizard recognized the multiple relationships between the two fact tables and the date dimension table and automatically added Order Date, Due Date, and Ship Date *role-playing dimensions* to your cube. Role-playing dimensions conserve storage space, save processing time, and improve database manageability.

Role-playing dimensions illustrate the difference between *database dimensions* and *cube dimensions*. A dimension's properties and data are contained in an Analysis Services database. This is a database dimension. A cube may contain one or several cube dimensions that reference the properties and data of a database dimension. When the database dimension is modified, the cube dimensions reflect those changes. However, cube dimensions have some properties that can be changed without changing the database dimension. For example, the name of a cube dimension can be different than the name of the corresponding database dimension.

In the next procedure, you will learn how cube dimensions are used to incorporate role-playing dimensions into a cube.

Review the structure of role-playing dimensions

1. In Solution Explorer, expand the Dimensions folder. There is a single Date *database dimension*.

   In the Dimensions pane of the Cube Structure tab, you can see that the AdventureWorks cube contains four versions of the date dimension: Due Date, Order Date, Ship Date, and Date. These cube dimensions reference the Date database dimension. When a cube contains role-playing dimensions, the Cube Wizard derives names for the cube dimensions based on the names of the fact table columns that are related to the dimension table. The dimension pane should look similar to this:

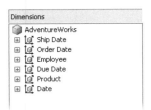

2. In the Cube Designer, click the Dimension Usage tab.

   The Dimension Usage tab shows the cube dimensions on rows and measure groups on columns. The rows in this grid show the name of the database dimension followed by the name of the cube dimension enclosed in parentheses.

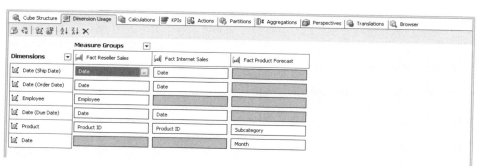

   The intersection of a dimension and measure group contains the information about how the dimension and measure group are related.

3. Select the cell in the grid at the intersection of the Date (Order Date) dimension and the Fact Reseller Sales measure group.

   An ellipsis button appears in the cell.

4. Click the ellipsis button.

   The Relationship pane in the Define Relationship dialog box shows that the Order Date role-playing cube dimension is created by relating the Fact Reseller Sales measure group to the Date database dimension by joining the dimension DateKey column to the measure group OrderDateKey column.

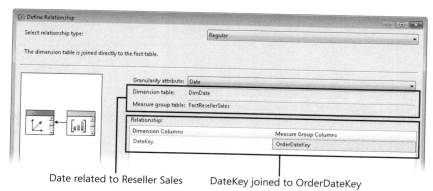

   Date related to Reseller Sales   DateKey joined to OrderDateKey

5. Click OK. Repeat steps 3 and 4 for the cell in the grid at the intersection of Date (Order Date) and Fact Internet Sales.

The Relationship pane in the Define Relationship dialog box shows that the Order Date dimension and the Fact Internet Sales measure group are related by joining the dimension DateKey column to the measure group OrderDateKey column, the same way that Fact Reseller Sales and Order Date are related.

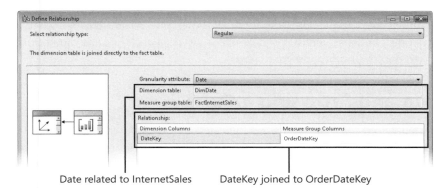

Date related to InternetSales   DateKey joined to OrderDateKey

If you like, you can repeat steps 3 and 4 to see that the Fact Reseller Sales and Fact Internet Sales measure groups are related to the Ship Date dimension on the measure group ShipDateKey column and are related to the Due Date dimension on the measure group DueDateKey column.

6. Click OK. Repeat steps 3 and 4 for the cell in the grid at the intersection of Date and Fact Product Forecast.

The Define Relationship dialog box shows that the date granularity of the forecast data is at the month level. In the Relationship pane, you can see that the Date dimension and the Fact Product Forecast measure group are related by joining on the MonthKey column.

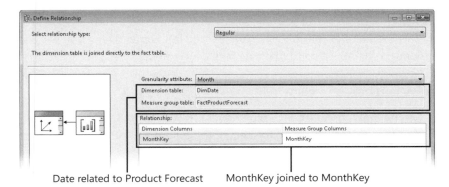

Date related to Product Forecast   MonthKey joined to MonthKey

You may have been wondering why the cube contains the Date dimension as well as the three role-playing date dimensions. The name of the measure group column,

MonthKey, that is used to create the relationship doesn't provide the Cube Wizard with any information that allows it to join to one of the role-playing date dimensions. So the wizard added the Date dimension to the cube and then related the Fact Product Forecast measure group to the Date dimension. Click OK.

In the two prior procedures, you first stepped through the Cube Wizard to select the fact tables and columns that were used to create measure groups and measures, selected the dimensions that were included in the cube, and gave the cube a name. You then reviewed the structure of the role-playing dimensions that the Cube Wizard created based on the multiple relationships between Internet and reseller sales data and the Date dimension. You are now ready to deploy and browse your cube.

Deploying and Browsing a Cube

You should view the dimensions and measures in a cube early in the development cycle. The most important thing you can do is verify that the values in the cube are consistent with the values in the source database and that the measures are aggregating correctly. You also need to ensure that you have not made any errors, to determine whether any data issues might affect the cube design, and to make sure that the dimensions and measures appear as anticipated. You may find that you need to rename measure groups, rename and format measures, modify the relationships between dimension members and measure groups, or even add more measures and measure groups.

Before you can browse a cube, you must first deploy your design to the Analysis Services server. As you progressed through the pages of the Cube Wizard, an XML file containing the cube design was created. You can see that file, AdventureWorks.cube, in the Cubes folder of the AdventureWorks SSAS project in Solution Explorer. When you deploy the cube, the contents of the XML file are copied to the Analysis Services server, the cube structure is created, and source data is then processed into the cube.

In the next few procedures, you will deploy and browse your cube. You will have an opportunity to review some of the concepts you learned in Chapter 4, and you will also see that your cube needs to be modified to make it more user-friendly.

Deploy and browse a cube

1. On the Build menu, click Deploy AdventureWorks SSAS. If the AdventureWorks SSAS database already exists on the server, the following dialog box may appear:

Click Yes and the prior version of the database is deleted and the current deployment continues.

When the AdventureWorks cube has been deployed and processed successfully, the message Deployment Completed Successfully appears in the Deployment Progress window.

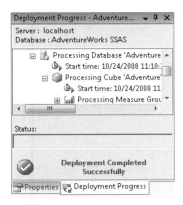

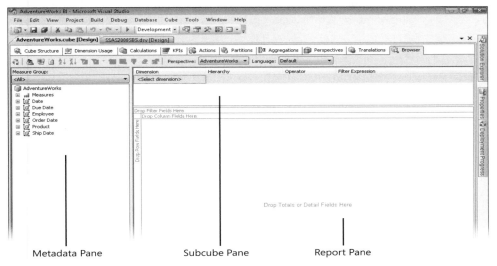

Metadata Pane   Subcube Pane   Report Pane

Note The BIDS cube browser is very convenient to use while you develop your cube, but it has not been designed for end users and cannot be deployed as a stand-alone application. You should have your report consumers and analysts use Microsoft Office Excel, Microsoft PerformancePoint Server, SQL Server Reporting Services, or another general purpose cube browser or reporting tool to view cube data.

2. In the Metadata pane, expand the Measures folder and then expand the Fact Internet Sales, Fact Product Forecast, and Fact Reseller Sales folders.

The names of the measure groups and measures are not very user-friendly. You will re-name them in a following procedure.

3. From the Metadata pane, drag the Order Quantity – Fact Internet Sales and Sales Amount – Fact Internet Sales measures one at a time to the Report pane and drop them in the area labeled Drop Totals Or Detail Fields Here.

    You can see that the measures are not formatted, making it difficult to see how large the numbers are. In a later procedure, you will learn how to format measures.

4. In the Metadata pane, expand the Product dimension.

    In the Metadata pane, you can see that the Product dimension contains attribute hier-archies marked with rectangle-shaped icons and user-defined hierarchies marked with pyramid-shaped icons.

    The List Price attribute does not appear because its *AttributeHierarchyEnabled* property is set to *False*. The Category, Subcategory, and Product attribute hierarchies do not ap-pear because their *AttributeHierarchyVisible* property has been set to False.

5. Drag the Product dimension from the Metadata pane to the Report pane and drop it on the area labeled Drop Row Fields Here. In the Report pane, point to the Category column header.

    When you point at the Category column header, a tooltip displays Category (Product By Category), indicating that the column contains the Category level of the Product by

Category user-defined hierarchy. When you drag a dimension onto the Report, the first user-defined hierarchy is used. If there are no user-defined hierarchies, the first attribute hierarchy is used.

Notice that the measures are left-aligned, making it difficult to compare numbers. In another procedure, you will right-align the measures.

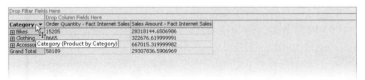

You now have a simple report displaying Internet sales by product categories. You can perform additional analysis by applying filters to your report.

Filter cube data

You can create a simple filter by dropping a hierarchy on the filter area of the Report pane and then selecting hierarchy members to include in the filter. The Subcube pane allows you to create more complex filters using operators such as Equal, Not Equal, In, Not In, and so on. Sometimes your report will contain rows or columns in which all of the cells are empty. You can choose to show or hide these rows using the Report pane Show Empty Cells option.

1. In the Metadata pane, expand the Order Date dimension. Drag the Order Date.Fiscal Date user-defined hierarchy to the Report pane and drop it on the area labeled Drop Filter Fields Here.

   Because of the multiple Date dimensions, the dimension name has been added as a prefix to the hierarchy names.

2. In the filter area of the Report pane, click the triangle next to Order Date.Fiscal Date, clear the (All) check box, and then select the FY 2009 check box.

3. Click OK.

   The report shows that AdventureWorks only sold bikes in 2009. Also notice that the triangle next to Order Date.Fiscal Date is blue, indicating that a filter has been applied to the hierarchy.

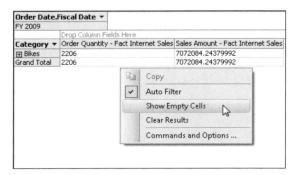

By default, the cube browser hides rows or columns where all of the values in the row or column are blank.

4. In a blank area of the Report pane, right-click and then select Show Empty Cells.

The report now displays Components, Clothing, and Accessories categories where all the values in the rows are blank. You can also see the Unknown member of the Category attribute.

Order Date.Fiscal Date ▾		
FY 2009		
	Drop Column Fields Here	
Category ▾	Order Quantity - Fact Internet Sales	Sales Amount - Fact Internet Sales
⊞ Bikes	2206	7072084.24379992
⊞ Components		
⊞ Clothing		
⊞ Accessories		
⊞ Unknown		
Grand Total	2206	7072084.24379992

5. In the Report pane, right-click the Category column header and select Expand Items.

6. Right-click the Subcategory column header and select Expand Items.

You can now see subcategories and individual products. Because most products were not sold in FY 2009, most of the report rows have no sales data.

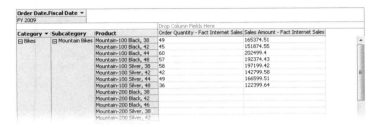

7. Right-click in the Report pane and select Show Empty Cells.

    Rows and columns with no data are now hidden.

Tip Always be aware of whether you are showing or hiding empty cells. Hiding empty cells often improves the readability of a report and reduces the amount of time it takes to execute a query and render a report. However, sometimes the empty cells are the most important information on a report. For example, if you have a report of sales by employee, you most definitely want to see the employees who made no sales.

The filter area of the Report pane allows you to create simple filters. You apply complex filters using the Subcube pane.

8. In the Subcube pane, select Product from the Dimension list, select Color from the Hierarchy list, select Not Equal from the Operator list, and then select Black and Red from the Filter Expression list. Click OK.

    Notice that the report no longer displays products that are Black or Red.

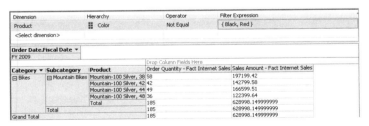

Browse a parent-child dimension with data members

In Chapter 4, you created the parent-child Employee dimension. Now that you have created a cube including the Employee dimension, you can see numeric data associated with the data members of this dimension.

But before you can create a report using the Employee dimension, you need to clear away the hierarchies, measures, and filters you added to the report in the previous procedure.

1. Click the Report pane, and on the Browser tab toolbar, click the Clear Results button.

Clicking the Clear Results button quickly removes all hierarchies and measures from the Report pane.

> **Note** If you have selected individual members of a hierarchy in the Report pane, removing the hierarchy does not change the selection of members. For example, if you were to drag the Order Date.Fiscal Date hierarchy back onto the Report pane, FY 2009 would still be the only hierarchy member selected.

The Clear Results pane removes all hierarchies and measures from the Report pane, but it does not clear the Subcube pane.

2. In the Subcube pane, right-click Product and select Delete.

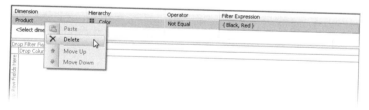

3. In the Metadata pane, from the Fact Reseller Sales measure group, drag the Order Quantity measure to the Report pane and drop it in the area labeled Drop Total Or Detail Fields Here.

4. Drag the Employee dimension from the Metadata pane to the Report pane and drop it in the area labeled Drop Row Fields Here.

5. In the Report pane, expand Ken Sánchez, expand Brian Welcker, and then expand Amy Alberts.

The report shows Order Amount for Amy Alberts in her role as a supervisor and as an employee. You can see that that the total value for her as a supervisor is her individual value plus the value of each of her team members.

CEO ▾	Manager	Supervisor	Employee	Order Quantity
⊟ Ken Sánchez	⊟ Brian Welcker	⊞ Syed Abbas		4948
		⊟ Amy Alberts	⊞ Amy Alberts (Direct)	2009
			⊞ Jae Pak	26231
			⊞ Rachel Valdez	6898
			⊞ Ranjit Varkey Chudukatil	14085
			Total	49223
		⊞ Stephen Jiang		160207
		Total		214378
	Total			214378

Browse your cube using alternative date hierarchies

In Chapter 4, you created two different month attributes in the Date dimension. The Month attribute contains a member for each month of each year. That is, January 2008 is a different member than January 2009. The Month Name attribute contains only one member for each of the twelve months of the year. That is, it contains January, February, March, and so on through December. The following procedure shows you why having these two attributes is useful.

1. On the Browser tab toolbar, click the Clear Results button.

2. In the Metadata pane, from the Fact Reseller Sales measure group, drag the Order Quantity measure to the Report pane and drop it in the area labeled Drop Total Or Detail Fields Here.

3. From the Order Date dimension, drag the Order Date.Month hierarchy to the Report pane and drop it on the area labeled Drop Row Fields Here.

   Because the Month hierarchy contains the combination of month name and year, it clearly labels time series data.

Month ▾	Order Quantity
July 2008	820
August 2008	2053
September 2008	1512
October 2008	1242
November 2008	2963
December 2008	2245
January 2009	852
February 2009	2132
March 2009	1642

4. From the Report pane, drag the Month column header to the Metadata pane and drop it when a red X appears next to the mouse pointer.

5. From the Order Date dimension, drag the Order Date.Month Name hierarchy to the Report pane and drop it in the area labeled Drop Row Fields Here. The report now shows sales by month where each month is the sum of sales from every year. The Month Name hierarchy is not useful for displaying time series data.
6. From the Order Date dimension, drag the Order Date.Calendar Year hierarchy onto the Report pane area labeled Drop Column Fields Here.

   Because the Month Name hierarchy only contains month names, you can use it to create crosstab reports showing seasonal trends or year-to-year growth.

	Calendar Year				
	CY 2008	CY 2009	CY 2010	CY 2011	Grand Total
Month Name	Order Quantity	Order Quantity	Order Quantity	Order Quantity	Order Quantity
January		852	3288	4637	8777
February		2132	5159	6371	13662
March		1642	3860	6601	12103
April		1260	5400	7134	13794
May		2965	7943	10127	21035
June		2204	6123	10260	18587
July	820	7502	9871		18193
August	2053	11044	15139		28236
September	1512	8868	14774		25154
October	1242	5355	7457		14054
November	2963	8075	10584		21622
December	2245	6342	10574		19161
Grand Total	10835	58241	100172	45130	214378

Tip It is useful to create two versions of week, month, and quarter attributes in a Date dimension. One version of each attribute should include the year, so that you can use it to label time series data. The other version of the attribute should not include the year, so that it can be put on one axis of a crosstab report with year on the other axis of the report.

The AdventureWorks cube contains both forecast and sales data, making it very easy to create reports comparing actual and predicted performance. But, because the forecast and sales data has different dimensionality and granularity, it's possible to create reports that can display misleading or confusing information. In the next procedure, you create a report showing the effect of having data with different dimensionality. After that, in the procedure titled "Browse Measure Groups with Different Granularity," you create a report showing the effects of having measure groups that contain different levels of detail.

Browse measure groups by unrelated date dimensions

1. On the Browser tab toolbar, click the Clear Results button.
2. Drag the Sales Amount – Fact Internet Sales, Sales Amount, and Sales Amount Forecast measures one at a time from the Metadata pane to the Report pane and drop them on the area labeled Drop Totals Or Detail Fields Here.
3. From the Order Date dimension, drag the Order Date.Calendar Year hierarchy to the Report pane and drop it on the area labeled Drop Row Fields Here.

   This report lets you compare actual and forecast sales by year. But you can see that the total value for Sales Amount Forecast is repeated for every year. This occurs because the Fact Product Forecast measure group is not related to the Order Date dimension.

Calendar Year ▼	Sales Amount - Fact Internet Sales	Sales Amount	Sales Amount Forecast
CY 2008	3266373.65660001	8065435.3053	95714000
CY 2009	6530343.52639999	24144429.654	95714000
CY 2010	9791060.2977012	32202669.4252	95714000
CY 2011	9720059.11000089	16038062.5977999	95714000
Unknown			95714000
Grand Total	29307836.5906969	80450596.9822993	95714000

Because the Fact Product Forecast measure group is related to the Date dimension, you can try to fix this report by replacing the hierarchy from the Order Date dimension with a hierarchy from the Date dimension.

4. Remove the Calendar Year hierarchy from the report. Drag the Calendar Year column header to the Metadata pane and drop it when a red X appears next to the mouse pointer.

5. In the Metadata pane, expand the Date dimension, drag the Date.Calendar Year hierar-chy to the Report pane, and drop it on the area labeled Drop Row Fields Here.

The report now displays different values for Sales Amount Forecast for each year. However, the total values of Sales Amount – Fact Internet Sales and Sales Amount are repeated for every year. This occurs because the Fact Internet Sales and Fact Reseller Sales measure groups are not related to the Date dimension.

Calendar Year ▼	Sales Amount - Fact Internet Sales	Sales Amount	Sales Amount Forecast
CY 2008	29307836.5906969	80450596.9822993	9513000
CY 2009	29307836.5906969	80450596.9822993	29009000
CY 2010	29307836.5906969	80450596.9822993	38782000
CY 2011	29307836.5906969	80450596.9822993	18410000
Unknown	29307836.5906969	80450596.9822993	
Grand Total	29307836.5906969	80450596.9822993	95714000

For this report to display properly, you need all three measure groups in the cube to have at least one date dimension in common. You will make this modification to the cube in a later procedure.

Browse measure groups with different granularity

1. Remove the Calendar Year hierarchy from the report.

2. From the Product dimension, drag the Product by Category hierarchy to the Report pane and drop it on the area labeled Drop Row Fields Here.

3. In the Report pane, expand the Bikes category.

The report shows sales and forecast data by category and by subcategory. Note that the value for Sales Amount Forecast is different for each category and subcategory.

4. In the Report pane, expand the Touring Bikes subcategory.

The report shows that the value of Sales Amount Forecast for the products in the Touring Bikes subcategory is the same as the subcategory total. This confusing result occurs because the product forecast is created at the subcategory level of detail and is not related to the Product attribute. In most cases, it is less confusing to display a blank cell when you browse a measure by an unrelated attribute or dimension. You will make this modification to the cube in a later procedure.

Category	Subcategory	Product	Sales Amount - Fact Internet Sales	Sales Amount	Sales Amount Forecast
⊟ Bikes	⊞ Mountain Bikes		9952759.56440052	26492684.3765005	1305000
	⊞ Road Bikes		14520584.0363004	29358206.9606999	11162000
	⊟ Touring Bikes	Touring-1000 Blue, 46	421980.390000001	1164973.1831	11786000
		Touring-1000 Blue, 50	357610.500000001	713790.558	11786000
		Touring-1000 Blue, 54	381451.200000001	361901.826	11786000
		Touring-1000 Blue, 60	350458.290000001	1370784.2244	11786000
		Touring-1000 Yellow, 46	410060.040000001	1016312.8294	11786000
		Touring-1000 Yellow, 50	359994.570000001	621193.2792	11786000
		Touring-1000 Yellow, 54	376683.060000001	290475.0888	11786000
		Touring-1000 Yellow, 60	333769.800000001	1184363.3013	11786000
		Touring-2000 Blue, 46	117840.45	321027.0281	11786000
		Touring-2000 Blue, 50	128774.1	157444.56	11786000
		Touring-2000 Blue, 54	106906.8	665395.2123	11786000
		Touring-2000 Blue, 60	98402.8500000001	537320.8659	11786000
		Touring-3000 Blue, 44	39344.55	94020.4842000001	11786000
		Touring-3000 Blue, 50	35632.8	312948.7051	11786000
		Touring-3000 Blue, 54	40829.25	249245.8693	11786000
		Touring-3000 Blue, 58	42313.95	168632.227	11786000
		Touring-3000 Blue, 62	47510.4	87773.6088000001	11786000
		Touring-3000 Yellow, 44	43798.65	314323.2401	11786000
		Touring-3000 Yellow, 50	43798.65	247948.6129	11786000
		Touring-3000 Yellow, 54	35632.8	161177.177	11786000
		Touring-3000 Yellow, 58	34690.45	96008.1262000001	11786000
		Touring-3000 Yellow, 62	37117.5	314430.2127	11786000
		Total	3844801.05	10451490.2198001	11786000
	Total		28318144.6506986	66302381.5569981	24253000
⊞ Components				11799076.6584	32948000
⊞ Clothing			322676.619999991	1777840.83909998	22893000
⊞ Accessories			667015.319999982	571297.9278	15620000
Grand Total			29307836.5906969	80450596.9822993	95714000

In this section you deployed and then browsed a cube. You discovered that the cube needs several modifications to improve its usability. The measure groups and measures need to be given names that are more user-friendly, the measures need to be formatted and right-aligned, the measure groups need to be related to a common date dimension, and the Sales Amount Forecast measure needs to display a blank cell when it is browsed by the Product attribute. In the next section you will use the Cube Designer to make these changes. You will also add a measure group, measures, and a calculation formula to the cube.

Using the Cube Designer to Modify a Cube

When you create a cube using the Cube Wizard, you select the data source view and fact tables that contain the source data, choose the measure groups and measures to include in the cube, select the dimensions for the cube, and provide a name for the cube. You will need to further enhance the cube using the Cube Designer.

The Cube Designer lets you configure properties for the cube, measure groups, measures, and cube dimensions. You can add or delete measure groups and measures and create calculation formulas. You can also add dimensions to your cube and modify the relationship between measure groups and dimensions. You can add many other powerful enhancements to your cube using the Cube Designer, and you will learn more about how to use Cube Designer in other chapters in this book. In this section, you make some basic modifications to your cube.

Adding User-Friendly Names to a Cube

The Cube Wizard assigns measure group and measure names based on the names of the fact tables and columns you selected to include in your cube. In many cases, relational database table and column names include abbreviated words and are very cryptic. In the next two procedures, you use the Cube Designer to give your measure groups and measures more user-friendly names.

Rename measure groups

1. In the Cube Designer, click the Cube Structure tab.

2. In the Measures pane, right-click the Fact Reseller Sales measure group and select Rename.

3. Change the name of the measure group to Reseller Sales.

4. Repeat steps 2 and 3 to change the name of the Fact Internet Sales measure group to Internet Sales and to change the name of the Fact Product Forecast measure group to Product Forecast.

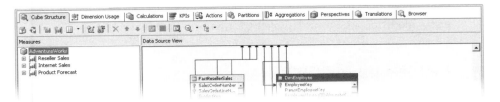

Rename measures

1. In the Measures pane, expand the Reseller Sales, Internet Sales, and Product Forecast measure groups. With the measure groups expanded, you can see all of the measures in your cube.

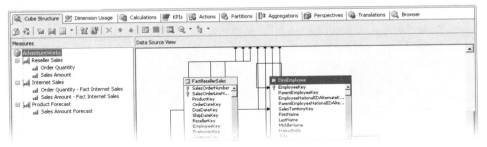

2. In the Reseller Sales measure group, right-click the Order Quantity measure and select Rename.

3. Change the name of the measure to Reseller Order Quantity.

4. Repeat steps 2 and 3 to rename the other measures in the cube as shown in the following table.

Measure Group	Measure Name	New Measure Name
Reseller Sales	Sales Amount	Reseller Sales Amount
Internet Sales	Order Quantity – Fact Internet Sales	Internet Order Quantity
Internet Sales	Sales Amount – Fact Internet Sales	Internet Sales Amount

The measure groups and measures in your cube now have more user-friendly names and should look like this:

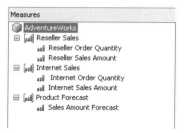

Renaming the measure groups and measures improves the usability of your cube. You can also make your cube more usable by formatting the measures.

Formatting Measures

Formatting measures makes it easier to read and compare the values in your cube. When you apply a format, you can add thousands separators and configure a fixed number of decimal places. You can apply a different format to a number depending on whether it is positive, negative, zero, or null. You can also precede negative numbers with a minus sign or enclose negative numbers in parentheses.

Analysis Services provides you with a list of named predefined formats, or you can create your own user-defined format strings. You can also apply a format to measures that contain strings or dates. You can learn more about applying format strings and get a list of all of the named formats and characters that you can use in a user-defined format in the SQL Server Books Online article "FORMAT_STRING Contents (MDX)."

The ability to format measures when you design your cube, sometimes referred to as *server-side formatting*, is very powerful. You only need to apply the format once, instead of having to format measures every time you create a report. However, for this to work, the reporting application that you use must be able to retrieve and apply the format information from Analysis Services.

You should be aware that many formats are sensitive to the current geographic locale that has been selected in the Windows operating system. For example, in some locations the thousands separator is a comma and the decimal placeholder is a period, while in other locations the use of these symbols is reversed. Also, a variety of standard date formats are used throughout the world.

Format measures

1. In the Measures pane in the Reseller Sales measure group, right-click Reseller Order Quantity and select Properties.

2. In the Properties window, select the *FormatString* property and then expand the list of property values. The *FormatString* property displays a partial list of named and user-defined format strings.

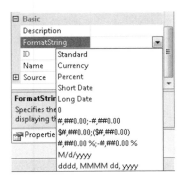

The particular format you need to use does not appear in the list, so you have to enter a user-defined format string.

3. Set the *FormatString* property value to #,#. The #,# format string will cause Reseller Order Quantity to be displayed as a thousands-separated integer.

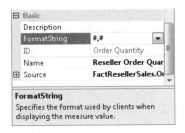

4. Repeat steps 1 and 3 to set the *FormatString* property value as shown in the following table.

Measure Group	Measure	Format String
Reseller Sales	Reseller Sales Amount	$#,#
Internet Sales	Internet Order Quantity	#,#
Internet Sales	Internet Sales Amount	$#,#
Product Forecast	Sales Amount Forecast	$#,#

Important Be very careful when using the Currency named format. The measure's currency symbol will change based on the country selected in the Windows operating system even though an exchange rate has not been applied to convert the value of the measure into the country's currency.

When you browsed your cube, you saw that you needed to rename measure groups and measures and apply formats to the measures. You have now taken care of these enhancements. You also saw that you needed to right-align the measures. The SQL Server Books Online article "Configuring Measure Properties" describes all of the measure properties that you can configure. You can also select a measure on the Cube Structure tab of the Cube Designer and view all of the measure properties in the Properties window. You will see that no property allows you to configure the alignment of a measure. Instead, you must align measures using your cube browser or reporting application. Later in this chapter, you will learn how to right-align measures in the Cube Designer browser.

Renaming measure groups and measures and applying formats to measures modifies the appearance of your cube, but they don't change its basic functionality. In the next section, you will change the interaction of the dimensions and measure groups in your cube.

Modifying the Interaction of Dimensions and Measure Groups

The Cube Designer allows you to add or delete dimensions from your cube and allows you to change how dimensions are related to measure groups. It also allows you to configure how the cube should behave when you browse a measure group by an unrelated dimension or attribute.

In the procedure titled "Review the Structure of Role-Playing Dimensions," you saw that when a fact table has multiple dimension keys related to the same dimension, the Cube Wizard creates multiple role-playing versions of that dimension in the cube. In the procedure titled "Browse Measure Groups by Unrelated Date Dimensions," you saw that when a cube has role-playing dimensions, the measure groups may not all be related to at least one common version of the dimension. In this section, you will modify your cube so that all the measure groups are related to the Date dimension.

Specify dimension usage

1. Click the Dimension Usage Tab.

   The Dimension Usage grid displays dimensions on rows and measure groups on columns. The intersection of a row and column shows how a measure group and dimension are related.

   The grid shows the Reseller Sales and Internet Sales measure groups are related to the Due Date, Order Date, and Ship Date role-playing dimensions and the Product Forecast measure group is related to the Date dimension.

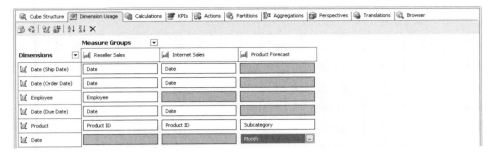

In the Internet Sales and Reseller Sales measure groups, Order Date is the primary role-playing date dimension and Due Date and Ship Date are of secondary importance. So Order Date is the Date dimension for these two measure groups. In this procedure, you will delete the Order Date dimension from the cube and then relate the Internet Sales and Reseller Sales measure groups to the Date dimension.

2. Right-click the Order Date dimension and select Delete.

> **Note** Deleting a cube dimension does not affect the corresponding database dimension. You have just deleted the Order Date cube dimension, but the Date database dimension still exists and is available for use.

3. In the Delete Objects dialog box, click OK.

4. Select the cell in the grid at the intersection of the Date dimension and the Reseller Sales measure group. An ellipsis button appears in the cell.

5. Click the ellipsis button.

6. In the Define Relationship dialog box, select Regular from the Select Relationship Type list. Expand the Granularity Attribute list.

The Granularity Attribute list shows the attributes in the Date dimension.

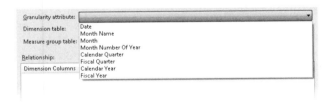

7. Select Date from the Granularity Attribute list.

In the Relationship pane, the Dimension Column has been set to DateKey, the column in the DimDate table used to create the key of the Date attribute.

8. In the Relationship pane, select OrderDateKey from the Measure Group Columns list.

You have now created a relationship between the Date dimension and the Reseller Sales measure group based on a join between the DateKey column in the DimDate table and the OrderDateKey column in the FactResellerSales table.

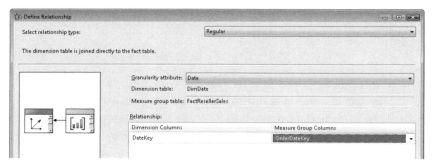

9. Click OK.

10. Repeat steps 4 through 9 to create a relationship between the Internet Sales measure group and the Date dimension.

You have used the Dimension Usage tab of the Cube Designer to make sure that all of the measure groups are related to the Date dimension. But sometimes you don't have a way to relate a measure group to a dimension or attribute. The Product Forecast measure group is related to the Date dimension and can't logically be related to the Due Date or Ship Date dimension. Because the lowest level of detail in the Product Forecast measure group is product subcategory, you cannot relate the measure group to the Product attribute.

When you browse a measure group by an unrelated dimension or attribute, by default Analysis Services will *ignore the unrelated dimension* and display a value based on the current member of all the dimensions related to the measure group. In this case, the value displayed does not change when members of the unrelated dimensions change, but changes when members of related dimensions change. This is the behavior you saw in the procedure titled "Browse Measure Groups with Different Granularity."

You can configure a measure group so that Analysis Services does not ignore unrelated dimensions or attributes. In this case, when you browse a measure group by an unrelated dimension or attribute, a blank cell is displayed.

Ignore unrelated dimensions

1. Click the Cube Structure tab. In the Measures pane, right-click the Product Forecast measure group, and select Properties.

2. In the Properties window, scroll up to the Advanced group and select the *IgnoreUnrelatedDimensions* property. Change the property value to *False*.

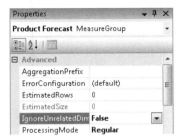

Adding Measures and Measure Groups to a Cube

You have used the Cube Designer to modify the measure groups, measures, and dimension relationships that were already in the cube you created using the Dimension Wizard. In the next two procedures, you will add new measures and a measure group to your cube.

Add measures to your cube

The Internet and reseller sales fact tables each have a column that contains the amount it costs to procure the product that was sold. If measures based on this column are added to the Internet Sales and Reseller Sales measure groups, you can compare sales and costs.

1. In the Measures pane of the Cube Structure tab, right-click the Reseller Sales measure group and select New Measure.

2. In the New Measures dialog box, expand the Usage list.

   The Usage list shows the various methods that can be used to aggregate the new measure. You will learn more about these aggregate functions in Chapter 6, "Creating Advanced Measures and Calculations."

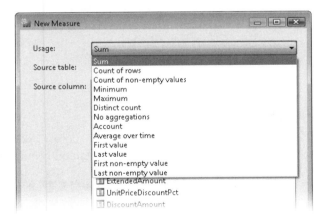

3. Select Sum from the Usage list.

4. Select TotalProductCost from the Source Columns list. The New Measure dialog box shows that you are going to create a new measure that is the sum of the values in the FactResellerSales table's TotalProductCost column.

5. Click OK. You will have a product cost measure in both the Reseller Sales and Internet Sales measure groups, so you need to ensure that the measure names are unique.

6. Right-click the Total Product Cost measure and select Properties. Change the name of the measure to **Reseller Product Cost** and change the value of the *FormatString* property to **$#,#**.

7. Repeat steps 1 through 6 to create the Internet Product Cost measure in the Internet Sales Measure group. You now have two new measures in your cube.

Add a measure group to a cube

You want to be able to use your cube to compare sales with sales quotas. To do this, you need to add a new measure group based on the FactSalesQuota table to your cube.

1. In the Cube Structure tab, right-click anywhere in the Measures pane and select New Measure Group.

The New Measure Group dialog box appears and shows a list of tables in the SSAS2008SBS data source view that have not yet been used to create a measure group.

2. In the New Measure Group dialog box, select the FactSalesQuota table.

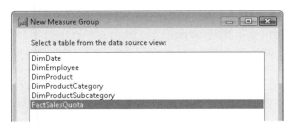

3. Click OK. After you created a cube using the Cube Wizard, you had to use the Cube Designer to change measure group and measure properties. You now need to make similar changes to your new measure group. You need to add user-friendly names, configure the *IgnoreUnrelatedDimensions* property, and format measures.

4. Right-click the Fact Sales Quota measure group and select Properties. In the Properties window, select the *Name* property and change its value to **Sales Quota**.

5. In the Properties window, scroll up to the Advanced group, select the *IgnoreUnrelatedDimensions* property, and set its value to *False*.

    The new measure group contains a measure for each numeric column in the fact table that is not already being used to relate the measure group to a dimension. It also contains a measure that contains the count of records in the fact table. You can delete the measures that you will not use.

6. Expand the Sales Quota measure group, right-click the Sales Quota Key, and select Delete. In the Delete Objects dialog box, click OK. Right-click the Fact Sales Quota Count measure and select Delete. In the Delete Objects dialog box, click OK. You also should format the new measure.

7. Right-click the Sales Amount Quota measure and select Properties. In the Properties window, select the *FormatString* property and change its value to $#,#.

    You have now added the new Sales Quota measure group containing the Sales Amount Quota measure to the cube.

Creating a Calculated Member

You can add calculation formulas to a cube by creating a new member in one of the cube's dimensions and storing the formula in the member. For example, in the next procedure, you will add a member to the Measures dimension that contains the formula for total sales equal to the sum of Internet and reseller sales. Frequently, *calculated members* are added to the measures dimension, but calculated members can also be added to a user-defined hierarchy in any of the other dimension in the cube. For example, you could create a new member in the Product by Category hierarchy named Primary Products that contains the sum of the Bikes and Components categories.

Create a calculated member

1. Click the Calculations tab of the Cube Designer.

2. In the Calculation Tools pane in the lower-left corner of the Calculations tab, verify that the Metadata tab is selected. Expand the Measures folder and the Fact Internet Sales and Fact Reseller Sales measure groups.

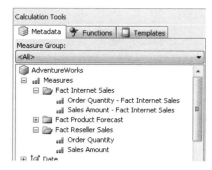

The Metadata tab of the Calculation Tools pane displays measures and dimensions retrieved from a cube that has been deployed to the Analysis Services server. Because you have not deployed the cube since you modified its properties, the user-friendly measure group and measure names are not displayed. You need to deploy the cube and reconnect the Calculations tab to refresh the metadata in the Calculation Tools pane.

3. On the Build menu, click Deploy AdventureWorks SSAS.

4. After the cube has been deployed and processed successfully, click the Reconnect button on the Calculations tab toolbar.

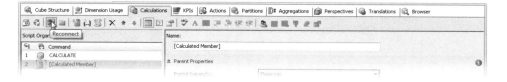

The new, user-friendly measure group and measure names now appear on the Metadata tab of the Calculation Tools pane.

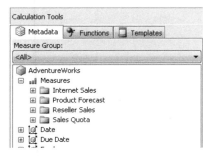

5. Click the New Calculated Member button on the Calculations tab toolbar.

A new calculated member appears in the Script Organizer pane and the Calculated Member Editor appears on the right side of the Calculations tab.

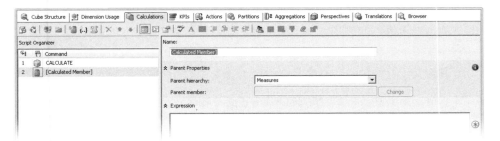

6. In the Calculated Member Editor pane, change the name of the calculated member to **[Total Sales Amount]**.

   If the calculated member name contains a space or any special characters, it must be enclosed in square brackets.

7. In the Calculation Tools pane Metadata tab, expand the Internet Sales and Reseller Sales measure groups.

8. Drag the Internet Sales Amount measure from the Calculation Tools pane to the Calculated Member Editor and drop it in the Expression text box.

9. In the Expression text box, type a space, plus symbol (+), and space to the right of the Internet Sales Amount measure.

10. Drag the Reseller Sales Amount measure from the Calculation Tools pane to the Calculated Member Editor pane and drop it in the Expression text box on the right of the plus symbol.

11. In the Format String text box, type **"$#,#"**. Make sure to include the quote symbols (") in the *FormatString* property value. The Calculated Member Editor should now look like this:

In this section, you renamed measure groups and measures to make your cube more user-friendly, you formatted measures to make the values in the cube easier to read, you modified the relationship between measure groups and dimensions so that all measure groups are related to the Date dimension, and you configured the *IgnoreUnrelatedDimensions* property so that blank cells are displayed when you browse by an unrelated dimension or attribute. You also added new measures, a new measure group, and a calculated member. You should now browse the cube so that you can view the effect of these changes.

Redeploying and Browsing a Cube

When you modify a cube, you should periodically browse the cube to verify that the effect of the changes are what you anticipate and that you have not introduced any errors. You should also verify that the values in the cube remain consistent with the source database.

Before you can browse the cube and view the changes, you must redeploy the cube design to the Analysis Services server. When you modified the cube, the changes to the design were recorded in the AdventureWorks.cube XML file. When you redeploy the cube, those changes are copied to the Analysis Services server, the structure of any changed measure groups is re-created, and then the source data is reloaded into the changed measure groups.

Redeploy and browse a cube

1. On the Build menu, click Deploy AdventureWorks SSAS.

2. After the cube has been deployed and processed successfully, click the Browser tab of the Cube Designer.

The browser displays the last report that you viewed. At the bottom of the browser you can see a warning message that says The Cube Has Been Reprocessed On The Server. To Prevent Possible Browsing Errors, Click Reconnect. To Hide This Message, Click Here. Any time you process a dimension or a cube, you have to reconnect the dimension or cube browser to the Analysis Services server. This causes the browser to retrieve the cube's metadata and re-execute the current report.

3. Click the Reconnect button.

4. Click the Report pane, and then on the Browser tab toolbar, click the Clear Results button.

5. In the Metadata pane, expand each measure group.

All of the measure groups and measures now have user-friendly names and the cube contains the new product cost measures, the new Sales Quota measure group, and the new Total Sales Amount calculated member.

6. Drag Internet Sales Amount, Reseller Sales Amount, Total Sales Amount, Sales Amount Forecast, and Sales Amount Quota one by one from the Metadata pane to the Report pane and drop them on the area labeled Drop Totals Or Detail Fields Here.

Applying a format to the measures has made them easier to read. However, they are not yet right-aligned.

Internet Sales Amount	Reseller Sales Amount	Total Sales Amount	Sales Amount Forecast	Sales Amount Quota
$29,307,837	$80,450,597	109,758,434	$95,714,000	$95,714,000

7. Right-click the Internet Sales Amount column header and select Commands And Options.

8. In the Commands And Options dialog box verify, that the Format tab is selected. In the General Commands section Select list, select Internet Sales Amount (Total). In the Text Format section, click the Align Right button.

The value in the Internet Sales Amount column immediately becomes right-aligned.

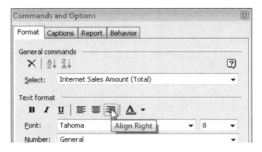

9. Repeat step 8 for Reseller Sales Amount, Total Sales Amount, Sales Amount Forecast, and Sales Amount Quota.

10. Close the Commands And Options dialog box. All of the values on the report are now right-aligned. If you put any of the other measures on a report, you have to use the Commands And Options dialog box to make them right-aligned.

Browse measure groups by unrelated dimensions and attributes

You modified the cube so that all of the measure groups are related to the Date dimension and configured the Product Forecast and Sales Quota measure groups to display blank values when browsed by unrelated dimensions and attributes. In this procedure, you will verify that these measure groups display blank values as expected.

1. From the Date dimension, drag the Date.Calendar Year hierarchy to the Report pane and drop it on the area labeled Drop Row Fields Here.

   The value for each of the measures varies from one year to the next because all of the measure groups are related to the Date dimension.

Calendar Year ▾	Internet Sales Amount	Reseller Sales Amount	Total Sales Amount	Sales Amount Forecast	Sales Amount Quota
CY 2008	$3,266,374	$8,065,435	11,331,809	$9,513,000	$9,513,000
CY 2009	$6,530,344	$24,144,430	30,674,773	$29,009,000	$29,009,000
CY 2010	$9,791,060	$32,202,669	41,993,730	$38,782,000	$38,782,000
CY 2011	$9,720,059	$16,038,063	25,758,122	$18,410,000	$18,410,000
Grand Total	$29,307,837	$80,450,597	109,758,434	$95,714,000	$95,714,000

2. Remove the Calendar Year hierarchy from the report.

3. Drag the Due Date dimension from the Metadata pane to the Report pane and drop it on the area labeled Drop Row Fields Here.

   You can see a grand total value for Sales Amount Forecast and Sales Amount Quota, but the values for each year are blank because the Product Forecast and Sales Quota measure groups are unrelated to the Due Date dimension.

Calendar Year ▾	Internet Sales Amount	Reseller Sales Amount	Total Sales Amount	Sales Amount Forecast	Sales Amount Quota
⊞ CY 2008	$2,986,977	$8,065,435	11,052,412		
⊞ CY 2009	$6,602,117	$24,144,430	30,746,547		
⊞ CY 2010	$9,346,328	$32,202,669	41,548,998		
⊞ CY 2011	$10,372,414	$16,038,063	26,410,476		
Grand Total	$29,307,837	$80,450,597	109,758,434	$95,714,000	$95,714,000

4. Remove the Calendar Year hierarchy from the report.

5. Drag the Product dimension from the Metadata pane to the Report pane and drop it on the area labeled Drop Row Fields Here. Expand the Bikes category and the Touring Bikes subcategory.

    You can see a grand total for Sales Amount Quota and category and subcategory val-ues for Sales Amount Forecast, but the other values for these two measures are blank. This occurs because forecast data is at the subcategory level of granularity and quotas are set for employees by month, but not for products.

Category	Subcategory	Product	Internet Sales Amount	Reseller Sales Amount	Total Sales Amount	Sales Amount Forecast	Sales Amount Quota
⊟ Bikes	⊞ Mountain Bikes		$9,952,760	$26,492,684	36,445,444	$1,305,000	
	⊞ Road Bikes		$14,520,584	$29,358,207	43,878,791	$11,162,000	
	⊟ Touring Bikes	Touring-1000 Blue, 46	$421,980	$1,164,973	1,586,954		
		Touring-1000 Blue, 50	$357,611	$713,791	1,071,401		
		Touring-1000 Blue, 54	$381,451	$361,902	743,353		
		Touring-1000 Blue, 60	$350,458	$1,370,784	1,721,243		
		Touring-1000 Yellow, 46	$410,060	$1,016,313	1,426,373		
		Touring-1000 Yellow, 50	$359,995	$621,193	981,188		
		Touring-1000 Yellow, 54	$376,683	$290,475	667,158		
		Touring-1000 Yellow, 60	$333,770	$1,184,363	1,518,133		
		Touring-2000 Blue, 46	$117,840	$321,027	438,867		
		Touring-2000 Blue, 50	$128,774	$157,445	286,219		
		Touring-2000 Blue, 54	$106,907	$665,395	772,302		
		Touring-2000 Blue, 60	$98,403	$537,321	635,724		
		Touring-3000 Blue, 44	$39,345	$94,020	133,365		
		Touring-3000 Blue, 50	$35,633	$312,949	348,582		
		Touring-3000 Blue, 54	$40,829	$249,246	290,075		
		Touring-3000 Blue, 58	$42,314	$168,632	210,946		
		Touring-3000 Blue, 62	$47,510	$87,774	135,284		
		Touring-3000 Yellow, 44	$43,799	$314,323	358,122		
		Touring-3000 Yellow, 50	$43,799	$247,949	291,747		
		Touring-3000 Yellow, 54	$35,633	$161,177	196,810		
		Touring-3000 Yellow, 58	$34,890	$96,008	130,899		
		Touring-3000 Yellow, 62	$37,118	$314,430	351,548		
		Total	$3,844,801	$10,451,490	14,296,291	$11,786,000	
	Total		$28,318,145	$66,302,382	94,620,526	$24,253,000	
⊞ Components				$11,799,077	11,799,077	$32,948,000	
⊞ Clothing			$322,677	$1,777,841	2,100,517	$22,893,000	
⊞ Accessories			$667,015	$571,298	1,238,313	$15,620,000	
Grand Total			$29,307,837	$80,450,597	109,758,434	$95,714,000	$95,714,000

6. Click the Save All button and close BIDS.

In this chapter, you learned how to create a cube using the Cube Wizard and how to modify a cube using the Cube Designer. When you created a cube using the wizard, you selected the data source view that references the fact tables that contain the data you wanted to load into the cube. You then selected the fact tables and columns that became the measure groups and measures in the cube and gave the cube a name. You used the Cube Designer to further enhance the cube by giving measure groups and measures user-friendly names, formatting measures, modifying dimension and measure group relationships to ensure that all measure groups were related to a common date dimension, and configuring measure groups to ignore unrelated dimensions and attributes. You then added new measures, measure groups, and a calculated member to the cube. You also learned how to browse a cube and validate its design.

Chapter 6
Creating Advanced Measures and Calculations

In this chapter, you will learn how to:

- Create measures using additive, pseudo-additive, semi-additive, and non-additive aggregate functions.

- Identify and navigate the cells in a cube using tuples and MDX functions.

- Create calculated members using MDX expressions.

- Apply conditional formatting using MDX expressions.

- Understand calculation precedence.

- Use calculation script statements to apply MDX formulas to a cube.

- Create key performance indicators (KPIs).

In Chapter 5, "Creating a Cube," you learned how to create a cube using the Cube Wizard and Cube Designer. When you created the cube, you combined descriptive dimension data with numeric measures. The cube you created aggregated measures by summing numeric values along the hierarchies contained in the dimensions. You learned how to create a simple calculated member that added the value of two measures. You also learned how to apply a format to the measures and calculated members.

In this chapter, you will learn how to create measures that aggregate using additive, pseudo-additive, semi-additive, and non-additive aggregate functions. Instead of summing, these measures will count rows, find minimum or maximum values, sum balances at a single point in time, or apply one of several other aggregation methods. You will learn basic Multidimensional Expressions (MDX) concepts and how to use MDX to create calculated members and calculation script assignment statements that contain complex formulas. You will also learn how to use MDX to conditionally apply formatting to a measure or calculated member. Finally, you will learn to create key performance indicators (KPIs) that combine expressions and graphics for actual, target, status, and trend values.

Using Aggregate Functions

It is very common to sum measures when you aggregate values along dimension hierarchies, but sometimes you need to apply a different aggregation method. For example, if you want to calculate average sales per customer, you divide total sales by number of customers. You can sum sales amount to get total sales, but to get the number of customers, you need to count customers, making sure to count each customer only once, regardless of how many purchases each customer has made. Suppose you want to compare customer sales and credit balances. For a single day, you can sum all customer values to get daily sales and credit balances. But suppose you want to look at monthly values. You want to sum daily sales, but if you sum daily credit balance, you will significantly overstate the value. Instead, you will probably want to use the credit balance on the last day of the month as the value for monthly credit balance.

Analysis Services provides a variety of *aggregate functions* to enable complex aggregation rules to be applied to a measure. The four categories of aggregate functions are additive, pseudo-additive, non-additive, and semi-additive. You determine which category an aggregate function belongs to based on how the values for the parent members in the dimension hierarchies are derived from the values of their children.

When a measure uses an additive aggregate function, the value of a parent hierarchy member is equal to the sum of the values of all its children. If a measure uses a pseudo-additive aggregate function, it does not perform addition, but you can determine the value of a parent dimension member by applying an aggregation rule to the values of the children of the member. For example, if a measure uses the *Max* aggregate function, the value of a parent is the maximum value of the children. Because the additive and pseudo-additive aggregate functions allow you to calculate the value of a parent from the value of its children, without examining any other data, these aggregate functions provide the fastest query performance. The term *pseudo-additive* does not yet have widespread acceptance, but this book will use the term, and we hope its popularity will grow.

When a measure uses a non-additive aggregate function, the value of a parent member can't be derived from the values of its children. The two non-additive aggregate functions are *None* and *DistinctCount*. No aggregate values are created by the *None* aggregate function. If a measure uses the *DistinctCount* aggregate function, the value of a parent member isn't the sum, average, or minimum of the values of its children. It may be the maximum value of its children, but this is not guaranteed. For example, the distinct count of customers for a quarter is not the sum of the values of the months in that quarter. If *DistinctCount* did simply sum the values, then any customers that appear in more than one month would be counted more than once. Instead, the list of customers for the quarter must be created and counted to get the value for the quarter. Because the *DistinctCount* aggregate function requires calculation at the granularity of the attribute that is being counted, this aggregate function provides the slowest query performance.

When a measure uses a semi-additive aggregate function, the value of a parent member is equal to the sum of its children, unless the member is in the time dimension. In the time dimension, the value of a parent member is equal to a point in time represented by one of its children. For example, if you wanted to measure beginning credit balance, you could use the *FirstChild* aggregate function. The value of the beginning credit balance for a month would be the sum of each customer's credit balance on the first day of the month. The value of the beginning credit balance for a quarter would be the value of the first month in the quarter. Academically, an aggregate function could be semi-additive along another dimension, but the time dimension is by far the most common occurrence, and the only one that Analysis Services natively supports. Table 6-1 provides a brief description of all of the aggregate functions.

TABLE 6-1 AGGREGATE FUNCTIONS

Aggregate Function	Category	Description
Sum	Additive	The value of a parent member is the sum of the values of its children. Sum is the default aggregate function.
Count	Additive	Counts number of rows in a fact table where are particular column is non-empty or counts fact table rows. The value of a parent member can also be calculated by summing of the values of its children.
Min	Pseudo-additive	The value of a parent member is the minimum value of its children.
Max	Pseudo-additive	The value of a parent member is the maximum value of its children.
DistinctCount	Non-additive	Counts unique values of a column in the fact table. The value of a member is determined by counting unique values for the member.
None	Non-additive	No aggregations are performed.
FirstChild	Semi-additive	The value of a parent member is the sum of the value of its children, except for a member in the Time dimension. In the Time dimension, the value of a parent member is the value of its first child.
LastChild	Semi-additive	The value of a parent member is the sum of the value of its children, except for a member in the Time dimension. In the Time dimension, the value of a parent member is the value of its last child.
FirstNonEmpty	Semi-additive	The value of a parent member is the sum of the value of its children, except for a member in the Time dimension. In the Time dimension, the value of a parent member is the value of its first non-empty child.
LastNonEmpty	Semi-additive	The value of a parent member is the sum of the value of its children, except for a member in the Time dimension. In the Time dimension, the value of a parent member is the value of its last non-empty child.
AverageOfChildren	Semi-additive	The value for a member derived by summing along all dimensions at the lowest level of granularity of the cube's time dimension and then averaging.
ByAccount	Semi-additive	The ByAccount aggregate function is used when the cube contains an account type dimension. The aggregate function applied to the measure is a property of the members of the Account dimension. This aggregate function will be covered in detail in Chapter 8, "Working with Account Intelligence."

Now that you have been introduced to aggregate functions, you are ready to add measures that use these functions to a cube. In the next several procedures, you will create measures using the *Count*, *Min*, and *DistinctCount* aggregate functions. Then you will browse the cube and compare the effect of using these different functions.

Create a measure using the *Count* aggregate function

In this procedure, you will add a measure that uses the *Count* aggregate function to count the number of rows in the FactResellerSales table. Measures that count the number of rows in a table or number of values in a column are frequently used as the denominator in a calculated measure that computes an average value. You can also use row count measures to validate a measure group. You can query the source data to find out how many rows are in a fact table and compare that with the value of the row count measure. Before you can add measures to the cube, you need to open this chapter's version of the AdventureWorks BI solution.

1. Use Business Intelligence Development Studio (BIDS) to open the AdventureWorks BI solution contained in the C:\Microsoft Press\Analysis Services 2008 SBS\Chapter 06\ AdventureWorks BI folder.

2. In Solution Explorer, expand the Cubes folder, right-click the AdventureWorks.cube, and select View Designer.

3. On the Cube Structure tab in the Measures pane, right-click the Reseller Sales measure group and select New Measure.

4. In the New Measure dialog box, expand the Usage list. The Usage list displays the types of aggregation rules you can apply to the new measure. Table 6-2 shows a correspondence between the aggregation rules displayed in the Usage list and the aggregate functions.

TABLE 6-2   USAGE LIST AGGREGATE FUNCTIONS

Usage List Item	Aggregate Function
Sum	*Sum*
Count of rows	*Count* (applied to fact table rows)
Count of non-empty values	*Count* (applied to a fact table column)
Minimum	*Min*
Maximum	*Max*
Distinct count	*DistinctCount*
No aggregations	*None*
Account	*ByAccount*
Average over time	*AverageOfChildren*
First value	*FirstChild*
Last value	*LastChild*
First non-empty value	*FirstNonEmpty*
Last non-empty value	*LastNonEmpty*

5. In the Usage list, select Count Of Rows. Click OK.

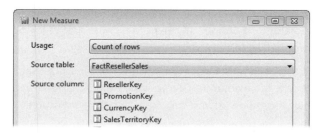

The new measure appears in the Reseller Sales measure group. Because the new measure usage is count of rows, its name is the name of the measure group followed by the word *count*.

6. Each row in the FactResellerSales table contains data from a single line of an order. You should rename the measure so that its name more clearly reflects the data it contains. Right-click the Reseller Sales Count measure and select Rename. Change the name of the measure to Reseller Order Line Count. You will also want to apply a format to the measure to make it easy to read.

7. Right-click the Reseller Order Line Count measure and select Properties. In the Properties window, set the value of the FormatString property to #,#. In the Properties window, you can also see that the value of the AggregateFunction property is Count.

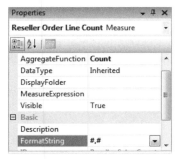

Creating a measure using the *Max* aggregate function

In this procedure, you will create a measure that displays the value from the FactResellerSales table row that contains the largest number of units based on the dimension members selected. You can use this type of measure to find products that are ordered in bulk.

1. In the Measures pane, right-click the Reseller Sales measure group and select New Measure.

2. In the New Measure dialog box Usage list, select Maximum and in the Source Column list, select Order Quantity. Click OK.

3. The new measure name, Maximum Order Quantity, is the measure usage combined with the name of the fact table column. The new measure actually displays the maximum quantity from an order line, so you should rename the measure.

4. Right-click the Maximum Order Quantity measure and select Rename. Change the name of the measure to Max Order Line Quantity. You should also apply a format to the measure.

5. Right-click the Max Order Line Quantity measure and select Properties. In the Properties window, set the value of the FormatString property to #,#. In the Properties window, you can also see that the value of the AggregateFunction property is Max.

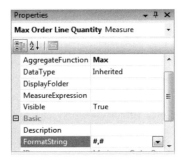

Creating measures using the *DistinctCount* aggregate function

In this procedure, you will create a measure that counts orders and a measure that counts resellers. You can use order count by time period to help gauge call center performance and use reseller count to measure product penetration. You can use either measure as the denominator in a calculated measure that computes an average. Because the fact table contains a record for each order line and an order may have multiple lines, a single order number may appear many times. Because a reseller may place multiple orders, a single reseller will most likely appear many times in the fact table. Because individual order numbers and resellers may appear multiple times in the fact table, the measures you create have to use the *DistinctCount* aggregate function.

1. In the Measures pane, right-click the Reseller Sales measure group and select New Measure.

2. In the New Measure dialog box Usage list, select Distinct Count and in the Source Column list, select SalesOrderNumber.

3. Click OK. A new measure group, Reseller Sales 1, has been created. BIDS will create a separate measure group for each distinct count measure that you create. When Analysis

Services processes a distinct count measure group, the SQL query used to select data from the fact table sorts the records by the distinct count column so that measure group physical data storage is optimized for the distinct count measure. Therefore, each distinct count measure should be in a separate measure group.

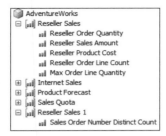

 Tip Because the SQL query executed when a distinct count measure group is processed sorts the fact records by the distinct count column, processing a measure group that contains a distinct count measure takes longer and uses more source database resources than processing a similar measure group that doesn't contain a distinct count measure. Because the *DistinctCount* aggregate function is non-additive, an Analysis Services query that contains a distinct count measure executes slower than a similar query that doesn't contain a distinct count measure.

4. The names of the new measure group and measure are not very user friendly, so you should rename them. Right-click the Reseller Sales 1 measure group and select Rename. Change the name of the measure group to Reseller Orders.

5. Right-click the Sales Order Number Distinct Count measure and select Rename. Change the name of the measure to Reseller Order Count. You will also want to apply a format to the new measure.

6. Right-click the Reseller Order Count measure and select Properties. In the Properties window, set the value of the *FormatString* property to #,#. In the Properties window, you can also see that the value of the *AggregateFunction* property is *DistinctCount*.

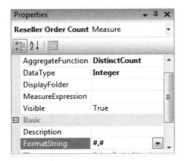

Now that you have created the Reseller Order Count measure, you are ready to create a measure that counts resellers.

7. Repeat steps 1 through 6 to create a new measure with the properties listed in the following table.

Property	Value
Usage	Distinct Count
Source Column	ResellerKey
Measure Group Name	Resellers
Measure Name	Reseller Count
FormatString	#,#

You have created four new measures. The Measures pane should now look like this:

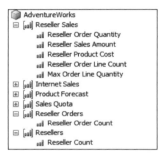

In the next procedure, you will deploy the Analysis Services project, process the database, and then browse the cube to view the new measures.

Deploy and browse the cube

1. On the Build menu, select Deploy AdventureWorks SSAS. If the AdventureWorks SSAS database already exists on the server, a dialog box may appear warning you that the database will be overwritten. If the warning appears, click Yes. The prior version of the database will be deleted and the current deployment will continue.

2. After the database has been successfully deployed and processed, click the Browser tab of the Cube Designer.

3. In the Metadata pane, expand the Measures folder and then expand the Reseller Orders, Reseller Sales, and Resellers measure groups.

4. Drag the Reseller Count, Reseller Order Count, Reseller Order Line Count, Max Order Line Quantity, and Reseller Order Quantity measures to the area labeled Drop Totals Or Detail Fields Here in the Report pane.

   The report shows the effect of using the *DistinctCount*, *Count*, *Max*, and *Sum* aggregate functions. It shows that 635 resellers placed 3,796 orders that had 60,855 order lines. The largest order line was for 44 units, and a total of 214,378 units were ordered.

Drop Filter Fields Here				
Drop Column Fields Here				
Reseller Count	Reseller Order Count	Reseller Order Line Count	Max Order Line Quantity	Reseller Order Quantity
635	3,796	60,855	44	214,378

5. Drag the Product dimension to the area labeled Drop Row Fields Here in the Report pane.

6. Expand the Accessories product category. The first two measures, Reseller Count and Reseller Order Count, are non-additive distinct count measures. You can easily see that a parent value of these two measures can't be derived from the value of the children. Because individual resellers order multiple products from the Accessories category, the sum of the subcategory values (Bike Racks, Bottles and Cages, and so on) is greater than the value of the parent category.

    The last three measures use additive or pseudo-additive *Count*, *Max*, and *Sum* aggregate functions. For these measures, you can derive the value of a parent from the value of the children. For the count and sum measures, Reseller Order Line Count and Reseller Order Quantity, the value of a parent is just the sum of the values of the children. For the max measure, Max Order Line Quantity, the value of the parent is the maximum of the values of the children.

Drop Filter Fields Here						
		Drop Column Fields Here				
Category ▼	**Subcategory**	Reseller Count	Reseller Order Count	Reseller Order Line Count	Max Order Line Quantity	Reseller Order Quantity
⊞ Bikes		587	3,153	24,800	30	75,015
⊞ Components		580	2,646	18,687	23	49,027
⊞ Clothing		475	2,410	12,267	44	64,497
⊟ Accessories	⊞ Bike Racks	155	468	468	29	2,838
	⊞ Bottles and Cages	170	444	444	26	2,571
	⊞ Cleaners	169	419	419	25	2,411
	⊞ Helmets	298	1,072	2,740	24	13,101
	⊞ Hydration Packs	142	341	341	20	2,028
	⊞ Locks	93	259	259	14	1,086
	⊞ Pumps	90	267	267	13	1,130
	⊞ Tires and Tubes	80	163	163	12	674
	Total	346	1,315	5,101	29	25,839
Grand Total		635	3,796	60,855	44	214,378

    If you are interested, you can expand the Helmets subcategory and verify the behavior of the measures as product values are aggregated into product category values.

Analysis Services contains semi-additive aggregate functions to enable you to include measures that represent balances in a cube. A *balance* is a count or sum at a particular point in time. One characteristic of a balance is that the same item may be counted or summed multiple times. For example, using shipping and receiving records, the inventory in a warehouse can be derived and recorded on a daily basis. An item may be counted multiple times, once for each day it is in the warehouse.

When you aggregate a measure that represents a balance, you want to avoid counting items more than once. The value of a parent member is equal to the sum of its children for every dimension except for the time dimension. For the time dimension, the value of a parent member is the value of one of its children. In the warehouse example, suppose there are two measures, Opening Inventory and Closing Inventory, supported by values recorded in the underlying relational data. Opening Inventory is the count of items at the beginning of the day and Closing Inventory is the count of items at the end of the day. For a month, the value of Opening Inventory is the value of Opening Inventory on the first day of the month, and the value of Closing Inventory is the value of Closing Inventory on the last day of the month. You can continue to aggregate up the time dimension in a similar fashion. For example, the Opening Inventory for a quarter is the Opening Inventory for the first month in the quarter, and the Closing Inventory for a year is the Closing Inventory for the fourth quarter. Continuing with our warehouse example, the Opening Inventory for the Bikes category is the sum of the Opening Inventory values for each of the children of Bikes (Mountain Bikes + Road Bikes + Touring Bikes).

When a measure uses the *FirstChild* or *LastChild* aggregate functions, the value of a parent member in the time dimension is equal to the first or last child of the member. This works well except in those situations where the first or last child is blank. In those situations, when the first child is blank, you may want to use the value of the first child that isn't blank. When the last child is blank, you may want to use the value of the last child that isn't blank. For example, suppose the warehouse is closed on weekends and holidays, and inventory is recorded only on workdays. For some months, the first or last day of the month occurs during a weekend or holiday. For those months, you will want the month value of Opening Inventory to be the value of Opening Inventory from the first workday of the month and Closing Inventory to be the value from the last workday of the month. To get this type of aggregation behavior, use the *FirstNonEmpty* and *LastNonEmpty* aggregate functions.

In the following procedure, you will create an inventory measure using the *LastNonEmpty* aggregate function.

Creating a measure using the *LastNonEmpty* aggregate function

1. Click the Cube Structure tab, right-click anywhere in the Measures pane, and then select New Measure.

2. In the New Measure dialog box Usage list, select Last Non-Empty Value.

3. In the Source Table list, select FactInventory. When you select a table in the Source Table list, the New Measure dialog box retrieves the list of columns from the table and refreshes the Source Column list.

4. In the Source Column list, select InStkUnit.

5. Click OK. Because this is the first measure created from the FactInventory table, Analysis Services created a new measure group named Fact Inventory.

6. Right-click the Fact Inventory measure group and select Rename. Change the name of the measure group to Inventory.

7. Right-click the Last In Stk Unit measure and select Rename. Change the name of the measure to Units In Stock.

8. Right-click the Units In Stock measure and select Properties. In the Properties window, set the value of the FormatString property to #,#. In the Properties window, you can also see that the value of the *AggregateFunction* property is *LastNonEmpty*.

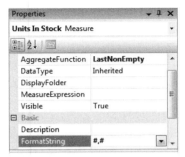

Deploy and browse the cube

1. On the Build menu, select Deploy AdventureWorks SSAS.

2. After the database has been successfully deployed and processed, click the Browser tab of the Cube Designer and then click the Reconnect button.

3. Click the Report pane and then click the Clear Results button.

4. Now we will focus on the information available about bike inventories. Drag the Product dimension to the Report pane where it says Drop Row Fields Here. Click the blue arrow next to Product by Category. Click the check box next to All to deselect everything and then click the check box next to Bikes to select only Bikes. Click OK.

5. Expand the Bikes member of the Category level.

6. In the Metadata pane expand the Inventory measure group and add the Units In Stock measure to the Report pane totals area. Notice that the 190 Bikes are the sum of 70 Mountain Bikes, plus 53 Road Bikes, plus 67 Touring Bikes.

7. Remove the Subcategory and Category levels of the Product by Category hierarchy from the report.

> **Tip** When removing hierarchy levels from a browser, remove the lowest level first and then work your way up the hierarchy. The upper hierarchy levels are filtering out the members of the lowest levels. If you remove all of the upper levels, your report may try to retrieve hundreds, thousands, or millions of members from the leaf level of the hierarchy.

8. Add the Date dimension to the Report pane rows area and then expand the CY 2009 member of the Calendar Year hierarchy. The value of Units In Stock for CY 2009 is not the sum of the four 2009 quarters. Instead, it is the value of CY 2009 Qtr 4. The Units In Stock measure is non-additive in the Date dimension.

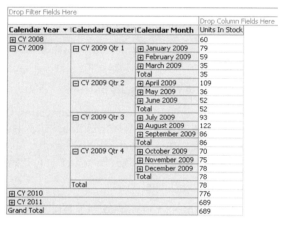

9. Click the Report pane and then right-click the Calendar Quarter column header and select Expand Items. The report shows that the value of Units In Stock for each quarter is the value of the last month in the quarter.

Calendar Year ▼	Calendar Quarter	Calendar Month	Units In Stock
⊞ CY 2008			60
⊟ CY 2009	⊟ CY 2009 Qtr 1	⊞ January 2009	79
		⊞ February 2009	59
		⊞ March 2009	35
		Total	35
	⊟ CY 2009 Qtr 2	⊞ April 2009	109
		⊞ May 2009	36
		⊞ June 2009	52
		Total	52
	⊟ CY 2009 Qtr 3	⊞ July 2009	93
		⊞ August 2009	122
		⊞ September 2009	86
		Total	86
	⊟ CY 2009 Qtr 4	⊞ October 2009	70
		⊞ November 2009	75
		⊞ December 2009	78
		Total	78
	Total		78
⊞ CY 2010			776
⊞ CY 2011			689
Grand Total			689

10. Expand January 2009. The report shows that the value of Units In Stock for January 2009 is the value of 31 January 2009.

The cube now contains several measures using a variety of aggregate functions. You can use these measures in complex formulas by creating calculated members. To create calculated members, you need to have a basic understanding of MDX.

Using MDX to Retrieve Values from a Cube

The formula in a calculated member needs to retrieve values from the cells in a multidimensional cube. If you have worked with a spreadsheet application, you already know how to retrieve values from the cells in a two-dimensional worksheet using spreadsheet formulas. Working with multidimensional data is not much different, although it is a bit harder to visualize and requires a different language, MDX, to retrieve values from the cells in a cube. To see how MDX refers to the values in the cells in a multidimensional cube, consider first how a Microsoft Office Excel formula in one cell refers to values in other cells in a two-dimensional worksheet.

Imagine that you are creating a worksheet that calculates the margin (sales minus cost) for three product categories. Traditionally, spreadsheet formulas have used row and column addresses to refer to cells.

	A	B	C	D
1	Category	Sales	Cost	Margin
2	Bikes	$28,318,145	$16,812,348	$11,505,797
3	Clothing	$322,677	$193,506	=B3-C3
4	Accessories	$667,015	$249,465	$417,550

The formula in cell D3 uses the address B3 to refer to Clothing Sales. The address B3 refers to the position of the cell, not to its meaning. When you copy the formula from cell D3 to cell D4, the address B3 must change to B4. This type of formula is called a *relative reference*; the formula's operands are relative to the cell's position and each copy of the formula appears slightly different.

In a worksheet, you can create a label for a range of cells and then use those labels in formulas. The same worksheet could have formulas that look like these:

	A	B	C	D
1	Category	Sales	Cost	Margin
2	Bikes	$28,318,145	$16,812,348	$11,505,797
3	Clothing	$322,677	$193,506	=Sales-Cost
4	Accessories	$667,015	$249,465	$417,550

The new formula in cell D3 uses the label Sales to refer to Clothing Sales. This time, the word *Sales* refers to the meaning of the cell, not to its position. The formula assumes that you want the Sales value that is on the same row as the formula. When you copy the formula from cell D3 to cell D4, the formula doesn't change. In MDX terminology, the formula implicitly uses the current member of the row axis.

Excel formulas that use labels are easy to understand. MDX expressions work in a very similar way. You can create a new calculated member in the Measures dimension that automatically refers to the current member of the Product dimension, or you can create a new calculated member in the Product dimension that automatically refers to the current measure. By creating a calculated member using MDX, you are in effect entering formulas into a set of cube cells the same way that you copy and paste formulas across a set of cells in an Excel worksheet. The power of an MDX calculated member comes from the fact that you don't have to enter the formula into each cell; a single formula automatically propagates to all the necessary cells. This works even when you change the dimensions on the axes.

A spreadsheet formula must often refer to a cell that is not on the same row or column as the cell containing the formula. For example, suppose you want to calculate the percentage that a specific product category contributed to total sales. Using traditional spreadsheet references, you would need to create a formula similar to the following:

	A	B	C
1	Category	Sales	Contribution
2	Bikes	$28,318,145	96.6%
3	Clothing	$322,677	=B3/B$5
4	Accessories	$667,015	2.3%
5	Grand Total	$29,307,837	100.0%

The formula in cell C3 refers to cell B5. To be able to copy the formula to the other cells in column C, it's necessary to add a dollar sign to "anchor" the row. This notation technique works, but it's clumsy and difficult to understand, and doesn't translate well to the multidimensional world. If you create the formula using labels, it looks like this:

	A	B	C
1	Category	Sales	Contribution
2	Bikes	$28,318,145	96.6%
3	Clothing	$322,677	= B3/Total Sales
4	Accessories	$667,015	2.3%
5	Grand Total	$29,307,837	100.0%

The reference *Total Sales* refers to cell B5. In this worksheet, each row and column has been given a name. You can refer to any cell by entering its row name and column name separated by a space. The result is remarkably readable. MDX, however, cannot simply use member names separated by spaces, because an online analytical processing (OLAP) cube typically contains many more than two dimensions. MDX uses a notation and terminology for referring to an explicit cell that can be best understood by seeing how to specify a point on a chart.

Imagine a mathematical line. A line has one dimension. In basic charting, if you want to specify a point on the line, you specify a single number or a single coordinate. On the following line, the coordinate for the marked point is 3.

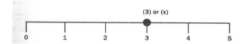

Now imagine an OLAP cube with one dimension. If you want to specify a value from the cube, you specify a single member from the dimension. This single value is the coordinate for the cell. In the following hypothetical cube, the coordinate for the marked cell is [February].

January	February	March	April
1,555	1,619	1,653	1,813

Imagine a mathematical grid. A grid has two dimensions. In basic charting, if you want to specify a point on the grid, you specify a pair of numbers or a double coordinate, typically enclosed in parentheses. On the following grid, the coordinate for the marked point is (3, 4):

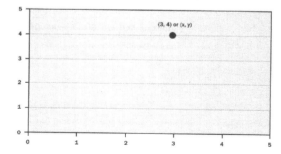

Now imagine an OLAP cube with two dimensions. If you want to specify a value from the cube, you specify a single member from each dimension. This double value is the coordinate for the cell. In the following hypothetical cube, the coordinate for the marked cell is ([March],[Road Bikes]).

	January	February	March	April
Mountain Bikes	283	305	319	328
Road Bikes	311	343	358	413
Touring Bikes	185	199	204	234

Imagine a three-dimensional mathematical space. In charting, to specify a point in the space, you specify three numbers, or a triple coordinate. In the following space, the coordinate for the marked point is (4, 2, 3).

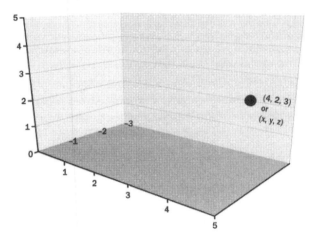

Now imagine an OLAP cube with three dimensions. Since three dimensions are harder to visualize, imagine the three dimensions of the cube as key columns. To specify a member from the cube, you specify a single member from each dimension. In the following hypothetical cube, the coordinate for the marked cell is ([Europe],[Road-750 Black, 52],[Qtr 1]).

Region	Product	Date	Units
All	All	All	10,762
Europe	All	All	3,305
Europe	Bikes	All	1,957
Europe	Road-750 Black, 52	All	80
Europe	Road-750 Black, 52	Qtr 1	32
Europe	Road-750 Black, 52	Mar	13

With more than two or three dimensions, it's usually easier to visualize a cube as a table with dimensions represented by key columns. To retrieve a single value from the cube—that is, to specify a single cell in the cube—you must specify one member from each dimension.

Watch for a pattern in the terminology for a coordinate as it includes more dimensions: A coordinate containing one dimension is a single coordinate. A coordinate containing two dimensions is a double coordinate. With three dimensions, it is a triple coordinate. With four dimensions, it is a quadruple coordinate; with five, a quintuple; with six, a sextuple; with seven, a septuple; and with eight, an octuple. When you get past four dimensions in a coordinate, each of the coordinate numbers ends in the suffix *-tuple*. The generic term for a coordinate that includes one or more dimensions is a *tuple*.

> **Note** Some people pronounce the first syllable of *tuple* to rhyme with *cup* (as in the word *quintuple*). Others pronounce it to rhyme with *coop* (as in the word *quadruple*). Each group considers the other uncivilized. Because this is a book, you don't have to know how I pronounce it.

As is the case with a mathematical coordinate, a tuple that contains more than a single dimension must be enclosed in parentheses. A tuple that contains one member from each attribute hierarchy of each dimension identifies a unique value in the cube. Remember that measures are considered to be a dimension, and you must include a measure within a tuple to uniquely identify a value.

Dimensions may include user-defined hierarchies as well as attribute hierarchies. If your tuple includes a member from a user-defined hierarchy, the ancestors of the member (parent, grandparent, and so on) are implicitly included in the tuple. When Analysis Services evaluates the tuple, it maps the members of the user-defined hierarchy to the corresponding members of the attribute hierarchies used to create the user-defined hierarchy.

If a cube contains several dimensions that have several attributes each, a tuple that contained the name of one member from every attribute hierarchy would be very long. Fortunately, you can use a very convenient bit of shorthand. When you omit a member of an attribute hierarchy, the current member of the hierarchy is used in its place. Most of the time, you can use the current member for all but one or two dimensions. The current member is understood by Analysis Services to be the member specified in report rows, columns, and filters. For example, in a report in the Browser tab, a cell at the intersection of Bikes and CY 2009 has current members of Bikes in the Product dimension and CY 2009 in the Date dimension.

A member name must be written using correct syntax. The basic syntax for a member name is *[DimensionName].[HierachyName].[LevelName].[MemberName]* or *[DimensionName].[HierarchyName].[AncestorName].[MemberName]*. If necessary, you can include multiple ancestor names. That is, you may need to include the parent, grandparent, and so on in the member name. You can also replace a member name with *&[MemberKey]*. For example, *[Product].[Product by Category].[Subcategory].[Touring Bikes]* and *[Product].[Product by Category].[All].[Bikes].[Touring Bikes]* are both valid names. *[Product].[Product by Category].[All].&[1].&[3]* is also a valid name, because 1 is the member key for Bikes and 3 is the member key for Touring Bikes.

Using this syntax uniquely identifies a member, but the member name syntax rules don't require inclusion of all of the parts of a name. However, leaving out a part of a member name may result in ambiguity that Analysis Services may not resolve as intended. For example, the member name *[All].[Bikes].[Touring Bikes]* is correctly formed but will return no data.

Creating Calculated Members

The simplest calculated members apply an arithmetic operation to a few measures. In Chapter 5, you created a simple calculated member that was the sum of two measures. In this section, you will create a calculated member that contains a ratio of two measures. The ratio will be one tuple that contains a single measure divided by another tuple that also contains a single measure. When a tuple contains only a measure, it is implicitly including the current member of each of the dimension attribute hierarchies.

The MDX formula in a calculated member is applied to the measures after they are aggregated. In some instances, aggregating numeric values and then applying a formula is not equal to applying a formula to numeric values and then aggregating the results. This holds true, for example, with multiplication and division. If you need to first apply a formula that multiplies or divides numbers and then sum or apply some other aggregate, you should create a named calculation or named query in the data source view. If you need to aggregate first and then apply a formula, you should create a calculated member.

Create a ratio calculation

1. In the Cube Designer, click the Calculations tab. In the Script Organizer, you can see the *CALCULATE* statement and the Total Sales Amount calculated member that you created in Chapter 5. Calculated members and statements are executed in the order that they appear in the Script Organizer. In the next step, you will create a new calculated member that will be executed after the Total Sales Amount calculated member.

2. In the Script Organizer, select the Total Sales Amount calculated member. On the Calculations toolbar, click the New Calculated Member button.

3. In the Calculated Member Editor, change the name to [Reseller Avg Sales]. Calculated members can be created in any dimension. This calculated member will belong to the Measures dimension.

4. Verify that Measures is selected in the Parent Hierarchy list. The next step is to create an MDX formula in the Expressions text box. The Calculation Tools pane contains items that you can drag to make creating a calculation easier.

5. On the Metadata tab in the Calculation Tools pane, expand the Measures folder and then expand the Reseller Sales and Resellers measure groups.

6. Drag Reseller Sales Amount from the Metadata tab to the Expression text box. The text [Measures].[Reseller Sales Amount] appears in the Expression text box. Because the Measures dimension doesn't contain hierarchies or levels, this is the fully qualified name of the Reseller Sales Amount measure.

7. Click to position the cursor at the end of the expression and then type a forward slash (/).

8. Drag Reseller Count from the Metadata tab to the end of the calculation in the Expression text box. The MDX formula in the Expression text box should read:

    ```
    [Measures].[Reseller Sales Amount]/[Measures].[Reseller Count]
    ```

9. Set the value of the *FormatString* property to "$#,#" (include the quote symbols in the property value).

10. In the Non-Empty Behavior list, select Reseller Count and click OK.

> **Important** The Non-Empty Behavior list provides a hint to Analysis Services that the calculated member will be empty when all of the selected measures are empty. Correctly setting this property can improve query performance.

11. In the Associated Measure Group list, select Reseller Sales. When you browse the cube, the calculated member will appear in the Reseller Sales measure group. The Calculated Member Editor will look like this:

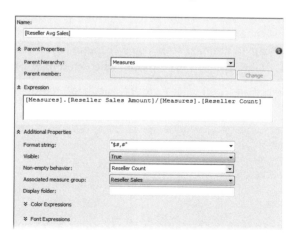

Applying Conditional Formatting

In Chapter 5, you learned how to configure a measure format string to improve the readability of a report. Calculated members (and the calculation script) provide you with many more formatting capabilities. You can configure font name, size, and color; font effects including bold, italic, underline, and strikeout; and cell background color for clients that support this feature. You can learn more about these options in the SQL Server 2008 Books Online article "Using Cell Properties (MDX)."

Now that you are a little more familiar with MDX, you can apply conditional formatting to a calculated member. Conditional formatting allows you to change the format of a member dynamically based on the value returned by an MDX expression. For example, if a measure is below target, you can make the value appear in a bold red font. To apply conditional formatting, you use the *IIF* function or a *CASE* statement combined with MDX expressions. In the next procedure, you will use the *IIF* function to change the background of the Reseller Avg Sales calculated member to green for a positive trend in sales or red to indicate that sales are declining.

Apply conditional formatting to a calculated member

1. On the Calculations tab in the Calculated Member Editor, expand the Color Expressions section.

2. Enter the following MDX expression in the Back Color text box.

> **Note** You can drag items from the Calculation Tools pane to make creating this expression easier, or you can copy the expression from the file C:\Microsoft Press\Analysis Services 2008 SBS\Chapter 06\MDX\Reseller Avg Sales Back Color.txt.

```
IIF(
   ([Measures].[Reseller Sales Amount],[Date].[Fiscal Year].&[2011])
    < ([Measures].[Reseller Sales Amount],[Date].[Fiscal Year].&[2010])
   ,255 /*Red*/
   ,65280 /*Lime*/)
```

This expression follows the standard syntax for an MDX immediate-if statement of *IIF(Logical_Expression, ValueIfTrue, ValueIfFalse)*. The logical expression compares two tuples that represent the value of Reseller Sales Amount for Fiscal Year 2010 and 2011.

Embedded within the expression are comments, which are enclosed within the /* and */ symbols. Comments are ignored when evaluating an expression, but they can be helpful for clarifying complex expressions or, as in this case, labeling a color code.

If you don't already know the color code that you want to use, you can click the button to the right of the Back Color box and choose a color. The code associated with that color will be inserted in the Back Color expression box.

You can now deploy the AdventureWorks SSAS project and browse the cube to see the new calculated member.

Deploy and browse the cube

1. On the Build menu, select Deploy AdventureWorks SSAS. You may notice that deploying the project occurs relatively quickly. When you create calculated members, you don't change the structure or data of any dimensions or cubes, you only modify the text of the calculation script. When you deploy the project, Analysis Services doesn't need to process any data. It just replaces the calculation script in the cube.

2. After the cube has been deployed and processed successfully, click the Browser tab of the Cube Designer. On the Browser tab toolbar, click the Reconnect button.

3. Click in a blank area of the Report pane and then click the Clear Results button on the Browser tab toolbar.

4. From the Metadata pane, add Reseller Sales Amount, Reseller Count, and Reseller Avg Sales to the Report pane totals area.

5. Add the Product dimension to the Report pane rows area and expand the Bikes Category. You should confirm that for each row of the report, Reseller Avg Sales is equal to Reseller Sales Amount divided by Reseller Count. Also notice that data displays with the background of Reseller Avg Sales in green, except for the Mountain Bikes and Road Bikes categories. For these two categories, sales declined between 2010 and 2011, so the background is red.

Drop Filter Fields Here				
	Drop Column Fields Here			
Category ▾	Subcategory	Reseller Sales Amount	Reseller Count	Reseller Avg Sales
⊟ Bikes	⊞ Mountain Bikes	$26,492,684	211	$125,558
	⊞ Road Bikes	$29,358,207	243	$120,816
	⊞ Touring Bikes	$10,451,490	133	$78,583
	Total	$66,302,382	587	$112,951
⊞ Components		$11,799,077	580	$20,343
⊞ Clothing		$1,777,841	475	$3,743
⊞ Accessories		$571,298	346	$1,651
Grand Total		$80,450,597	635	$126,694

Calculating Contribution

A tuple such as *([Reseller Sales Amount])*, which uses an explicit member name from one dimension, is very common in MDX expressions. A tuple such as *([Reseller Sales Amount],[2010])*, which uses explicit member names from two or more dimensions, is less common. Usually, when you explicitly include members from more than one dimension in a tuple, you use functions that operate on the current member of a hierarchy to retrieve another member in the hierarchy. This gives your MDX expression greater flexibility, like an Excel formula that retrieves values from a different row or column.

Suppose you want to calculate what percent each product or product category contributes to the total sales for all products. This expression would have two component values: a numerator (Sales for the current product) divided by a denominator (Sales for All Products). The numerator will change from product to product, but the denominator always retrieves the member from the All level of the product dimension.

In this procedure, you'll create a calculated member that displays the percentage that a category contributes to the total sales for all products.

Create a percent of total calculation

1. In the Cube Designer, click the Calculations tab and then click the Reconnect button.

2. In the Script Organizer, select Reseller Avg Sales and then click the New Calculated Member button on the Calculations toolbar.

3. In the Calculated Member Editor, change the name to [Product % of Total].

4. Enter the following MDX expression in the Expression text box.

 Note You can drag items from the Calculation Tools pane to make creating this expression easier, or you can copy the expression from the file C:\Microsoft Press\Analysis Services 2008 SBS\Chapter 06\MDX\Product % of Total.txt.

```
([Measures].[Reseller Sales Amount])/
([Measures].[Reseller Sales Amount],[Product].[Product by Category].[All])
```

The tuple in the numerator is going to retrieve Reseller Sales Amount in the context of the rows, columns, and filter of your report. The denominator is also going to retrieve Reseller Sales Amount, but it will ignore any member of the Product By Category hierarchy that appears on the report. Instead, it will retrieve the value of Reseller Sales Amount from the All member of Product By Category.

5. Select "Percent" from the Format String list.

6. In the Non-Empty Behavior list, select Reseller Sales Amount and click OK.

7. In the Associated Measure Group list, select Reseller Sales. You can group related measures and calculated members in folders by giving each the same value for the Display Folder property.

8. In the Display Folder text box, type Product %. The Calculated Member Editor should look similar to the following image.

Name:

[Product % of Total]

☆ Parent Properties ⓘ

Parent hierarchy: Measures ▾

Parent member: [   ] Change

☆ Expression

```
([Measures].[Reseller Sales Amount])/
([Measures].[Reseller Sales Amount],[Product].[Product by Category].[All])
```

☆ Additional Properties

Format string: "Percent" ▾

Visible: True ▾

Non-empty behavior: Reseller Sales Amount ▾

Associated measure group: Reseller Sales ▾

Display folder: Product %

⯆ Color Expressions

⯆ Font Expressions

Calculating the relative contribution to the total is a comparatively easy calculation to create in a spreadsheet. In every cell, the denominator is anchored to the cell that contains the total. Creating a formula that calculates a value's contribution to the value of its parent is more difficult. For dates, you can create a formula that divides month values by quarter subtotals and then copy this formula to all the month cells. You could also create a formula that divides quarter subtotals by the year total. Then you could copy the set of cells for the months and quarters and paste it into the cells for all the other years. This exercise is not too difficult, because at every level a parent has the same number of children. But if the number of children varies from one parent to the next, creating the percent of parent spreadsheet report becomes very tedious.

If you could create a formula that divides a value by the value of its parent, you could use a single formula in all the cells of the report. A spreadsheet, however, has no conception of a hierarchy. Analysis Services is aware of hierarchies, and one of its remarkable strengths is the ability of expressions to use the hierarchical relationships in dimensions.

In this next procedure, you'll create a calculated member that displays the percentage that a member of the Product Category hierarchy contributes to its parent's sales.

Create a percent of parent calculation

The Product % of Parent calculated member that you need to create is very similar to the Product % of Total calculated member that you have already created. Unfortunately, you can't copy a calculated member when the Calculated Member Editor is displayed. So in this procedure, you will switch to the Script View of the Calculations tab, copy the Product % of Total calculated member, and then modify it to become Product % of Parent.

1. On the Calculations toolbar, click the Script View button to open the Script Editor.

The Script Editor replaces the Calculated Member Editor. In the Script Editor, you see the complete MDX statements used to create each of the calculated members. Each calculated member statement begins with *CREATE MEMBER* and ends with a semicolon (;). In the Script Editor, you can copy the Product % of Total calculated member and then modify it.

 Important The first statement in the Calculation Script is *CALCULATE*. Don't delete or comment out this statement. If you do, you will not be able to retrieve any data from your cube.

2. Select the statement that creates the Product % of Total calculated member.

```
CREATE MEMBER CURRENTCUBE.[Measures].[Product % of Total]
  AS ([Measures].[Reseller Sales Amount])/
([Measures].[Reseller Sales Amount],[Product].[Product by Category].[All]),
FORMAT_STRING = "Percent",
NON_EMPTY_BEHAVIOR = { [Reseller Sales Amount] },
VISIBLE = 1 ,  DISPLAY_FOLDER = 'Product %' ,  ASSOCIATED_MEASURE_GROUP = 'Reseller Sales'  ;
```

3. Copy the statement and then paste it at the end of the calculation script.

 Tip The Calculation Script will be much easier to read if you enter a blank line between each statement. MDX ignores white space, so it is a best practice to employ spacing and indenting for readability.

4. Change the name of the calculated member to Product % of Parent.

5. In the denominator of the expression, change [Product].[Product by Category].[All] to [Product].[Product by Category].CurrentMember.Parent. The code for the Product % of Parent calculated member should look like this:

```
CREATE MEMBER CURRENTCUBE.[Measures].[Product % of Parent]
  AS ([Measures].[Reseller Sales Amount])/
 ([Measures].[Reseller Sales Amount],[Product].CURRENTMEMBER.PARENT),
FORMAT_STRING = "Percent",
NON_EMPTY_BEHAVIOR = { [Reseller Sales Amount] },
VISIBLE = 1 ,  DISPLAY_FOLDER = 'Product %' ,  ASSOCIATED_MEASURE_GROUP = 'Reseller Sales'  ;
```

Now the denominator of the formula will be equal to the value of the parent of the current member of the Product by Category hierarchy. For example, if the Mountain Bikes subcategory is on rows, the value of the denominator will be the value for the Bikes category.

This expression works well for all members of the Product by Category hierarchy except the All member. Because the All member belongs to the top level of the hierarchy, it does not have a parent and the Product % of Parent calculated member will return an error. You need to change the expression in the create member statement to first test whether the current member of the Product by Category hierarchy is the All member.

6. In the calculated member, change the expression from

```
([Measures].[Reseller Sales Amount])/
([Measures].[Reseller Sales Amount],[Product].[Product by Category].CURRENTMEMBER.
PARENT)
```

to the following:

```
IIF([Product].[Product by Category].CurrentMember
    IS [Product].[Product by Category].[All]
  ,1
  ,([Measures].[Reseller Sales Amount],[Product].[Product by Category].
CurrentMember)/
    ([Measures].[Reseller Sales Amount],[Product].[Product by Category].
CurrentMember.Parent)
  )
```

> **Note** You can drag items from the Calculation Tools pane to make creating this expression easier, or you can copy the expression from the file C:\Microsoft Press\Analysis Services 2008 SBS\Chapter 06\MDX\Product % of Parent.txt.

The code for the Product % of Parent calculated member should now look like this:

```
CREATE MEMBER CURRENTCUBE.[Measures].[Product % of Parent]
  AS IIF([Product].[Product by Category].CurrentMember IS [Product].[Product by Category].[All]
  ,1
  ,([Measures].[Reseller Sales Amount],[Product].[Product by Category].CurrentMember)/
    ([Measures].[Reseller Sales Amount],[Product].[Product by Category].CurrentMember.Parent)
  )
,
FORMAT_STRING = "Percent",
VISIBLE = 1 ,   DISPLAY_FOLDER = 'Product %' ,   ASSOCIATED_MEASURE_GROUP = 'Reseller Sales'  ;
```

The first parameter of the *IIF* function determines whether the current member of Product by Category is the All member. If it is, the function returns a 1; otherwise, it returns the percent of parent value.

7. Click the Check Syntax button. If your calculation script contains a syntax error, you will not be able to switch back to the Calculated Member editor.

8. In the Check Syntax dialog box, click OK. If you received a syntax error that you cannot resolve, you can replace the new *CREATE MEMBER* statement with the contents of the C:\Microsoft Press\Analysis Services 2008 SBS\Chapter 06\MDX\Product % of Parent Complete.txt file.

9. Click the Form View button.

```
                                                 Form View
 ,255 /*Red*/
 ,65280 /*Lime*/),
```

You can see the new calculated member in the Calculated Member editor.

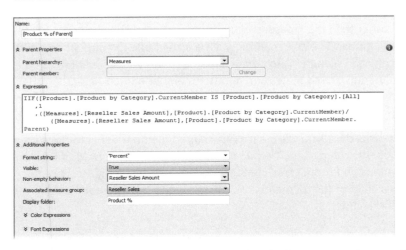

You must deploy the AdventureWorks SSAS project before you can browse the cube and see the two new calculated members.

Deploy and browse the cube

1. On the Build menu, select Deploy AdventureWorks SSAS.

2. After the cube has been deployed and processed successfully, click the Browser tab of the Cube Designer and then click the Reconnect button on the Browser tab toolbar.

3. Remove Reseller Count and Reseller Avg Sales from the report.

4. In the Metadata pane, expand the Product % folder and add the Product % of Parent and Product % of Total calculated members to the Report pane totals area. The report shows that Mountain Bike sales ($26,492,684) are 39.96% of parent Bike sales ($66,302,382) and 32.93% of total product sales ($80,450,597).

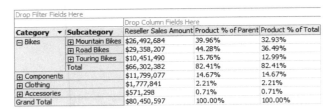

Category ▾	Subcategory	Reseller Sales Amount	Product % of Parent	Product % of Total
⊟ Bikes	⊞ Mountain Bikes	$26,492,684	39.96%	32.93%
	⊞ Road Bikes	$29,358,207	44.28%	36.49%
	⊞ Touring Bikes	$10,451,490	15.76%	12.99%
	Total	$66,302,382	82.41%	82.41%
⊞ Components		$11,799,077	14.67%	14.67%
⊞ Clothing		$1,777,841	2.21%	2.21%
⊞ Accessories		$571,298	0.71%	0.71%
Grand Total		$80,450,597	100.00%	100.00%

You may want to verify the functionality of these two calculated members by expanding one of the Bike subcategories and reviewing the Product level values.

Creating Calculated Members Outside of the Measures Dimension

Because the name *Calculated Member* implies manipulating numbers, and because most calculated members are created in the measures dimension, it is easy to forget that you can create calculated members in any dimension. When you create a calculated member in a dimension other than the measures dimension, you must specify where in the dimension the member will appear. The new member will be a child of a member in one of the hierarchies. One very common scenario is to create a member named Continental US that is the sum of the 48 continental United States and another member named Alaska And Hawaii that is the sum of those two states. These two calculated members would then be a child of the United States member in the Customer dimension Customers By Geography user-defined hierarchy.

In the next procedure, you will create a calculated member equal to the sum of the Bikes and Components categories. The calculated member will be a child of the All member of the Product dimension Product by Category user-defined hierarchy. Because the new calculated member is a child of the All member, it will belong to the Category level of the Product By Category hierarchy.

Create a non-measures dimension calculation

1. In the Cube Designer, click the Calculations tab and then click the Reconnect button.

2. In the Script Organizer, select the Product % of Parent member and on the Calculations toolbar, click the New Calculated Member button.

3. In the Calculated Member Editor, change the name to [Bikes & Components].

4. In the Parent Hierarchy list, expand the Product dimension, select Product By Category, and click OK.

5. Click the Change button next to the Parent Member selection area. In the Select Parent Member dialog box, select the All member. The Bikes & Components calculated member is now a member of the Product dimension Product by Category user-defined hierarchy. It will be a child of the All member and be in the Category level. Click OK.

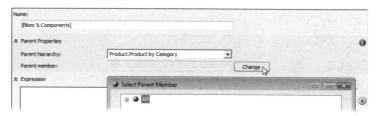

6. In the Expression text box, enter the following MDX expression, which uses the SUM function to add two tuples:

```
SUM({[Product].[Product by Category].[Category].&[1]
  ,[Product].[Product by Category].[Category].&[2]})
```

You can drag items from the Calculation Tools pane to make creating this expression easier. You will need to expand the Product dimension, the Product By Category hierarchy, and the Category level. Then drag the Bikes member and the Components member to the Expression text box. When you drag the members to the Expression text box, the member names are replaced by the member keys. The member key for Bikes is 1 and the member key for Components is 2. Alternatively, you can copy the expression from the file C:\Microsoft Press\Analysis Services 2008 SBS\Chapter 06\MDX\Bikes & Components.txt.

> **Tip** I find it difficult to remember what key belongs to what member, so I often replace member keys with the member name. If you do this, remember to remove the ampersand (&).

The Bikes & Components calculated member does not include a measure. Instead, for each cell in the cube, the calculated member uses the current member of the measures dimension. When you browse the cube, you will see that the Bikes & Components member can be used to sum any measure or measure dimension calculated member that appears in the cube.

Leave the *FormatString* property blank so that you can see how the Bikes & Components calculated member interacts with the cube's measures.

Deploy and browse the cube

1. On the Build menu, select Deploy AdventureWorks SSAS.

2. After the cube has been deployed and processed successfully, click the Browser tab of the Cube Designer and then click the Reconnect button on the Browser tab toolbar.

3. Click in the Report pane and then click the Clear Results button on the Browser tab toolbar.

4. Add the Reseller Sales Amount, Reseller Count measures, and the Reseller Avg Sales calculated member to the Report pane totals area.

5. Add the Product dimension to the Report pane rows area. Notice that the value Reseller Avg Sales for Bikes & Components is not correct—$78,101,458 divided by 1,167 is equal to $66,925.

Drop Filter Fields Here			
	Drop Column Fields Here		
Category ▾	Reseller Sales Amount	Reseller Count	Reseller Avg Sales
⊞ Bikes	$66,302,382	587	$112,951
⊞ Components	$11,799,077	580	$20,343
⊞ Clothing	$1,777,841	475	$3,743
⊞ Accessories	$571,298	346	$1,651
⊞ Bikes & Components	$78,101,458	1,167	$133,294
Grand Total	$80,450,597	635	$126,694

Two MDX expressions are at the intersection of Bikes & Components and Reseller Avg Sales. Because Bikes & Components appears after Reseller Avg Sales in the Calculations tab Script Organizer and in the calculation script, its expression is used to calculate the value of the cell. The cell displays the sum of Reseller Avg Sales for Bikes and Reseller Avg Sales for Components. "Last expression wins" is the simple rule for which formula gets applied to a cell. And to be clear, this doesn't mean that each calculated member gets evaluated one after the other. No—all but the last calculated member that applies to a cell is ignored.

Because it makes more sense for the cell to display the result of the Reseller Avg Sales expression, in the next procedure, you will change the order of the calculated members.

Modify calculated member precedence

1. In the Cube Designer, click the Calculations tab.

2. In the Script Organizer, drag the Bikes & Components calculated member to the area above Reseller Avg Sales. This reordering in the Script Organizer is effectively equivalent to setting the SOLVE_ORDER property.

3. On the Build menu, select Deploy AdventureWorks SSAS.

4. After the cube has been deployed and processed successfully, click the Browser tab of the Cube Designer and then click the Reconnect button on the Browser tab toolbar. The report shows that the Reseller Avg Sales calculated member is now being applied to the intersection of Bikes & Components and Reseller Avg Sales. The value of the cell is now equal to Reseller Sales Amount divided by Reseller Count. Also note that the Reseller Avg Sales calculated member formatting is being applied.

Category	Reseller Sales Amount	Reseller Count	Reseller Avg Sales
⊞ Bikes	$66,302,382	587	$112,951
⊞ Components	$11,799,077	580	$20,343
⊞ Clothing	$1,777,841	475	$3,743
⊞ Accessories	$571,298	346	$1,651
⊞ Bikes & Components	$78,101,458	1,167	$66,925
Grand Total	$80,450,597	635	$126,694

But notice that the value of Reseller Count is not correct. You have a total of only 635 resellers, but the report shows that 1,167 resellers purchased Bikes & Components. It is appropriate for the Bikes & Components calculated member to sum Reseller Sales Amount, but it is not appropriate to sum the distinct count Reseller Count measure. Bikes & Components needs to apply a different function based on the aggregate function of the measures to which it is being applied.

Use the *AGGREGATE* MDX function

When the *AGGREGATE* MDX function is used in a calculated member, the calculated member summarizes measures based on the measure's *AggregateFunction* property.

1. In the Cube Designer, click the Calculations tab.

2. Select the Bikes & Components calculated member.

3. In the Expression text box, replace the *SUM* function with the *AGGREGATE* function. The formula in the expression box is now:

```
AGGREGATE({[Product].[Product by Category].[Category].&[1]
  ,[Product].[Product by Category].[Category].&[2]})
```

4. On the Build menu, select Deploy AdventureWorks SSAS.

5. After the cube has been deployed and processed successfully, click the Browser tab of the Cube Designer and then click the Reconnect button on the Browser tab toolbar. The report shows that the Bikes & Components value of Reseller Count is a more reasonable 628. The Bikes & Components calculated member is summing the Reseller Sales Amount measure, but it is performing a distinct count for the Reseller Count measure.

Drop Filter Fields Here

Category	Reseller Sales Amount	Reseller Count	Reseller Avg Sales
⊞ Bikes	$66,302,382	587	$112,951
⊞ Components	$11,799,077	580	$20,343
⊞ Clothing	$1,777,841	475	$3,743
⊞ Accessories	$571,298	346	$1,651
⊞ Bikes & Components	$78,101,458	628	$124,365
Grand Total	$80,450,597	635	$126,694

In this section, you added new measure and dimension members to a cube by creating calculated members. You can also modify the value of existing measures and dimensions using calculated scripts.

Calculation Scripting

When you first create a cube, a default MDX script that defines calculations in the cube is also created. This script is identified by the Calculate command that appears first in the Script Organizer of the Calculation tab of the Cube Designer. You add to this script every time you create a new calculated member. This script tells the server to calculate the entire cube on the first pass. The MDX expressions and statements that you add to the MDX script then get resolved in the order in which they appear in the Script Organizer.

You can use the debugging features in Microsoft Visual Studio to observe the interaction of calculations during execution of the MDX script. As you step through the script, you use the debugger's cube browser to review the calculations and calculated members at each step. You can also make changes to the script while debugging to correct any problems that you find.

Suppose you want to motivate your sales staff to get an earlier start on their annual quotas. You would like to increase the first-quarter quotas by 20 percent, but you don't want to change the annual quotas. In the next procedure, you will add an assignment statement to the calculation script to make this change.

Create a script assignment

1. In the Cube Designer, click the Calculations tab.

2. On the Calculations toolbar, click the Script View button.

3. Enter the following MDX statements after the *CALCULATE* statement and before the statement that creates the Total Sales Amount calculated member.

```
SCOPE([Measures].[Sales Amount Quota]);
  ([Date].[Calendar Quarter].[CY 2010 Qtr 1])
    = ([Date].[Calendar Quarter].[CY 2010 Qtr 1]) * 1.2;
END SCOPE;
```

> **Note** You can drag items from the Calculation Tools pane to make creating this statement easier, or you can copy the expression from the file C:\Microsoft Press\Analysis Services 2008 SBS\Chapter 06\MDX\Sales Amount Quota.txt.

The calculation script now looks like this:

```
CALCULATE;

SCOPE([Measures].[Sales Amount Quota]);
   ([Date].[Calendar Quarter].[CY 2010 Qtr 1])
     = ([Date].[Calendar Quarter].[CY 2010 Qtr 1]) * 1.2;
END SCOPE;

CREATE MEMBER CURRENTCUBE.[Measures].[Total Sales Amount]
```

The *SCOPE* statement is used to define a *subcube*—a specific collection of cube cells. Any MDX statements that you include between the *SCOPE* and *END SCOPE* statements apply only to this subcube. Therefore, in this procedure, the MDX statements affect only the Sales Amount Quota measure. The MDX statement increases the first-quarter sales quota by 20 percent.

4. On the Debug menu, select Start Debugging. Because you modified the calculation script, the AdventureWorks SSAS project will be deployed. When the project is successfully deployed, the calculation debugger starts. The *CALCULATE* statement is highlighted, indicating that script execution has stopped at this statement.

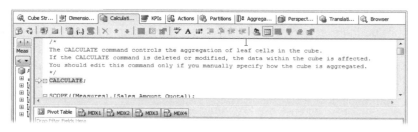

> **Tip** Several windows—Autos, Call Stack, and so on—may open below the Debugger browser pane. You can unpin and hide these windows to provide more room for the debugger and browser. Unpin the windows by clicking the pushpin icon in the upper-right corner of each window.

Before you execute the statements in the calculation script, you want to create a report in the Report pane that has appeared below the calculation script. Then you can execute the statements in the calculation script one at a time and see how they affect the values in the report.

5. On the Metadata tab, expand the Measures folder, expand the Sales Quota measure group, and drag the Sales Quota Amount measure to the totals area on the Pivot Table tab of the Report pane.

6. Drag the Date dimension to the rows area of the Pivot Table. Expand the CY 2010 member of the Calendar Year level. Because the *CALCULATE* statement has not yet been executed, the data cells of the report are empty.

7. On the BIDS Debug toolbar, click the Step Over button.

Now that the *CALCULATE* statement has been executed, data appears in the report. The cells affected by the last executed calculation script statement display highlighted in yellow.

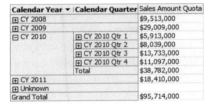

Calendar Year ▾	Calendar Quarter	Sales Amount Quota
⊞ CY 2008		$9,513,000
⊞ CY 2009		$29,009,000
⊟ CY 2010	⊞ CY 2010 Qtr 1	$5,913,000
	⊞ CY 2010 Qtr 2	$8,039,000
	⊞ CY 2010 Qtr 3	$13,733,000
	⊞ CY 2010 Qtr 4	$11,097,000
	Total	$38,782,000
⊞ CY 2011		$18,410,000
⊞ Unknown		
Grand Total		$95,714,000

The value of CY 2010 Qtr 1 is $5,913,000. The value of CY 2010 is $38,782,000. The value for all time is $95,714,000. The next two statements will modify these values.

8. Click the Step Over button two more times. The script assignment statement that increases the first quarter sales quota by 20 percent has now been executed. The change in the value for CY 2010 Qtr 1 has "bubbled up" the Calendar Date hierarchy and increased the value of the CY 2010 and All members.

Calendar Year ▾	Calendar Quarter	Sales Amount Quota
⊞ CY 2008		$9,513,000
⊞ CY 2009		$29,009,000
⊟ CY 2010	⊞ CY 2010 Qtr 1	$7,095,600
	⊞ CY 2010 Qtr 2	$8,039,000
	⊞ CY 2010 Qtr 3	$13,733,000
	⊞ CY 2010 Qtr 4	$11,097,000
	Total	$39,964,600
⊞ CY 2011		$18,410,000
⊞ Unknown		
Grand Total		$96,896,600

Because you wanted to increase the value of the quota for CY 2010 Qtr1 but didn't want to increase the CY 2010 quota, you need to further modify the calculation script.

9. On the BIDS Debug toolbar, click the Stop Debugging button.

10. In the Script Editor, insert a line after the *SCOPE* statement and enter **FREEZE**;. The script now looks like this:

```
SCOPE([Measures].[Sales Amount Quota]);
FREEZE;
    ([Date].[Calendar Quarter].[CY 2010 Qtr 1])
      = ([Date].[Calendar Quarter].[CY 2010 Qtr 1]) * 1.2;
END SCOPE;
```

The *FREEZE* statement prevents any changes to the current subcube except the explicit changes made in the following statements. The *FREEZE* statement allows the change to CY 2010 Qtr 1 but prevents the change from bubbling up the Calendar Date hierarchy.

11. On the Debug menu, select Start Debugging.

12. On the Debug toolbar, click the Step Over button four times. The report shows that the value for CY 2010 Qtr 1 has increased by 20 percent, but if you compare the report in this step to the report in step 7, you can see that the values for the CY 2010 and All members remain unchanged.

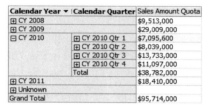

Calendar Year ▾	Calendar Quarter	Sales Amount Quota
⊞ CY 2008		$9,513,000
⊞ CY 2009		$29,009,000
⊟ CY 2010	⊞ CY 2010 Qtr 1	$7,095,600
	⊞ CY 2010 Qtr 2	$8,039,000
	⊞ CY 2010 Qtr 3	$13,733,000
	⊞ CY 2010 Qtr 4	$11,097,000
	Total	$38,782,000
⊞ CY 2011		$18,410,000
⊞ Unknown		
Grand Total		$95,714,000

13. On the Debug toolbar, click the Stop Debugging button.

Creating KPIs

Key performance indicators (KPIs) have captured the attention of the business world in recent years. A KPI measures the progress that a business is making toward meeting its goals. In Analysis Services, a KPI provides a visual representation of these comparative metrics over time, rather than just displaying the numbers. The visual representation is based on your input and shows whether the progress against goals is positive, neutral, or negative by using graphical images such as a stoplight that displays a green, yellow, or red light according to the specified business rules.

You create a KPI in the Cube Designer. For each KPI, you develop expressions that calculate the KPI's value, goal, current status, and trend. The Value expression represents where the business is today and is sometimes referred to as an *actual* when comparing it to a goal. The Goal expression defines the business goal, such as a constant value or perhaps a 20 percent increase in sales from the previous year. The Status expression measures how the Value compares to the Goal. Typically, you associate a visual icon, such as a stoplight or a gauge, to the Status value to express whether the result is positive or negative. The Trend expression is used to compare the current Status value with the value of Status at a previous point in time. As with Status, you can assign a graphic to illustrate whether the trend is positive, negative, or neutral.

Because the MDX expressions in a KPI may become complicated, it is useful to create calculated members for the values you need in your KPIs and then just use the calculated members when you create the KPI itself. For particularly complex calculations, it is a good technique to build simple calculated members and then build other calculations from them. In this procedure, you will create Forecast Variance, Forecast Variance Status, and Forecast Variance Trend calculated members in just such a stepwise building fashion.

KPI expressions are calculated after all the calculated members and assignment statements in the calculation script are evaluated. If you create calculated members to use in your KPIs, you can determine where the calculated members appear in the Calculations tab Script Organizer. This gives you greater control over when the expressions are evaluated.

The KPI you will create compares actual sales to forecast sales.

Create calculated members for a KPI

1. In the Cube Designer, click the Calculations tab and then click the Reconnect button.

2. Click the Form View button.

3. In the Script Organizer, select the last calculated member (Product % of Parent) in the Script Organizer. On the Calculations toolbar, click the New Calculated Member button.

4. In the Calculated Member Editor, change the name to [Forecast Variance].

5. In the Expression text box, enter this MDX expression:

```
([Measures].[Total Sales Amount]-[Measures].[Sales Amount Forecast])
/[Measures].[Sales Amount Forecast]
```

All the MDX expressions in this procedure are contained in the file C:\Microsoft Press\ Analysis Services 2008 SBS\Chapter 06\MDX\KPI.txt.

6. Create a new calculated member named [Forecast Variance Status]. Analysis Services provides status and trend indicators that can display three states. These states can be interpreted as high, medium, and low—or acceptable, marginally acceptable, and not acceptable. If you are going to use these indicators, then the status and trend expressions that you create should return a 1, 0, or –1 for high (acceptable), medium (marginally acceptable), and low (not acceptable). It is worth noting that the cube does not care whether these calculations make sense—the status conditions are made available and should be defined from a business application perspective. If you are using a client application that provides its own indicators, you need to configure the status and trend expressions to return values based on the requirements of that client.

Configure the expression as shown in the following table.

Condition	Status	Return Value
Actual sales – forecast < –2.5%	Not acceptable	–1
–2.5 <= Actual sales – forecast < 0	Marginally acceptable	0
Actual sales – forecast > 0	Acceptable	1

7. In the Expression text box, enter the following MDX expression:

```
CASE
  WHEN [Measures].[Forecast Variance] < -0.025
        THEN -1
  WHEN [Measures].[Forecast Variance] < 0
        THEN 0
  ELSE 1
END
```

This expression uses the MDX *CASE* statement. The *CASE* statement evaluates the WHEN conditions in order until one of the conditions evaluates to *True*. It then returns the value of the associated THEN expression. If none of the WHEN conditions is satisfied, the *CASE* statement returns the value of the optional ELSE expression.

8. Create a new calculated member named [Forecast Variance Trend].

9. In the Expression text box, enter the following MDX expression:

```
CASE
  WHEN ([Measures].[Forecast Variance]) < ([Date].[Calendar Date].
PREVMEMBER,[Measures].[Forecast Variance])
        THEN -1
  WHEN ([Measures].[Forecast Variance]) = ([Date].[Calendar Date].
PREVMEMBER,[Measures].[Forecast Variance])
        THEN 0
  ELSE 1
END
```

The *PREVMEMBER* function returns the Previous Member at the same level in the hierarchy. For example, if the current member is the month of February, the *PREVMEMBER* function will return the month of January. To use these new calculated members in a KPI, you have to deploy the project to the Analysis Services server.

10. On the Build menu, select Deploy AdventureWorks SSAS.

Now that you have calculated members created specifically for use in your KPI, you are ready to create the KPI itself.

Create a KPI

1. In the Cube Designer, click the KPIs tab.

2. Click the New KPI button.

3. Set the KPI properties as shown in the following table. You can drag calculated members from the Calculation Tools pane to the KPI Editor pane to make creating the KPI expressions easier. The Sales Amount Forecast measure is in the Product Forecast measure group, and the rest of the values are calculated members.

Property	Value
Name	Sales Amount Forecast
Value Expression	[Measures].[Total Sales Amount]
Goal Expression	[Measures].[Sales Amount Forecast]
Status Indicator	*Road Signs*
Status Expression	[Measures].[Forecast Variance Status]
Trend Indicator	*Status Arrow*
Trend Expression	[Measures].[Forecast Variance Trend]

Having calculated members created to use in the KPI makes the KPI easier to create and understand. The KPI Editor should look like the following image.

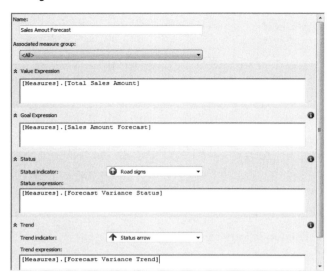

4. Now that the Sales Amount Forecast KPI is created, you need to deploy the AdventureWorks SSAS project before you can display the KPI. On the Build menu, select Deploy AdventureWorks SSAS.

5. After the cube has been deployed and processed successfully, stay on the KPI tab, click the Reconnect button, and then click the Browser View button.

6. In the KPI Browser, select Date from the Dimension list, select Calendar Date from the Hierarchy list, select Equal from the Operator list, and then select CY 2009 Qtr 4 from the Filter Expression list. Click OK.

7. Click in the KPI Browser. The values in the filter are applied to the KPI and the browser is refreshed. In this time period, the actual value failed to meet the goal and the trend is negative.

8. In the KPI Browser, change the Filter Expression list value to CY 2010 Qtr 1 and click OK. Click in the KPI Browser. The KPI shows that actual sales exceeded forecast and the trend is positive in CY 2010 Qtr 1.

Dimension	Hierarchy	Operator	Filter Expression			
Date	Calendar Date	Equal	{ CY 2010 Qtr 1 }			
<Select dimension>						

Display Structure	Value	Goal	Status	Trend	Weight	
Sales Amout Forecast	$6,679,874	$5,913,000	⬆	↑		

9. Click the Save All button and then select Close Solution from the File menu.

In this chapter, you learned how to create measures that aggregate data using additive, pseudo-additive, semi-additive, and non-additive aggregate functions. These aggregate functions enable you to create measures that can count values or table rows, count unique instances of a value, find minimum or maximum values, or find balances for a given time period. You learned to create measures using the Cube Structure tab of the Cube Designer. In the New Measure dialog box, you selected the aggregation method you wanted to use and the table and column that contain the measure's source data.

You also learned basic MDX concepts and how to create calculated members and MDX calculation script assignment statements. MDX expressions allow you to create formulas similar to spreadsheet formulas, but MDX expressions are more flexible and more powerful. You created new values in a cube using calculated members and modified existing cube values by adding an assignment statement to the calculation script. Finally, you created a key performance indicator (KPI) that displayed actual and target values and status and trend indicators.

This chapter has provided you basic information about MDX, calculated members, and MDX scripting. If you would like to learn more, you should read *Microsoft SQL Server 2008 MDX Step by Step* by Bryan Smith and C. Ryan Clay (Microsoft Press, 2009).

In Chapter 7, "Advanced Dimension Design," you will learn how to create reference, fact, and many-to-many dimensions. You can use a reference dimension to avoid duplicating data when attributes appear in more than one dimension. You can use a fact dimension when dimension attributes appear in a fact table. Many-to-many dimensions solve the problem of counting more than once when a single fact record is related to multiple members in a dimension.

Chapter 7
Advanced Dimension Design

In this chapter, you will learn how to:

- Create a referenced dimension.

- Create a degenerate dimension.

- Add a fact dimension to a cube.

- Create a many-to-many dimension.

In Chapter 6, "Creating Advanced Measures and Calculations," you learned how to create measures using additive, pseudo-additive, semi-additive, and non-additive aggregate functions. You also learned basic MDX concepts and created calculated members and script assignment statements. You then created a KPI that used calculated members for its status and trend expressions.

In this chapter, you will learn how to use advanced dimension capabilities. Some attributes appear in more than one dimension. You can create a single dimension for these attributes and then add it to a cube as a reference dimension. A reference dimension allows you to share common attributes across multiple dimensions.

Sometimes a fact table contains attributes. For example, a fact table may contain invoice numbers. If the fact table is at the invoice grain, each row of the fact table will contain a unique invoice number. Even if the fact table is at the invoice line grain, there will still be a high ratio of unique invoice numbers compared to total rows in the table. Because of the high cardinality of the invoice numbers, they won't be used for grouping, but rather will be used for detail reporting or made available for drillthrough. You can create a dimension containing the invoice numbers and then add the dimension to the cube as a fact dimension.

In most instances, a single record in a fact table is related to only one dimension record— that is, there is a one-to-many relationship between the dimension table and the fact table. However, in some circumstances a single fact record is related to multiple dimension records. Because of the many-to-many relationship between the dimension table and the fact table, it becomes very easy to double-count fact records. If you add the dimension to your cube as a many-to-many dimension, Analysis Services aggregates the fact data without double-counting any records.

Dimension Usage

In Chapter 5, "Creating a Cube", you were introduced to dimension usage as the way in which a dimension is related to a measure group in a cube. So far, you've dealt with a dimension that has either *No Relationship* or a *Regular* relationship with a measure group. A dimension has a *Regular* relationship with a measure group when each fact table record is related to one dimension table record.

Analysis Services provides alternative dimension usage relationship types to accommodate other ways that a dimension and a measure group can be related. Sometimes multiple dimensions may share a common set of attributes that are contained in a snowflake dimension table. A snowflake dimension has a *Referenced* relationship with a measure group when the fact table is indirectly related to the snowflake dimension table. Attributes that are unique for each fact record can be stored in a fact table. A dimension has a *Fact* relationship with a measure group when the dimension is created from attributes stored in the measure group's fact table. A single fact record may be related to multiple dimension records. In this case, a dimension has a *Many-to-Many* relationship type with the measure group.

Creating Reference Dimensions

You might want to use a *Referenced* relationship type in two situations. The first is when a snowflake dimension table is shared by multiple dimensions. The second is when the attributes of a dimension are not all stored in the same data source. In either case, the fact table contains a dimension key column that you can use to create a direct relationship to a dimension table, and the dimension table contains a foreign key column that you can use to create a relationship to a second dimension table. The fact table is indirectly related to the second dimension table by means of the first dimension table.

You can use a *Referenced* relationship type when a fact table contains a dimension key column that can be used to create a direct relationship to the first dimension table, and that dimension table contains a foreign key column that can be used to create a relationship to a second dimension table. This way, the fact table can be related to the second dimension table even though it doesn't contain a dimension key to the second dimension. The fact table is indirectly related to the second dimension table by means of the first dimension table.

The most common example of an indirectly related dimension table is when geography attributes are stored in a single table and then related to various dimensions: customer, supplier, employee, facility, and so on. You could have the geography attributes and hierarchies appear in each of these dimensions, but that makes developing and maintaining these dimensions more difficult. If you have to make a change to one of the geography attributes, you have to modify every dimension that contains the attribute. Instead, you can create a separate geography dimension and then use the customer, supplier, employee, and facility dimensions to create an indirect relationship between the geography dimension and the measure groups in your cube.

In the next three procedures, you will add three dimensions—Customer, Reseller, and Geography—to your Analysis Services database. You will add Customer and Reseller to the cube, and they will have a *Regular* relationship type with the measure groups in the cube. You will also add the Geography dimension to the cube. Because none of the fact tables contains a Geography dimension key, you will use Customer and Reseller as intermediate dimensions to relate the Geography dimension to the cube's measure groups using the *Referenced* relationship type.

Add dimensions to a cube

1. Use Business Intelligence Development Studio (BIDS) to open the AdventureWorks BI solution contained in the C:\Microsoft Press\Analysis Services 2008 SBS\Chapter 07\ AdventureWorks BI folder.

   Before you can add a dimension to a cube, you must add the dimension table to a data source view, and you need to create relationships to other tables in the data source view. The DimCustomer, DimGeography, and DimReseller tables have already been added to the SSAS2008SBS data source view. In the next steps, you will review these tables.

2. In Solution Explorer, expand the Data Source Views folder, right-click SSAS2008SBS.dsv, and select Open.

3. In the Diagram pane of the Data Source View Designer, select the Internet Sales diagram. The DimCustomer and DimGeography tables have been added to this diagram. The FactInternetSales table is directly related to the DimCustomers table and indirectly related to the DimGeography table.

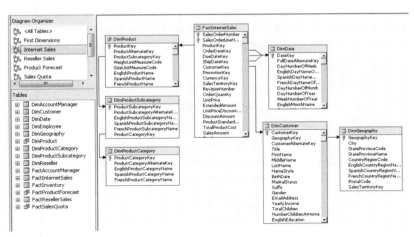

4. In the Diagram pane of the Data Source View Designer, select the Reseller Sales diagram. The DimReseller and DimGeography tables have been added to this diagram. The FactResellerSales table is directly related to the DimResellers table and indirectly related to the DimGeography table.

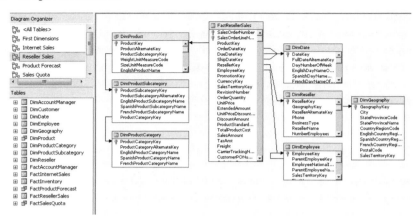

The properties of each object (data source, data source view, dimension, cube, and so on) in an Analysis Services project are stored in individual XML files. After you create an object in one project, you can copy the file and add it to a different project. The XML files for the Customer, Geography, and Reseller dimensions are ready for you to add to your project.

> **Important** Objects in an Analysis Services database can contain references to other objects. These references are made using object IDs. For example, a dimension contains a data source view ID, and a data source view contains one or many data source IDs. If you add an object's XML file to a project, the project must contain the other objects referenced by the added object. Alternatively, you can edit the object's XML file and update the IDs.

5. In Solution Explorer, right-click the AdventureWorks SSAS project, point to Add, and then select Existing Item.

6. In the Add Existing Item dialog box, browse to the C:\Microsoft Press\Analysis Services 2008 SBS\Chapter 07 folder. Select Customer.dim, Geography.dim, and Reseller.dim and then click Add.

   These three files will be copied to the C:\Microsoft Press\Analysis Services 2008 SBS \Chapter 07\AdventureWorks BI\AdventureWorks SSAS folder, the same folder that contains all of the other AdventureWorks SSAS project files. The added dimensions will now appear in the Dimensions folder. You should use the Dimension Designer to view the properties of these dimensions.

7. In Solution Explorer, right-click Geography.dim and select View Designer. The Geography dimension contains several attributes and the Geography user-defined hierarchy. It is important to notice that the key attribute is Geography Key. None of the fact tables contains a GeographyKey column, but the Customer and Reseller dimensions do contain a Geography Key attribute.

8. In Solution Explorer, right-click Reseller.dim and select View Designer. The Reseller dimension contains a few attributes and a couple of user-defined hierarchies. Reseller, which contains the name of businesses that sell Adventure Works products, is the key attribute and is used to relate the Reseller dimension to measure groups created using data from the FactResellers table. The Reseller dimension also contains the Geography Key attribute. This attribute will be used when Reseller is the intermediate dimension in the relationship between the Geography dimension and the Reseller Sales measure group. Because the Geography Key attribute will not be used for reporting, its *AttributeHierarchyVisible* property is set to *False*.

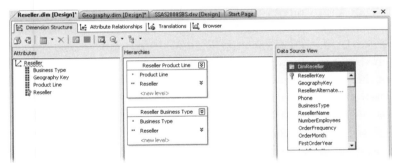

9. In Solution Explorer, right-click Customer.dim and select View Designer. Customer is the key attribute and is used to relate the Customer dimension to the Internet Sales measure group. The Customer dimension also contains a Geography Key attribute that will be used as the intermediate attribute in the relationship between the Geography dimension and the Internet Sales measure group. Again, its *AttributeHierarchyVisible* property is set to *False*.

Now that you have Customer, Geography, and Reseller database dimensions, you can add them as cube dimensions to the AdventureWorks cube. When the dimensions are added to the cube, you can configure the Geography dimension usage so that it has a *Referenced* relationship type with the Reseller Sales and Internet Sales measure groups.

Add a referenced dimension to a cube

1. In Solution Explorer, expand the Cubes folder, right-click AdventureWorks.cube, and select Open.

2. In the Cube Designer, on the Cube Structure tab, right-click in the Dimensions pane and select Add Cube Dimension.

3. In the Add Cube Dimension dialog box, select Customer, Geography, and Reseller.

4. Click OK. The new cube dimensions appear in the Dimensions pane.

5. In the Cube Designer, click the Dimension Usage tab.

The Reseller dimension has a *Regular* relationship with the Reseller Sales measure group. Because the SSAS2008SBS data source view contains a relationship between the DimReseller and FactResellerSales tables, a *Regular* relationship is created automatically when the dimension is added to the cube. The Dimension Usage grid shows this relationship by displaying the granularity attribute, Reseller, at the intersection of the Reseller dimension and the Reseller Sales measure group. In a similar fashion, the Dimension Usage grid shows that the Customer dimension has a *Regular* relationship with the Internet Sales measure group, with Customer serving as the granularity attribute. Because the DimGeography table is not directly related to any fact tables, the Geography dimension is not related to any measure groups.

You need to add relationships between the Geography dimension and the Reseller Sales and Internet Sales measure groups.

6. Select the cell at the intersection of the Geography dimension and the Reseller Sales measure group and click the ellipsis button (...) that appears.

7. In the Define Relationship dialog box, select *Referenced* from the Select Relationship Type list.

Note The term "referenced" doesn't clearly communicate to me how the dimension is related to the measure group. I like to remember that a *Referenced* relationship type means the dimension is *indirectly* related to the measure group. When you have a *Referenced* (think indirect) relationship type, you need to select which intermediate dimension will be used in the relationship. The intermediate dimension will be in the middle of the *Referenced* (indirect) relationship. The intermediate dimension has a direct relationship to both the measure group and the reference dimension.

The intermediate dimension must already be related to the measure group. These dimensions are displayed in the Intermediate Dimension list.

8. In the Intermediate Dimension list, select Reseller. After you select the intermediate dimension, you need to choose the attributes used to relate the intermediate and reference dimensions.

9. In the Reference Dimension Attribute list, select Geography Key. In the Intermediate Dimension Attribute list, select Geography Key.

   The Materialize option is selected by default. When a *Referenced* relationship is materialized, the relationship between the fact records and the members of the referenced dimension becomes part to the cube's physical storage structure. This improves query performance, but may cause the cube to take longer to process. If the option is not selected, only the relationship between the fact records and the intermediate dimension is stored in the cube. This means that Analysis Services has to derive the aggregated values for the members of the referenced dimension when a query is executed, resulting in slower query performance.

   The Define Relationship dialog box should look like this:

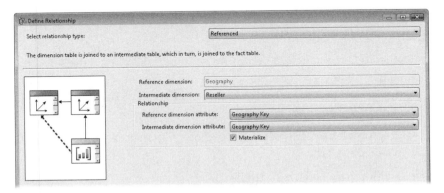

10. Click OK. Repeat steps 6 through 9 to create a relationship between the Geography dimension and the Internet Sales measure group. Use Customer as the intermediate dimension. The Define Relationship dialog box should look like the following image.

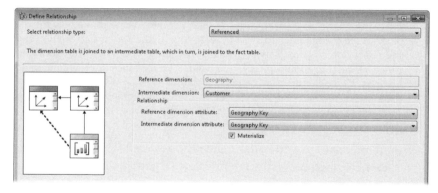

11. Click OK. You have created *Referenced* relationships between the Geography dimension and the Reseller Sales and Internet Sales measure groups. The *Referenced* relationship type icon appears at the intersection of the dimension and the two measure groups to help you more easily identify this special type of relationship.

You are now ready to deploy the AdventureWorks SSAS database and browse the cube using the Geography dimension.

Deploy and browse the cube

1. On the Build menu, select Deploy AdventureWorks SSAS. If the AdventureWorks SSAS database already exists on the server, a dialog box may appear warning that the database will be overwritten. If the warning appears, click Yes to delete the prior version of the database and continue with the current deployment.

2. After the cube has been deployed and processed successfully, click the Browser tab of the Cube Designer.

3. In the Metadata pane, expand the Measures folder, expand the Internet Sales and Reseller Sales measure groups, and then add the Internet Sales Amount and Reseller Sales Amount measures to the Report pane totals area.

    Even though the Geography dimension is indirectly related to the measure groups by means of the Customer and Reseller dimensions, in the cube browser it appears just like any of the other dimensions.

4. In the Metadata pane, drag the Geography dimension to the rows area of the Report pane. Each country in the Geography dimension has a different value for Internet Sales Amount. This shows that the Geography dimension is related to the Internet Sales measure group. The varying amounts for Reseller Sales show that the Geography dimension is also related to the Reseller Sales measure group.

Country Region ▼	Internet Sales Amount	Reseller Sales Amount
⊞ Australia	$9,051,766	$1,594,335
⊞ Canada	$1,966,991	$14,377,926
⊞ France	$2,640,526	$4,607,538
⊞ Germany	$2,890,708	$1,983,988
⊞ United Kingdom	$3,387,491	$4,279,009
⊞ United States	$9,370,355	$53,607,801
Grand Total	$29,307,837	$80,450,597

You should be aware that the Geography dimension does not have the same meaning for the two measure groups. Because the dimension is related to the Internet Sales measure group using the Customer intermediate dimension, in the context of the Internet Sales measure group it represents customer geography. For the Reseller Sales measure group, Reseller is the intermediate dimension, so in the context of this measure group it represents reseller geography. If you want to be clearer about what the Geography dimension represents or if you have a measure group that is related to both the Customer and Reseller dimensions, you could add the Geography dimension to the cube twice, once as a Customer Geography role-playing dimension and once as a Reseller role-playing dimension.

Creating a Fact Dimension

A fact table may have columns that contain descriptive attributes. If the attributes have *low cardinality*—meaning that the values in the column are repeated and the number of distinct values is low compared to the number of fact records—you should create a dimension table and replace the attribute columns in the fact table with a column containing a dimension key. If the attributes have a high or even one-to-one cardinality—meaning a unique value for each fact table record—it is best to not create a dimension table. In this case, the attributes as a group are referred to as a *degenerate dimension*. You can create an Analysis Services dimension from the degenerate dimension attribute columns in a fact table.

Analysis Services treats a degenerate dimension the same way it treats a dimension created using data from a dimension table. The degenerate dimension must be processed before any measure groups related to the dimension are processed. So when you have a degenerate dimension, Analysis Services processes all of the fact table records at least twice: once when the degenerate dimension is processed and once when the measure group is processed.

When you create a degenerate dimension, you need to take some precautions. You need to be careful because a degenerate dimension may contain a very large number of members. Very large dimensions use a lot of storage space and take a long time to process. Queries that request all of the dimension members use a lot of server resources and are slow to execute, and the volume of data returned by the query may be overwhelming. You should ensure that reports that request data from a degenerate dimension include a filter so that only a relatively few members are requested. It's common to filter a report containing a degenerate dimension by day or hour, by individual, or by transaction.

Degenerate dimension attributes are usually values that provide an alternative to the fact table primary key as a way to uniquely identify a fact record. Examples include a prescription number, a point-of-sale system transaction number, or an inventory control number. These attributes are rarely used for analysis, but may be useful for reporting or filtering. For example, you wouldn't want to group by transaction line-item numbers, but you might want a report that shows transaction line-item numbers, quantity, and amount for a customer.

You may want to create a degenerate dimension for two additional reasons. Analysis Services only allows you to drill through to data that is contained in a dimension or measure group. If you have textual attributes in a fact table that you want to be able to display via drillthrough, those attributes must be contained in a dimension. You will learn how to enable drillthrough in Chapter 10, "Interacting with a Cube." You may also need to use a degenerate dimension when you create a many-to-many dimension. You will learn more about many-to-many dimensions in the next section of this chapter.

Creating a degenerate dimension and creating a fact dimension are not the same thing. You create a fact dimension when you add a degenerate dimension to a cube and relate the degenerate dimension to a measure group using the *Fact* relationship type. The benefit of creating a fact dimension occurs when you are using ROLAP storage and perform a drillthrough operation. In this case, Analysis Services can retrieve the dimension and fact data from the fact table using a single query. Otherwise, there is no performance difference between using a *Fact* relationship type and using a *Regular* relationship type.

In the next three procedures, you will create a degenerate dimension using the Dimension Wizard, modify it using the Dimension Designer, and then create a fact dimension. You will create a degenerate dimension that contains the sales order number and sales order line number for all reseller sales, and then you will make the dimension a fact dimension related to the Reseller Sales measure group. This dimension will let you select a single order and then display the order's line items.

Create a degenerate dimension

1. In Solution Explorer, right-click the Dimensions folder and select New Dimension. On the Welcome To The Dimension Wizard page, click Next.

2. On the Select Creation Method page, verify that Use An Existing Table is selected and click Next.

3. On the Specify Source Information page, verify that in the Data Source View list, SSAS2008SBS is selected.

4. In the Main Table list, select FactResellerSales. Selecting a fact table as the data source for the dimension means that it will be a degenerate dimension. No dimension property identifies a degenerate dimension.

   The dimension key attribute needs to be created from a column or columns that uniquely identify each record in the data source table. The SalesOrderNumber and SalesOrderLineNumber columns form the FactResellerSales composite primary key and therefore uniquely identify each FactResellerSales record. The Cube Wizard automatically displays these primary key columns in the Key Columns list.

5. Verify that SalesOrderNumber and SalesOrderLineNumber are selected in the Key Columns list.

   At the bottom of the wizard page, you can see that the *Name Column* property is blank and there is a warning message about specifying a name column. By default, the names of attribute members come from the attribute's key column. If you don't want to use the key column, you can select an alternative name column. If you have multiple key columns, the Cube Wizard doesn't know which key column to use for the attribute member names and requires you to select a name column. The OrderLineDescription column is a named calculation that contains the SalesOrderNumber combined with SalesOrderLineNumber. This column can be used as the name for the key attribute.

6. In the Name Column list, select OrderLineDescription. The Specify Source Information page should look like this:

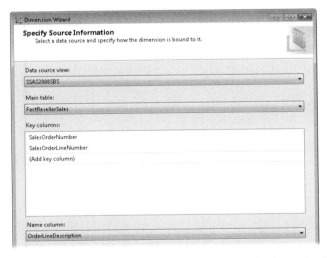

7. Click Next. The Select Related Tables page displays all of the tables that are related to the main table selected on the previous page. When the main table is a fact table, there may be many related dimension tables. In this exercise, you don't want to include any of the dimension table data in the degenerate dimension.

8. On the Select Related Tables page, clear all of the tables.

9. Click Next. The Specify Dimension Attributes page lists all of the columns in the data source table. The key attribute is already selected. By default, the Dimension Wizard names the key attribute using the name of the first key column—SalesOrderNumber. The granularity of the key attribute is actually the second key column—SalesOrderLineNumber—so you will rename the key attribute.

10. Click Sales Order Number and change the attribute name to **Order Line**.

    You also need an attribute that displays the order number, but because SalesOrderNumber is already being used as one of the key attribute key columns, the Specify Dimension Attributes page doesn't display the attribute. Instead of creating the attribute using the wizard, you have to use the Dimension Designer to create this attribute.

    You may want to display an order's Carrier Tracking Number and Customer PO Number, so add these attributes to the dimension. You only want these attributes for reporting purposes and not for analytical purposes, so you will disable browsing by these attributes.

11. On the Select Dimension Attributes page, select Carrier Tracking Number and Customer PO Number. For these two attributes, clear the Enable Browsing check box. The Dimension Wizard automatically selects any foreign keys contained in the data source table. These don't make useful attributes in a degenerate dimension.

12. Clear the following attributes: Due Date Key, Employee Key, Order Date Key, Ship Date Key, Reseller Key, Product Key. You will create a dimension containing three attributes, as shown in the following image.

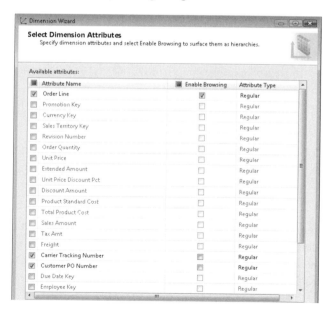

13. Click Next. On the Completing The Wizard page, change the name of the dimension to **Reseller Orders** and then click Finish.

In the Dimension Designer, you can see that the dimension contains an attribute containing the Order Line, but no attribute contains the Order Number. In the next procedure, you will create the Order Number attribute using the Dimension Designer.

Modify the degenerate dimension

1. In the Dimension Designer, drag SalesOrderNumber from the FactResellerSales table in the Data Source View pane to the Attributes pane. A new attribute will be created from the SalesOrderNumber column.

2. Right-click the Sales Order Number attribute and select Rename. Change the name of the attribute to **Order Number**.

You can now add the Reseller Orders degenerate database dimension to the AdventureWorks cube and you can create a *Fact* relationship between the Reseller Orders cube dimension and the Reseller Sales measure group.

Add a fact dimension to a cube

1. In Solution Explorer, expand the Cubes folder, right-click AdventureWorks.cube, and select View Designer.

2. In the Cube Designer, click the Dimension Usage tab.

3. Right-click the designer workspace and select Add Cube Dimension.

4. In the Add Cube Dimension dialog box, select Reseller Orders.

5. Click OK. When you add the Reseller Orders dimension to the cube, the Cube Designer detects that the dimension's key attribute is based on columns in the FactResellerSales table and creates a relationship between Reseller Orders and the Reseller Sales measure group. The cell at the intersection of the Reseller Orders dimension and the Reseller Sales measure group shows that Reseller is used as the granularity attribute in the relationship and displays the *Fact* relationship type icon.

Dimensions	Reseller Sales	Internet Sales	Product Forecast	Sales Quota	Reseller Orders
Date (Ship Date)	Date	Date			Date
Employee	Employee			Employee	Employee
Date (Due Date)	Date	Date			Date
Product	Product ID	Product ID	Subcategory		Product ID
Date	Date	Date	Month	Month	Date
Customer		Customer			
Geography		Customer			
Reseller	Reseller				Reseller
Reseller Orders	Order Line				Order Line

You can now deploy the cube and create a report that displays line item quantities for a reseller order.

6. On the Build menu, select Deploy AdventureWorks SSAS.

7. After the cube has been deployed and processed successfully, click the Browser tab of the Cube Designer. On the Browser tab toolbar, click the Reconnect button.

8. Click the Report pane and then click the Clear Results button.

9. Drag Reseller Order Quantity to the Report pane totals area.

10. Expand the Reseller Orders dimension and drag the Order Number hierarchy to the Report pane filter area.

11. Click the triangle next to Order Number, clear the (All) check box, select SO43659, and click OK.

12. Drag the Order Line hierarchy to the rows area of the Report pane. The report shows the quantity ordered for each line of order number SO43659.

> **Tip** Be very careful when browsing a cube using attributes that contain a very large number of members, like Order Line. You should first add an attribute or hierarchy that can be used as a filter to reduce the number of members of the very large attributes that appear on the report.

Creating a Many-to-Many Dimension

Typically, a record in a fact table is related to only one record in a dimension table, but a dimension record may be related to many fact table records. For example, each order line is for a single product, but that product may have many order lines. The product dimension and the sales measures have a *one-to-many relationship*. When a dimension and a measure a have one-to-many relationship, the total value of the measure is equal to the sum of the values of the measure of each of the individual dimension members.

In some situations, a single record in a fact table can be related to multiple records in a dimension table. For example, the Adventure Works sales department often has several account managers working with a single reseller. When the reseller places an order, all the account managers are credited with the order. In this case, there is a *many-to-many relationship* between account managers and orders.

> **Note** Many-to-many relationships are common. A medical patient may have many physicians and many diagnoses. Products may have multiple features, accessories, or option packages and may be designed or marketed by teams of employees. People work in teams, groups, or work shifts.

When there is a many-to-many relationship, you must be careful to make sure that values are not double-counted. Adventure Works can create a report that shows the sales amount for each account manager. On the report, the sales amount for each manager is correct, but because some orders are credited to multiple sales managers, the sum of sales amount for all account managers is greater than the total sales made by Adventure Works.

Analysis Services provides the capability of having a *Many-to-Many* relationship in a cube without double-counting any values. Creating the *Many-to-Many* relationship requires two dimensions and two measure groups. Obviously, you must have a dimension and a measure group for which you want to create a *Many-to-Many* relationship. You must also have an intermediate measure group that contains the *Many-to-Many* relationship and an intermediate dimension that has a *Regular* relationship to both the measure group and the intermediate measure group.

> **Tip** Analysis Services implements a *Many-to-Many* relationship in a manner similar to the way it implements a referenced dimension. Queries may execute more slowly because the values for attribute members in the many-to-many dimension are resolved when the query is executed.

You are now ready to create a *Many-to-Many* relationship between the Account Manger dimension and the Reseller Sales measure group. You will use the Account Manager measure group and the Reseller Orders dimension as the intermediate measure group and intermediate dimension. The Reseller Sales measure group and Reseller Orders dimension already exist, but you will have to add the Account Manager dimension and Account Manager measure group to your Analysis Services project. Then you will create the *Many-to-Many* relationship.

Add a database dimension

The data source tables for the Account Manager dimension and intermediate fact table have already been added to the SSAS2008SBS data source view. Before you add the Account Manager dimension to your project, you should review these tables.

1. In Solution Explorer, expand the Data Source Views folder, right-click SSAS2008SBS.dsv, and select Open.

2. In the Diagram pane of the Data Source View Designer, select the Account Manager diagram. The Account Manager diagram shows the FactAccountManager table that contains the *Many-to-Many* relationship between the DimAccountManager table and the FactResellerSales table. The relationship is based on the AccountManagerKey and SalesOrderNumber columns.

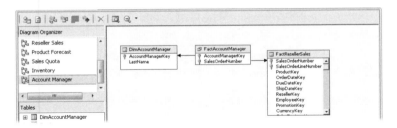

The Account Manager dimension has already been created and its properties are stored in an XML file. You need to add this file to your project.

3. In Solution Explorer, right-click the AdventureWorks SSAS project, point to Add, and select Existing Item.

4. In the Add Existing Item dialog box, browse to the C:\Microsoft Press\Analysis Services 2008 SBS\Chapter 07 folder, select Account Manager.dim, and click Add. The Account Manager dimension will now appear in the Dimensions folder. You should use the Dimension Designer to view the properties of this dimension.

5. In the Dimensions folder, right-click Account Manager.dim and select View Designer. The Account Manager dimension is very simple. It contains a single, key attribute that displays an account manager's last name. The Account Manager attribute key column is AccountManagerKey.

You have added the Account Manager dimension to the AdventureWorks SSAS database. You must now add the Account Manager measure group to your cube. The Account Manager measure group contains the *Many-to-Many* relationship between account managers and orders and will serve as the intermediate measure group between the Account Manager dimension and the Reseller Sales measure group.

Create an intermediate measure group

1. In Solution Explorer, right-click AdventureWorks.cube and select View Designer.

2. In the Cube Designer, click the Cube Structure tab.

3. Right-click in the Measures pane and select New Measure Group.

4. In the New Measure Group dialog box, select FactAccountManager and click OK.

5. Right-click the Fact Account Manager measure group, select Rename, and change the name of the measure group to **Account Manager**. The Account Manager measure group contains a single measure that displays the count of records in the FactAccountManager table. This measure isn't useful for analysis, so you will hide it.

6. Expand the Account Manager measure group, right-click the Fact Account Manager Count measure, and select Properties.

7. In the Properties window, change the value of the *Visible* property to *False*. You can change the order of the measure groups in a cube. It is easier to configure the many-to-many dimension if the Reseller Sales and Account Manager measure groups are next to each other.

8. Drag the Account Manager measure group up to below the Reseller Sales measure group. The Measures pane should now look like the following image.

Add a many-to-many dimension to a cube

1. In the Cube Designer, click the Dimension Usage tab. In the Dimension Usage grid, the cells in the Account Manager measure group column are all empty except for the cell in the Reseller Orders dimension row. This cell shows that the Reseller Orders dimension has a *Regular* relationship with the Account Manager measure group. The relationship is at the Order Number level of granularity.

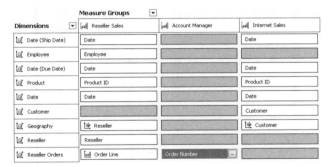

2. In the Dimension Usage tab workspace, right-click and select Add Cube Dimension.

3. In the Add Cube Dimension dialog box, select Account Manager and click OK. The Dimension Usage grid shows that the Account Manager dimension is not related to any measure group except Account Manager. It has a *Regular* relationship to the Account Manager measure group at the Account Manager level of granularity.

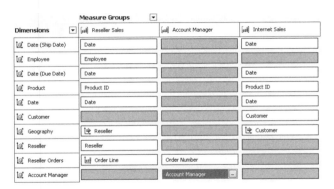

4. Select the cell in the grid at the intersection of the Account Manager dimension and the Reseller Sales measure group and click the ellipsis button that appears.

5. In the Select Relationship Type list, select Many-To-Many.

6. In the Intermediate Measure Group list, select Account Manager.

7. Click OK. In the Dimension Usage grid, the cell at the intersection of the Account Manager dimension and Account Manager measure group now displays the *Many-to-Many* relationship type icon and shows that the relationship between the dimension and measure group is at the Account Manager level of granularity.

Dimensions	Reseller Sales	Account Manager	Internet Sales
Date (Ship Date)	Date		Date
Employee	Employee		
Date (Due Date)	Date		Date
Product	Product ID		Product ID
Date	Date		Date
Customer			Customer
Geography	Reseller		Customer
Reseller	Reseller		
Reseller Orders	Order Line	Order Number	
Account Manager	Account Manager	Account Manager	

8. On the Build menu, select Deploy AdventureWorks SSAS.

9. After the cube has been deployed and processed successfully, click the Browser tab of the Cube Designer. On the Browser tab toolbar, click the Reconnect button. The report appears exactly the same as it appeared after step 12 of the procedure titled "Add a Fact Dimension to a Cube" earlier in the chapter.

10. Drag the Account Manager dimension to the rows area to the left of the Order Line column in the Report pane.

11. Click in a blank area of the Report pane, right-click the Account Manger column header, and select expand items. The report shows that the account managers Dobney and Ellerbrock both received credit for order number SO43659. But notice that the last row of the report shows that the total number of items ordered is 26. The items do not get counted more than once.

Order Number ▾		
SO43659		

		Drop Column Fields Here
Account Manager ▾	**Order Line** ▾	Reseller Order Quantity
⊟ Dobney	SO43659 Line 01	1
	SO43659 Line 02	3
	SO43659 Line 03	1
	SO43659 Line 04	1
	SO43659 Line 05	1
	SO43659 Line 06	2
	SO43659 Line 07	1
	SO43659 Line 08	3
	SO43659 Line 09	1
	SO43659 Line 10	6
	SO43659 Line 11	2
	SO43659 Line 12	4
	Total	26
⊟ Ellerbrock	SO43659 Line 01	1
	SO43659 Line 02	3
	SO43659 Line 03	1
	SO43659 Line 04	1
	SO43659 Line 05	1
	SO43659 Line 06	2
	SO43659 Line 07	1
	SO43659 Line 08	3
	SO43659 Line 09	1
	SO43659 Line 10	6
	SO43659 Line 11	2
	SO43659 Line 12	4
	Total	26
Grand Total		26
		26

12. Remove Order Line and then remove Order Number from the report. The report now shows the quantity of items for which each account manager has received credit. The sum of Reseller Order Quantity for all the managers is 319,858 items. This amount is greater than the total of items ordered, 214,378, because some orders are credited to more than one account manager.

Drop Filter Fields Here	
	Drop Column Fields Here
Account Manager ▾	Reseller Order Quantity
Bradley	19,706
Brown	43,831
D'Hers	42,396
Dobney	19,100
Ellerbrock	19,100
Erickson	21,324
Gilbert	45,545
Johnson	42,784
Tamburello	21,843
Walters	44,229
Grand Total	214,378

13. Click the Save All button and select Close Project from the File menu.

In this chapter, you learned how to relate a dimension to a measure group using a *Referenced* relationship type. The referenced dimension is related to the measure group by means of an intermediate dimension. The *Referenced* relationship type allows you to reuse a dimension that contains attributes that are shared by multiple dimensions and it allows you to create a relationship between a measure group and a dimension that are not stored in the same data source. You learned how to create a degenerate dimension from high cardinality attributes contained in a fact table and then how to join the dimension to a measure group using a *Fact* relationship type. Finally, you learned how to create a relationship between a dimension and a measure group using a *Many-to-Many* relationship type. The *Many-to-Many* relationship type uses both an intermediate measure group and an intermediate dimension. The

Many-to-Many relationship type enables Analysis Services to avoid counting values more than once.

In the next chapter you will learn how to use Account Intelligence to provide the functionality needed to perform financial analytics. You will create an Account type dimension to contain a chart of accounts and the information needed to designate how values should summarize along the account dimension. You will also configure a measure group to apply various aggregate functions based on the information contained in the account dimension.

Chapter 8
Working with Account Intelligence

In this chapter, you will learn how to:

- Build an Account dimension to support Financial Analysis.

- Define and manage custom rollup (unary) operators.

- Apply Financial Business Intelligence properties.

- Create non-additive measures.

- Create a custom member rollup formula.

- Work with a Scenario dimension.

In previous chapters, you learned how to build dimensions and measure groups from standard data warehouse tables. You can use the techniques you learned to meet most analytical requirements. When you need to perform financial analysis, there are several special requirements that need additional cube design and aggregation rules. In this chapter, you'll learn about the special tools that Analysis Services provides to handle these special requirements. You will learn how to create an Account dimension and a financial measure group. Additionally, you will expand your experience with calculations by building a financial ratio (a non-additive measure). When defining an Account dimension, you will learn how to use custom rollup operators to specify how aggregation needs to behave for Account dimension member rollup. When other special rollup rules are desired, you will learn how to create a custom rollup formula for defining the calculation rule for rollup for select account dimension members.

In the last section of this chapter, you'll learn how to create a Scenario dimension. The Scenario dimension is not unique to financial analysis, but it is very common in financial analysis to enable the display and comparison of multiple sets of measures for the Account dimension including actual, budget, and forecast values.

In this chapter, you will browse the data contained in the DimAccount table and then use the Dimension Wizard to create an Account dimension based on the DimAccount table. In addition, you will work with the Business Intelligence Wizard to extend the Account dimension's definition and to modify dimension properties specific to the needs of Account and Scenario dimensions. Additionally, you will extend the financial analysis cube measures by learning to create non-additive measures from calculations using Account dimension members as a custom formula.

Designing a Financial Analysis Cube

Before you begin to enable financial analysis within a cube, it is important to review the requirements of financial analysis. A finance or treasury department deals with many types of financial reporting, including, but not limited to:

- Profit and loss statements

- Balance sheets

- Cash flow statements

- Statutory quarter and annual reports

In Chapter 4, "Creating Dimensions," you created standard, time, and parent-child dimensions. In this chapter, when you create an Account dimension, you will have to perform some additional steps to configure the way Account dimension members aggregate. Sometimes the account values need to sum to a parent, sometimes the account values are subtracted, and sometimes account values should not aggregate into a parent value at all. Consider, for example, a typical profit and loss report:

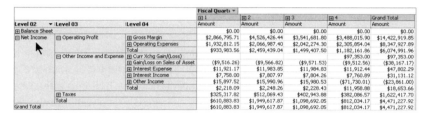

The component values of the Net Income report include Operating Profit, Other Income And Expense, and Taxes. Most values are managed and displayed as positive numbers unless values can be both positive and negative over time. To properly calculate the Net Income Total, the report needs to subtract Taxes from the sum of the Operating Profit Total and Other Income And Expense Total. Statistical accounts in financial reports often contain statistical account values, such as Headcount, or inventory amount values that may change in value over time. These statistical account types are common informational values that should not be added to the balance sheet total or net income total values. Nor should these values be summed across time (in other words, Headcount should not be summed across four quarters).

Working with Account Intelligence

In this section, you will learn how to use the Dimension Wizard and the Account Intelligence features of the Business Intelligence Wizard to add financial analysis to the AdventureWorks cube. The Account Intelligence features depend on the relational table used to create the Account dimension. This relational table must contain a record for each account and a parent-child relationship that defines the hierarchy of the chart of accounts. It must also contain a column with the unary operators that determine how an account aggregates into its parent account. Additionally, the table must contain a column specifying the member's account type. When adding Account Intelligence to your Account dimension, you will identify and map each account to specific account types. For example, you will identify Account dimension members as Assets, Expenses, or Income, just to name a few account types. Finally, the relational data source needs to include a fact table that contains the Account dimension keys and the numeric values for each account.

In the following procedure, you will explore the data in the DimAccount table to view the underlying columns and structure needed for the Account dimension. Later in this chapter, you will use this table to create a new Account dimension to add financial analysis capabilities to your cube.

Explore the DimAccount Table

1. Using Business Intelligence Development Studio (BIDS), open the AdventureWorks BI solution contained in the C:\Microsoft Press\Analysis Services 2008 SBS\Chapter 08 \AdventureWorks BI folder.

2. In Solution Explorer, expand the Data Source Views folder, right-click SSAS2008SBS.dsv, and select View Designer.

3. In the Diagram Organizer pane, select Finance. In the Diagram pane, right-click the header of the DimAccount table and select Explore Data. You can see the specific columns that will be used when designing the Account dimension: AccountDescription, AccountType, and Operator. The parent-child relationship structure of the table is contained in the AccountKey and ParentAccountKey columns. Additionally, note that the Operator column is composed of plus (+), minus (-), and tilde (~) characters to identify aggregation behavior for each account attribute member. The Operator column values represent the aggregation behavior for each account, where the plus sign means sum the account value, the minus sign means subtract the account value, and the tilde sign means that no aggregation is to be performed.

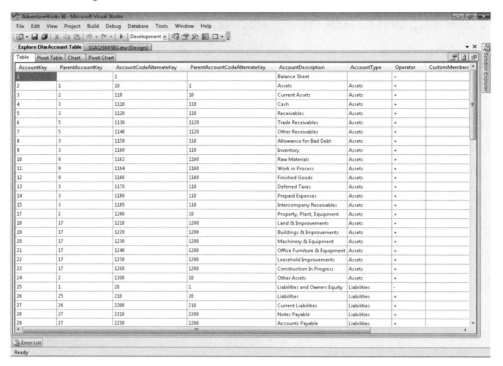

 Note The AccountType and Operator attributes will be assigned when you apply the Account Intelligence properties using the Business Intelligence Wizard.

4. Close the Explore Data window and the Data Source View designer.

Now that you have become familiar with the data that will be loaded into the Account dimension, you are ready to begin creating the Account dimension.

Creating an Account Dimension

You use the Dimension Wizard to create the initial structure of the Account dimension. As you work through the steps of the wizard, you will select the data source table, the key attribute, and other attributes that you want to include in the dimension. You'll also set some of the more important attribute properties. But for financial analysis, the dimension design for the Account dimension will not be complete. You will need to use the Business Intelligence Wizard to set additional properties to further enhance your Account dimension.

 Note Analysis Services uses account and time information to enable specialized dimension behavior. It is not enough to just define the dimension as an Account or Time dimension. Some attributes within the dimension have types that must also be set to be compatible with the dimension type. This is best completed when using the Business Intelligence Wizard.

Use the Dimension Wizard to create the Account dimension

1. In Solution Explorer, right-click the Dimensions folder and select New Dimension. On the Welcome To The Dimension Wizard page, click Next.

2. Verify that Use An Existing Table is selected and click Next.

3. Verify that SSAS2008SBS has been selected from the Data Source View list.

4. Select DimAccount from the Main Table list. The Dimension Wizard recognizes the primary key of the main table as the key attribute and selects this column in the Key Column and Name Column lists. The primary key of the DimAccount table is the AccountKey column.

5. Verify that AccountKey has been selected in the Key Columns list.

6. Select AccountDescription from the Name Column list and then click Next. The Dimension Wizard lists all the other table attributes for inclusion within the dimension.

7. Verify that Account Key and Parent Account Key have been selected. Select Account Type and Custom Members and then click Next.

8. Rename the dimension **Account** and click Finish. The wizard will open the Dimension Designer for the dimension.

In the next procedure, you will give the Account dimension attributes more user-friendly names and process the dimension for browsing using the BIDS Dimension Designer.

Use the Dimension Designer to edit the Account dimension

1. Right-click the Parent Account Key attribute and rename it **Accounts**. This attribute contains the hierarchical structure of the chart of accounts.

2. Right-click the Account Key attribute and rename it **Account**. This attribute contains each individual account. Your screen should look like this:

3. On the Build menu, select Deploy AdventureWorks SSAS. If the AdventureWorks SSAS database already exists on the server, a dialog box may appear warning that the database will be overwritten. If the warning appears, click Yes. The prior version of the database will be deleted and the current deployment will continue.

4. After the dimension processes, select the Browser tab on the Dimension Designer for the Account dimension. Expand a few members of the Accounts hierarchy to see the chart of accounts.

5. Close the Dimension Designer.

You will now add the new Account dimension and the Fact Finance measure group to the AdventureWorks cube. After you add these to the cube, you will observe how the Account dimension behaves before Account Intelligence is applied.

Create the Finance measure group and add the Account dimension to the cube

1. Expand the Cubes folder in Solution Explorer and double-click the AdventureWorks cube to open it in the Cube Designer.

2. In the Measures pane of the Cube Structure tab, right-click the AdventureWorks folder and select New Measure.

3. From the Source Table list, select FactFinance. In the Source Column list, select Amount and click OK. A new measure group is added to the cube. The measure group name defaults to the source table name. In the next step, you will give the measure group a more user-friendly name.

4. Right-click the Fact Finance measure group, select Rename, and change the name of the measure group to **Finance**.

5. Right-click the Amount measure and select Properties.

6. In the Measure Properties window, select $#,##0.00;($#,##0.00) from the *FormatString* property list.

7. Right-click in the Dimensions pane and select Add Cube Dimension.

8. Select Account from the Select Dimension list and click OK.

9. Select the Dimension Usage tab and you will be able to see that the Account dimension is related to the Finance measure group at the Account Key granularity level.

In the next procedure, you will browse the cube to observe the aggregation behavior. Note that at this point Account Intelligence has not yet been applied to the Account dimension or to the Finance measure group.

View the Account dimension aggregation behavior

1. On the Build menu, select Deploy AdventureWorks SSAS. When the project has been deployed, select the cube Browser tab to observe the Account dimension behavior.

2. In the Metadata pane, expand the Measures folder and expand the Finance measure group. Drag the Amount measure to the Drop Totals Or Details Here area of the Report pane.

3. In the Metadata pane, expand the Account dimension and drag the Accounts hierarchy from the Account dimension to the Drop Row Fields Here area of the Report pane.

4. In the Report pane, expand the Balance Sheet and Net Income members. Expand Operating Profit and Other Income And Expense under Net Income. Your cube should look like this:

Level 02	Level 03	Level 04	Amount
⊟ Balance Sheet	⊞ Assets		$553,505,459.26
	⊞ Liabilities and Owners Equity		$553,505,459.26
	Total		$1,107,010,918.52
⊟ Net Income	⊟ Operating Profit	⊞ Gross Margin	$181,455,968.33
		⊞ Operating Expenses	$50,055,025.20
		Total	$231,510,993.53
	⊟ Other Income and Expense	⊞ Curr Xchg Gain/(Loss)	$86,484.00
		⊞ Gain/Loss on Sales of Asset	($180,008.68)
		⊞ Interest Expense	$225,723.59
		⊞ Interest Income	$147,002.28
		⊞ Other Income	$223,183.45
		Total	$502,384.64
	⊞ Taxes		$7,243,791.01
	Total		$239,257,169.18
⊞ Statistical Accounts			$12,372,325.00
Grand Total			$1,358,640,412.70

You can see that the value of every parent member in the Accounts hierarchy is the sum of its children. This aggregation behavior will not satisfy the requirements of financial analysis. For example, the report shows that Assets and Liabilities sum to give a Balance Sheet Total of more than $1 billion. Instead, Liabilities should be subtracted from Assets to give a Balance Sheet Total of $0. You can also see that Net Income is not calculated correctly. Fortunately, Analysis Services allows you to configure how each child account will aggregate into its parent account so that it will perform financial calculations correctly.

In the next procedure, you will use the Business Intelligence Wizard to specify the aggregation mode for each account by using the Unary Operator. When you explored the DimAccount table in the SSAS2008SBS.DSV earlier in this chapter, you noted the Operator column, which contains values that represent how each account will aggregate into its parent account. The Business Intelligence Wizard will set the value of the *UnaryOperatorColumn* property to the Operator column.

Define the Unary Operator for aggregation behavior

1. In Solution Explorer, right-click the Account dimension and select Add Business Intelligence. On the Welcome To The Business Intelligence page, click Next.

2. On the Choose Enhancement page, select Specify A Unary Operator and click Next.

3. On the Specify A Unary Operator page, select Operator from the Source Column list and click Next. On the Completing The Wizard page, click Finish.

4. On the Build menu, select Deploy AdventureWorks SSAS.

5. When deployment is complete, on the Browser tab of the Cube Designer, click the Reconnect button on the browser toolbar. Your chart of accounts report will now look like this:

Level 02 ▾	Level 03	Level 04	Amount
⊟ Balance Sheet	⊞ Assets		$553,505,459.26
	⊞ Liabilities and Owners Equity		$553,505,459.26
	Total		$0.00
⊟ Net Income	⊟ Operating Profit	⊞ Gross Margin	$86,226,249.61
		⊞ Operating Expenses	$50,055,025.20
		Total	$36,171,224.41
	⊟ Other Income and Expense	⊞ Curr Xchg Gain/(Loss)	$86,484.00
		⊞ Gain/Loss on Sales of Asset	($180,008.68)
		⊞ Interest Expense	$225,723.59
		⊞ Interest Income	$147,002.28
		⊞ Other Income	$223,183.45
		Total	$50,937.46
	⊞ Taxes		$7,243,791.01
	Total		$28,978,370.86
Grand Total			$28,978,370.86

Net Income is adding and subtracting accounts as desired and the Balance Sheet is aggregating Assets and Liabilities correctly so that the total is $0.

The Unary Operator controls the aggregation of accounts for rolling up within the Account dimension hierarchy. But you need to determine how the aggregation is behaving over time. In the next step, you will add the Date dimension to the browser and observe how values aggregate over time.

6. On the Metadata pane of the Browser tab, expand the Date dimension and drag the Fiscal Date hierarchy to the Drop Column Fields Here section of the report pane. Expand the FY 2009 member. Your chart of accounts report should now look like this:

			Fiscal Year ▾ Fiscal Quarter					
			⊟ FY 2009					⊞ FY 2010
			⊞ FY 2009 Qtr 1	⊞ FY 2009 Qtr 2	⊞ FY 2009 Qtr 3	⊞ FY 2009 Qtr 4	Total	
Level 02 ▾	Level 03	Level 04	Amount	Amount	Amount	Amount	Amount	Amount
⊟ Balance Sheet	⊞ Assets		$20,497,941.83	$32,283,937.98	$29,523,486.72	$30,480,648.48	$112,786,015.01	$193,130,
	⊞ Liabilities and Owners Equity		$20,497,941.83	$32,283,937.98	$29,523,486.72	$30,480,648.48	$112,786,015.01	$193,130,
	Total		$0.00	$0.00	$0.00	$0.00	$0.00	$0.00
⊟ Net Income	⊟ Operating Profit	⊞ Gross Margin	$6,011,745.71	$9,585,526.44	$7,430,681.80	$7,199,915.90	$30,227,869.85	$24,727,4
		⊞ Operating Expenses	$3,654,632.15	$3,919,127.40	$3,900,624.30	$4,380,744.04	$15,855,127.89	$14,414,9
		Total	$2,357,113.56	$5,666,399.04	$3,530,057.50	$2,819,171.86	$14,372,741.96	$10,312,5
	⊟ Other Income and Expense	⊞ Curr Xchg Gain/(Loss)					$97,353.00	$4,643.00
		⊞ Gain/Loss on Sales of Asset	($9,516.26)	($9,566.82)	($9,571.53)	($9,512.56)	($38,167.17)	($56,280.2
		⊞ Interest Expense	$11,921.17	$11,983.85	$11,984.83	$11,912.44	$47,802.29	$70,618.2
		⊞ Interest Income	$7,758.00	$7,807.97	$7,804.26	$7,760.89	$31,131.12	$45,999.8
		⊞ Other Income	$15,897.52	$15,990.96	$15,980.53	($71,730.01)	($23,861.00)	$89,997.7
		Total	$2,218.09	$2,248.26	$2,228.43	$11,958.88	$18,653.66	$13,742.0
	⊞ Taxes		$325,317.82	$512,069.43	$402,943.88	$382,086.57	$1,622,417.70	$2,938,54
	Total		$2,034,013.83	$5,156,577.87	$3,129,342.05	$2,449,044.17	$12,768,977.92	$7,387,75
Grand Total			$2,034,013.83	$5,156,577.87	$3,129,342.05	$2,449,044.17	$12,768,977.92	$7,387,75

Notice that for all accounts, the FY 2009 value is equal to the sum of the four FY 2009 quarters. This is appropriate for the Net Income accounts, but it is not the desired behavior for the Balance Sheet accounts. For the Balance Sheet accounts, the value for FY 2009 should equal the value of FY 2009 Qtr 4.

Financial analysis accounts that represent flows, such as income and expense accounts, need to sum when they are aggregated over time. Accounts that represent balances, such as inventory and assets, need to use the last value when they are aggregated over time. For example, the inventory level for a month needs to equal the inventory level of the last day of the month, and the inventory level of a quarter needs to equal the inventory level of the last quarter of the month.

This means that one measure in your cube, Amount, must apply a different aggregation function depending on the account type of the member in the Account dimension. To enable this behavior in Analysis Services, you must perform three procedures: in the Analysis Services database, you will need to configure the aggregation function for each account type, you will need to map the dimension table account types to the Analysis Services database account types, and you will need to apply the *ByAccount* aggregation function to the Amount measure.

Configure account type mappings

In this procedure, you will assign the aggregation function for each account type.

1. In Solution Explorer, right-click AdventureWorks SSAS and select Edit Database.

2. In the Database Designer, on the General tab in the Account Type Mapping section, select Income from the Name list at the bottom of the screen, and in the same row, select Sum from the Aggregation Function list.

3. Repeat step 2 to add additional account type mappings to the AdventureWorks SSAS database as shown in the following table.

Name	Aggregation Function
Expense	Sum
Flow	Sum
Balance	LastNonEmpty
Asset	LastNonEmpty
Liability	LastNonEmpty
Statistical	LastNonEmpty

When you complete this step, the Account Type Mapping section should look like this:

 Tip You can add additional account types in the Account Type Mapping section. You can also add alternative spellings in the Alias column. The Business Intelligence Wizard can use the values in the Alias column to map dimension account types to database account types.

4. On the BIDS toolbar, click the Save All button. Close the Database Designer.

Add Account Intelligence to the Cube

In this procedure, you will map dimension account types to the database account types you configured in the prior procedure.

1. In Solution Explorer, expand the Dimensions folder, right-click the Account dimension, and select Add Business Intelligence to start the Business Intelligence Wizard.

2. On the Welcome page, click Next. On the Choose Enhancement page, select Define Account Intelligence and click Next.

    One of the steps for defining Account Intelligence for the Account dimension is to iden-tify which dimension attributes define the accounts, the chart of accounts, and the type of account for each dimension member.

3. On the Configure Dimension Attributes page, select Include for the Chart Of Accounts row, and in the Dimension Attribute column, select Accounts. Be careful here, because the Dimension Attribute column will default to Account.

4. Select Include for the Account Name row. Verify that the wizard selects Account in the Dimension Attribute column.

5. Select Include for the Account Type row. Verify that the wizard selects Account Type in the Dimension Attribute column.

    The Configure Dimension Attributes page should look like this:

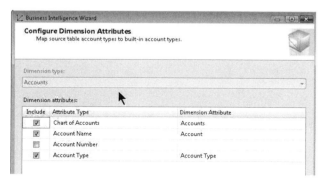

6. Click Next. The next page of the Business Intelligence Wizard asks you to map the ac-count types present in the Account dimension with the database account types you configured in the prior procedure. The Source Table Account Types column lists all of the account types in the Account dimension. In the Built-In Account Types column, the wizard has attempted to provide a match from the database account types. You need to review the matches to make sure that they are correct.

7. On the Define Account Intelligence page, verify that the value in the Built-In Account Types column correctly corresponds to the value in the Source Table Account Types col-umn as shown in the following table.

Source Table Account Types	Built-In Account Types
Assets	Asset
Balances	Balance
Expenditures	Expense
Flow	Flow
Liabilities	Liability
Revenue	Income
Statistical	Statistical

Your screen should now look like the following image.

8. Click Next. On the Completing The Wizard page, click Finish.

Each dimension account type is now mapped to a database account type. Each database account type has been assigned an aggregation function. You can tell Analysis Services to apply these aggregation functions by setting a measure's *AggregateFunction* property to *ByAccount*.

Apply the *ByAccount* aggregation function

1. Select the Cube Structure tab in the Cube Designer. In the Measures pane, expand the Finance measure group.

2. Right-click the Amount measure and select Properties. In the Properties window, set the value of the *AggregateFunction* property to *ByAccount*.

3. On the Build menu, select Deploy AdventureWorks SSAS.

4. Select the Browser tab and click the Reconnect button. You will now see that the Balance Sheet accounts are aggregated using the *LastNonEmpty* aggregation function. The FY 2009 Total value for each of these accounts is equal to the FY 2009 Qtr 4 value. The Net Income accounts are aggregated using the *Sum* aggregate function. The FY 2009 Total value for each of these accounts is equal to the sum of the four FY 2009 quarters. Analysis Services is satisfying the requirements of financial analysis by having a single measure that applies a different aggregation based on account type.

Working with Non-Additive Financial Measures

Quantitative analysis isn't always limited to the additive or semi-additive measures that you have created in the previous procedures. Averages, ratios, and percentages can often reveal important trends and are consequently relevant to many types of analysis. These types of calculations must be added to a cube as calculated measures, because they won't aggregate correctly across *any* dimension. The components of these calculations have distinct aggregation rules that must be performed separately for each component, after which the necessary multiplication or division can be performed. These types of calculations are known as *non-additive measures*.

In this section, you will create a non-additive measure, commonly used in financial analysis, that divides the value of a measure value for one financial account by the value of the same measure for a different financial account. Each account has different aggregation properties.

Creating a Non-Additive Calculated Member

Financial analysis often includes ratios that are derived from monetary and statistical values. One such ratio is Operating Profit per Employee, calculated by dividing Operating Profit by Headcount, which are two members of the Account dimension. More accurately, the numerator in this operation is the Amount measure for Operating Profit, which is the aggregation of its children accounts. Likewise, the denominator for this ratio is the Amount measure for Headcount, which is a statistical account often available in financial systems to track the number of employees at distinct points over time.

Create a non-additive calculated member for displaying the Operating Profit by Employee

1. Click the Calculations tab of the AdventureWorks cube designer. Scroll to the bottom of the list of calculations in the Script Organizer pane, select the last calculation, and then click the New Calculated Member button in the Calculations toolbar.

> **Important** If the New Calculated Member button is disabled, you may be viewing the Calculations tab in Script View mode. Select the Form View button on the Calculations toolbar to put the Calculations tab in Form View mode and the New Calculated Member button will be enabled.

2. Enter **[Operating Profit by Employee]** as the name of the calculation.

3. In the Expression text box, enter the following MDX expression:

```
([Account].[Accounts].&[48],[Measures].[Amount])/
```

```
([Account].[Accounts].&[96],[Measures].[Amount])
```

This MDX expression uses the keys for the Operating Profit and Headcount members of the Account dimension. As an alternative, you could use the member names and enter the following MDX expression:

```
([Account].[Accounts].[Operating Profit],[Measures].[Amount])/
```

```
([Account].[Accounts].[Headcount],[Measures].[Amount])
```

The choice of whether to use keys or member names in an MDX expression is not easy. Using member names makes the formula easier to read; however, member names or keys may change. You should chose to use member names or member keys based on which one is least likely to change. In financial applications, keys tend to be more stable than member names.

4. From the Format String list select Currency, from the Non-Empty Behavior list select Amount, and from the Associated Measure Group list select Finance.

5. On the Build menu, select Deploy AdventureWorks SSAS to activate the calculation.

6. Select the Browser tab on the Cube Designer, click the Reconnect button on the browser toolbar, click the Report pane, and then click the Clear Results button on the browser tool bar to reset the Report pane.

7. In the Metadata pane, expand the Finance measure group and then drag the Operating Profit By Employee calculated member to the Drop Totals Or Detail Fields Here area of the Report pane.

8. In the Metadata pane, expand the Date dimension and drag the Fiscal Date hierarchy to the rows area.

9. Expand the FY2009 year so that your report looks like this:

Fiscal Year ▾	Fiscal Quarter	Operating Profit by Employee
⊟ FY 2009	⊞ FY 2009 Qtr 1	$19,163.52
	⊞ FY 2009 Qtr 2	$44,617.32
	⊞ FY 2009 Qtr 3	$27,795.73
	⊞ FY 2009 Qtr 4	$21,854.05
	Total	$111,416.60
⊞ FY 2010		$56,662.40
⊞ FY 2011		$41,919.43
Grand Total		$132,011.77

In the last procedure, you created a calculated member to display operating profit by employee. Analysis Services also enables you to use MDX formulas to calculate a measure for select accounts in the Account dimension.

In the next procedure, you will define a custom formula for a rollup value for the statistical account, Average Unit Price. The formula resides within the DimAccount table used to build the Account dimension. You will first review the formula within the table.

Add a custom rollup formula to the Account dimension

1. In Solution Explorer, expand the Data Source Views folder and double-click AdventureWorks.dsv to open the Data Source View Designer.

2. In the Tables pane, right-click the DimAccount table and select Explore Data.

3. In the Explore Data window, scroll to the bottom and find the row with Account Key equal to 98. For this row, the value in the AccountDescription column is Average Unit Price, and the CustomMembers column contains the following MDX expression:

```
[Account].[Accounts].&[50]/
```

```
[Account].[Accounts].&[97]
```

If you find the rows with AccountKey equal to 50 and 97 and look at the values in the AccountDescription column, you can determine that the MDX expression for Average Unit Price is equivalent to the following MDX expression:

```
[Account].[Accounts].[Net Sales]/
```

```
[Account].[Accounts].[Units]
```

You can use the Dimension Designer to configure the Account dimension so that if there is an MDX expression in the CustomMembers column, that expression will be used to calculate the value for the dimension member. Storing the MDX expression in the source dimension table is an alternative to using calculated members.

4. Close the Explore DimAccount Table window and close the Data Source View Designer.

5. In Solution Explorer, expand the Dimensions folder, right-click the Account dimension, and select View Designer. Right-click the Accounts parent-child attribute and select Properties.

6. Select the *CustomRollupColumn* property and then click the ellipsis button that appears on the right.

7. In the Custom Rollup Column dialog box Source Column list, select CustomMembers and click OK.

8. On the Build menu, select Deploy AdventureWorks SSAS. When processing is complete, close the Dimension Designer.

9. Switch to the Cube Designer and select the Browser tab. Click the Reconnect button and click the Clear Results button.

10. From the Metadata pane, drag the Amount measure to the Drop Totals Or Detail Fields Here area of the Report pane. Drag the Accounts hierarchy to the Drop Row Fields Here area of the Report pane.

11. Right-click in the Report pane and select Show Empty Cells. The Statistical Accounts and Unknown members of the Accounts hierarchy appear. Expand the Statistical Accounts member to display the Average Unit Price and Units members.

12. Expand the Net Income, Operating Profit, and Gross Margin members to display the Net Sales member. You can see that Average Unit Price is equal to Net Sales divided by Units.

Level 02 ▾	Level 03	Level 04	Level 05	Amount
⊞ Balance Sheet				$21,366,847.84
⊟ Net Income	⊞ Net Income			
	⊟ Operating Profit	⊟ Gross Margin	⊞ Gross Margin	
			⊞ Net Sales	$127,234,148.59
			⊞ Total Cost of Sales	$41,007,898.98
			Total	$86,226,249.61
		⊞ Operating Expenses		$50,055,025.20
		⊞ Operating Profit		
		Total		$36,171,224.41
	⊞ Other Income and Expense			$50,937.46
	⊞ Taxes			$7,243,791.01
	Total			$28,978,370.86
⊟ Statistical Accounts	⊞ Average Unit Price			$631.99
	⊞ Headcount			$274.00
	⊞ Square Footage			$390,000.00
	⊞ Statistical Accounts			
	⊞ Units			$201,323.00
	Total			
⊞ Unknown				
Grand Total				$28,978,370.86

Working with a Scenario Dimension

It is common for many sets of financial analysis measures to include charts of account values for budget, forecast, and actual measure values. Adding a Scenario dimension is an easy way to accomplish this requirement within your financial analysis cube. You learned that dimensions by default include an All member that is the sum of all members of the dimension. Having an All member in the Scenario dimension is not desirable because it does not make sense to sum budget, forecast, and actual values into a single All value.

In the next procedure, you will create a Scenario dimension to enable budget and actual account measure analysis. You will also use the Dimension Designer to modify the property to remove the All aggregation behavior for the Scenario dimension. You will review the data in the FactFinance and DimScenario tables and then use the Dimension Wizard to create the Scenario dimension.

Create a Scenario dimension

1. In Solution Explorer, right-click SSAS2008SBS.dsv and select View Designer. In the Tables pane of the Data Source View Designer, right-click the DimScenario table and select Explore Data. You can see that the DimScenario table contains rows for Actual, Budget, and Forecast scenarios.

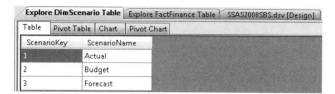

2. Close the Explore Data window. In the Tables pane, right-click the FactFinance table and select Explore Data. You can see that the FactFinance table contains a ScenarioKey column containing keys that map to the Actual, Budget, and Forecast rows in the DimScenario table.

3. Close the Explore Data window and the Data Source View designer. Right-click the Dimensions Folder in Solution Explorer and select New Dimension. On the Welcome To The Dimension Wizard page, click Next.

4. On the Select Creation Method page, verify that Use An Existing Table is selected and click Next.

5. On the Specify Source Information page, verify that SSAS2008SBS has been selected from the Data Source View list. Select DimScenario from the Main table list.

6. Verify that ScenarioKey has been selected from the Key Columns list and then select ScenarioName from the Name Column list. Click Next.

7. On the Select Dimension Attributes page, click Scenario Key to put the text box into edit mode and change the name of the attribute to **Scenario**. Click Next.

8. On the Completing The Wizard page, change the name of the dimension to **Scenario** and click Finish.

You will now add the Scenario dimension to the cube.

Add the Scenario dimension to the cube

1. In Solution Explorer, right-click AdventureWorks.cube and select View Designer. On the Cube Structure tab, right-click in the Dimensions pane and select Add Cube Dimension.

2. In the Add Cube Dimension dialog box, select Scenario from the Select Dimension list. Click OK.

3. Select the Dimensional Usage tab. You will see that the Scenario dimension is related to the Finance measure group at the Scenario Key granularity level.

4. On the Build menu, select Deploy AdventureWorks SSAS.

5. Select the Browser tab, and then on the Browser tab toolbar, click the Reconnect button. Click in the Report pane and then click the Clear Results button on the Browser tab toolbar. Right-click in the Report pane and select Show Empty Cells so that empty cells will not be visible.

6. From the Metadata pane, drag the Accounts hierarchy to the rows area of the Report pane. In the Level 02 column header, click the drop-down arrow, clear the (All) check box, and select Net Income. Click OK.

7. Drag the Scenario dimension to the columns area of the Report pane and drag the Amount measure to the totals area of the Report pane. Your report should look like this:

Drop Filter Fields Here			
	Scenario ▾		
	Actual	Budget	Grand Total
Level 02 ▾ Level 03	Amount	Amount	Amount
⊞ Net Income	$20,680,620.86	$8,297,750.00	$28,978,370.86
Grand Total	$20,680,620.86	$8,297,750.00	$28,978,370.86

The cube is displaying Actual values and Budget values for the Accounts. But the cube is also summing these values to generate a total, which doesn't provide meaningful information. To remove the total summing for the Scenario members, set the *IsAggregatable* property for the Scenario attribute in the dimension to *False*. This step removes the All member from the attribute hierarchy so that a total value is not calculated.

Remove the All member from the Scenario dimension

1. In the Scenario Dimension Designer, select the Dimension Structure tab for the Scenario dimension.

2. Right-click the Scenario attribute and select Properties. In the Properties window, set the value of the *IsAggregatable* property to *False*.

3. On the Build menu, select Deploy AdventureWorks SSAS.

4. In the Cube Designer, select the Browser tab, and then on the Browser tab toolbar, click the Reconnect button. A Total value no longer appears in the Scenario dimension and only the values for the leaf level members Actual and Budget are shown.

Level 02 ▾	Level 03	Scenario ▾	
		Actual	Budget
		Amount	Amount
⊞ Net Income		$20,680,620.86	$8,297,750.00
Grand Total		$20,680,620.86	$8,297,750.00

Now your Scenario dimension can be used to compare scenarios with the appropriate aggregation behavior.

In this chapter, you learned to enable financial analysis in an Analysis Services database. You created an Account dimension, and in the Account dimension, you implemented unary operators that control how a child account aggregates into a parent account. You also configured database account types, dimension account types, and the *ByAccount* aggregation function so that a single measure could implement different aggregations based on account type. You created financial calculations using calculated members and custom rollup formulas. Finally, you created a Scenario dimension, and using the *IsAggregatable* property, you disabled the All member so that Actual, Budget, and Forecast scenarios would not be summed. In the next chapter, you will learn how to implement foreign currency conversions and how to enable multiple languages in your Analysis Services database.

Chapter 9
Currency Conversion and Multiple Languages

In this chapter, you will learn how to:

- Enable multiple currency conversion for analysis and reporting.

- Add multiple language translation to existing dimensions, measure groups, measures, and calculated members.

In Chapter 8, "Working with Account Intelligence," you learned how to use the Business Intelligence Wizard to create a financial accounting dimension and how to manage aggregation for rolling up and summing financial accounting measures over time to support the special requirements for financial analysis. All of the financial measure values for all of the measure groups that you have created so far have been displaying the values in U.S. dollars and only English language terminology has been displayed for dimension attribute members and measure captions. But many companies are international and have operating entities in multiple countries, each with its own foreign language and currency. Such international companies therefore have additional requirements for their analysis cubes, including the support for currency conversion and supporting end user localization for viewing cube data in their native language.

In this chapter, you will learn how to enable your cube to support a variety of currency conversion schemes and how to add language translations to existing dimensions and measure groups, measures, and calculations.

Supporting Foreign Currency Conversion

Companies doing business in multiple countries often need to convert financial data from and to multiple currencies. Currency conversion may need to be applied to any measure that represents a monetary value and is commonly applied to financial measures such as sales amount, expenses, assets, and salaries. To perform currency conversions for your financial measures, you first need to determine and understand several key business operational requirements for the conversion. Understanding the financial data collection and conversion requirements and the corresponding dimensions and measure groups needed for the conversion calculations, as well as how to capture and define this information within the cube, is the topic of this section.

Before implementing foreign currency conversion, you need to know your company's foreign financial business data collection and reporting requirements. International companies can apply several data collection and reporting approaches, depending on the characteristics and requirements of their financial measures (for example, foreign country sales amounts, foreign expenses, foreign asset values, and other financial currency measures).

One approach is to load all financial facts into the cube with values in their original currency. The cube then converts the values into a single target (or pivot) currency for corporate consolidation, rollup, and reporting. The single target currency is usually the currency of the country where the corporate headquarters are located. For example, sales transactions in euros, British pounds, and U.S. dollars are loaded into the cube in their original currency values. The cube converts all of the values into euros for corporate rollup and reporting. This is referred to as a *many-to-one* type of currency conversion.

Another approach handles the scenario in which all financial values have been converted into the single target (or pivot) currency before they are loaded into the cube. After the values are loaded into the cube, they are ready for corporate consolidation, rollup, and reporting. The cube can then convert the values into multiple currencies so that any corporate entity can create reports in its local currency. For example, sales transactions are all converted into euros and then loaded into the cube. The values are ready for corporate rollup and reporting. The cube then converts the values into British pounds when someone from Wales executes a report and converts the values into U.S. dollars when someone from New York executes a report. This approach is referred to as a *one-to-many* type of currency conversion.

Another approach is a combination of the previous two approaches. All financial facts are loaded into the cube with values in their original currency. The cube can then convert the values into multiple currencies. For example, sales transactions in euros, British pounds, and U.S. dollars are loaded into the cube in their original currency values. The cube converts all of the values into euros when someone at headquarters executes a corporate report. The cube also converts the values into British pounds when someone from Wales executes a report and converts the values into U.S. dollars when someone from New York executes a report. This approach is referred to as a *many-to-many* type of currency conversion.

Whichever business requirement and approach your company uses needs to be identified so that you can set the appropriate rules in the cube to support your company's currency conversion requirements.

After you have determined the required conversion approach for your sales transaction and financial fact data, you need to determine how to identify the currency for each financial fact record so that the cube will know what conversion rate is required to perform the conversion calculation. You identify the currency by defining a fact table column that contains a currency identifier code. Many companies use the currency codes provided by the International Organization for Standardization (ISO 4217), which defines a set of three-character codes for each currency used in the world today.

When you know which transactions and financial fact records will require foreign currency conversion and the currency used to record each value, you need to determine what exchange rate to use for the currency conversion calculations. International exchange rates fluctuate several times a day. Some companies use a daily exchange rate that is available from many external services. Other companies may only need to perform conversion weekly or monthly and therefore use an average of the exchange rates across the period representing the weekly or monthly time period for their transactions. Thus, another key informational component you need to know to enable currency conversion is what exchange rate value you need to use based on the granularity of the time dimensions of the transactions (daily, weekly, monthly, or annually).

To support currency conversion, your data warehouse needs to include some additional tables to supply the informational components reviewed so far. First, you need a currency dimension that lists all of the currencies your company will be converting. The currency dimension is used to determine the currency for the sales transaction and financial fact values. Second, you need a fact table that contains and tracks the exchange rates for each currency over time.

After you have added the currency dimension and exchange rate measure group to your cube, you can use the Business Intelligence Wizard to define your currency conversion approach and requirements. The wizard creates the set of calculations (MDX scripts) within the cube to perform the calculations that convert the currencies on demand. You can define one or more currency conversion approaches using the Business Intelligence Wizard so that you are not limited to only one approach. If you have some measures that are converted monthly and some that are converted quarterly, you can define multiple conversion approaches to meet these requirements.

Now that you are familiar with the financial business operational approaches and the dimension and fact table data required for currency conversion, you will learn how foreign currency conversion support has been set up within the DimCurrency and FactCurrencyRate tables of the SSAS2008SBS database. You will then use the Business Intelligence Wizard to enable multiple currency support. You will browse the cube and observe how the sales information can be viewed in multiple currencies.

In the following procedure, you will review the data in the DimCurrency and FactCurrencyRate tables and the relationships of the DimCurrency table with the Date Dimension and the Fact Reseller Sales tables. You will explore the data and see how the currency and exchange rates are identified among the dimension and fact tables. The Adventure Works company example uses the *one-to-many* type of currency conversion, in which all of the sales transactions are already converted into U.S. dollar values before they are loaded into the cube. These values are converted back to their original local currencies for reporting and analysis. For example, when you view sales for European entities, the values are converted to British pounds or euros.

Review the DimCurrency and FactCurrencyRate tables

1. Use Business Intelligence Development Studio (BIDS) to open the AdventureWorks SSAS solution contained in the C:\Microsoft Press\Analysis Services 2008 SBS \Chapter 09\AdventureWorks BI folder.

2. In Solution Explorer, expand the Data Source View folder, right-click SSAS2008SBS.dsv, and select View Designer.

3. In the Diagram Organizer pane, select the Currency diagram. Your screen should look like this:

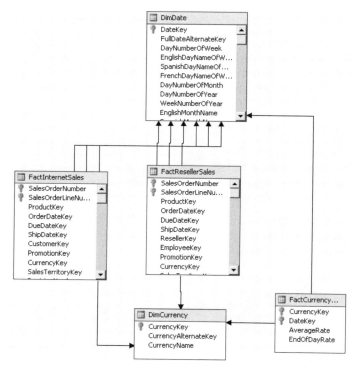

4. Right-click the DimCurrency table and select Explore Data. You will see that the CurrencyAlternativeKey column contains the ISO 4217 currency codes.

5. Close the Explore DimCurrency Table window. In the Currency diagram, right-click the FactCurrencyRate table and select Explore Data. You will see that this table contains two exchange rates: AverageRate and EndOfDayRate. The EndOfDayRate is available if the conversion requirement calls for using the last rate for the day for that currency. Alternatively, the AverageRate is available and represents the daily average exchange rate for use rather than the EndOfDayRate value. The rate you use is determined by your company's requirements.

6. Close the FactCurrencyRate table Explore Data window and close the Data Source View Designer.

In the next procedure, you will create the Currency dimension from the DimCurrency table.

Create the Currency dimension

1. In Solution Explorer, right-click the Dimensions folder and select New Dimension to launch the New Dimension Wizard. On the Welcome To The Dimension Wizard page, click Next.

2. Verify that Use An Existing Table is selected and then click Next.

3. On the Specify Source Information page, verify that SSAS2008SBS is selected in the Data Source View list. In the Main Table list, select DimCurrency.

4. In the Key Columns list, verify that Currency Key is selected. In the Name Column list, select CurrencyName and then click Next.

5. On the Select Dimension Attributes page, verify that the Currency Key check box is selected. In the Attribute Type column, click Regular and then click the arrow that appears on the right. Expand Currency, select Currency Name, and click OK.

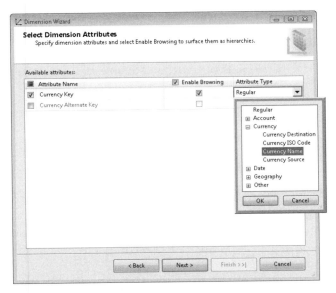

You have just set the *Type* property for the Currency Key attribute. This enables the Business Intelligence Wizard to know which attribute to use to obtain the original foreign currency.

6. Click Next. On the Completing the Wizard page, name the dimension **Currency** and click Finish.

7. In the Dimension Designer, right-click the Currency dimension and select Properties. In the Properties window, verify that the *Type* property is set to *Currency*.

8. Close the Dimension Designer.

In the next procedure, you will add the FactCurrencyRate measure group to your cube and set the value of the measure group's *Type* property to *ExchangeRate*. This measure group will be used when defining the currency conversion rules using the Business Intelligence Wizard.

Add the Currency Rate measure group to the cube

1. In Solution Explorer, expand the Cube folder and double-click the AdventureWorks cube to open the Cube Designer.

2. On the Cube Structure tab, right-click the Measures pane and select New Measure Group.

3. In the New Measure Group dialog box, select the FactCurrencyRate table and click OK. The Fact Currency Rate measure group will be added to the cube.

4. In the Measures pane of the Cube Designer, right-click the Fact Currency Rate measure group, select Rename, and change the name of the measure group to **Currency Rate**.

5. Right-click the Currency Rate measure group and select Properties. In the Properties window, set the value of the *Type* property to **ExchangeRate**.

6. Expand the Currency Rate measure group and delete the End Of Day Rate and Fact Currency Rate Count measures. Keep the Average Rate measure. You will be using the Average Rate for setting up currency conversion in this procedure and therefore do not need the other measures. Having multiple rates is common; the Business Intelligence Wizard allows you to select different rates for different measures if desired.

7. Right-click the Average Rate measure and select Properties. In the Properties window, set the value of the *FormatString* property to **$#,##0.000000;($#,##0.000000)**.

Normally you would not need to set the *FormatString* property for this measure because it is used in calculating values during currency conversion and not usually used for display or reporting. You do want to set this format value now for use when you view the Average Rate while browsing the cube to observe the currency conversion and to see that your conversion is working as defined.

In the next procedure, you will add the Currency dimension to the cube. When the dimension is added to the cube, you will view the Dimensional Usage tab of the Cube Designer to see how the dimension is related to the measure groups in the cube. Finally, you will deploy the project and process the currencies and exchange rates into the cube.

Add the Currency dimension to the cube

1. On the Cube Structure tab of the Cube Designer, right-click in the Dimensions pane and select Add Cube Dimension.

2. In the Add Cube Dimension dialog box, select Currency and click OK.

3. Click the Dimension Usage tab. You can see that the Currency dimension is related to the Reseller Sales, Internet Sales, Reseller Orders, Resellers, and Currency Rate measure groups at the Currency Key granularity level.

4. On the Build menu, select Deploy AdventureWorks SSAS. If the AdventureWorks SSAS database already exists on the server, a dialog box may appear warning that the database will be overwritten. If the warning appears, click Yes. The prior version of the database will be deleted and the current deployment will continue.

You have created the Currency Rate measure group and added the Currency dimension to the cube. In the next procedure, you will use the Business Intelligence Wizard to implement the many-to-one type of currency conversion in the AdventureWorks cube. The wizard will add MDX statements to the cube's calculation script. It will also create a new dimension named Reporting Currency.

Implement currency conversion using the Business Intelligence Wizard

1. In Solution Explorer, right click the AdventureWorks cube and select Add Business Intelligence. Click Next on the Welcome To The Business Intelligence Wizard page.

2. On the Choose Enhancement page, select Define Currency Conversion and click Next. The wizard will inspect the cube for measure groups that are related to a dimension where the value of the *Type* property is *Currency*. From these measure groups, the wizard will select a measure group where the value of the *Type* property is *ExchangeRate*. Verify that the wizard has selected Currency Rate from the Select The Measure Group That Contains Exchange Rates list.

3. On the Set Currency Conversion Options page of the wizard, select US Dollar from the Specify The Pivot Currency list and click OK. The pivot currency is the standard against

which all other exchange rates are measured. The value of the exchange rate for this currency is always 1.

4. From the Select How You Entered Your Exchange Rates list, select Canadian Dollar. Then select N US Dollar Per 1 Canadian Dollar. Your selections should look like this:

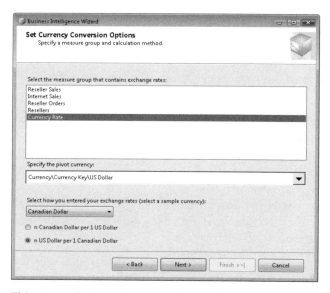

This step tells the wizard that the exchange rates in the currency rate fact table represent the number of pivot currency units equal to 1 unit of the foreign currency. For example, the exchange rate in the fact table for Canadian Dollars is set to $0.630231 USD per $1 CAD. This information enables the wizard to correctly create the MDX expressions in calculation script that will be used to convert currency values.

5. Click Next. On the Select Members page, select Reseller Sales Amount, Reseller Product Cost, Internet Sales Amount, and Internet Product Cost from the Measures list. Currency conversion will be applied to these measures. The Exchange Rate Measures column will default to Average Rate. The Select Members page should look like the following image.

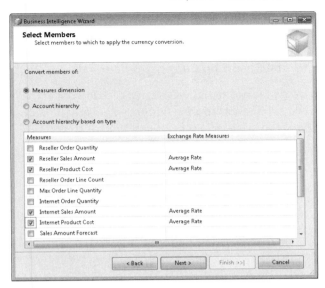

6. Click Next. On the Select Conversion Type page, notice that the wizard provides three currency conversion types: Many-To-Many, Many-To-One, and One-To-Many. The Adventure Works data warehouse has been designed to support the one-to-many currency conversion type—in this case, all the reseller and Internet sales transactions are loaded in U.S. dollar values, but they need to be analyzed and reported in Canadian dollars, euros, British pounds, and other currencies in addition to the default US Dollar pivot currency.

7. On the Select Conversion Type page, select One-To-Many and then click Next.

8. On the Specify Reporting Currencies page, select the Reporting Currencies check box. The wizard will respond by selecting all of the currencies listed on the page.

9. Click Next. The wizard displays a summary of the currency conversion rules. A new dimension, Reporting Currency, will be generated by the wizard for use when selecting reporting currencies. The wizard will also add MDX statements to the cube's calculation script.

10. Click Finish. If you expand the Dimensions folder in Solution Explorer, you will see the new Reporting Currency dimension. If you select the Calculations tab of the Cube designer and click the Script View button on the Calculations toolbar, you will be able to view the MDX statements the wizard added to the calculation script. If your currency conversion requirements change, it is possible to modify these statements, but it is usually easier to rerun the Business Intelligence Wizard to make any needed changes.

In the next procedure, you will use the Dimension Usage tab to create a relationship between the new Reporting Currency dimension and the Currency Rate measure group.

Set dimension usage for the Reporting Currency dimension

1. On the Dimension Usage tab of the Cube Designer, click the cell at the intersection of the Reporting Currency dimension and the Currency Rate measure group. Click the ellipsis button (...) that then appears in that intersection.

2. In the Define Relationship dialog box, select Regular from the Select Relationship Type list.

3. From the Granularity Attribute list, select Currency Key.

4. In the Relationship pane, the Dimension Columns value will default to CurrencyKey. From the Measure Group Columns list, select CurrencyKey. Your screen should look like this:

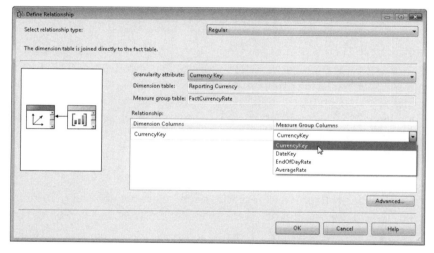

5. Click OK. You are now ready to deploy the AdventureWorks SSAS database and browse the cube to verify that currencies are being converted correctly.

Deploy the project and browse the cube

1. On the Build menu, select Deploy AdventureWorks SSAS.

2. When the database has been successfully deployed and processed, click the Browser tab of the Cube Designer.

3. In the Metadata pane, expand the Measures folder and then expand the Reseller Sales measure group.

4. Drag the Reseller Sales Amount and Reseller Product Cost measures to the Report pane and drop them in the area labeled Drop Totals Or Detail Fields Here. By default, the report shows the values in U.S. dollars.

5. Expand the Geography dimension. Drag the Geography hierarchy to the report pane and drop it in the area labeled Drop Row Fields Here.

6. Expand the Date dimension. Drag the Date.Fiscal Date hierarchy to the Report pane and drop it in the area labeled Drop Column Fields Here.

   In the next step, you will select July 1, 2010 from the Fiscal Date hierarchy.

7. Expand the Fiscal Year column header, clear the (All) check box, expand FY 2011, expand FY 2011 Qtr 1, expand July 2010, and select 1 July 2010. Click OK.

   The report should display Reseller Sales Amount and Reseller Product Cost by Country Region for a single day, 1 July 2010.

Drop Filter Fields Here				
	Fiscal Year ▾			
	⊞ FY 2011		Grand Total	
Country Region ▾	Reseller Sales Amount	Reseller Product Cost	Reseller Sales Amount	Reseller Product Cost
⊞ Australia	$49,825	$66,596	$49,825	$66,596
⊞ Canada	$501,046	$498,264	$501,046	$498,264
⊞ France	$55,465	$52,702	$55,465	$52,702
⊞ Germany	$180,041	$222,475	$180,041	$222,475
⊞ United Kingdom	$152,484	$158,087	$152,484	$158,087
⊞ United States	$1,726,789	$1,849,385	$1,726,789	$1,849,385
Grand Total	$2,665,651	$2,847,508	$2,665,651	$2,847,508

Now you will add the Reporting Currency dimension to enable viewing the Reseller Sales Amount and Unit Price in other currencies.

8. In the Metadata pane, expand the Reporting Currency dimension. Drag Currency Key to the Report pane and drop it on Drop Filter Fields Here.

9. In the Metadata pane, expand the Currency Rate measure group. Drag the Average Rate measure to the Report pane and drop it to the right of Reseller Product Cost. The Average Rate measure displays $1.000000 because the US Dollar is the pivot currency. Notice that the Reseller Sales Amount grand total is $2,665,651.

Currency Key ▾			
US Dollar			
	Fiscal Year ▾		
	⊞ FY 2011		
Country Region ▾	Reseller Sales Amount	Reseller Product Cost	Average Rate
⊞ Australia	$49,825	$66,596	$1.000000
⊞ Canada	$501,046	$498,264	$1.000000
⊞ France	$55,465	$52,702	$1.000000
⊞ Germany	$180,041	$222,475	$1.000000
⊞ United Kingdom	$152,484	$158,087	$1.000000
⊞ United States	$1,726,789	$1,849,385	$1.000000
⊞ Unknown			$1.000000
Grand Total	$2,665,651	$2,847,508	$1.000000

10. In the Report pane filter area, expand the Currency Key attribute, clear the US Dollar check box, select United Kingdom Pound, and click OK. The cube will convert Reseller Sales Amount and Reseller Product Cost from U.S. dollar values to the British pound values for all the regions. Your screen should look like the following image.

| Currency Key ▼ | | | |
| United Kingdom Pound | | | |

	Fiscal Year ▼		
	⊞ FY 2011		
Country Region ▼	Reseller Sales Amount	Reseller Product Cost	Average Rate
⊞ Australia	$34,563	$46,198	$1.441545
⊞ Canada	$347,576	$345,645	$1.441545
⊞ France	$38,476	$36,559	$1.441545
⊞ Germany	$124,894	$154,331	$1.441545
⊞ United Kingdom	$105,778	$109,665	$1.441545
⊞ United States	$1,197,874	$1,282,918	$1.441545
⊞ Unknown			$1.441545
Grand Total	$1,849,162	$1,975,316	$1.441545

In step 9, you saw that the Reseller Sales Amount grand total in U.S. dollars was
$2,665,651. The Average Rate measure shows that on 1 July 2010, the value of the
British pound was 1.441545 U.S. dollars. The report from this step shows that the cube
is applying the MDX statements created by the Business Intelligence Wizard and calculating that $2,665,651 U.S. dollars equal $1,849,162 British pounds.

11. Repeat step 10 and change the Reporting Currency filter from United Kingdom Pounds
to EURO. The values for Reseller Sales Amount and Reseller Product Cost will now display in their euro values based upon the exchange rate of $0.880359 USD for each EUR
for the date filtered in the Fiscal Year hierarchy.

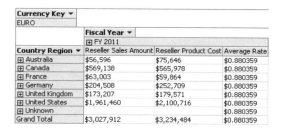

| Currency Key ▼ | | | |
| EURO | | | |

	Fiscal Year ▼		
	⊞ FY 2011		
Country Region ▼	Reseller Sales Amount	Reseller Product Cost	Average Rate
⊞ Australia	$56,596	$75,646	$0.880359
⊞ Canada	$569,138	$565,978	$0.880359
⊞ France	$63,003	$59,864	$0.880359
⊞ Germany	$204,508	$252,709	$0.880359
⊞ United Kingdom	$173,207	$179,571	$0.880359
⊞ United States	$1,961,460	$2,100,716	$0.880359
⊞ Unknown			$0.880359
Grand Total	$3,027,912	$3,234,484	$0.880359

Supporting Foreign Language Translation

In the previous section, you learned how to implement currency conversion to accommodate multiple currencies within your cube for reporting and analysis. You can also apply
translations to your cube to display the labels on rows and columns in different languages.
Together, currency conversion and translation enables you to provide an analytical solution
that displays local currency and local language.

When browsing your cube, member captions are the labels for attributes that appear as
headers in rows and columns. By default, these captions correspond to the name that you
assign to an attribute. In this section, you will learn how to add translations to dimensions,
measure groups, measures, and calculated members. You will learn how to replace the default caption with a translated caption and use translated names for dimension members
stored as attributes in a dimension table.

> **Note** The Business Intelligence Design Studio lets you test and view translations in its browsers for cubes and dimensions. End-user experience with translation depends on the client application used to connect to and browse the cube. Not all tools offer translation capabilities, so verify that your client applications support translations before adding translations to your cube.

In the following procedure, you will add French translations to the Date dimension as well as to folder captions for measure groups and measures within the cube.

Add translated captions and attribute values

1. In Solution Explorer, right-click the Date dimension and select View Designer.

2. Select the Translations tab. On the Translations tab toolbar, click the New Translation button.

3. In the Select Language dialog box, scroll down and select French (France). Click OK. A new column named French (France) appears on the Translation page.

4. The first row contains Date, the English name of the dimension. In the first row in the French (France) column, enter Temp.

5. Starting with the third row, enter the following French captions for the dimension attributes.

Attribute	French Caption
Date	Temp
Calendar Year	Annee Civile
Calendar Quarter	Quart de Civile
Fiscal Quarter	Quart Fiscal
Fiscal Year	Exercice Budgetaire

> **Note** Don't worry about typing special accent characters for foreign language captions at this time. This is just an example for you to understand how to add translations to a dimension.

Your screen should look like the following image.

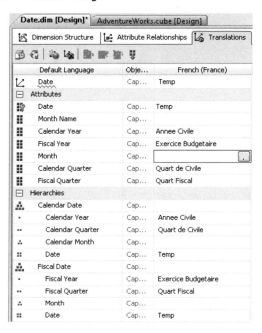

Notice that when you provided a French caption for an attribute, a French caption for the hierarchy levels appeared.

6. In the Attributes section, click the cell at the intersection of the Month row and the French (France) column and then click the ellipsis button that will appear.

7. In the Attribute Data Translation dialog box, enter **Mois** in the Translated Caption text box. In the Translation Columns list, select FrenchMonthName.

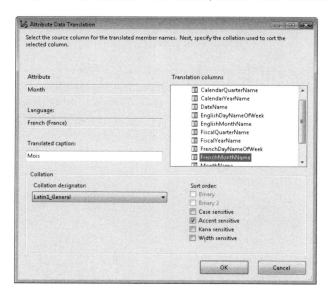

In this step, you assigned a French caption for the attribute and also assigned a column in the dimension table that contains French month names.

8. Click OK. An icon appears in the cell containing the French caption for the Month attribute.

9. Return to the Cube Designer for the AdventureWorks cube and select the Translation tab.

10. On the Translation tab toolbar, click the New Translation button. In the Select Language dialog box, select French (France) and click OK.

11. Add the French translations as shown in the following table.

Measure or Calculated Member	French Caption
Reseller Sales	Ventes de Revendeur
Reseller Sales Amount	Quantite de Ventes de Revendeur
Internet Sales	Ventes d'Internet
Internet Sales Amount	Quantite de Ventes d'Internet
[Measures].[Total Sales Amount]	Tout Ventes

Deploy the project and browse the cube

1. On the Build menu, select Deploy AdventureWorks SSAS.

2. When the database has been successfully deployed and processed, click the Browser tab of the Cube Designer and then click Reconnect.

3. Click the Clear Results button on the Browser toolbar.

4. In the Metadata pane, expand Measures, expand the Internet Sales and Reseller Sales measure groups, and then expand the Date dimension. Notice that all the captions are in English.

5. Expand the Geography dimension, drag the Geography hierarchy to the Report pane, and drop it on the rows area. Expand the Country Region column header, clear the (All) check box, select France, and click OK.

6. Drag the Date.Calendar Date hierarchy of the Date dimension to the Report pane columns area.

7. Drag the Reseller Sales Amount to the Drop Totals Or Detail Fields area in the Report pane.

8. Expand the Reporting Currency dimension and drag the Currency Key to the filter area of the Report pane. Expand the Currency Key attribute, clear the (All) check box, select EURO, and click OK. The report shows the values of Reseller Sales for France in euros across several calendar years.

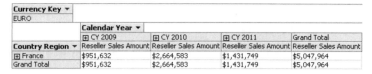

Currency Key ▼				
EURO				
	Calendar Year ▼			
	⊞ CY 2009	⊞ CY 2010	⊞ CY 2011	Grand Total
Country Region ▼	Reseller Sales Amount	Reseller Sales Amount	Reseller Sales Amount	Reseller Sales Amount
⊞ France	$951,632	$2,664,583	$1,431,749	$5,047,964
Grand Total	$951,632	$2,664,583	$1,431,749	$5,047,964

9. Find the Language list, which is located just below the Browser tab. Select French (France) from the Language list.

   Because EURO is selected from the Currency Key attribute, the report displays values in euros. Because French (France) is selected from the Language list, the cube provides French translations.

10. In the report, expand the CY 2009 and CY 2009 Qtr 3 members to display the months in French. Notice that the browser Measures and Dimension pane Metadata pane names are in French as well.

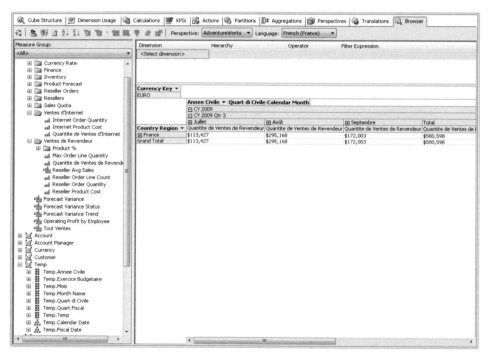

You should also note that in the Metadata pane, there are French captions for two measure groups, several measures, one calculated member, and several attributes.

11. Close BIDS.

In this chapter, you have learned how to implement currency conversion in a cube. Based on your company's requirements, you can design a cube that converts many currencies into a single currency, converts a single currency into many currencies, or converts many currencies into many currencies. To implement currency conversion, you must have a dimension that contains a list of currencies. You must also have a fact table that contains exchange rates. You can then use the Business Intelligence Wizard to configure currency conversion. The wizard will add MDX statements to the cube's calculation script and also create a new dimension named Reporting Currency. After the wizard is complete, you need to remember to use the Dimension Usage tab of the Cube Designer to create a relationship between the Reporting Currency dimension and the measure group that contains the exchange rates.

You also learned how to add multiple languages to a dimension and a cube in this chapter, to be able to present data with captions and labels in the language appropriate to the user, and you discovered that when you select a different reporting language, some translations are provided by the cube automatically.

In Chapter 10, "Interacting with a Cube," you will learn how to add interactive capabilities to a cube by creating actions and enabling dimension and cube writeback. You can add a URL action to a cube that enables users to open a Web page related to the content of the cube, a drillthrough action that allows users to view detail data, or a reporting action that lets users open a Reporting Services report. Enabling dimension and cube writeback allows users to modify dimension members and cube values.

Chapter 10
Interacting with a Cube

In this chapter, you will learn how to:

- Create a URL action.

- Create a drillthrough action.

- Create a reporting action.

- Enable dimension writeback and add or modify dimension members.

- Enable cube writeback and add or modify measure values.

Throughout the preceding chapters of this book, you have been making changes to dimensions and cubes to take advantage of Analysis Services native functionality. Now you are ready to explore the features that enable Analysis Services to interact with other applications. *Actions* enable Analysis Services to provide additional information to a client application that can be used to perform a certain task or invoke another application. For example, an action can return a URL and instructions to open a Web browser to a client application. *Writeback* allows client applications to add, modify, and delete dimension members and to modify measure values.

In this chapter, you will learn how to create a URL action that opens a Web browser and displays a Live Search page. You will create a drillthrough action that displays detail data. You will also create a reporting action that executes a Reporting Services report. You will then learn how to enable dimension and cube writeback and how to modify Analysis Services data.

Implementing Actions

You already know that the purpose of an online analytical processing (OLAP) application is to provide users with valuable information to drive business decisions. Actions provide another mechanism by which users can gather information and take steps based on the information they find in cubes. You can add actions to a cube that users will later execute. An action is always initiated by a user or client application and relates to an object in a cube. That object might be a dimension member or a particular cell, which is then used as a parameter for the action. Not all client applications are able to execute actions, so make sure you understand the capability of the client application before creating actions in your cube.

You can add several types of actions to a cube. A URL action is useful for navigating to a particular Web site based on cube data. For example, you might want to visit a customer's Web site after viewing that customer's data in a cube, or you might want to access information from an internal reporting Web server to get more information about a particular product you're analyzing. Another popular action type is *drillthrough*, which you can implement to provide immediate access to the most detailed data stored in your cube. If you're using Microsoft SQL Server 2008 Reporting Services, you can use the Reporting action to link a report to a cube object.

Creating Standard Actions

The Cube Designer in Business Intelligence Development Studio (BIDS) includes an Actions tab. You can define an action on this tab by specifying the action name, action target, the action type, and the action expression that generates a string used to run the action. An *action target* is the portion of the cube to which the action relates and is the object that the user clicks to launch the action. The *action expression* is a Multidimensional Expression (MDX) that evaluates as a string relevant to the action type. Each action type has its own syntax requirements, but generally you include the MDX *CURRENTMEMBER* function in the action expression to link the object to the current cube context.

In this procedure, you'll add a new URL action that opens a Web page and executes a search for a product category or subcategory.

Create a URL action

1. Use Business Intelligence Development Studio (BIDS) to open the AdventureWorks BI solution contained in the C:\Microsoft Press\Analysis Services 2008 SBS\Chapter 10 \AdventureWorks BI folder. You will need to deploy the AdventureWorks SSAS database before you can create an action. This ensures that the database design contained in BIDS and on the Analysis Services server are both the same.

2. On the Build menu, select Deploy AdventureWorks SSAS. If the AdventureWorks SSAS database already exists on the server, a dialog box may appear warning that the database will be overwritten. If the warning appears, click Yes. The prior version of the database will be deleted and the current deployment will continue.

3. After the database has been successfully deployed and processed, expand the Cubes folder in Solution Explorer, right-click the AdventureWorks.cube, and select View Designer.

4. In the Cube Designer, click the Actions tab. On the Actions tab toolbar, click New Action.

5. In the Action Editor, change the name of the action to **Internet Search**.

6. An action target is the location in the cube where the action can be executed. An action target has a target type and a target object. You can choose from several target

types. If you select Cube, the action is available for all cube objects—every dimension, hierarchy, level, and member, and every cell containing a measure. Alternatively, you can limit an action to certain members within a dimension. If you select Dimension Members as the target type, the action is available for all members of the dimension that you specify as the target object. Similarly, you can select Hierarchy or Level to limit the availability of the action to members of the specified hierarchy or level. You can limit the action even further if you select a target type of Attribute Members. Another option is to use Cells as the target type. Unlike the Cube target type, Cells does not include members of a dimension—it includes only the cells containing numeric values.

In the Target Type list, select Hierarchy Members. You want the action to execute an Internet search on product categories or subcategories, so select a target object that contains these dimension members.

7. Expand the Target Object list, expand the Product dimension, select Product By Category, and click OK. You can enter an MDX expression in the Condition text box to further limit the scope of the target. In this case, you will limit the action so that it applies only to the Category and Subcategory levels of the Product By Category hierarchy.

8. In the Condition text box, enter the following MDX expression:

```
[Product].[Product by Category].Level IS [Product].[Product by Category].[Category] OR
[Product].[Product by Category].Level IS [Product].[Product by Category].[Subcategory]
```

> **Note** You can drag and drop items from the Calculation Tools pane to make creating this expression easier, or you can copy the expression from the file C:\Microsoft Press\Analysis Services 2008 SBS\Chapter 10\MDX\InternetSearch.txt.

You need to select the type of action that you want to create. Because you want the action to start a Web browser and open a URL, choose URL. The other action types available are Dataset and Rowset, which return either a dataset or rowset from Analysis Services–generated queries that the client application can send to Analysis Services or other data sources, and Statement, which generates other MDX, DMX (Data Mining Extensions), or SQL (Structured Query Language) database commands that can be executed by the client application. If you want to create a custom action that allows the user or client application to invoke any other application, select the Proprietary action type.

9. In the Action Content section of the editor, verify that URL is selected from the Type list. The Action Expression text box contains the string that will be passed to the application that is started by the action. In this case, the action will start a Web browser, so the Action Expression text box needs to contain a URL. You want this to be a dynamic URL that contains a constant that provides the address of the Web site and then an MDX expression that includes the text that you want to search. The key to a dynamic URL is the use of an MDX expression that returns a key value, a name, or other attribute property based on the current context of the cube. You can retrieve the current value of a dimension member by using the MDX *CURRENTMEMBER* function.

10. In the Action Expression text box, enter the following MDX expression:

```
"http://search.live.com/results.aspx?q="
+ [Product].[Product by Category].CurrentMember.Name
+ "&form=QBLH"
```

> **Note** You can copy the expression from the file C:\Microsoft Press\Analysis Services 2008 SBS\Chapter 10\MDX\InternetSearch.txt.

The Action Editor should now look like the following image.

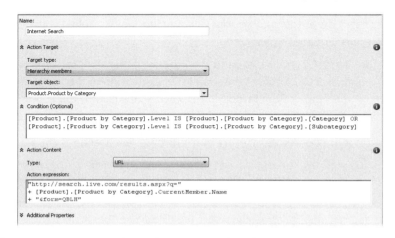

Before you can execute the action, you need to deploy your project. After the project is successfully deployed, you can browse the cube and execute the URL action that you just created.

Deploy and browse the cube

1. On the Build menu, select Deploy AdventureWorks SSAS.

2. After the cube has been deployed and processed successfully, click the Browser tab in the Cube Designer.

3. In the Metadata pane, expand the Measures folder, expand the Reseller Sales measure group, and then add the Reseller Sales Amount measure to the Report pane totals area.

4. Drag the Product dimension from the Metadata pane to the Report pane rows area.

5. In the Category column, expand the Bikes member and then expand the Mountain Bikes member. Now that your report contains product categories and subcategories, you can execute the URL action.

6. Click the report pane and then click and right-click the Mountain Bikes member. You can see the Internet Search action on the shortcut menu.

7. Select Internet Search. Internet Explorer opens with a Live Search page similar to this.

8. Close Internet Explorer. When you created the URL action, you applied a condition so that the action would only be enabled for product categories and subcategories. In the next step, you will verify that the action is not enabled for products.

9. Switch back to BIDS. In the Report pane of the cube browser, click and then right-click Mountain-100 Black, 38. The Internet Search option does not appear on the shortcut menu because the URL action is available only for product categories and subcategories.

Creating Drillthrough Actions

Drillthrough actions provide quick access to the lowest level of detail stored in a cube. When you create a drillthrough action, you select dimension attributes and measures that are returned as columns of data when the action is executed. When a user viewing a summary value executes the action, the client application executes the drillthrough query supplied by Analysis Services to return and display a set of rows containing the detailed data behind the summary value. Contrary to the action name, a drillthrough action does not access data stored in the source relational database. Any data that you want to be available for drillthrough must be contained in the cube's dimensions and measures. In the next procedure, you will create a drillthrough action that displays reseller sales detail data.

Create a drillthrough action

1. In the Cube Designer, click the Actions tab.

2. On the Actions tab toolbar, click the New Drillthrough Action button.

3. In the Action Editor, change the name of the action to **Reseller Sales Details**. In the "Create a URL Action" procedure earlier in this chapter, you learned that an action has an action target, which is the location in the cube where the action can be executed. You also learned that every action target has a target type and a target object. Because you are creating a drillthrough action, the target type is Cell. The target type is not displayed, to prevent you from changing it. The target object must be all of the measures in the cube or all of the measures in one of the cube's measure groups. In this procedure, since you are enabling drillthrough for reseller sales detail data, you will enable the drillthrough action for measures in the Reseller Sales measure group.

4. In the Measure Group Members list, select Reseller Sales.

> **Tip** If you don't want the action to be enabled for all of the measures in a measure group, enter an MDX expression in the Condition text box that is true only for the measures for which you want the action to be enabled.

5. You can use the Drillthrough Columns section of the Action Editor to configure the columns of data that will be returned by the action. In the Drillthrough Columns section, expand the <Select Dimensions> list and select the Reseller dimension.

6. Click the empty cell in the Return Columns column, expand the list, and select the Reseller attribute. Click OK. The Drillthrough Columns section should now look like this:

7. Repeat steps 5 and 6 to add the following dimensions and return columns to the drillthrough columns that will be returned by the action.

Dimension	Return Columns
Date	Date
Reseller Orders	Order Line
Measures	Reseller Order Quantity
	Reseller Sales Amount

You can restrict the maximum number of rows that will be returned when a drillthrough action is executed. Using this option prevents Analysis Services from sending an overwhelmingly large number of rows back when the client application executes the parameterized query.

8. Expand the Additional Properties section and in the Maximum Rows text box, type **10**. The Drillthrough Action editor should now look like this:

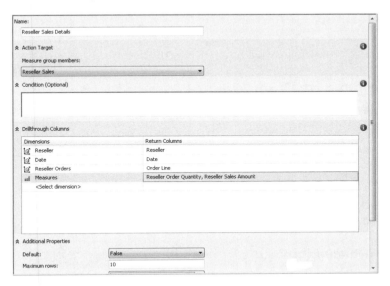

Deploy and browse the cube

Before you can execute the action, you need to deploy your project. After the project is successfully deployed, you can browse the cube and execute the drillthrough action that you just created.

1. On the Build menu, select Deploy AdventureWorks SSAS.

2. After the cube has been deployed and processed successfully, click the Browser tab of the Cube Designer. On the Browser tab toolbar, click Reconnect.

3. In the Metadata pane, expand the Internet Sales measure group and add the Internet Sales Amount measure to the Report pane totals area.

4. Click the Report pane and then right-click the Reseller Sales Amount value for the Mountain-100 Black, 38 product. The Reseller Sales Details drillthrough action will appear on the shortcut menu.

5. Select Reseller Sales Details. The Data Sample Viewer dialog box appears and displays the 10 orders for the Mountain-100 Black, 38 product. You may want to expand the width of each column so that you can see the entire column name.

[$Reseller].[Reseller]	[$Date].[Date]	[$Reseller Orders].[Order Line]	[Reseller Sales].[Reseller Order Quantity]	[Reseller Sales].[Reseller Sales Amount]
Original Bicycle Supply Company	1 July 2008	SO43661 Line 07	3	6074.982
Capable Sales and Service	1 July 2008	SO43664 Line 02	4	8099.976
Latest Sports Equipment	1 July 2008	SO43665 Line 07	2	4049.988
Yellow Bicycle Company	1 July 2008	SO43667 Line 04	1	2024.994
Trusted Catalog Store	1 July 2008	SO43676 Line 04	3	6074.982
Great Bikes	1 July 2008	SO43683 Line 08	4	8099.976
Sports Sales and Rental	1 July 2008	SO43695 Line 08	5	10124.97
Two-Wheeled Transit Company	1 August 2008	SO43844 Line 01	4	8099.976
Suburban Cycle Shop	1 August 2008	SO43848 Line 03	1	2024.994
Sharp Bikes	1 August 2008	SO43853 Line 05	2	4049.988

Data Sample Viewer (first 1000 records)

6. In the Data Sample Viewer dialog box, click Close. When you created the drillthrough action, you selected the Reseller Sales measure group as the action target. In the next step, you will verify that the action is not enabled for measures in the Internet Sales measure group.

7. Right-click the Internet Sales Amount value for the Mountain-100 Black, 38 product. Note that the Reseller Sales Details action doesn't appear on the shortcut menu.

Modify a drillthrough action

You can also use the Action tab of the Cube Designer to modify an existing action. The Reseller Sales Details action displays only 10 rows of data, no matter how many detail records have been aggregated to create the summary value. In this procedure, you will modify the action so that it returns all of the detail rows. To prevent the action from returning too many rows, you will only enable the action if the summary value has 200 or fewer detail records. If the summary value has more than 200 detail records, a user will not be able to execute the action. In order to view detail data, the user will have to drill down further into the cube or apply a filter.

1. In the Cubes Designer, click the Actions tab.

2. In the Action Organizer pane, select the Reseller Sales Details action. The Measure Group Members list shows that the action is enabled for all of the measures in the Reseller Sales measure group. You can further restrict the scope of where the action is enabled by entering an MDX expression in the Condition text box.

3. In the Condition text box, enter the following MDX expression:

```
[Measures].[Reseller Order Line Count] < 201
```

Note You can copy the expression from the file C:\Microsoft Press\Analysis Services 2008 SBS\Chapter 10\MDX\ResellerSalesDetails.txt.

Because the action is enabled only when a summary value has 200 or fewer detail records, you no longer need to use the *MaximumRows* property to restrict the number of records returned by the action.

4. Clear the Maximum Rows text box. The Reseller Sales Details action should now look like this:

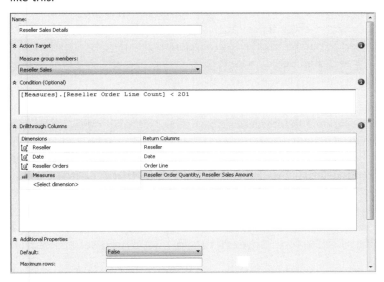

5. On the Build menu, select Deploy AdventureWorks SSAS.

6. After the cube has been deployed and processed successfully, click the Browser tab of the Cube Designer. On the Browser tab toolbar, click Reconnect.

7. Remove Internet Sales Amount from the report and add the Reseller Order Line Count measure to the Report pane totals area.

8. Click the Report pane. Right-click the Reseller Sales Amount or Reseller Order Line Count value for the Mountain-100 Black, 38 product and select Reseller Sales Details. The Data Sample Viewer dialog box appears and displays all of the detail records. You may want to expand the width of each column so that you can see the entire column name.

9. In the Data Sample Viewer dialog box, click Close.

10. In this step, you will verify that the action is not enabled if the summary value has more than 200 detail records. Notice that the value of Reseller Order Line Count for the Mountain-200 Silver, 42 product is 480. This product has more than 200 detail records. Right-click the Reseller Sales Amount or Reseller Order Line Count value for the Mountain-200 Silver, 42 product. The Reseller Sales Details action doesn't show up on the shortcut menu because there are more than 200 orders for this product.

Linking to Reporting Services Reports

When Reporting Services is part of your business intelligence (BI) infrastructure, you can easily create actions that execute these reports. While the focus of this book is not Reporting Services, you need to complete several procedures to configure Internet and Reporting Services security and then deploy a Reporting Services report. After the report is deployed, you can create an action that executes the report.

The enhanced security environment of Windows Vista (and Windows Server 2008) requires that you modify the default Internet Explorer security configuration if you want to deploy a report to the local instance of Reporting Services. You must also add yourself to the Reporting Services Content Manager security role. In the next two procedures, you will make these security modifications. You can learn more about these issues in the document *How to: Configure a Report Server for Local Administration on Windows Vista and Windows Server 2008* (*http://technet.microsoft.com/en-us/library/bb630430.aspx*).

Configure Internet Explorer Security to allow Reporting Services administration

1. On the Microsoft Windows task bar, click Start, select All Programs, right-click Internet Explorer, and select Run As Administrator.

2. In the User Account Control dialog box, select Allow.

3. From the Internet Explorer Tools menu, select Internet Options.

4. In the Internet Options dialog box, click the Security tab, select Trusted Sites, and then click Sites.

5. In the Trusted Sites dialog box, clear the Require Server Verification (https:) For All Sites In This Zone check box.

6. In the Add This Website To The Zone text box, type **http://localhost**.

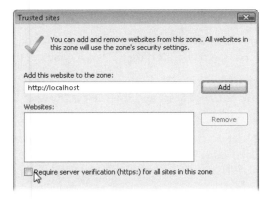

7. Click Add and then click Close.

8. In the Internet Options dialog box, click OK.

Configure Reporting Services Security to allow Reporting Services administration

1. In the address bar in Internet Explorer, type the URL **http://localhost/reports** and press ENTER.

2. In the Connect To Localhost dialog box, type the user name and password of a user configured as an Administrator on the local computer. Click OK.

> **Tip** Report Manager may be slow to start the first time you connect to it. Be patient—it will start after a few moments. After Report Manager has been started, it responds quickly to additional requests.

3. In Report Manager, click the Properties tab and then click New Role Assignment.

4. On the New Role Assignment page, in the Group Or User Name text box, enter your Windows domain and user name and then select Content Manager.

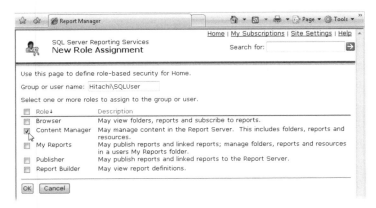

5. Click OK and then close Internet Explorer.

   You have completed the changes to Internet Explorer and Report Manager. In the next few steps, you will test these changes to confirm that you now have permission to manage Reporting Services.

6. On the Microsoft Windows task bar, click Start and then select Internet Explorer.

7. In Internet Explorer, type in the URL **http://localhost/reports** and press ENTER. Because of the security configuration changes you made, Internet Explorer may need to open a new window and will display this warning.

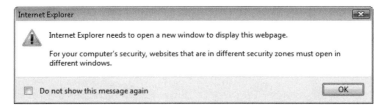

8. In the Internet Explorer warning dialog box, click OK.

9. In the Connect To Localhost dialog box, in the User Name text box, enter your Windows domain and user name. In the Password text box, enter your password and then click OK.

   The Report Manager Home page will appear. If you can see the Properties tab on the Report Manager home page, you have correctly configured Internet Explorer and Reporting Services security.

You now have the security permissions you need to deploy a Reporting Services report. A Reporting Services report has already been created for you. In the next procedure, you will add the project containing this report to the AdventureWorks BI solution and then deploy the report. After the report is deployed, you will be able to create a report action that executes the report.

Deploy a Reporting Services Report

1. Switch back to BIDS and select Add Existing Project from the File menu.

2. In the Add Existing Project dialog box, browse to the C:\Microsoft Press\Analysis Services 2008 SBS\Chapter 10\Report Project folder, select the Report Project.rptproj file, and click Open. In Solution Explorer, you should see the Report Project project, and in the Reports folder, you should see the ResellerSalesReport report.

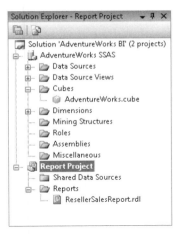

To execute this report, you need to deploy it to Reporting Services. The project has already been configured to deploy reports to the local computer.

3. Select the Report Project project or the ResellerSalesReport report in Solution Explorer. On the Build menu, select Deploy Report Project. When the report has been successfully deployed, the message "Deploy: 1 succeeded, 0 failed, 0 skipped" appears in the Output window.

 Tip The Output window may be pinned open, making your screen cluttered. You can close or unpin it to conserve screen space.

4. You should execute the report to verify that it has been successfully deployed and is functioning properly. Switch back to Report Manager in Internet Explorer and click Refresh. The SSAS 2008 SBS Reports folder will appear in Report Manager. This folder contains the report that you deployed in step 2.

5. On the Report Manager page, select the SSAS 2008 SBS Reports folder. You will be able to see the ResellerSalesReport.

6. On the SSAS 2008 SBS Reports page, select ResellerSalesReport. The ResellerSalesReport report appears but doesn't display any data. The report contains a parameter that you must populate with the name of a Reseller. The report will then display the sales for that Reseller by product subcategory.

7. In the Reseller filter box, type **Active Life Toys** and click View Report. The ResellerSalesReport appears, confirming that you have properly deployed the report. The report should look like this:

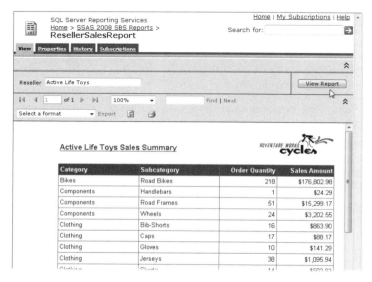

8. Close Internet Explorer.

You have configured Internet Explorer and Reporting Services security so that you can administer the local instance of Reporting Services. You have also successfully deployed and viewed a Reporting Services report. In the next procedure, you will create an Analysis Services action that will provide a parameter value and then execute the report.

Create a reporting action

1. Switch back to BIDS. In the Cube Designer, click the Actions tab. On the Actions tab toolbar, click the New Reporting Action button.

2. In the Action Editor, change the name of the action to **Reseller Sales Summary**.

In the next two steps, you must select the Action Target type and object. The report displays sales for a single reseller, so you want the target type to be Attribute Members and the target object to be the Resellers attribute.

3. Expand the Target Type list and select Attribute Members.

4. Expand the Target Object list, expand the Reseller dimension, select the Reseller attribute, and click OK. The Action Editor should look like this:

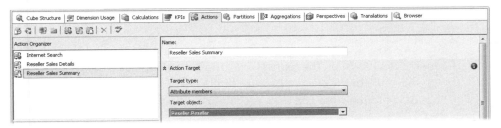

In the Report Server section of the Action Editor, you enter the name of the server and the path of the report that you want the action to execute. The report path includes the Reporting Services virtual directory, the name of the folder(s) that contain the report, and the report name.

5. In the Report Server section Server Name text box, type **localhost**.

6. In the Report Path text box, type **ReportServer?/SSAS 2008 SBS Reports/ ResellerSalesReport**. When the Reporting Action is executed, it can send parameter values to the report that will be run. You can use the Parameters section of the Action Editor to give the name of a report parameter and the value that you want to pass to the parameter. You can pass a value to the parameter that uses an MDX expression containing the *CURRENTMEMBER* function. This way, the parameter value is based on the current context of the cube.

The ResellerSalesReport report contains a parameter named Reseller. In the next four steps, you will configure the Reporting Action to pass the name of a reseller into this parameter.

7. Expand the Parameters section. In the Parameter Name column, click <Add parameter> and then type **Reseller** in the Parameter Name column.

8. Select the cell in the Parameter Value column and click the ellipsis button that appears.

9. In the MDX Builder dialog box, enter the following MDX expression:

```
[Reseller].[Reseller].CURRENTMEMBER.NAME
```

> **Note** You can drag and drop items from the Metadata and Functions pane in the MDX Builder dialog box to make creating this expression easier, or you can copy the expression from the file C:\Microsoft Press\Analysis Services 2008 SBS\Chapter 10\MDX \ResellerSalesSummary.txt.

10. Click OK and then press ENTER. The Report Server and Parameters section of the Action editor should look like this:

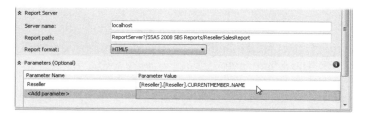

You have created a reporting action that will execute the ResellerSalesReport Reporting Services report. When the report is run, the action populates the report's Reseller parameter with the name of the current Reseller. In the next procedure, you will deploy the changes you have made to the cube and then execute the reporting action.

Deploy and browse the cube

1. On the Build menu, select Deploy AdventureWorks SSAS.

2. After the cube has been deployed and processed successfully, click the Browser tab of the Cube Designer. On the Browser tab toolbar, click Reconnect.

3. Remove the Product, Subcategory, and Category attributes and the Reseller Order Line Count measure from the report.

4. Add the Reseller dimension to the Report pane rows area and expand the Specialty Bike Shop member. The report should look like this:

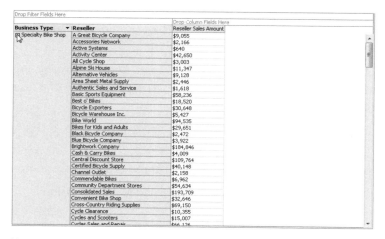

You can now execute the reporting action. When you right-click a Reseller, the Reseller Sales Summary action appears in the shortcut menu.

5. Click the Report pane. In the Reseller column, click Activity Center. When the cell is selected, right-click Activity Center and select Reseller Sales Summary.

The reporting action starts Internet Explorer and executes the report. Before the report is displayed, you must provide your user name and password so that Reporting Services can verify that you have permission to view the report.

6. In the Connect To Localhost dialog box, enter your Windows domain and user name into the User Name text box and then enter your password in the Password text box. The Connect To Localhost dialog box should look similar to this.

7. Click OK. The Reseller Sales Summary report is displayed. The Reseller parameter has been populated with Activity Center, the name of the reseller for which you executed the reporting action.

8. Close Internet Explorer.

Using Writeback to Modify Analysis Services Data

The purpose of business intelligence (BI) is to provide you with information that you can use to make decisions to improve the performance of your organization. So far, you have been using Analysis Services to provide information. You have viewed data from Analysis Services using a cube browser and executed actions that pass data and instructions for using that data from Analysis Services to other applications. You have been a consumer of information provided by Analysis Services. You can use that information to make decisions that are usually expressed as numbers. *Writeback* allows you to interactively record these numbers in Analysis Services.

One important decision-making activity is planning. Planning provides an opportunity to anticipate the future and also to look back and see the truth of the adage "life is what happens while you are making other plans." Planning has interesting challenges because it's an interactive process. Rather than simply looking at historical values generated by business systems, you typically enter planning values based on what you anticipate for the future. To effectively use the planning capabilities of Analysis Services, you need a client application that supports Analysis Services writeback. In this section, you'll learn how to create and administer a cube that uses writeback to enable interactive forecasting. This cube will allow you to create a quarterly forecast for product categories.

Enabling Dimension Writeback

Typically, creating a forecast requires multiple iterations. You create a first-pass forecast and have meetings to discuss the ramifications. Then you create a second-pass forecast and have meetings to discuss those ramifications. Often, it's important to keep track of each interim stage of the process. A *Scenario* dimension allows you to give a name to each pass of the forecast. You often need to add additional members to the Scenario dimensions during the course of the planning cycle. Analysis Services allows you to create a dimension that you can modify dynamically—that is, you can write-enable a dimension.

When you write back data to an Analysis Services dimension, the data is stored in the dimension table in the source database. The AdventureWorks SSAS database already contains a scenario dimension based on data stored in the DimScenario table contained in the SSAS2008SBS data mart. In this procedure, you will view the data in the DimScenario table, enable writeback on the Scenario dimension, add a new member to the Scenario dimension, and then refresh the view of the DimScenario table to see the new dimension member.

Enable dimension writeback

1. In Solution Explorer, expand the Data Source Views folder, right-click SSAS2008SBS.dsv, and select Open.

2. In the Diagram Organizer pane of the Dimension Designer, select the Product Forecast diagram. The DimScenario dimension table has been added to the data source view and appears in the Product Forecast diagram. It is joined to the FactProductForecast fact table on the ScenarioKey column.

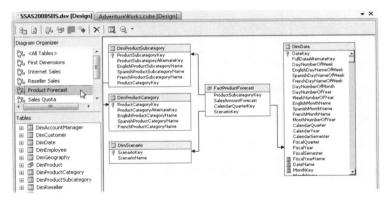

3. Right-click the DimScenario table header and select Explore Data. The DimScenario table contains records for Actual, Budget, and Forecast scenarios only.

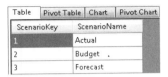

4. You can modify the Scenario dimension and enable writeback so that you can use Analysis Services to add members to the Scenario dimension. In Solution Explorer, expand the Dimensions folder, right-click Scenario.dim, and select View Designer.

5. In the Attributes pane, right-click the Scenario dimension and select Properties.

6. In the Properties window, change the value of the *WriteEnabled* property to *True*. You must deploy this change to the Analysis Services server before you can write back data to the dimension.

7. On the Build menu, select Deploy AdventureWorks SSAS. After the project has been deployed successfully, click the Browser tab of the Dimension Designer.

8. The Scenario dimension contains a member called Forecast. It identifies the first-round forecast values. You also want to do a second forecast iteration, so you will need to add the Revised Forecast member to the dimension. Right-click in the Level And Members pane and select Writeback.

9. Right-click the Forecast member and select Create Sibling. A new member is added to the dimension. The member doesn't have a name, so a text box in edit mode is ready for you to enter a name for the new member.

10. Type **Revised Forecast** in the text box and press ENTER. You have added a new member to the Scenario dimension.

You can refresh the view of the dimension's source data to verify that the new dimension member has also been added to the DimDimension table.

11. Select the Explore DimScenario Table tab and click the Resample Data button.

The Revised Forecast dimension member has been inserted into the DimScenario table.

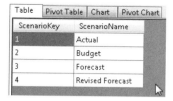

Enabling Cube Writeback

In Analysis Services, you can write-enable a measure group so that you can modify the value of a measure. When you write values to the cube, they are initially stored in memory, in what is called the *writeback cache*, but they are visible to you only in your current session. You may then make the values permanent by committing the changes so they will be written to a relational database table and processed into the measure group on the server, making the new values available to other users. When you write-enable a measure group, you must specify the database and table that will contain the writeback values.

In the following procedure, you will make it possible to update and insert product forecast values. You will write-enable the Product Forecast measure group and specify the database table that will hold the writeback values.

Enable cube writeback

1. In Solution Explorer, right-click AdventureWorks.cube and select View Designer.

2. Click the Partitions tab. All of the data in a cube is stored in partitions. Every measure group must have at least one partition but could have many. You will learn more about partitions in Chapter 14, "Managing Partitions and Database Processing." For now, the important thing to note is that when you write-enable a measure group, a new partition that contains the writeback values is created.

3. Expand the Product Forecast measure group and right-click the Fact Product Forecast partition.

4. Select Writeback Settings. The Enable Writeback dialog box appears. In this dialog box, you can specify the name of the table that will contain the writeback values. This table will be created the next time the measure group is processed. You select the database that will contain the writeback table by selecting a data source. Remember that in Chapter 3, "Accessing Source Data," you learned that a data source contains the information that Analysis Services uses to connect to a database. The writeback table does not have to be in the same database that contains the measure group's fact table. You can also select the writeback partition storage mode. In MOLAP storage mode, after writeback values are written to the writeback table, they are processed into the Analysis Services. In ROLAP mode, the writeback values are stored only in the relational database.

5. Accept all of the default values in the Enable Writeback dialog box.

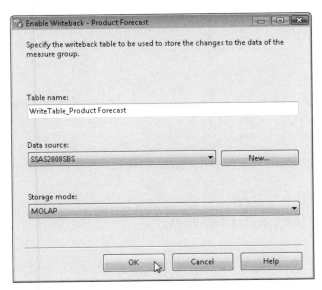

6. Click OK. A new partition for the Product Forecast measure group appears on the Partitions tab.

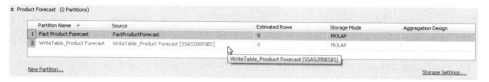

7. Before you can write back data to the Product Forecast measure group, you must deploy your changes to Analysis Services. On the Build menu, select Deploy AdventureWorks SSAS.

After the project has been deployed successfully, you are ready to begin the next procedure, in which you will write back data to the Product Forecast measure group. You will first update values the values in the cube by using the *UPDATE CUBE* MDX statement. These new values will be temporarily stored in the writeback cache. You will then commit these changes to the cube, so that Analysis Services will write records to the writeback table in the relational database and process these records into the writeback partition.

Analysis Services can only write values to the lowest level of a cube. To change the value of an aggregation, Analysis Services must *allocate* the change to the lowest level of the cube. By default, Analysis Services will allocate the updated value evenly across the lower levels. In this procedure, you will see how Analysis Services allocates values across the lower levels of the cube.

Not all client applications are able to take advantage the writeback functionality of Analysis Services. For example, neither the cube browser in BIDS nor Microsoft Office Excel 2007 are able to perform writeback. If your client application cannot perform writeback, you may need to add a custom-coded extension to the application. A client application uses the *UPDATE CUBE* MDX statement to write back values to a cube. Some client applications make it appear that they are writing data back to an aggregate value. In reality, they are using an *UPDATE CUBE* statement to allocate the aggregate value across leaf-level values.

Writeback cube values

In this procedure, you will use SQL Server Management Studio to execute MDX statements that let you view and modify forecast values. You will learn more about MDX statements in Chapter 11, "Retrieving Data from Analysis Services."

1. On the Microsoft Windows task bar, click Start, point to All Programs, expand the Microsoft SQL Server 2008 folder, and then select SQL Server Management Studio.

2. In the Connect To Server dialog box, select Analysis Services from the Server Type list. In the Server Name text box, type **localhost**.

3. Click Connect.

4. On the File menu, point to Open and select File. In the Open File dialog box, browse to the C:\Microsoft Press\Analysis Services 2008 SBS\Chapter 10\MDX folder, select the Writeback.mdx file, and click Open.

> **Tip** You can click the Auto Hide button on the Object Explorer pane to free up additional space on your screen, if desired.

5. In the Available Databases drop-down menu, select AdventureWorks SSAS. The MDX Query Editor should look like this:

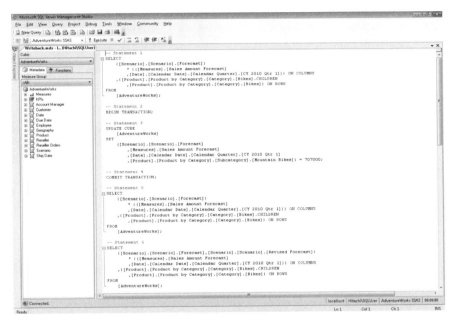

6. The Writeback.mdx file contains a series of MDX statements that select data from the Product Forecast measure group. It also contains statements that write back values. Statement 1 selects the initial forecast values. In the Query Editor, select Statement 1 and click Execute.

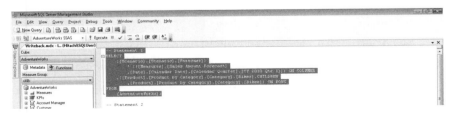

The results pane will appear below the query pane and will display these forecast values.

The value for Mountain Bikes appears low. You can use writeback to correct this value. MDX Statements 2, 3, and 4 will update the value in the cube and then commit this change so that it will be added to the writeback table in the relational database and processed into the writeback partition in the cube.

7. Select and execute Statement 2, Statement 3, and Statement 4. You must execute these statements one at a time.

8. You should verify that the value for Mountain Bikes has been correctly updated. Statement 5 will select the forecast values. Execute Statement 5. You can see that the value for Mountain Bikes is now correct.

9. You now want to create a revised forecast. First, execute a query to show that the Revised Forecast scenario doesn't contain any values. Execute Statement 6. The query results should look like this:

For the revised forecast, you would like the value of Bikes to be $2,500,000. Because Bikes is an aggregate value, Analysis Services will allocate the $2,500,000 across the three Bike subcategories.

10. Execute Statement 7, Statement 8, and Statement 9. You must execute these statements one at a time.

11. Now execute a query to confirm that the data was updated correctly. Execute Statement 10. You can see that the *UPDATE CUBE* statement equally allocated the $2,500,000 across the three subcategories.

12. Click the Save All button and close BIDS. Close SQL Server Management Studio.

In this chapter, you have learned how to enable the interactive functionality of Analysis Services. You created URL, drillthrough, and reporting actions. You then learned how to enable dimension and cube writeback and how to add and modify dimension members and measure values. In the next chapter, you will learn more about creating MDX queries and how to create reports using the Excel 2007 PivotTable feature and Reporting Services.

Chapter 11
Retrieving Data from Analysis Services

In this chapter, you will learn how to:

- Create a perspective and access a cube using a perspective.

- Create MDX queries.

- Create an Excel 2007 PivotTable report using data from Analysis Services.

- Use an Excel 2007 PivotTable report to execute actions, view KPIs, and drill to detail.

- Create a SQL Server Reporting Services report using data from Analysis Services.

Your cube contains many dimensions and measures from several subject areas: sales, finance, production, and inventory. It can serve as a source of information for multiple workgroups or departments across your organization. Although this centralization is beneficial for users, application developers, and IT administrators, it might be difficult for users to find their way to the information they need. Some might even feel a bit overwhelmed by the large amount of information and numerous features in your cube. To help make your cube easier to comprehend and navigate, you can create *perspectives* that limit the number of dimensions, measures, calculations, actions, and KPIs that users see when they are browsing or querying a cube. A perspective allows you to create a view of a subset of a cube that can be more easily comprehended by users.

While developing your Analysis Services database, you've periodically verified your work by browsing a dimension or cube using Business Intelligence Management Studio (BIDS) or SQL Server Management Studio (SSMS), and you were briefly introduced to Reporting Services reporting actions in Chapter 10, "Interacting with a Cube." However, you have not yet created a report using a reporting or visualization application that could be part of your BI system's presentation layer. Reporting and visualization tools use MDX queries to request data from Analysis Services. In this chapter, you will learn how to create MDX queries and then learn how to use SQL Server 2008 Reporting Services and Microsoft Office Excel 2007 to create reports that use data from an Analysis Services database.

Creating Perspectives

A cube may contain multiple perspectives. Usually each perspective displays a subset of the cube that is related to a common subject area or that is required by a group of users. To reporting and visualization applications, a perspective appears just like a cube. However, it is important to note that you cannot apply security to a perspective. You will learn in Chapter 12, "Implementing Security," that you can only secure databases, dimensions, and cubes. If a user has access to a cube, the user has access to all of the perspectives in that cube.

Create a perspective

Let's assume that some users of your cube want to use the cube to analyze sales data. To help these analysts narrow their focus to include only the objects in the cube that pertain to sales analytics, you want to create a perspective for these users. In the following procedure, you will use the Perspectives tab of the Cube Designer to create a Sales perspective and select sales-related cube objects to be visible in the perspective.

1. Use Business Intelligence Development Studio (BIDS) to open the AdventureWorks BI solution contained in the C:\Microsoft Press\Analysis Services 2008 SBS\Chapter 11 \AdventureWorks BI folder.

2. In Solution Explorer, expand the Cubes folder, right-click the AdventureWorks.cube, and select View Designer.

3. In the Cube Designer, click the Perspectives tab and then click the New Perspectives button on the designer toolbar button.

4. In the Perspective Details pane, select the Perspective Name text box, change the name of the perspective to **Sales**, and press ENTER.

5. A check box next to each object in the cube indicates whether the item will appear in the perspective. Because you want to create a perspective that includes only objects that pertain to sales data, you will clear some of these check boxes to keep some cube objects from appearing in the perspective. Clear the check boxes next to the Inventory, Reseller Orders, and Resellers measure groups.

   You can see that the check boxes next to the Reseller Order Count, Reseller Count, and Units in Stock measures have also been cleared. When you clear a check box and remove a measure group from the perspective, you also remove all of the measures in the measure group from the perspective.

You can also see that the Fact Account Manager Count Measure check box is selected. However, this measure will not appear in the perspective because the value of its *Visible* property is *False*. Because there are no visible measures in the Account Manager measure group, it will also not be visible.

6. You can also remove individual measures from your perspective. In the Reseller Sales measure group, clear the check box next to the Max Order Line Quantity and Reseller Product Cost measures. In the Internet Sales measure group, clear the check box next to the Internet Product Cost measure.

7. A list of the dimensions in the cube appears below the list of measure groups and measures. You can use the list of dimensions to remove an entire dimension from a perspective, or you can remove individual attribute and user-defined hierarchies. Clear the check boxes next to the Due Date, Reseller Orders, Scenario, and Ship Date dimensions. When you remove a dimension from a perspective, you also remove all of its attribute and user-defined hierarchies.

8. Expand the Product dimension and clear the check boxes next to the Size By Color hierarchy and the Product ID and Status attributes.

9. A list of the KPIs, Actions, and Calculations in the cubes appears below the list of dimensions. Clear the check boxes next to the Reseller Sales Summary action and all of the calculations except Total Sales Amount.

Before you can browse the Sales perspective, you must first deploy the AdventureWorks SSAS database. After the database has been deployed successfully, you will be able to use the browser in the Cube Designer to compare the dimensions and measures available in the AdventureWorks cube and the Sales perspective.

Deploy and browse the cube

1. On the Build menu, select Deploy AdventureWorks SSAS. If the AdventureWorks SSAS database already exists on the server, a dialog box may appear warning that the database will be overwritten. If the warning appears, click Yes. The prior version of the database will be deleted and the current deployment will continue.

2. After the cube has been deployed and processed successfully, click the Browser tab of the Cube Designer.

3. In the Metadata pane, expand the Product dimension. Expand the Measures folder and then expand the Reseller Sales measure group. The Metadata pane displays the dimensions and measures available in the AdventureWorks cube.

4. Switch to the Sales perspective and compare the available measures and dimensions. On the designer toolbar, expand the Perspective list and select Sales.

5. In the Metadata pane, expand the Product dimension. Expand the Measures folder and expand the Reseller Sales measure group. You can see that the Sales perspective contains fewer dimensions, attribute and user-defined hierarchies, measure groups, and measures. Because irrelevant objects have been removed, the Sales perspective is easier to comprehend than the AdventureWorks cube.

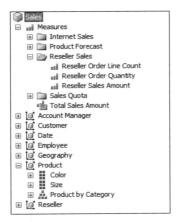

In Chapter 6, "Creating Advanced Measures and Calculations," you learned how to use MDX expressions to create calculated members and calculation script statements. In the next section, you will learn that you can also use MDX to create queries to retrieve information from an Analysis Services cube or perspective.

Creating MDX Queries

An MDX query is different from an MDX expression. An *expression* is a formula that calculates a single value. A *query* is a command that can retrieve many values from a cube, usually to create a report. The cube browser in the Cube Designer, like other reporting and data visualization applications used with Analysis Services, allows you to drag and drop dimensions and measures and generates MDX queries behind the scenes to retrieve values from a cube. You can use these tools to create reports without writing any MDX queries of your own. So why should you learn how to create an MDX query? Learning MDX will allow you to take advantage of some of the more advanced features of Analysis Services to create exactly the dataset you need. You can use MDX queries to understand and debug complex MDX expressions. Also, although almost all reporting applications that can access Analysis Services data can generate MDX queries for you, many reporting applications also allow you to manually enter an MDX query. Finally, you may find that a report returns unexpected results or executes more slowly than expected. If you understand MDX queries, you can view and execute the MDX query generated by the reporting application and troubleshoot the problem.

The most common use of an MDX query is to extract values from an OLAP cube to populate a report. A cube has dimensions, but a report does not. Reports have axes (typically, a row axis, a column axis, and a filter axis). An axis can include members from more than one dimension. Also, a report usually doesn't display all of the data contained in a cube. Therefore, an MDX query must consist of the instructions to extract a subset of data from a dimensional data structure and display it across multiple axes.

If you write Structured Query Language (SQL) queries, you'll recognize the clauses used to create an MDX query: SELECT, FROM, and WHERE. The SELECT clause defines which dimension members to include on each axis of the report and the FROM clause names the cube or perspective that is being queried. The optional WHERE clause restricts values returned by the query to specific dimension members.

You can use the MDX Query Editor provided in SQL Server Management Studio (SSMS) to create and execute MDX queries. The MDX Query Editor provides a Query pane where you can enter and edit MDX Queries. You select a cube or perspective and its measures and dimensions are displayed in the Metadata pane. You can then drag items from the Metadata pane to the Query pane. When you have created an MDX query, you can have SSMS validate the query by clicking Parse on the toolbar or Query menu, and you can execute the query by pressing F5 or clicking Execute on the toolbar or Query menu. After the query has executed, the results are displayed below the Query window in the Results window, and any error or additional information about the execution of the query will appear in the Messages window.

Create a simple MDX Query

1. On the Microsoft Windows task bar, click Start, point to All Programs, expand the Microsoft SQL Server 2008 folder, and then select SQL Server Management Studio.

2. In the Connect To Server dialog box, select Analysis Services from the Server Type list. In the Server Name text box, type **localhost**. Click Connect.

3. On the View menu, select Object Explorer. In Object Explorer expand the Databases folder, right-click AdventureWorks SSAS, point to New Query, and select MDX.

   In SSMS, the Object Explorer window is pinned open by default. You may find that the combination of the Object Explorer window and the Metadata pane of the MDX Query Editor consume too much screen space. If this is the case, you can unpin the Object Explorer window by clicking the Auto Hide button in the upper-right corner.

   In the Metadata pane of the MDX Query Editor, you can select a cube or perspective from the Cube list and then the cube or perspective and all of its measures, KPIs, and dimensions will appear on the Metadata tab. You can then drag items from the Metadata tab onto the Query pane.

4. In the Metadata pane Cube list, select Sales.

5. In the Query Editor, enter the following MDX query:

```
-- Query 1
SELECT
FROM
  [Sales];
```

Note You can enter text and drag items from the Metadata pane and drop them in the Query pane to create the queries in this section or you can copy the queries from the file C:\Microsoft Press\Analysis Services 2008 SBS\Chapter 11\MDX\MDX Queries.txt.

This first query is the simplest possible query you can execute. Because the query contains no measures or dimension measures, Analysis Services resolves the query using the default measure and the default member of each attribute hierarchy in every dimension. If a perspective does not have a value specified for the *DefaultMeasure* property, Analysis Services uses the default measure of the cube. If the cube doesn't have a default measure, the first measure defined on the Cube Structure tab of the BIDS Cube Designer is the default measure. If an attribute does not have a value specified for the *DefaultMember* property, Analysis Services uses the All member as the default member of the attribute hierarchy. If the All member of the attribute has been disabled by setting the value of the *IsAggregatable* property to *False*, Analysis Services uses the first member of the attribute as the default member of the attribute hierarchy.

Note You can add a comment to an MDX query simply by entering two adjacent hyphens (**--**) or two slash characters (**//**), and Analysis Services will ignore everything from that point to the end of the line. Comments can appear before or after the text of the query and can even be inserted between lines of a query. You can also create multiple-line comments. Start the comment with a slash followed by an asterisk (**/***) and end the comment with an asterisk followed by a slash (***/**). Adding comments to a query is particularly helpful when you have a long query in which the logic can be difficult to follow.

6. Select the entire text of Query 1 and then click Execute on the toolbar. Highlighting only the MDX you want to execute allows Analysis Services to ignore any queries that are not selected. A single number without row or column headers will appear in the Results window.

   Neither the AdventureWorks cube nor the Sales perspective has a default measure. The number 214,378 represents the value of the Reseller Order Quantity measure, which is the first measure defined in the AdventureWorks cube.

You can create queries that are more interesting by adding sets of members to the column or row axis. A set must contain one or more members. You can create a set by enclosing a comma-separated list of tuples inside of braces, by using an MDX function that returns a set, or by using an MDX expression that Analysis Services can convert into a set. In the query, you must specify on which axis the set should appear.

In the following procedure, you will first create a simple query with a set that contains only one member and then gradually make it more complex. The first query illustrates how to use a specific measure. Reseller Order Quantity represents a single member of the Measures dimension, so the query you create in the following procedure contains a set with one member.

Create a query with rows and columns

1. In the Query Editor, position the cursor at the end of the last line of Query 1, press ENTER twice, and then enter the following MDX query:

```
-- Query 2
SELECT
  [Measures].[Reseller Order Quantity] ON COLUMNS
FROM
  [Sales];
```

2. Select the entire text of Query 2 and on the toolbar click Execute. Because you specified the name of a measure on the columns axis of the query, the results display a column header.

   You can add additional members to the column axis. If you have a single member on an axis, Analysis Services can infer that the member is a set. If you have more than one member, you need to explicitly create a set by enclosing the list of members in braces ({}). You will now create a query that contains a set with two members from the Measures dimension.

3. In the Query Editor, position the cursor at the end of the last line of Query 2, press ENTER twice, and then enter the following MDX query:

```
-- Query 3
SELECT
  {[Measures].[Reseller Sales Amount],[Measures].[Internet Sales Amount]} ON COLUMNS
FROM
  [Sales];
```

4. Select the entire text of Query 3 and then click Execute on the toolbar. The results display the measures in two columns.

   You learned about tuples in Chapter 6. The set on the column axis consists of two positions. Each position corresponds to a tuple, and each tuple contains a single member. If you want, you can add parentheses around each tuple, writing the set as {([Measures].[Reseller Sales Amount]), ([Measures].[Internet Sales Amount])} to show that each member is a separate tuple within the set. If the first tuple in a set consists of a single member, each subsequent tuple in that set must be a member of the same hierarchy.

   You can also add a set to the row axis. In MDX, if you create a query that has only one axis, it must be the column axis. If you create two axes, one must be the column axis and one must be the row axis, although it doesn't matter in which order they appear within the query.

   In the previous queries, you created a set by listing individual members of the Measures dimension. You can also create a set by using an MDX set function. In the next query, you will use the *MEMBERS* function, which returns all of the members from a hierarchy or a level.

5. In the Query Editor, position the cursor at the end of the last line of Query 3, press ENTER twice, and then enter the following MDX query:

```
-- Query 4
SELECT
   {([Measures].[Reseller Sales Amount]),([Measures].[Internet Sales Amount])} ON
COLUMNS
   ,NON EMPTY [Date].[Calendar Year].MEMBERS ON ROWS
FROM
   [Sales];
```

> **Note** Add the *NON EMPTY* keyword before the set on an axis to prevent an empty row or column from being returned by the query.

6. Select the entire text of Query 4 and then click Execute on the toolbar.

	Reseller Sales Amount	Internet Sales Amount
All	$80,450,597	$29,307,837
CY 2008	$8,065,435	$3,266,374
CY 2009	$24,144,430	$6,530,344
CY 2010	$32,202,669	$9,791,060
CY 2011	$16,038,063	$9,720,059

> **Note** The terms COLUMNS and ROWS are simply aliases for the true names of the axes, Axis(0) and Axis(1) respectively. The underlying names make it clearer to understand why a single-axis report must include a COLUMNS axis but not a ROW axis. Technically, an MDX query can have up to 128 axes, with aliases for the first five: COLUMNS, ROWS, PAGES, SECTIONS, and CHAPTERS.

On the row axis, the *MEMBERS* function displays only the members from the Calendar Year attribute hierarchy of the Date dimension. Even though the individual years are not indented below the All member, all the members of the Calendar Year hierarchy are in the set.

Because each dimension is composed of one or more attribute hierarchies, you must include both the dimension and hierarchy name when using the *MEMBERS* function. The exception is the Measures dimension, which does not contain a hierarchy.

You can filter the data in a query by including a set in the WHERE clause. In the following query you will add a WHERE clause to your query to limit the dataset returned.

Create a query with a WHERE clause

1. In the Query Editor, position the cursor at the end of the last line of Query 4, press ENTER twice, and then enter the following MDX query:

```
-- Query 5
SELECT
  {([Measures].[Reseller Sales Amount]),([Measures].[Internet Sales Amount])} ON
COLUMNS
  ,NON EMPTY [Date].[Calendar Year].MEMBERS ON ROWS
FROM
  [Sales]
WHERE
  {([Geography].[Country].&[United Kingdom])};
```

2. Select the entire text of Query 5 and then click Execute on the toolbar. Compared to Query 4, the results of this query show smaller amounts for Reseller Sales Amount and Internet Sales Amount, because only sales to the United Kingdom are displayed.

	Reseller Sales Amount	Internet Sales Amount
All	$4,279,009	$3,387,491
CY 2008	(null)	$291,591
CY 2009	$841,758	$591,587
CY 2010	$2,160,146	$1,298,249
CY 2011	$1,277,105	$1,206,065

3. Close SQL Server Management Studio.

In this section, you learned how to create a very basic MDX query. You can learn more about MDX in *Microsoft SQL Server 2008 MDX Step by Step* by Bryan Smith and C. Ryan Clay (Microsoft Press, 2009).

Accessing Analysis Services Using Excel 2007

You can use Analysis Services as a data source for the Office Excel 2007 PivotTable and PivotChart features. The Excel 2007 PivotTable feature allows you to create reports and cross-tab reports that will let you pivot, filter, add and remove dimensions, drill down, drill up, and drillthrough data. You can use the Excel 2007 PivotChart feature to create powerful data visualizations. Because most business users are already familiar with Excel, they can easily begin accessing data from Analysis Services.

Excel 2007 provides many more powerful features you can use to format and analyze data with PivotTable dynamic views than can be covered in this book. This section is limited to covering those features that are particularly important when you are using PivotTable with Analysis Services. In this section, you will create an Analysis Services data source and a basic PivotTable report. You will then learn how to do the following:

■ Improve the appearance of your report by hiding field headers and using the expand/collapse buttons.

■ View empty rows and columns.

■ Execute Analysis Services actions.

- Sort and filter data.

- Create a top 100 report.

- Display member properties.

- Display KPIs.

- View and modify data sources.

If you have not previously used Excel with Analysis Services, you will need to create an Office Data Connection (ODC) file using the Data Connection Wizard. When you complete the Data Connection Wizard, the Import Data dialog box appears, which you can then use to create a PivotTable report.

Create a dynamic view using the Excel 2007 PivotTable feature

1. On the Windows task bar, click Start, point to All Programs, expand the Microsoft Office folder, and then select Microsoft Office Excel 2007.

2. On the Office Ribbon, click the Data tab. In the Get External Data group, click From Other Sources and select From Analysis Services to open the Data Connection Wizard.

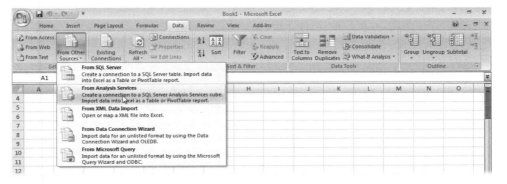

3. On the Connect To Database Server page, type **localhost** in the Server Name text box and verify that Use Windows Authentication has been selected. Click Next.

   The Select Database And Table page displays a list of all of the Analysis Services data-bases that exist on the server that you selected on the previous page and to which you have access. When you select a database, the page displays all of the cubes and per-spectives contained in that database. The Type column of the list indicates whether an item is a cube or a perspective.

4. On the Select Database And Table page, verify that AdventureWorks SSAS is selected in the Select The Database That Contains The Data You Want list and that the Connect To A Specific Cube Or Table check box is selected.

5. Select the Sales perspective from the list of cubes and perspectives. The Select Database And Table page should show that you are creating a connection to the Sales perspective in the AdventureWorks SSAS database.

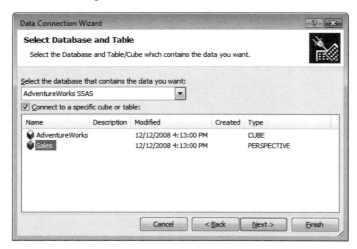

6. Click Next. On the last page of the wizard, you need to give the Office Data Connection file a file name and a friendly name that will be easy for users to understand. You will also have an opportunity to add a description and keywords that can be used to search for the file.

7. On the Save Data Connection File And Finish page, change the Description to **Sales perspective in the AdventureWorks cube on the local computer** and change the Friendly Name to **Sales Perspective**.

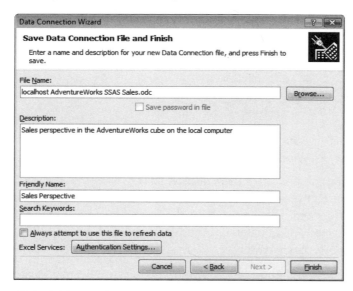

Click Finish. You have just created an Office Data Connection file (ODC). By default, these files are stored in a user's Documents\My Data Sources folder.

8. The Import Data dialog box appears, enabling you to create a PivotTable report or PivotTable and PivotChart dynamic views that are linked so that changes made in a

single Field List are applied to both the table and the chart. Or you can skip creating PivotTable or PivotChart dynamic views and only create the ODC file. The dialog box also lets you select where the data will be placed in the Excel workbook. By default, a PivotTable chart will be created in cell A1. In the Import Data dialog box, click OK.

A PivotTable report is added to the Sheet1 worksheet and the PivotTable Field List appears, by default, on the right side of the Excel window. The Fields section of the PivotTable Field List displays the measures and calculated measures, KPIs, and dimensions contained in the Analysis Services cube. Below the Fields section, the Layout section of the PivotTable Field List shows which measures and calculated measures are being displayed and which hierarchies have been placed on the rows, columns, and filter axes of the report.

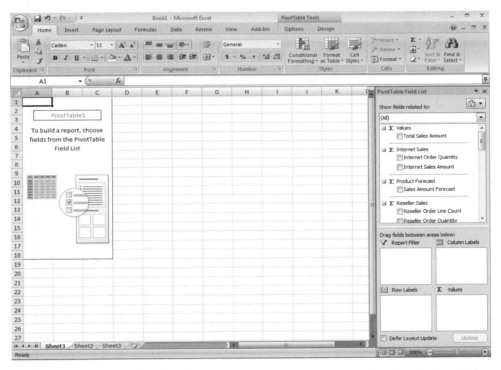

9. You can add items to the PivotTable report by selecting them in the PivotTable Field List. In the PivotTable Field List Fields section, select Reseller Sales Amount. The Reseller Sales Amount measure now appears in the PivotTable report and in the Values area of the Layout Section of the PivotTable Field List.

10. In the PivotTable Field List, locate the Date dimension and select the Date.Calendar Date hierarchy. By default, when you select a hierarchy, the hierarchy is placed on the rows axis of the PivotTable report, but because the value of the Date dimension *Type* property is Time, the Calendar Date hierarchy is placed on the column axis. The hierarchy also appears in the Column Labels area of the Layout section.

11. Locate the Product dimension and select the Product By Category hierarchy. The Product By Category hierarchy is placed on the rows axis of the report and in the Row Labels area of the Layout section. The PivotTable report should now look like this:

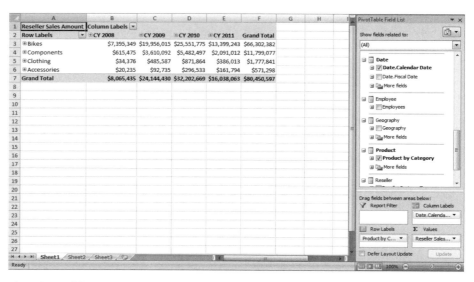

12. The PivotTable report contains Row Labels and Column Labels field headers that you can use to select, sort, and apply a filter to dimension members. In the report, expand the Row Labels list and clear the check boxes next to Clothing, Accessories, and Unknown. Click OK.

13. You can click the plus sign (+) buttons on the report to expand a parent hierarchy member and display its child members. Click the plus sign next to the Bikes member and the Components member. You have modified the PivotTable report so that it should now look like this:

Reseller Sales Amount	Column Labels				
Row Labels	⊿ ⊕CY 2008	⊕CY 2009	⊕CY 2010	⊕CY 2011	Grand Total
⊟Bikes	$7,395,349	$19,956,015	$25,551,775	$13,399,243	$66,302,382
⊕Mountain Bikes	$4,545,337	$9,190,838	$8,854,263	$3,902,247	$26,492,684
⊕Road Bikes	$2,850,012	$10,765,177	$11,294,381	$4,448,637	$29,358,207
⊕Touring Bikes			$5,403,131	$5,048,360	$10,451,490
⊟Components	$615,475	$3,610,092	$5,482,497	$2,091,012	$11,799,077
⊕Handlebars		$53,643	$88,711	$28,238	$170,591
⊕Bottom Brackets			$30,793	$21,034	$51,826
⊕Brakes			$45,187	$20,831	$66,019
⊕Chains			$5,686	$3,692	$9,378
⊕Cranksets			$124,249	$79,693	$203,943
⊕Derailleurs			$44,321	$25,888	$70,209
⊕Forks		$49,673	$28,259		$77,932
⊕Headsets		$35,932	$25,010		$60,942
⊕Mountain Frames	$371,588	$1,400,332	$2,067,909	$873,844	$4,713,672
⊕Pedals			$94,061	$53,423	$147,484
⊕Road Frames	$243,887	$1,618,392	$1,631,377	$356,197	$3,849,853
⊕Saddles			$37,832	$17,997	$55,829
⊕Touring Frames			$1,032,154	$610,174	$1,642,328
⊕Wheels		$452,122	$226,948		$679,070
Grand Total	$8,010,824	$23,566,107	$31,034,272	$15,490,255	$78,101,458

The field headers, expand/collapse buttons, and the PivotTable Field List detract from the appearance of the report. Fortunately, these can be hidden. However, when they are hidden, you can no longer use them to change your report. In the following procedure, you will learn how to hide the field headers, expand/collapse buttons, and the PivotTable Field List. You will then make the Field List visible and learn an alternative method for selecting dimension members and expanding and collapsing hierarchy parent members.

Hide field headers and expand/collapse buttons

1. On the PivotTable Tools Ribbon Options tab in the Show/Hide group, click Field List, click +/- Buttons, and then click Field Headers.

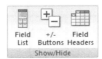

The PivotTable report now has a much cleaner, easier-to-read appearance.

	A	B	C	D	E	F
1	Reseller Sales Amount					
2		CY 2008	CY 2009	CY 2010	CY 2011	Grand Total
3	Bikes	$7,395,349	$19,956,015	$25,551,775	$13,399,243	$66,302,382
4	Mountain Bikes	$4,545,337	$9,190,838	$8,854,263	$3,902,247	$26,492,684
5	Road Bikes	$2,850,012	$10,765,177	$11,294,381	$4,448,637	$29,358,207
6	Touring Bikes			$5,403,131	$5,048,360	$10,451,490
7	Components	$615,475	$3,610,092	$5,482,497	$2,091,012	$11,799,077
8	Handlebars		$53,643	$88,711	$28,238	$170,591
9	Bottom Brackets			$30,793	$21,034	$51,826
10	Brakes			$45,187	$20,831	$66,019
11	Chains			$5,686	$3,692	$9,378
12	Cranksets			$124,249	$79,693	$203,943
13	Derailleurs			$44,321	$25,888	$70,209
14	Forks		$49,673	$28,259		$77,932
15	Headsets		$35,932	$25,010		$60,942
16	Mountain Frames	$371,588	$1,400,332	$2,067,909	$873,844	$4,713,672
17	Pedals			$94,061	$53,423	$147,484
18	Road Frames	$243,887	$1,618,392	$1,631,377	$356,197	$3,849,853
19	Saddles			$37,832	$17,997	$55,829
20	Touring Frames			$1,032,154	$610,174	$1,642,328
21	Wheels		$452,122	$226,948		$679,070
22	Grand Total	$8,010,824	$23,566,107	$31,034,272	$15,490,255	$78,101,458

You must display the PivotTable Field List to select the dimension members that appear on the rows and columns of your report.

2. In the Show/Hide group, click Field List. In the Fields section of the PivotTable Field List, point to the Product By Category hierarchy and click the triangle that appears on the right.

3. In the Select Field dialog box, select both Clothing and Accessories and click OK.

4. You can expand and collapse a parent hierarchy member using a shortcut menu or by double-clicking the member. In the PivotTable report, right-click Accessories, point to Expand/Collapse, and select Expand.

5. Double-click Clothing. The report now looks like this:

	A	B	C	D	E	F
1	**Reseller Sales Amount**					
2		**CY 2008**	**CY 2009**	**CY 2010**	**CY 2011**	**Grand Total**
3	**Bikes**	$7,395,349	$19,956,015	$25,551,775	$13,399,243	$66,302,382
4	Mountain Bikes	$4,545,337	$9,190,838	$8,854,263	$3,902,247	$26,492,684
5	Road Bikes	$2,850,012	$10,765,177	$11,294,381	$4,448,637	$29,358,207
6	Touring Bikes			$5,403,131	$5,048,360	$10,451,490
7	**Components**	$615,475	$3,610,092	$5,482,497	$2,091,012	$11,799,077
8	Handlebars		$53,643	$88,711	$28,238	$170,591
9	Bottom Brackets			$30,793	$21,034	$51,826
10	Brakes			$45,187	$20,831	$66,019
11	Chains			$5,686	$3,692	$9,378
12	Cranksets			$124,249	$79,693	$203,943
13	Derailleurs			$44,321	$25,888	$70,209
14	Forks		$49,673	$28,259		$77,932
15	Headsets		$35,932	$25,010		$60,942
16	Mountain Frames	$371,588	$1,400,332	$2,067,909	$873,844	$4,713,672
17	Pedals			$94,061	$53,423	$147,484
18	Road Frames	$243,887	$1,618,392	$1,631,377	$356,197	$3,849,853
19	Saddles			$37,832	$17,997	$55,829
20	Touring Frames			$1,032,154	$610,174	$1,642,328
21	Wheels		$452,122	$226,948		$679,070
22	**Clothing**	$34,376	$485,587	$871,864	$386,013	$1,777,841
23	Bib-Shorts		$101,863	$64,877		$166,740
24	Caps	$2,687	$9,388	$13,801	$5,666	$31,541
25	Gloves		$88,796	$102,156	$16,823	$207,775
26	Jerseys	$28,256	$110,244	$290,005	$150,805	$579,309
27	Shorts		$49,262	$179,301	$113,640	$342,203

Your report now displays row and column axes. You can also add a hierarchy to the filter axis. When you apply a filter, you may significantly reduce the amount of data that appears on the report. This may cause some of the rows or columns of the report to be empty.

By default, the PivotTable report hides a row (or column) if there are no values for the entire row (or column). This is often very helpful, because you usually don't need to view an empty row or column, and a report with many empty rows and columns consumes a lot of space and can be difficult to read. Sometimes, however, the most important information conveyed by a report is the dimension member associated with an empty row or column. For example, in the next procedure, you will create a report that allows you to select a Reseller and then display the products that the Reseller has not ordered.

Add a filter and display empty rows and columns

1. In the PivotTable Field List, locate the Reseller dimension folder, expand the More Fields folder, right-click the Reseller hierarchy, and select Add To Report Filter.

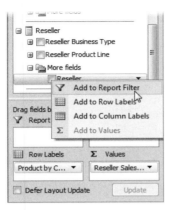

The Reseller hierarchy is added to the Report Filter area and appears in the Report Filter area of the Layout section of the PivotTable Field List.

2. In the Report Filter area, expand the Reseller list, expand the All member, and select Active Life Toys. Click OK.

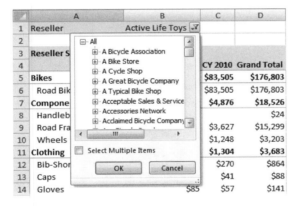

Many subcategories no longer appear on the report because Active Life Toys has not ordered these products. CY 2008 and CY 2011 no longer appear on the report because they did not make any orders during these two years.

3. On the PivotTable Tools Ribbon Options tab in the PivotTable group, expand the Options list and select Options.

4. In the PivotTable Options dialog box, click the Display tab and select Show Items With No Data On Rows and then select Show Items With No Data On Columns. Notice that the dialog box displays the Show Expand/Collapse Buttons option and the Display Field Captions And Filter Drop Downs option. These options are toggled on and off when you click the +/- Buttons and Field Headers buttons on the Office Ribbon.

5. Click OK. The report now displays all of the product subcategories, enabling you to identify the products that Active Life Toys has not purchased.

	A	B	C	D	E	F	G
1	Reseller	Active Life Toys ↴					
2							
3	**Reseller Sales Amount**						
4		CY 2008	CY 2009	CY 2010	CY 2011	Unknown	Grand Total
5	**Bikes**		$93,298	$83,505			$176,803
6	Mountain Bikes						
7	Road Bikes		$93,298	$83,505			$176,803
8	Touring Bikes						
9	**Components**		$13,650	$4,876			$18,526
10	Handlebars		$24				$24
11	Bottom Brackets						
12	Brakes						
13	Chains						
14	Cranksets						
15	Derailleurs						
16	Forks						

Note Displaying empty rows and columns will not display combinations of dimension members that do not exist in the dimension. For example, if the Product dimension doesn't contain any White bicycles, displaying empty rows on a report with the Product dimension Category and Color attribute hierarchies on rows does not cause the combination of Bikes and White to appear on the report.

To execute an Analysis Services Action in an Excel PivotTable report, you right-click a cell, point to Additional Actions, and then click the action that you want to execute. If no action has been defined for the cell or if the criterion specified in the action's *Condition* property is not met, No Actions Defined appears on the cell's shortcut menu and you won't be able to execute an action.

The Excel PivotTable also has a built-in action called Show Details that can be executed from cells that contain a measure. If you select Show Details from the cell's shortcut menu, Excel executes a drillthrough action that requests the key attribute of every dimension related to the current measure group and all of the measure group's measures.

In Chapter 10, you created the Internet Search URL action and defined it on the Product By Category hierarchy. You also created the Reseller Sales Details drillthrough action and defined it on the Reseller Sales measure group. In the next procedure, you will execute these two actions and the Excel Show Details action.

Execute Analysis Services actions

1. In the PivotTable report, right-click a product category or subcategory, point to Additional Actions, and select Internet Search. Internet Explorer opens with a Live Search page similar to this.

2. Close Internet Explorer and switch back to Excel.

3. Right-click Reseller Sales Amount for Road Bikes in CY 2009, point to Additional Actions, and select Reseller Sales Details. A new worksheet containing the results of the drillthrough action will be added to your Excel workbook. This new worksheet contains the columns you selected when you created the Reseller Sales Details action.

4. Select worksheet Sheet1 to switch back to the worksheet that contains the PivotTable report.

5. In the PivotTable report, right-click the cell at the intersection of Road Bikes and CY 2009 and select Show Details.

   The Excel PivotTable executes a drillthrough action that requests the key attribute of every dimension related to the Reseller Sales measure group and all of its measures. This data is inserted as a new worksheet in your Excel workbook.

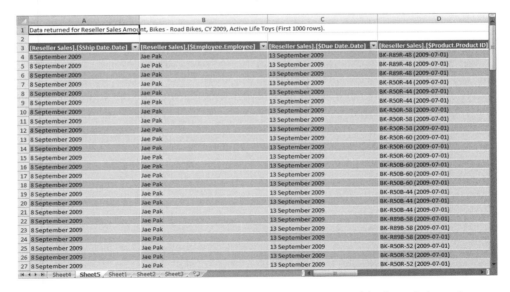

In the next procedure, you will create a new PivotTable report on a blank worksheet that displays the Adventure Works company's top 100 Internet customers. Creating the report requires two steps. First you will apply a filter that selects the top 100 rows, and then you will sort the rows by Internet Sales Amount in descending order.

Create a top 100 report

1. Select worksheet Sheet2 and then click the Data tab on the Office Ribbon.

2. You have already created a connection to the Sales perspective of the Analysis Services AdventureWorks cube. Now you can reuse that connection. In the Get External Data group, click Existing Connections to open the Existing Connections dialog box. The friendly name, Sales Perspective, and the description of the connection that you created earlier appear in the Connections In This Workbook and Connection Files On This Computer sections of the dialog box.

3. In the Existing Connections dialog box, select the Sales Perspective connection and click Open.

4. In the Import Data dialog box, click OK.

5. A new PivotTable has been added to worksheet Sheet2. Now add the Internet Sales Amount measure and the Calendar Date hierarchy to the report. In the PivotTable Field List, select Internet Sales Amount. Locate the Date dimension and select the Date. Calendar Date hierarchy.

   The natural thing to do next is to add the Customer hierarchy to the report. However, because the Customer hierarchy contains a large number of members, it is better to first apply the top 100 filter and then add the hierarchy to the report.

6. Locate the Customer dimension, expand the More Fields folder, point to the Customer attribute, and click the triangle that appears on the right. A shortcut menu containing Label Filters and Value Filters items appears. The Label Filters item allows you to create filters based on the attributes in the Customers dimension. The Value Filters item allows you to create filters based on the measures in the cube. Point to and hover your mouse over the Labels Filters and Value Filters items to see the variety of filtering options that are available.

7. Point to Value Filters in the shortcut menu and select Top 10.

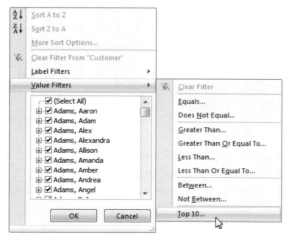

The Top 10 Filter dialog box contains four lists that let you configure the filter. In the fourth list, you select a measure. A ranking based on this measure is assigned to the members of the attribute. In the first list, you can choose to the show the top-ranked or the bottom-ranked members. The second list lets you set the threshold. In the third list, you can select Items, Percent, or Sum. If you select Items, the filter returns a count of members equal to the threshold. If you select Sum, the filter returns members until the cumulative total of the measure is at least as great as the threshold. If you select Percent, the filter returns members until the cumulative total of the measure reaches the threshold percent of the grand total of the measure. Note that the measure you select in the Top 10 filter does not have to be one of the measures being displayed on the report.

8. In the Top 10 Filter dialog box, change 10 to **100**. Click OK.

9. Now that you've applied a filter to the Customer hierarchy, you can add it to the report. Right-click the Customer attribute and select Add To Row Labels. The top 100 Internet customers now appear on the report, but they are sorted by name, not by sales amount. The Top 10 filter assigned a ranking to each customer, but it did not sort them. You will need sort the customers.

10. In the Field section of the Field List, point to the Customer attribute, click the triangle that appears on the right, and select More Sort Options.

11. In the Sort dialog box, select Descending (Z To A) By and then select Internet Sales Amount from the list.

    By default, the members are sorted by the Grand Total column of the measure that you select. However, you can choose to sort by a different column. In your report, sort the customers by the value in the column containing CY 2011 data.

12. Click More Options. In the More Sort Options dialog box, select Values In Selected Column. Change the value of the selected column from F3 to **E3**. Click OK.

13. In the Sort dialog box, click OK. The report is now sorted in descending order by the value of CY 2011 Internet sales.

	A	B	C	D	E	F
1	Internet Sales Amount	Column Labels				
2	Row Labels	⊕CY 2008	⊕CY 2009	⊕CY 2010	⊕CY 2011	Grand Total
3	Turner, Jordan			$4,448	$6,752	$11,201
4	Zheng, Lacey			$5,105	$6,143	$11,248
5	Lopez, Marco			$4,401	$6,067	$10,468
6	Gray, Ariana			$4,551	$5,978	$10,529
7	Munoz, Larry			$5,484	$5,584	$11,068
8	Cai, Lisa			$6,453	$5,016	$11,469
9	Vazquez, Frank		$2,182	$2,345	$4,996	$9,523
10	Tang, Katrina		$2,443	$2,440	$4,913	$9,796
11	Goel, Colleen		$2,182	$2,335	$4,905	$9,422
12	Kapoor, Ronald		$2,182	$2,370	$4,900	$9,452
13	Straatsma, Gerrit		$2,443	$2,295	$4,876	$9,615
14	Anand, Clarence		$3,375	$2,320	$4,871	$10,566
15	Vazquez, Ricky		$3,375	$2,335	$4,870	$10,580
16	Rubio, Latasha		$3,375	$2,330	$4,870	$10,575

Now that you have identified the Adventure Works company's top 100 Internet customers, you would like to be able to contact them with a special offer. You want to add each customer's telephone number and e-mail address to the report. However, if you look in the Field List, you can see that these attributes are not available. The Customer dimension does contain Email Address and Phone attributes, but because these are high-cardinality attributes, the value of the *AttributeHierarchyEnabled* property has been set to *False*, and the attributes are available only as member properties. In the next procedure, you will learn how to add member properties to a report.

> **Tip** If you point to a dimension member in an Excel 2007 PivotTable report and pause for a moment, a tooltip appears, displaying all of the member's member properties.

Display member properties

1. Select the Row Labels cell or one of the cells containing a customer name. On the Office PivotTable Tools Ribbon, Options tab, in the Tools group, expand the OLAP Tools list and select Property Fields.

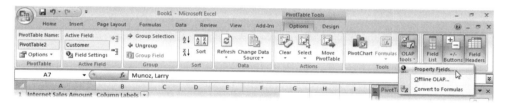

2. In the Choose Property Fields For Dimension dialog box, select Email Address and click the Add button (>), then select Phone and click the Add button (>) again.

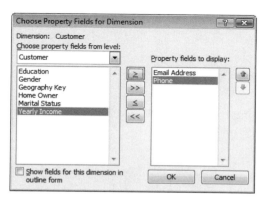

3. Click OK. The report now shows each customer's e-mail address and telephone number.

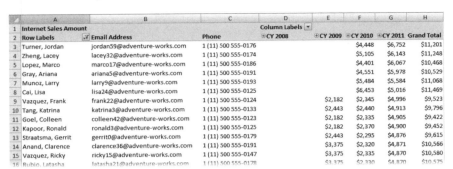

	Email Address	Phone	CY 2008	CY 2009	CY 2010	CY 2011	Grand Total
1	Internet Sales Amount		Column Labels				
2 Row Labels	Email Address	Phone	CY 2008	CY 2009	CY 2010	CY 2011	Grand Total
3 Turner, Jordan	jordan59@adventure-works.com	1 (11) 500 555-0176			$4,448	$6,752	$11,201
4 Zheng, Lacey	lacey32@adventure-works.com	1 (11) 500 555-0174			$5,105	$6,143	$11,248
5 Lopez, Marco	marco17@adventure-works.com	1 (11) 500 555-0186			$4,401	$6,067	$10,468
6 Gray, Ariana	ariana5@adventure-works.com	1 (11) 500 555-0191			$4,551	$5,978	$10,529
7 Munoz, Larry	larry9@adventure-works.com	1 (11) 500 555-0193			$5,484	$5,584	$11,068
8 Cai, Lisa	lisa24@adventure-works.com	1 (11) 500 555-0125			$6,453	$5,016	$11,469
9 Vazquez, Frank	frank22@adventure-works.com	1 (11) 500 555-0124		$2,182	$2,345	$4,996	$9,523
10 Tang, Katrina	katrina3@adventure-works.com	1 (11) 500 555-0133		$2,443	$2,440	$4,913	$9,796
11 Goel, Colleen	colleen42@adventure-works.com	1 (11) 500 555-0123		$2,182	$2,335	$4,905	$9,422
12 Kapoor, Ronald	ronald3@adventure-works.com	1 (11) 500 555-0125		$2,182	$2,370	$4,900	$9,452
13 Straatsma, Gerrit	gerrit0@adventure-works.com	1 (11) 500 555-0179		$2,443	$2,295	$4,876	$9,615
14 Anand, Clarence	clarence36@adventure-works.com	1 (11) 500 555-0191		$3,375	$2,320	$4,871	$10,566
15 Vazquez, Ricky	ricky15@adventure-works.com	1 (11) 500 555-0147		$3,375	$2,335	$4,870	$10,580
16 Rubio, Latasha	latasha21@adventure-works.com	1 (11) 500 555-0178		$3,375	$2,330	$4,870	$10,575

You can display an Analysis Services KPI in an Excel PivotTable dynamic view. Each KPI is composed of Value and Goal items that are numeric values and Status and Trend items that are graphical indicators. The KPIs in a cube are displayed in the PivotTable Field List. Like measures, KPIs can only be added to the Values area of a PivotTable report. In the next procedure, you will create a new PivotTable report on a blank worksheet and then add the Sales Amount Forecast KPI to the report.

Display KPIs

1. Select worksheet Sheet3 and then click the Data tab on the Office Ribbon.

2. In the Get External Data group, click Existing Connections. In the Existing Connections dialog box, select the Sales Perspective connection and then click Open.

3. In the Import Data dialog box, click OK.

4. You can now add the KPI to the PivotTable report by selecting the individual KPI items in the Field List. In the Field List, locate and expand the KPIs folder, expand the Sales Amount Forecast KPI, and select Value (Total Sales Amount), Goal, Status, and Trend.

By default, the column names are the combined names of the KPI and the individual item, such as Sales Amount Forecast, Sales Amount Forecast Goal, Sales Amount Forecast Status, and Sales Amount Forecast Trend. These names are long and consume a lot of space. You can improve the appearance of the report by renaming the columns.

5. In the Field List Layout section, click Sales Amount Forecast and select Value Field Settings.

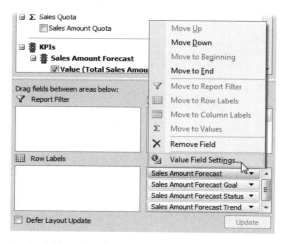

6. In the Value Field Settings dialog box, change the value of Custom Name to **Total Sales Amount**. Click OK.

7. Repeat steps 5 and 6 to rename the following KPI items:

Value	New Name
Sales Amount Forecast Goal	Goal
Sales Amount Forecast Status	Status
Sales Amount Forecast Trend	Trend

8. Displaying a KPI by itself is usually not very useful. Most likely, you will want to slice the KPI by the dimensions contained in the cube. In the Field section of the Field List locate the Date dimension, right-click the Date.Calendar Date hierarchy, and select Add To Row Labels.

9. In the PivotTable report, right-click CY 2008, point to Expand/Collapse, and select Expand Entire Field. The report now shows the Sales Amount Forecast KPI by Quarter.

Row Labels	Values Total Sales Amount	Goal	Status	Trend
⊟ CY 2008	$11,331,809	$9,513,000	✓	⬆
⊞ CY 2008 Qtr 3	$4,647,157	$3,886,000	✓	⬆
⊞ CY 2008 Qtr 4	$6,684,652	$5,627,000	✓	⬇
⊟ CY 2009	$30,674,773	$29,009,000	✓	⬇
⊞ CY 2009 Qtr 1	$5,860,884	$4,750,000	✓	⬆
⊞ CY 2009 Qtr 2	$6,167,833	$5,068,000	✓	⬇
⊞ CY 2009 Qtr 3	$10,277,073	$10,537,000	◐	⬇
⊞ CY 2009 Qtr 4	$8,368,983	$8,654,000	✗	⬇
⊟ CY 2010	$41,993,730	$38,782,000	✓	⬆
⊞ CY 2010 Qtr 1	$6,679,874	$5,913,000	✓	⬆
⊞ CY 2010 Qtr 2	$8,357,875	$8,039,000	✓	⬇
⊞ CY 2010 Qtr 3	$13,670,537	$13,733,000	◐	⬇
⊞ CY 2010 Qtr 4	$13,285,444	$11,097,000	✓	⬆
⊟ CY 2011	$25,758,122	$18,410,000	✓	⬆
⊞ CY 2011 Qtr 1	$11,386,315	$8,051,000	✓	⬆
⊞ CY 2011 Qtr 2	$14,371,807	$10,359,000	✓	⬇
⊞ CY 2011 Qtr 3			✓	⬇
⊞ CY 2011 Qtr 4			✓	⇨
⊟ Unknown			✓	⬇
⊞ Unknown			✓	⇨
Grand Total	$109,758,434	$95,714,000	✓	⬆

When you create an Excel PivotTable report that uses Analysis Services data, Excel reads the information that it needs to connect to Analysis Services from an Office Data Connection file and stores the information in the Excel workbook. The connection information is not displayed on the PivotTable report, so if you want to know the data source of the report, you need to know how to view the connection information stored in the workbook. You may also want to change this connection information. For example, you may want to change the report so that it retrieves data from an Analysis Services database located on a different server. Finally, when the information in an Office Data Connection file becomes out of date, you will want to update or delete the ODC file.

In the next procedure, you will view and update the connection information in an Excel workbook. You will save the changes to an ODC file and then learn how to delete an out-of-date ODC file.

View and modify data connections

1. On the PivotTable Tools Options tab in the Data group, expand the Change Data Source list and select Connection Properties. The Connection Properties dialog box appears and displays the name and description of the connection that the PivotTable report is using to access data in Analysis Services. The Usage tab contains properties that allow you to configure when the PivotTable report's data gets refreshed, whether formatting information from Analysis Services will be applied to the data in the report, and the maximum number of records that will be returned when you execute the built-in Show Details drillthrough command.

2. In the Connection Properties dialog box, change the Connection Name to **AdventureWorks Cube** and the Description to **AdventureWorks cube on the local computer**.

3. Click the Definition tab. The Definition tab's *Connection File* property shows the location of the ODC file that is the source of this connection's information. You can click Browse to retrieve connection information from a different ODC file. You can change the Analysis Services database that the PivotTable connects to by modifying the Data Source and Initial Catalog properties in the Connection String text box. A connection string is simply a string of text that specifies certain data source connection properties, usually in the form Property=Value, separated by semicolons. Data Source is the server and Initial Catalog is the database. You can change the cube or perspective by modifying the *Command Text* property.

4. Change the value of the *Command Text* property to **AdventureWorks** to connect to the full cube, instead of just the Sales perspective. The Connection Properties dialog box should look like this:

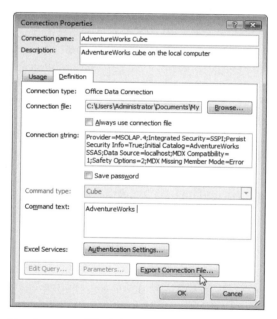

You have modified the connection information in the Excel workbook, but you have not yet changed the ODC file. If you want to save the connection information without changing the ODC file, click OK. Because the connection information in the workbook will be different from information in the ODC file, the link between the workbook and ODC file will be broken. If you want to change the ODC file, you must export the information.

5. Click Export Connection File. The File Save dialog box appears. You can update the ODC file you used to create the PivotTable report by saving to the same location and with the same file name, or you can create a new ODC file by changing either the loca-

tion or file name. Because you changed the connection information so that it references the AdventureWorks cube, in the next step you'll change the file name to create
a new ODC file.

6. Change the file name to **localhost AdventureWorks SSAS AdventureWorks.odc** and
click Save.

7. In the Connection Properties dialog box, click OK. The PivotTable report is now con-
nected to the AdventureWorks cube. Because the AdventureWorks cube contains
everything in the Sales perspective, the PivotTable report will not change. However,
in the Field List you will be able to see measures, KPIs, and dimensions that are in the
AdventureWorks cube but not in the Sales perspective.

> **Tip** If an ODC file becomes outdated, you may want to delete it so that nobody tries to
> create a PivotTable report using out-of-date connection information. You can't delete an
> ODC file using Excel, however. Instead, use Windows Explorer to browse to the folder con-
> taining the ODC file (default folder is Documents\My Data Sources) and delete the file.

8. Close Microsoft Excel. Save the file as **SSAS Reports.xlsx**.

Creating Reporting Services Reports

You can create Reporting Services reports that use Analysis Services data. Because SQL Server
2008 Reporting Services is an enterprise reporting solution, your organization's report developers will be able to create reports from Analysis Services data that can then be distributed
to individuals throughout your organization or accessed on demand through a Web browser.

Although Reporting Services provides many features to manage enterprise-scale reporting requirements, Reporting Services reports are not quite as flexible as the Excel 2007
PivotTable and PivotChart features. In a Reporting Service report, you can filter, drill down,
drill up, and drillthrough to other reports, but you can't pivot data and you can't add and
remove dimensions from the rows and columns of the report. If you want to give business
users more reporting flexibility, you can create a Report Model that uses Analysis Services
data and users can then create their own reports using Report Builder.

In this section, you will create a Reporting Services report that connects to the
AdventureWorks SSAS database. When you create the report, you will use the Reporting
Services graphical Query Designer to create the MDX query that the report will execute to
retrieve data from Analysis Services. You will then learn how to use the Query Designer in
Query mode to modify the MDX query.

Before you can create a report, you must create a Reporting Services project. BIDS allows you
to create multiple projects in a single solution, enabling you to keep all of the code related to
a solution in a single location. In the next procedure, you will add a Reporting Services project to the AdventureWorks BI solution.

Create a Reporting Services project

1. Switch back to BIDS and close any open designer windows. In Solution Explorer, collapse any expanded folders.

2. On the File menu, point to New and select Project.

3. In the Templates pane in the New Project dialog box, select Report Server Project.

4. Change the name of the project to **AdventureWorks SSRS**.

5. In the Solution list, select Add To Solution. By default, BIDS will create a new solution for the Reporting Services project, so you must change the value of the *Solution* property so that the new project is added to the solution you already are working on. When you select Add To Solution, BIDS changes the value of the Location text box so that the Reporting Services project will be saved to the same folder that contains the already existing AdventureWorks SSAS Analysis Services project.

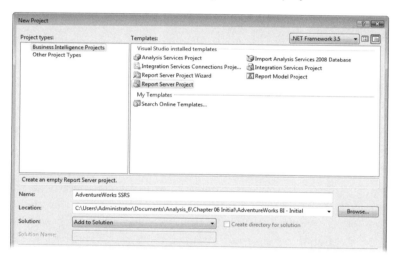

6. Click OK. The AdventureWorks SSRS project now appears below the AdventureWorks SSAS project in Solution Explorer. Because the solution now contains two projects, the AdventureWorks BI solution is now visible as the first item in Solution Explorer.

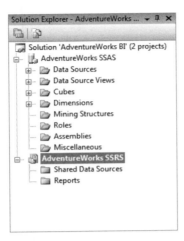

Now that you have created a Reporting Services project, you are ready to create a report. In the following procedure, you will create a Reporting Services report using the Report Wizard. First the wizard will guide you through steps to create a connection to Analysis Services, then you will use Query builder to select the data you want to display in the report, and finally you will apply a report template and arrange the data on the rows and columns of the report.

Create a Reporting Services report

1. In Solution Explorer, right-click Reports and select Add New Report.

2. On the Welcome To The Report Wizard page, click Next.

3. On the Select The Data Source page of the wizard, you provide the information Reporting Services needs to locate and connect to the AdventureWorks SSAS database. First change the name of the new data source to **AdventureWorks SSAS**.

4. In the Type list, select Microsoft SQL Server Analysis Services and then click Edit.

5. In the Connection Properties dialog box, enter **localhost** as the Server Name and from the Select Or Enter A Database Name list, select AdventureWorks SSAS. The Select The Data Source page should look like the following image.

6. Click OK.

7. Click Next. On the Design The Query page, click Query Builder. The Query Builder opens in Design mode. Design mode provides a graphical query designer that is very similar to the Browser tab of the BIDS Cube Designer. In the next few steps, you will design a query that retrieves the product category and subcategory, year, and total sales data from the AdventureWorks cube.

8. Drag the Product dimension from the Metadata pane to the Data pane (the area marked Drag Levels Or Measures Here To Add To The Query). In the Data pane, right-click the Product column and select Delete Product. The Data pane will display a message that says No Rows Found. Click To Execute The Query. Don't worry—as soon as you add a measure to the Data pane, the query will return data.

9. Expand the Date dimension, expand the Date.Calendar Year hierarchy, and drag the Calendar Year level from the Metadata pane to the Data pane.

10. Expand the Measures folder and drag Total Sales Amount from the Metadata pane to the Data pane. The query now returns data and should look like the following image.

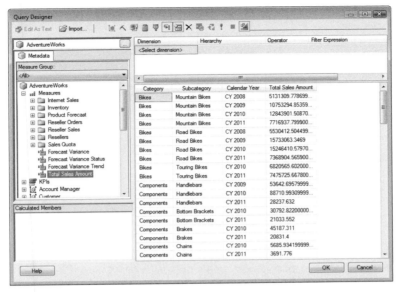

11. Click OK. The Design The Query page now displays the MDX query that you created using the Query Designer. This query appears more complicated than the queries you created in the section titled "Creating MDX Queries" earlier in this chapter, because the Query Designer is explicitly requesting dimension and cell properties.

    Now that you have created an MDX query, the wizard will guide you through arranging the data on the rows and columns of the report and selecting a report template.

12. On the Design The Query page, click Next.

13. On the Select The Report Type page, select Matrix and click Next.

14. On the Design The Matrix page, select both Category and Subcategory and then click Rows. Select Calendar_Year and click Columns. Select Total_Sales_Amount and click Details, and then select Enable Drilldown. When drilldown is enabled, only the first attribute on rows and columns will be displayed when the user opens the report. The user can then expand these attributes to display more granular detail. The Design The Matrix page should look like the following image.

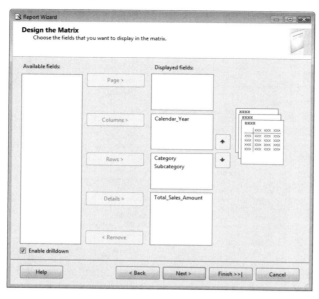

15. Click Next. On the Choose The Matrix Style page, select the Slate style templates, and click Next.

16. On the Completing The Wizard page, change the name of the report to **Product by Year**. In the lower-left corner of the page, select Preview Report and then click Finish. You report will be displayed on the Preview tab of the Report Designer. Because you enabled drilldown, the product categories are collapsed and product subcategories are not visible.

17. Expand the Bikes category. The Report Designer should look like this:

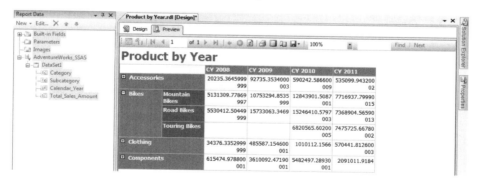

You have used the Query Designer's graphical tools to create the MDX query that retrieves the data displayed in the report. You can also create a report and directly enter the MDX query text, or you can modify the MDX query text of an existing report. In the next procedure, you will learn how to use the Query Designer in Query mode to modify the text of the MDX query. You will change the MDX query so that it also returns product names.

Important If you rename or delete attributes that already appear on the report, your changes to the MDX query will break the report.

Modify the MDX query

1. In the Report Designer, click the Design tab. In the Report Data window, right-click DataSet1 and select Query. The Query Designer dialog box opens in Design mode. To edit the text of the MDX query, you must change the Query Designer from Design mode to Query mode.

2. On the Query Designer toolbar, click the Design Mode button.

3. In the Query pane, select the MDX query and press DELETE. Enter the following query:

```
SELECT
  NON EMPTY { [Measures].[Total Sales Amount] } ON COLUMNS
  ,NON EMPTY { ([Product].[Product by Category].[Product].ALLMEMBERS
    * [Date].[Calendar Year].[Calendar Year].ALLMEMBERS ) } ON ROWS
FROM
  [AdventureWorks]
```

 Note You can copy the query from the file C:\Microsoft Press\Analysis Services 2008 SBS \Chapter 11\MDX\Report.mdx.

4. On the Query Designer toolbar, click the Execute Query button or, in the Data pane, click Click To Execute The Query. The query results now include a column containing product names.

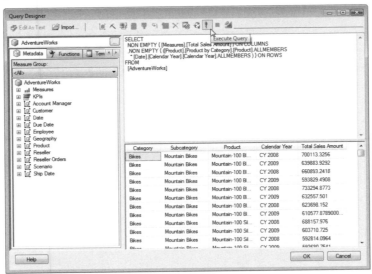

5. On the Query Designer toolbar, click Design Mode. If you switch from Query mode back to Design mode, all of the changes you made while the designer was in Query mode will be lost. The following warning will appear.

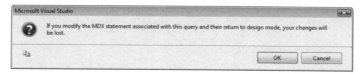

6. Click Cancel. In the Query Designer, click OK. In the Report Data window, you can see that DataSet1 now includes Product.

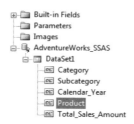

7. Drag Product from DataSet1 to below matrix1_Subcategory in the Row Groups area of the Grouping pane.

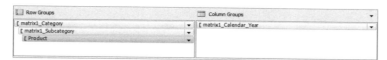

Product will be added to the report as a column to the left of the Subcategory column.

8. Click the Preview tab and expand the Bikes category. When you expand the Bikes category, both the Subcategory and Product columns appear. You need to configure the report so that you have to expand the Subcategory column to display the Product column.

9. Click the Design tab. In the Row Groups area, right-click Product and select Group Properties. In the Group Properties dialog box, select Visibility. On the Visibility page, select Hide, select Display Can Be Toggled By This Report Item, and then select Subcategory from the list of report items.

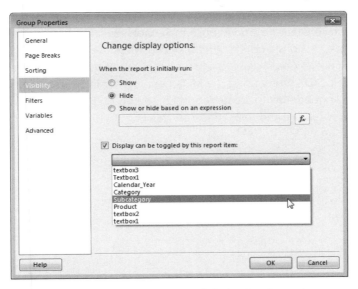

10. Click OK. In the Report Designer, click the Preview tab.

11. Expand the Bikes category and then expand the Mountain Bikes subcategory. Your report should now look like this:

Product by Year

		Product	CY 2008	CY 2009	CY 2010	CY 2011
⊞ Accessories			20235.3646	92735.3533999 998	590242.5866	535099.943199 998
⊟ Bikes	⊟ Mountain Bikes	Mountain-100 Black, 38	700113.3256	639883.9292		
		Mountain-100 Black, 42	660893.2418	593829.4908		
		Mountain-100 Black, 44	733294.8773	632557.501		
		Mountain-100 Black, 48		623698.152	610577.878900 001	
		Mountain-100 Silver, 38	688157.976	603710.725		

12. From the File menu, select Save All and then close BIDS. You may also close SQL Server Management Studio.

In this section, you have learned how to create a Reporting Services report that uses an Analysis Services data source. You can greatly improve the appearance of the report by applying additional formatting to the columns and values, but covering those topics is beyond the scope of this book. You can learn much more about creating reports and using Reporting Services enterprise features in *Microsoft SQL Server 2008 Reporting Services Step by Step* by Stacia Misner (Microsoft Press, 2009).

In this chapter, you learned about retrieving data from Analysis Services using MDX queries, the Excel 2007 PivotTable feature, and Reporting Services. Because a cube can contain many dimensions, measures, actions, and KPIs that may overwhelm some users, you first created a perspective that only allowed access to a limited number of these items. You then learned how to create a basic MDX query using the MDX query editor in SQL Server Management Studio. Finally, you learned how to create reports based on Analysis Services data using the Excel 2007 PivotTable feature and Reporting Services.

Chapter 12
Implementing Security

In this chapter, you will learn how to:

- Grant server and database-level administrative rights.

- Control access to data at the cube, dimension, and cell levels.

Your Analysis Services database has been designed to provide you valuable insight into your business. As such, it represents a sensitive source of information—one that needs to be properly secured.

Properly implemented security ensures administrators have just those permissions they require to perform their duties and end users have access only to the data appropriate to their responsibilities within the business. In this chapter, you will be introduced to the Analysis Services role-based security model and will employ server and database-level roles to configure appropriate access.

Understanding Roles

Analysis Services manages access to the various objects under its control. These objects include databases, dimensions, and cubes as well as the configuration of the Analysis Services service itself. Through roles, various rights to these objects are associated with users. Users may belong to one or more roles, accumulating the rights associated with each role.

Membership in Analysis Services roles is restricted to valid Windows users and groups. This allows Analysis Services to take advantage of the robust security infrastructure provided by Windows as well as the policies and practices around this infrastructure that are already in place in many organizations.

As a general best practice, we recommend that you assign membership in Analysis Services roles to domain-level Windows groups. For the purposes of the exercises in this chapter, however, you will violate this recommendation and employ a local Windows group. After you have completed the exercises in the chapter, we encourage you to remove this local group from your system.

Create a local Windows group

1. On the Windows task bar, click the Start button to open the Start menu.

2. From the Start menu, right-click Computer and select Manage from the shortcut menu to launch the Computer Management console. If you receive a User Account Control

prompt, press Continue to proceed. The Computer Management console is an interface providing administrative access to many of the more frequently managed aspects of your computer. These include local Windows users and groups.

3. Under System Tools on the left side of the Computer Management console, locate the item labeled Local Users And Groups.

4. Click the triangular symbol to the left of this item to expand it, exposing the Users And Groups folders. The folders under the Local Users And Groups item represent the collection of Windows users and groups managed by the local system. Through these folders, you can add new local users and groups.

5. Right-click the Groups folder and select New Group from the shortcut menu to open the New Group dialog box.

6. In the New Group dialog box, enter **SsasUsers** for the Group Name.

7. Click the Create button to create the SsasUsers group and then click the Close button to return to the Computer Management console. A local Windows group named SsasUsers is now in place on your computer. You will assign this group membership to various Analysis Services roles in exercises throughout this chapter. Individual Windows users assigned membership within the SsasUsers group, of which there are currently none, would obtain access to Analysis Services through roles associated with this group. You can now close the Computer Management console, though you will want to return to it after you complete this chapter to remove the SsasUsers group from your computer.

Securing Administrative Access

Within Analysis Services, administrative rights are assigned at two levels. The broadest administrative rights are granted through the built-in server role. More limited rights are assigned through custom database roles. In the sections that follow, you will explore the use of these roles to assign appropriate administrative access within Analysis Services.

Assigning Server-Level Administrative Access

Analysis Services comes preconfigured with a single, server-level role. This role, referred to as the *server role*, is the only server-level role permitted within Analysis Services, and it cannot be dropped or modified beyond changes to its membership.

The server role has full administrative rights within Analysis Services, permitting members of the role to create, alter, or drop any object hosted by the server and to access any data associated with these objects. Members of the server role may also alter server-level configuration settings and start traces as described in Chapter 16, "Advanced Monitoring and Management Tools." These rights are highly permissive, so membership in the server role should be limited to those persons with ultimate responsibility for the integrity of the Analysis Services service.

In the following exercise, you will use SQL Server Management Studio to assign membership within the server role.

Assign membership to the server role

1. Start SQL Server Management Studio and connect to Analysis Services.

2. From Object Explorer, right-click the Analysis Services server and select Properties from the shortcut menu to open the Analysis Services Properties dialog box, which is divided into three pages: General, Language/Collation, and Security. Each of these pages is accessible through a list on the left side of the dialog box. For the purposes of this exercise, you will use the Security page. This is the page through which Windows users and groups are added to the server role.

3. Navigate to the Security page by selecting the Security item in the list on the left side of the Analysis Services Properties dialog box. The Security page is very straightforward. In the center of the page is a list of those Windows identities currently assigned membership to the server role. Below and to the right of this list are two buttons for adding and removing members. That's all there is to the page.

   Before moving forward with the exercise, take a minute to review the members of the server role as presented on the Security page. If Analysis Services has been left to its default settings, as has ours, you will likely see no members listed here. This implies there are no members of the server role, but obviously, you have server-level administrative rights. Your hidden membership in this role is explained in the sidebar titled "Built-In Administrator Access" later in this chapter.

4. From the Security page, click the Add button to open the Select Users Or Groups dialog box.

5. In this dialog box, click the Object Types button and select Groups in the resulting dialog box. Leave the other check boxes selected and click OK to return to the Select Users Or Groups dialog box.

Through these last steps, you have configured the dialog box to evaluate your entry as either a Windows user account, group, or built-in security principle. Without expanding the evaluation to include Windows groups, you cannot add a group to the server role in the following steps.

Before moving on, notice that the text box labeled Locations in the Select Users Or Groups dialog box identifies the local computer, which will be used as the authority for the Windows group you are about to identify. If you were attempting to add a domain user account or group to the server role, you would need to use the Locations button to the right of this text box to set the location to the appropriate domain name.

6. In the text box labeled Enter The Object Names To Select, enter the name of the local Windows group created in the previous exercise, **SsasUsers**.

7. Click the Check Names button to verify the group's existence and then click OK to add the group to the server role.

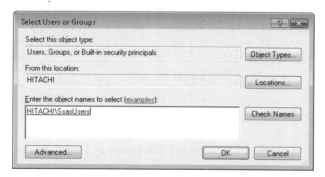

On the Security page, you should now see the SsasUsers group listed as a server administrator. Clicking the OK button at the bottom of the Analysis Services Properties dialog box would complete this process and return you to SQL Server Management Studio. For the purposes of this chapter, including the SsasUsers group in the server role is too permissive and will invalidate the remaining exercises. So, in the following steps, you will remove this group from the server role.

8. On the Security page, select the SsasUsers group from the list of server administrators. Notice that the Remove button at the lower-right side of the page is now enabled.

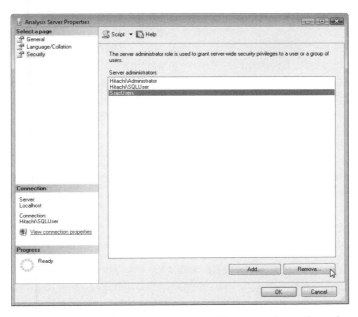

9. Click the Remove button to remove this group from the role.

10. Click OK to close the Analysis Services Properties dialog box and then close SQL Server Management Studio.

Built-In Administrator Access

Local and domain administrators are preconfigured as members of the Analysis Services server role. This assignment is controlled through the *Security\BuiltinAdminsAreServerAdmins* property accessible as an advanced option on the General page of the Analysis Server Properties dialog box. Setting this property from its default value of *True* (1) to *False* (0) revokes system administrators' membership in the Analysis Services server role.

Although revoking access is helpful for improving security, it does not fully prevent system administrators from obtaining administrative access to Analysis Services. The *Security\BuiltinAdminsAreServerAdmins* property, like most Analysis Services configuration settings, is recorded in plain text in an .ini file accessible to system administrators. An administrator locked out of Analysis Services only needs to modify this file to regain access. For this and many other reasons, you should carefully consider who has administrative access to systems within your environment.

Assigning Database-Level Administrative Access

Database roles provide rights to objects within a specific database. These rights include both administrative and data access rights, the latter of which are explored in subsequent sections of this chapter.

By granting a database role full control, you are assigning it the broadest available rights within a database. These include the right to create, modify, delete, and process any object in the database, execute backups and database-level traces, manage database security, and access all data associated with database objects. Full control should be reserved for those select individuals with responsibility for the administration of a database if those individuals are not included in the server role.

When responsibilities are limited to processing, database roles can be granted processing rights to specific dimensions and cubes. When granted at the database level, processing rights extend to all dimensions and cubes within the database. The right to process an object does not confer the right to access that object's data, so that processing administrators may be granted appropriate rights without exposing sensitive information.

Other specialized operations simply require the right to retrieve structural information about objects within a database. Database roles can be assigned the right to read the definitions of various objects including dimensions and data sources. As with processing rights, the application of this right to the database extends the right to all objects within the database. In addition, the assignment of the read definition right does not confer the right to data access.

As a general best practice, we recommend that you assign administrative rights to database roles dedicated to administrative purposes. Users can be members of multiple roles, and through these multiple assignments, they can acquire the combination of administrative and data access rights they require to perform their duties.

In the following exercise, you will create a database role intended for individuals who need to process database objects. These might be individuals responsible for the maintenance of dimensions and cubes as part of an ETL (extraction, transformation, and loading) process.

Create a database role for processing administrators

1. Use Business Intelligence Development Studio (BIDS) to open the AdventureWorks BI solution contained in the C:\Microsoft Press\Analysis Services 2008 SBS\Chapter 12 \AdventureWorks BI folder.

2. In Solution Explorer, locate the Roles folder. The Roles folder represents the collection of roles defined within an Analysis Services database. Through this folder, you can create new roles and edit existing ones.

> **Note** The Roles folder is presented in both BIDS and in SQL Server Management Studio. The same functionality is provided in both interfaces, allowing you to create and edit existing roles. This creates the potential for roles on the server to differ from those in an Analysis Services project. You should be aware that database roles defined on the server (through SQL Server Management Studio or other means) may be overwritten when an Analysis Services database is deployed from BIDS. The Analysis Services Deployment Wizard, described in Chapter 15, "Managing Deployment," provides several options for handling differences in security during database deployment.

3. Right-click the Roles folder and select New Role from the shortcut menu. This will add a new role named Role.role to the Roles folder and open the Role Designer for this object. The Role Designer is organized as a series of tabs that allow you to configure a role. Through the designer's default General tab, the role description is set and database level rights are assigned. The role name is also displayed but cannot be altered. This must be done through Solution Explorer.

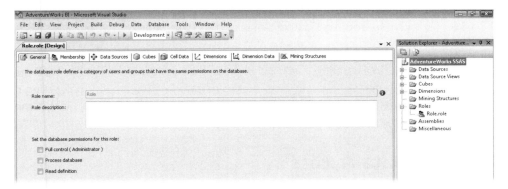

4. Right-click Role.role in Solution Explorer and select Rename from the shortcut menu. Rename the role **Processing Administrators.role**. At the resulting prompt, click Yes.

5. Navigate to the General tab of the Role Designer. In the Role Description text box, enter a short description identifying this role as intended for those responsible for the processing of this database's objects.

As a recommended best practice, you should employ precise, easy-to-interpret names and descriptions for your database roles. As the number of roles within your database proliferates, unambiguous names and descriptions assist with effective security management.

On the General tab, notice the three check boxes just below the Role Description text box. The check box labeled Full Control (Administrator) grants the role full rights to the database, as previously described. These rights include the database-level processing and read definition rights listed separately on this page.

For processing administrators, only processing rights are required. You can set these individually for cubes and dimensions within the database using the Cubes and Dimensions pages, respectively. Or, you can simply assign this right to all cubes and dimensions through the database-level assignment supported by the General tab, as you will do in the following step.

6. On the General tab, select the check box labeled Process Database. The Processing Administrators role is now assigned the right it requires to process all cubes and dimensions within the database. However, many graphical interfaces supporting processing, such as SQL Server Management Studio's Object Explorer, require you to browse the structures of the database in order to issue processing commands. If you want processing administrators to process objects through such interfaces, you will need to grant the role the right to read object definitions.

7. On the General tab, select the check box labeled Read Definition.

8. Now that you have assigned rights to the role, the last step is to define role membership through the Membership tab. Navigate to the Membership tab, and as in the last exercise, add the SsasUsers group to the role. Remember to use the Object Types button to enable the addition of Windows groups.

9. Save the changes to this role by selecting Save All from the File menu.

10. Select Deploy AdventureWorks SSAS from the Build menu. A dialog box may appear warning you that the database will be overwritten. If you see the warning, click Yes to complete the deployment.

Securing Data Access

Through database roles, access to data is tailored to the needs of your users. Because all Analysis Services data is accessed through cubes, your first step is to grant access to one or more cubes. After you grant this permission, you can then limit the data accessible through these cubes using dimension data and cell-level restrictions.

Granting Access to Cubes

Database roles are not permitted access to the data in cubes unless specifically granted (or overridden by full control rights as previously described). By granting a role Read access to a cube, you enable the members of the role to access all dimension and measures within the cube except where restricted by dimension data and cell-level constraints assigned to the role. Through Read/Write access, the same level of Read access is permitted, and write-back features accessible through the cube are generally enabled where specifically permitted through dimension, partition, and cell-level settings.

In the following exercise, you will create a database role with Read access to the data in the AdventureWorks cube. This role will be modified over the remaining exercises in this chapter.

Create a database role with access to the AdventureWorks cube

1. In Solution Explorer, right-click the Roles folder and select New Role from the shortcut menu. A new role, Role 1.role, is added to the Roles folder and the Role Designer for this object is presented.

2. Using Solution Explorer, rename the role from Role 1.role to **North American Analysts.role**. As before, click Yes at the prompt.

3. On the General tab of the Role Designer, enter a short description identifying this role as intended for those responsible for the analysis of data related to countries in North America.

   In the next exercise, you will implement dimension data restrictions limiting the members of this role to data related to countries in North America. In this exercise, you simply need to enable access to the AdventureWorks cube. This is done through the Cubes tab.

4. Navigate to the Cubes tab and review the list of cubes available through the database. Notice each cube is assigned a default access right of None. The None access right assignment indicates the North American Analysts role is not currently granted access to the data in these cubes.

5. A drop-down list to the right of the AdventureWorks cube allows you to grant this role Read access to its data. Use the drop-down list to change the access level from None to Read.

The role is now configured to provide Read access to the AdventureWorks cube. This is your first step in defining a role tailored to the needs of your users, the North American analysts. Before going any further, you should save your changes to the role.

6. Save the changes to this role by selecting Save All from the File menu.

> **Note** In later steps, you will assign membership to the role. As a general best practice, it is recommended that you define all dimension and cell data restrictions on a role before granting membership.

The Local Cube/Drillthrough Access Right

In the previous exercise, you may have noticed that some additional rights were assigned to cubes through the Role Designer's Cube tab. These include processing rights, discussed earlier in this chapter, and local cube/drillthrough access rights.

The assignment of local cube/drillthrough access rights determines whether members of a role are granted the rights required to execute two relatively advanced MDX statements, *DRILLTHROUGH* and *CREATE GLOBAL CUBE*. The *DRILLTHROUGH* statement allows the underlying rows of a cell to be retrieved. The *CREATE GLOBAL CUBE* statement allows cube data to be extracted to a local cube file for offline analysis.

Both statements support powerful forms of analysis, but each one accesses raw data in a way that bypasses certain calculations that typically take place in a cube. The *CREATE GLOBAL CUBE* statement entails the additional risk of extracting large volumes of data to a highly transportable structure. For this reason, local cube/drillthrough access is assigned a default value of None and should be left in this state unless clearly defined and understood requirements dictate otherwise.

Restricting Access to Dimension Members

Dimension data security settings are used to limit the members of a dimension accessible to a role. These restrictions are defined through allowed and denied sets.

An allowed set defines the set of attribute hierarchy members a role is permitted to access. A denied set defines the set of attribute hierarchy members to which a role is denied access. Although both allowed and denied sets can be applied to an attribute hierarchy to limit its accessible members, most implementations simply employ one or the other.

The allowed and denied sets are defined as sets of members from the associated attribute hierarchy. These sets are assembled using explicit declarations as well as MDX set-building expressions. The former is the easiest to assemble; the later is the most dynamic.

By limiting access to the members of a single attribute hierarchy, all other hierarchies in the dimension are restricted based on relationships between the attributes defined at design time. By relying on relationships, you can implement consistent restrictions across a dimension with relative ease.

In the following exercise, you will define an allowed set permitting the North American Analysts role access to those data related to countries in North America.

Permit the database role to access data associated with North America

1. In Solution Explorer, right-click the North American Analysts role created in the previous exercise. Select View Designer from the shortcut menu to return to the appropriate Role Designer.

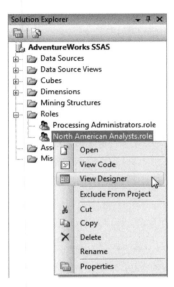

2. On the Role Designer, navigate to the Dimension Data tab.

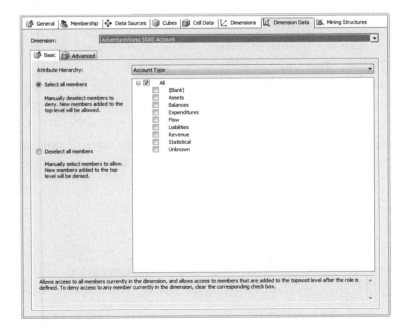

Through the Dimension Data tab, allowed and denied sets are defined on selected attribute hierarchies. The Dimension Data tab itself is divided into Basic and Advanced tabs. The Basic tab is the default and supports the assembly of explicitly defined allowed and denied sets using a hierarchical display of the members of the selected attribute hierarchy. The Advanced tab supports the assembly of more complex sets using MDX expressions. It also exposes additional options explained in the sidebar titled "Default Members and Visual Totals" later in this chapter.

At the top of the Dimension Data tab is the Dimension drop-down list, through which you identify the dimension containing the attribute hierarchy you intend to restrict. The drop-down list presents both database-level dimensions as well as cube dimensions for those cubes to which the role has been granted access. A restriction applied to a cube dimension affects the data available through that one, specific cube dimension. Applying a restriction to a database-level dimension impacts all cube dimensions based on it.

3. Using the Dimension drop-down list, select the AdventureWorks cube's Geography dimension. You will need to scroll past the database-level dimensions in order to locate the cube dimensions.

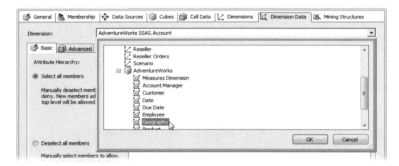

After you select the Geography dimension, click OK to close the list. The Attribute Hierarchy drop-down list at the top of the Basic tab is automatically populated with a list of the attribute hierarchies available through the Geography cube dimension.

4. From the Attribute Hierarchy drop-down list, select the Country attribute hierarchy. Notice the tree view below it is automatically populated with a list of the hierarchy's members.

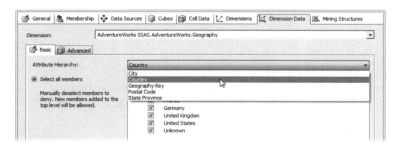

By selecting and deselecting members in the tree view, an explicitly defined allowed or denied set is assembled for you. Which is assembled depends on the option selected to the left of the tree. If the first option, Select All Members (which is the default), is selected, then your interactions with the tree view are reflected in a denied set. The other option, Deselect All Members, supports the assembly of an allowed set.

5. Select the option labeled Deselect All Members and notice all selections in the tree view are cleared.

6. In the tree view, select the Canada and United States members. Notice that the All Geography member is automatically selected. The All Geography member is made accessible whenever any member of the hierarchy is accessible.

7. Navigate to the Advanced tab and review the definition of the allowed set assembled through the Basic tab.

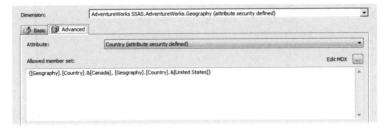

The allowed set defined through interaction with the Basic tab is presented in the Allowed Set text box. You can see it employs an explicitly defined set containing two member references, [Geography].[Country].&[Canada] and [Geography].[Country].&[United States]. (Although Mexico is part of North America, there is no Mexico member within the Country attribute hierarchy, so Mexico does not appear in the set.)

The member references in the allowed set employ member keys to identify Country members. You could modify the set's definition within the text box to employ member names, or you could assemble a complex set expression using the MDX Expression

Builder accessible through the Edit MDX button just above the text box. For the purposes of this exercise, you can leave the allowed set as is.

This role is now properly restricted per your requirements. Your next step should be to assign membership and then save and deploy your changes.

8. Navigate to the Role Designer's Membership tab, and as in previous exercises, add the SsasUsers group to the role. Remember to use the Object Types button to enable the addition of Windows groups.

9. Save the changes to this role by selecting Save All from the File menu.

10. On the Build menu, select Deploy AdventureWorks SSAS. With the changes deployed, the North American Analysts role is now limited to just the data associated with the available North American countries. To see this in action, in the next step you will browse the AdventureWorks cube's data through this role.

11. In Solution Explorer, right-click the AdventureWorks cube and select View Designer to open the Cube Designer.

12. In the Cube Designer, navigate to the Browser tab. If the Cube Designer had been previously open, you may need to click the Reconnect button to access the cube.

13. From the Browser tab's toolbar, locate the Change User button. It is positioned between the Process and Reconnect buttons. Click the Change User button to launch the Security Context dialog box.

Through the Security Context dialog box, you can connect to Analysis Services while impersonating a Windows user or a member of one or more database roles. Depending on your selections, when you return to the Browser tab, a message below the toolbar identifies the security context through which you are accessing cube's data. This is a very handy way to verify your security configuration.

14. Select the Roles option in the Security Context dialog box and use its associated drop-down list to select the North American Analysts role. Click OK to close the list and then click OK again to close the dialog box and return to the Browser tab. Notice that the informational message just below the toolbar indicates that you are impersonating the North American Analysts role.

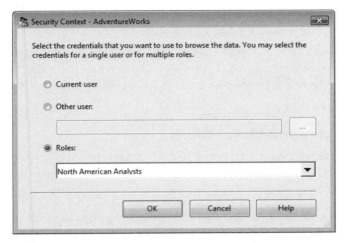

15. Expand the Geography dimension and drag the Geography user hierarchy to rows.

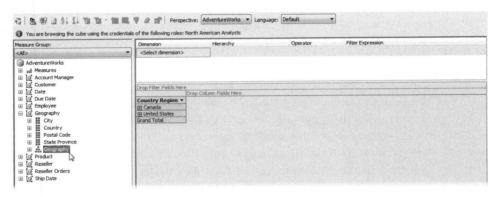

Notice that only the Canada and United States members of the hierarchy's Country-level are presented. Other countries, such as France and Germany, not identified in the allowed set, are not accessible. Notice, too, that the hierarchy's (All) member, All Geography, is presented as the Grand Total.

16. Drag the Reseller Sales Amount measure from the Reseller Sales measure group to details. Notice that the Grand Total value, the value for the hierarchy's (All) member, reflects the sum of all values and not just that of the accessible Canada and United States members.

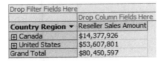

The (All) member represents the aggregation of all members within a hierarchy, regardless of their accessibility. Through the visual totals setting discussed in the following sidebar, "Default Members and Visual Totals," you can alter this behavior, but you should do so only following careful consideration.

Before moving on, try interacting with other hierarchies within the Geography dimension. Notice that the members of each of these hierarchies are limited to those directly or indirectly associated with the Canada and United States Country members. Although the allowed set is defined only against the Country attribute hierarchy, all data in the dimension are affected automatically through relationships defined in the dimension.

Default Members and Visual Totals

The Dimension Data tab's Advanced tab provides access to two security settings in addition to the allowed and denied sets explored in the last exercise. These settings allow you to define a default member for the role and enable visual totals.

The default member setting is fairly straightforward. Using either an explicit member reference or an MDX expression, you can assign the role a default member different from that associated with the attribute hierarchy. For example, if you were to define a United States–specific role with an allowed set of just the United States Country member, you might consider assigning the role a default member of United States, [Geography].[Country].&[United States], instead of the attribute hierarchy's default member, All Geography.

Although in certain scenarios the assignment of a role-specific default member might be useful, in many others it can be problematic. For example, when a user is a member of two roles with competing default members, Analysis Services arbitrarily elects which one to employ. In another example, two users in different roles may issue the same query but return different values because default member assignments differ. Role-specific default members should be carefully considered before being employed.

The visual totals setting also requires careful consideration. By enabling visual totals, you are asking Analysis Services to recalculate the value of the (All) member based on restrictions defined in the allowed and denied sets. In addition to the performance overhead of recalculating this member, two users with differing access to a dimension's data employing a single query may return differing results. Although this is problematic, the presentation of (All) member totals not matching the aggregation of available child members can also cause difficulties. We recommend you work with end-user representatives to determine the right strategy for your databases.

The Dimensions Page

Through the Role Designer's Dimensions tab, database-level dimension processing and read definition rights are assigned as described earlier in this chapter. Access rights can also be defined for both database-level and cube dimensions. These access rights have been the source of much confusion.

Dimensions may be assigned an access right or Read or Read/Write access. Neither of these assignments actually confers access to data, however. Instead, they determine whether a role is granted write permissions to a write-enabled dimension.

The default access right assignment for database-level dimensions is Read. For cube dimensions, the access right is configured to be inherited from the associated database-level dimension. Using options presented on the Dimensions page, you can alter these settings, but for the vast majority of Analysis Services databases, there is no need to do so.

Restricting Access to Cells

By default, all cells within a cube to which the members of a database role have been granted access are readable. Through cell data security settings, you can define access on a cell-by-cell basis. When enabled, the level of access granted to a cell is evaluated using a logical MDX expression. If the logical expression evaluates to *True*, the level of access it controls is granted, but if the logical expression evaluates to *False*, that level of access is denied. Through cell data security settings, any of three levels of access can be evaluated: Read, ReadContingent, and Read/Write.

The Read and ReadContingent access levels are evaluated to determine whether the current cell is readable. The two access levels are not mutually exclusive, but in most cell data security configurations, only one or the other is evaluated. With Read access, a cell is readable if the associated logical expression evaluates to *True* for the current cell. With ReadContingent access, a cell is readable if the associated logical expression evaluates to *True* for the current cell if that cell is not derived from other cells. If the cell is derived, the underlying cells are evaluated using the logical expression; the current cell is readable if each of these evaluates to *True*.

The Read/Write access level is evaluated to determine whether the current cell is writable. For write-back to succeed, Read/Write access must also be granted on the cube and a write-back partition must have been established. This permission only works in conjunction with many other settings.

In the following exercise, you define cell data security for the North American Analysts role, limiting access to finance data for the fiscal year 2009.

Limit database role access to financial data for a given fiscal year

1. Using Solution Explorer, open the Role Designer for the North American Analysts role.
2. On the Cubes tab, enable Read access to the Finance cube.

3. Navigate to the Cell Data tab. Through the Cell Data tab, logical expressions for determining various levels of access are defined for the cells of a cube. The evaluation of a particular level of access is enabled by selecting its associated check box and entering a logical expression in the text box below it. Before these can be enabled, the cube whose cells are to be evaluated must first be identified. This is done through the Cube drop-down list at the top of the page.

4. Using the Cube drop-down list, select the Finance cube.

5. Select the check box labeled Enable Read Permissions to enable the evaluation of the Read access level.

6. In the text box below it, enter the following MDX logical expression:

```
(NOT [Measures].CurrentMember Is [Measures].[Amount]) OR
([Date].[Fiscal Year].CurrentMember Is [Date].[Fiscal Year].[FY 2009])
```

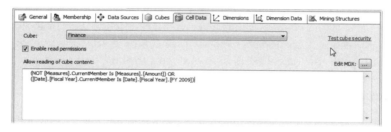

The logical expression evaluates the current cell to determine its readability. If the current cell is associated with a measure other than Amount, the measure associated with the Finance measure group, the cell is readable. If the current cell is associated with this measure, then if the current fiscal year associated with the cell is FY 2009 the cell is also readable. Otherwise, the cell is unreadable to the members of this role. Through this logic, you permit the members of the North American Analysts role access to financial data, but only for FY 2009—because analysis of finance data from multiple years may be considered sensitive and out-of-scope for this role.

7. Save the changes to this role by selecting Save All from the File menu.

8. On the Build menu, select Deploy AdventureWorks SSAS. A dialog box may appear warning that the database will be overwritten. If you see the warning, click Yes to complete deployment.

9. In Solution Explorer, right-click the Finance cube and select View Designer to open the Cube Designer. Navigate to the Cube Designer's Browser tab.

10. Click the Change User button to launch the Security Context dialog box.

11. Select the Roles option and use its associated drop-down list to select the North American Analysts role. Click OK to close the list and then click OK again to close the dialog box and return to the Browser tab. Notice that the informational message just below the toolbar indicates that you are impersonating the North American Analysts role.

12. Drag the Account dimension's Accounts hierarchy to rows and the Date dimension's Fiscal Date hierarchy to columns. Drag the Finance measure group's Amount measure to details. Notice that for all but fiscal year 2009, cells return the value *#N/A*. This the default value used to indicate that a cell is not readable. Through the North American Analysts role, you have full access to the members of the Accounts and Fiscal Date hierarchies, but those cells associated with the Amount measure and not with fiscal year 2009 are prohibited.

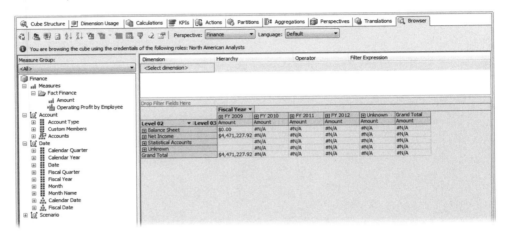

13. Close BIDS.

> **Note** Remember to remove the SsasUsers local group from your system.

Dynamic Security

Both dimension data and cell data security employ MDX expressions to determine data availability. Using MDX, you can implement quite complex criteria for data access.

One of the more interesting applications of MDX expressions within dimension and cell data security is to implement what is referred to as *dynamic security*. Dynamic security employs the identity of the current user in an expression to evaluate, for that specific individual, which members are in an allowed or denied set or to determine whether a specific cell is accessible.

The implementation of dynamic security is complex, and its evaluation on an individual-by-individual basis adds quite a bit of overhead to data access. Still, there are situations in which dynamic security is appropriate and preferable to other security approaches. These situations and the implementation of dynamic security in various scenarios are explored in *Microsoft SQL Server 2008 MDX Step-by-Step* by Bryan C. Smith and Ryan Clay (Microsoft Press, 2009).

In this chapter, you have learned to implement security. You have learned how to grant full administrative rights within Analysis Services by using SQL Server Management Studio to add Windows users and groups to the server role. You have also learned how to grant database, cube, dimension, dimension member, and cell level access by creating a role in an Analysis Services database, adding Windows users and groups to the role, and then granting permissions to the role.

Chapter 13
Designing Aggregations

In this chapter, you will learn how to:

- Design aggregations using the Aggregation Design Wizard.

- Improve aggregation design by creating attribute relationships and user-defined hierarchies.

- Control the aggregation of an attribute using the *AggregationUsage* property.

- Design an individual aggregation.

- Improve aggregation design by using long-term estimates of data volume.

- Enable Analysis Services query logging.

- Design aggregations based on logged queries using the Usage-Based Optimization Wizard.

In Chapter 2, "Understanding OLAP and Analysis Services," you learned that Analysis Services provides two major benefits: sophisticated data analysis capabilities and fast query response. In subsequent chapters, you learned how to create an Analysis Services database that provides many analytical capabilities. In this chapter, you will learn how to design aggregations, precalculated summary values, in order to enable fast query response.

Understanding Aggregation Design

An Analysis Services measure group appears to contain every possible summarized value by every attribute contained in every dimension in the measure group. In this chapter, you will be working with a simplified cube that contains only Product, Date, and Employee dimensions and Reseller Sales and Internet Sales measure groups. You can query the Reseller Sales measure group at the lowest level of detail and find out, for example, that Amy Alberts sold six units of Product ID BK-M47B-40 on August 1, 2009, for $3,888. You can also query the cube at a higher level of detail to discover that 58,241 products were sold in calendar year (CY) 2009 for $24,144,430. No matter what level of detail you request, Analysis Services returns values as if every level of detail is stored in the measure group.

Even very simple measure groups such as the one used for the step-by-step procedures in this chapter have the potential to become very large. The source database, SSAS2008SBS, contains 606 different products, 290 employees, and 1,279 dates. This means that there could potentially be 606 × 290 × 1,279 = 224,771,460 detail rows in the FactResellerSales table, one row for every possible combination of products, employees, and dates. In reality, the products were introduced gradually over time, and each product was not sold by every employee every day, so the FactResellerSales table actually contains 60,855 rows. However, even though the fact table contains only 60,855 detail rows, the measure group can display up to 224,771,460 detail levels cells for each measure. Of course, most of these cells would be empty.

When you think about the potential size of a measure group, you must also include the aggregated values. A measure group must appear to contain a summarized value for every possible combination of members from each attribute hierarchy in every dimension. Even though three of them are hidden, there are six total attribute hierarchies in the Product dimension: Category, Subcategory, Product, Size, Color, and Product ID that contain 5, 38, 505, 20, 11, and 607 members, respectively. (There are only four categories, but remember that by default each attribute hierarchy contains an All member.) The Employee dimension contains the Employees parent-child hierarchy, which has 290 members, and the Date dimension contains four attribute hierarchies: Calendar Year, Calendar Quarter, Month, and Date, which contain 5, 15, 43, and 1,280 members. The Reseller Sales measure group also contains two measures, Reseller Order Quantity and Reseller Sales Amount. So this simple measure group must appear to contain $5 \times 38 \times 505 \times 20 \times 11 \times 607 \times 290 \times 5 \times 15 \times 43 \times 1,280 \times 2 = 30,677,787,381,120,000,000$ values. Even with this small sample database, the measure group must appear to contain 504,112,848,264,235 times as many values as the fact table contains rows! This is a very clear example of data explosion, which was introduced in Chapter 2. Data explosion is a major issue when you work with OLAP cubes, because it can cause an OLAP database to consume a large amount of disk space and can cause measure groups to take a very long time to process.

The simplest way to avoid data explosion is to avoid storing aggregations altogether and instead calculate them on demand. But when you have a large data warehouse, this option quickly takes its toll on query performance, because requesting a single high-level summary value from a measure group could require retrieving and summarizing a very large number of detail values. The challenge of OLAP is to make queries as fast as possible while avoiding data explosion. Microsoft SQL Server 2008 Analysis Services provides several features that allow the database administrator to control and fine-tune the relationship between the physical size of a measure group and the time it takes to process the measure group and the speed of the queries. In fact, Analysis Services provides options that allow for both compact data files and responsive queries.

Analysis Services provides for compact data files and responsive queries by creating some, but usually not all, of the possible aggregations in a measure group. Although you can easily create a measure group without aggregations—none of the measure groups created previously in this book have any aggregations—aggregations can make a tremendous difference in query time for large measure groups. You can use the Aggregation Design Wizard and the Usage-Based Optimization Wizard to design aggregations. These wizards allow you to make a tradeoff between creating more aggregations to improve query response time at the cost of using more storage space and increasing processing time. Regardless of how many aggregations you design, a measure group always appears to contain every possible aggregated value. When you request a summary value from a measure group, Analysis Services uses whatever aggregations are available to retrieve the value as quickly as possible. For example, suppose you request Reseller Sales Amount for CY 2010, but this aggregated value has not been precalculated and stored in the measure group. If the aggregated values for Reseller Sales Amount for the Calendar Quarter attribute exist in the measure group, Analysis Services can quickly retrieve the four quarters of CY 2010 and calculate the year total.

Don't confuse an aggregated value with an aggregation. An *aggregated value* is a single summary value retrieved from a measure group. An *aggregation* is all the possible combinations of the members of one level from each attribute hierarchy in every dimension in a measure group. Consider the three aggregations that could be created just from the Color and Size attribute hierarchies in the Product dimension and a single measure. One aggregation would contain a single value equal to the summary value for all colors and all sizes. A second aggregation would contain 10 values equal to the 10 different colors summarized for all sizes. A third aggregation would contain 19 values equal to the 19 different sizes summarized for all colors. Of course, this is a simple example. The Product dimension contains other attribute hierarchies, and even the simple measure group used in this chapter contains other dimensions. Remember that an aggregation contains summarized values for the members of one level of every attribute hierarchy in every dimension in a measure group.

Aggregations are physically stored in measure group partitions. A *partition* in Analysis Services is the physical location of the data stored in a measure group. Each measure group in a cube has one or more corresponding partitions. Because every cube has at least one measure group, every cube has at least one partition. Each time you create an additional measure group, another partition is created. Queries run faster against a partitioned cube because Analysis Services only needs to read data from the partitions that contain the answers to the queries. Queries can run even faster when the partition also stores aggregations, the precalculated totals for measures. Analysis Services often can retrieve the aggregated value faster than it can calculate the same value from the detail data at query time.

Using the Aggregation Design Wizard

After you develop a measure group, you can use the Aggregation Design Wizard to design aggregations. A greater number of aggregations provides faster query response time, but uses more disk space and takes longer to process. So, when you use the Aggregation Design Wizard, you will be asked to restrict the number of aggregations that are designed by limiting the estimated amount of storage space the aggregations will use, by setting a limit for the performance gain the aggregations will provide, or by manually stopping the wizard while it is designing aggregations. The wizard, assuming that all queries are equally likely, will design the combination of aggregations that provide the best tradeoff between increased query performance and increased storage space given the restriction you have set. The wizard uses a sophisticated algorithm that considers the number of records in the fact table, the number of members in each attribute hierarchy, and the attribute relationships in a dimension. The wizard looks for aggregations that summarize many fact records into a few values and aggregations that can be used to calculate other aggregate values quickly. The wizard designs the aggregations that provide the greatest improvement in query performance compared to disk storage space first, so as you design more and more aggregations, the additional benefit from each additional aggregation decreases.

The Aggregation Design Wizard will also compare the potential number of values in an aggregation with the number of fact records that will be processed into a measure group partition. The wizard will not create an aggregation if the number of values in the aggregation is more than one-third the number of fact records. Suppose the wizard is considering an aggregation design that contains the leaf level of the Subcategory attribute hierarchy (37 members), the leaf level of the Date attribute hierarchy (1,279 members), and the All level of all other attribute hierarchies. This aggregation will have $37 \times 1,279 = 47,323$ values. If less than $47,323 \times 3 = 141,969$ fact records are being processed into the measure group, then the wizard will not create this aggregation, as they are not likely to improve query performance greatly.

The potential number of aggregations in a measure group can become very large. An aggregation contains either the All member or the members of the leaf level of every attribute hierarchy. Analysis Services will not create an aggregation that contains the leaf level of every attribute hierarchy in the cube. This aggregation would be redundant with the leaf level of the cube. Therefore, the number of potential aggregations in a measure group is equal to $2^N - 1$, where N is the number of attribute hierarchies that have an All level. The simple measure group used in this chapter has 12 attribute hierarchies, so it has 4,095 potential aggregations.

Because it can take the Aggregation Design Wizard a long time to consider every possible aggregation in a measure group, the wizard does not consider whether to use the All member or the leaf level members of every attribute hierarchy when it designs aggregations. Instead, the wizard uses the following criteria to create a pool of attributes that are eligible to be considered when it designs aggregations:

- The attribute is used as the granularity attribute to relate the dimension to the measure group.

- The attribute is a parent attribute in a parent-child hierarchy; that is, the value of the attribute's *Usage* property is *Parent*.

- The value of the attribute's *AggregationUsage* property is *Unrestricted*.

- The attribute is used as the top level of a user-defined hierarchy.

- The attribute is a child level in a natural hierarchy (i.e., the attribute is used as a level in a user-defined hierarchy and is also the source attribute in an attribute relationship with another attribute that is used as a higher level in the same hierarchy).

The last two criteria indicate that creating user-defined hierarchies and attribute relationships are important steps to take when designing aggregations. The dimensions in the cube used in this chapter have had all of their user-defined hierarchies removed, and every attribute only has a relationship with the key attribute. You will first design aggregations with these dimensions, then you will create attribute relationships and user-defined hierarchies, and then you will re-run the Aggregation Design Wizard to see the impact of attribute relationships and user-defined hierarchies on aggregation design.

In the following procedure, you will use the Aggregation Design Wizard to design aggregations in the Reseller Sales measure group.

Create an aggregation design

1. Use Business Intelligence Development Studio (BIDS) to open the AdventureWorks BI solution contained in the C:\Microsoft Press\Analysis Services 2008 SBS\Chapter 13 \AdventureWorks BI folder.

2. In Solution Explorer, expand the Cubes folder, right-click AdventureWorks.cube, and select View Designer.

3. In the Cube Designer, select the Aggregations tab. The Aggregations tab displays all of the measure groups contained in the cube and any aggregation designs that have been created. You will need to start the Aggregation Design Wizard to design an aggregation.

4. Right-click the Reseller Sales measure group and select Design Aggregations.

5. On the Welcome To The Aggregation Design Wizard page, click Next.

6. On the Review Aggregation Usage page, expand the Employee, Product, and Date dimensions if necessary. The Review Aggregation Usage page displays every attribute in the measure group. This page allows you to change the value of the attribute's *AggregationUsage* property. Be aware that when you change the value of this attribute property, it is changed for the attribute for the entire cube. The value of this property affects aggregation design as shown in Table 13-1.

TABLE 13-1 **Effect of *AggregationUsage* Property Value on Aggregation Design**

Value	Effect
Default	The Aggregation Design Wizard will consider whether to use the All member or the leaf level members of the attribute hierarchy if it is in the pool of eligible attributes.
Full	The attribute hierarchy leaf level members will be included in every aggregation design.
None	The attribute hierarchy All member will be included in every aggregation design. This option is not available if the attribute hierarchy doesn't have an All member, that is, if the value of the attribute's *IsAggregatable* property is *False*.
Unrestricted	The Aggregation Design Wizard will consider whether to use the All member or the leaf level members of the attribute hierarchy whether or not it is in the pool of eligible attributes.

Note The Review Aggregation Usage page displays all attributes in the measure group even if the level of the attribute is below the granularity attribute and even if the attribute can't be used in an aggregation because the value of its *AttributeHierarchyEnabled* property is *False*. In this case, the Employee Sort, List Price, and Month Number of Year attributes all have their *AttributeHierarchyEnabled* property set to *False*, but they still show up on this page.

7. Click Next. On the Specify Object Counts page, expand the Employee, Product, and Date dimensions. The Specify Object Counts page displays the attribute hierarchies that belong to the pool of eligible attributes and any attributes that have their *AggregationUsage* property set to *Full*. The Employee, Product ID, and Date attributes are in the pool of eligible attributes because they are the granularity attributes used to relate their dimensions to the Reseller Sales measure group. The Employees attribute is in the pool because it is a parent attribute in a parent-child hierarchy.

The algorithm that the wizard uses to design aggregations considers the count of fact records and members in each attribute in the measure group. The dimensions and attributes have a red wavy underline because the counts don't yet exist. You can either manually enter values or you can have the wizard query the source database.

Tip If any of the fact or dimension tables are very large or involve complex views or named queries that contain complex SQL, having the wizard query the source database to get a count of the number of fact records and attribute members may take a long time. As an alternative, you can enter these values manually.

8. Click Count. The wizard retrieves the counts from the SSAS2008SBS database. Because the measure group has only one partition, the Estimated Count and the Partition Count value for ResellerSales is the same. The wizard populates the Estimated Count value for

the attributes but leaves the Partition Count value blank or equal to zero. In this case, the aggregation designer will use each attribute's Estimated Count value. In Chapter 14, "Managing Partitions and Database Processing," you will learn to create multiple partitions for a measure group. If a measure group contains multiple partitions, then a particular partition may not contain all of the members of a dimension. For example, you could create separate partitions for each year. You would then want to change the value of Partition Count for the Date attribute to 365. The Specify Objects Counts page for the SSAS2008SBS database should look like this.

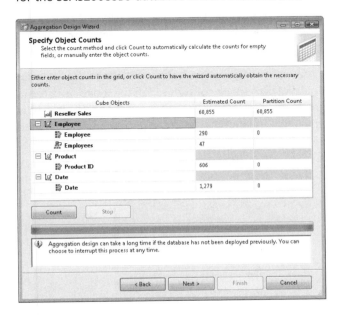

Note When the wizard retrieves counts from the source database or when you enter counts, the values of the measure group and partition *EstimatedRows* property and the values of the attributes' *EstimatedCount* property are updated.

9. Click Next. On the Set Aggregation Options page, select Performance Gain Reaches and verify that the percentage value is 30. The Set Aggregation Options page lets you place a restriction limiting the aggregations that will be designed by the wizard. If you select the Estimated Storage Reaches option, you can set a limit in megabytes (MB) or gigabytes (GB) to specify how much disk storage space the aggregates can use. The amount of storage is an estimate, because until the aggregates are actually calculated, the number of values that will actually be created is unknown. If you select the Performance Gain Reaches option, you can set a limit based on a percentage of the total performance gain that can be achieved by creating aggregations. You can also select the I Click Stop option. You can then watch the aggregation designer and click Stop when you think an appropriate aggregation design has been achieved.

No matter which option you select, the wizard will try various combinations of aggregations until it exhausts all possibilities for the specified limit that you have set. You have no control over which specific aggregations it selects. For most databases, using the default Performance Gain Reaches 30% option provides enough aggregation for very good performance. If you later find that queries are executing too slowly, you can add aggregations then.

10. Click Start. As the wizard designs aggregations, you can watch its progress in the graph. You can stop the wizard at any time if you decide to change the options for designing aggregations and want to restart the design process. When the wizard finishes its calculations, the number of aggregations that have been designed displays at the bottom of the page.

In the graph, you can see the relationship between the increase in performance (on the y-axis) and the amount of disk space consumed (on the x-axis) as a result of the current aggregation design. At some point, the amount of disk space required is more costly than the benefits gained by relatively little improved query performance. The goal of aggregation optimization is to get the best performance increase without unnecessarily consuming disk space. When aggregation design is complete, the Set Aggregation Options page should look like this.

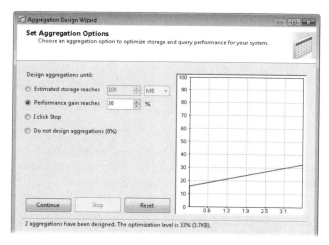

Note that two aggregations have been designed. In the procedures titled "Modify Attribute Relationships" and "Create User-Defined Hierarchies" later in this chapter, you will modify the design of the Product dimension so that the number of attributes in the pool of attributes eligible for the aggregation designer to consider is increased. In the procedure titled "Redesign Aggregations," you will then create another aggregation design for the FactResellerSales measure group and see that the new aggregation design contains more aggregations.

11. Click Next. On the Completing The Wizard page, accept the default name, verify that Save The Aggregations But Do Not Process Them is selected, and click Finish. As you stepped through the pages of the Aggregation Design Wizard, the property values, attribute and partition record counts, and aggregation design were added to the XML files containing the design of the AdventureWorks cube, but the aggregations are not calculated and stored. Aggregations are not created until the measure group partition is processed. The Completing The Wizard page allows you to deploy the design changes you have made and process the aggregations, or you can just save the aggregation design but not deploy and process. It most instances, you will just save the aggregations, because you will often want to design aggregations for other partitions and measure groups before you deploy and process.

    The Aggregations tab of the Cube Designer now displays the aggregation design you have just created.

    The Standard View of the Aggregations tab shows in the Aggregations column that the aggregation design contains three aggregations. This is one more aggregation than was designed by the Aggregation Design Wizard. You can use the Advanced View on the Aggregation tab to view the individual aggregations in an aggregation design. Looking at the individual aggregations will help you understand why the aggregation design contains three aggregations.

12. On the Aggregations tab toolbar, click Advanced View.

13. Verify that Reseller Sales is selected from the Measure Group list and select AggregationDesign from the Aggregation Design list. Expand the Employee, Product, and Date dimensions. The Advanced View should display three aggregations.

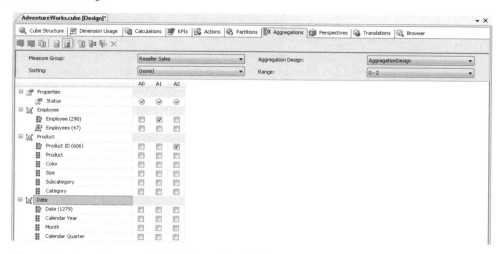

The attribute and parent-child hierarchies in the measure group are displayed on rows and the three aggregations are represented by the columns A0, A1, and A2. If a hierarchy is selected, then the corresponding aggregation contains the leaf level members of that hierarchy. Otherwise, the aggregation contains the members of the hierarchy's top level. This will be the All member, unless the hierarchy doesn't contain an All member.

One of the aggregations has no selected hierarchies. This aggregation contains the top level of every hierarchy and so contains the most highly summarized values in the partition. This aggregation will frequently be added to an aggregation design, and the other two aggregations are the aggregations that were designed by the Aggregation Design Wizard.

Attribute Relationships, User-Defined Hierarchies, and Aggregation Design

In Chapter 4, "Creating Dimensions," you learned how to create attribute relationships and user-defined hierarchies. This section will review why it is critically important to create attribute relationships and how attribute relationships and user-defined hierarchies affect aggregation design.

Attribute relationships identify the natural hierarchies that exist in a dimension. In a natural hierarchy, each child member has only one parent member, so the value of any member at any level of a natural hierarchy can be calculated by aggregating the member's descendants at one of the lower levels of the hierarchy. For example, to find the value for a year, you can aggregate the quarters of that year. You can also aggregate the months or you can aggregate the individual days.

Analysis Services can use natural hierarchies two ways to improve query performance. First, when you execute a query, Analysis Services checks to see if the needed aggregate values have been stored in memory cache. If not, Analysis Services will look in memory for the values of descendants that can be aggregated. Even if you don't create aggregations, you should still create attribute relationships so that Analysis Services can take advantage of descendant values stored in memory cache. Second, Analysis Services can use natural hierarchies to design aggregations that are stored on disk. Retrieving an aggregate value from disk (or retrieving and aggregating the aggregate values of members of a lower level of a natural hierarchy) is faster than retrieving and aggregating the lowest level of detail from disk.

When you created aggregations in the procedure titled "Design Aggregations" earlier in the chapter, the Aggregation Design Wizard considered only four attributes—Employee, Employees, Product ID, and Date—because these are the only attributes in the pool of attributes eligible to be considered by the aggregation designer. You can make more attributes eligible to be considered for inclusion in an aggregation design by creating attribute relationships and user-defined hierarchies. Creating attribute relationships identifies the natural hierarchies that Analysis Services can use to create aggregations. Creating user-defined hierarchies signals to Analysis Services that you anticipate users will frequently query Analysis Services using that hierarchy.

In the simplified database used in this chapter, all attributes are related to the dimension's key attribute, and all user-defined hierarchies have been removed. In the next two procedures, you will create attribute relationships and user-defined hierarchies. Then, in the procedure titled "Redesign Aggregations," you use the Aggregation Design Wizard and find that more attributes are available for aggregation and that the aggregation design contains more aggregations.

Modify attribute relationships

In this procedure, you will modify the attribute relationships in the Product dimension to indicate to Analysis Services that the Category, Subcategory, Product, and Product ID attributes form a natural hierarchy.

1. In Solution Explorer, expand the Dimensions folder, right-click Product.dim, and select View Designer.

2. In Dimension Designer, select the Attribute Relationships tab. You can see in the Attribute Relationships pane that every attribute is related to the key attribute, Product ID. Analysis Services is unable to take advantage of the natural hierarchy that exists in the Product dimension. For example, to derive a value for a Category, Analysis Services must aggregate the values of all of the Product IDs that belong to that category.

3. Right-click the Product ID – Subcategory relationship and select Edit Attribute Relationship to display the Edit Attribute Relationship dialog box, which you can use to create a natural hierarchy. The Source Attribute identifies the "child" attribute and the Related Attribute identifies the "parent" attribute.

4. Change the name of the Source Attribute to Product and click OK.

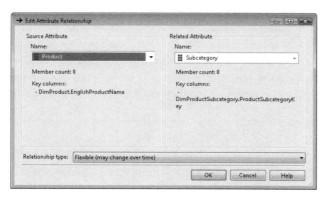

5. Right-click the Product ID – Category relationship and select Edit Attribute Relationship.

6. Change the name of the Source Attribute to Subcategory and click OK. The Attribute Relationships tab now displays the Category, Subcategory, Product, and Product ID natural hierarchy.

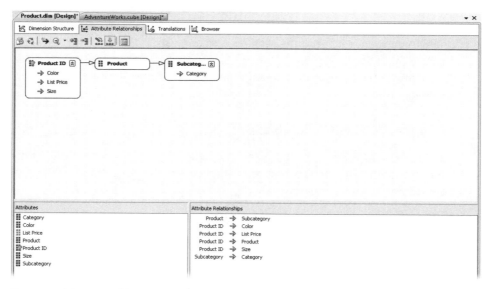

Because this natural hierarchy has been defined, Analysis Services now knows that it can derive a Category value by aggregating Subcategory values, and it can derive a Subcategory value by aggregating Product values.

Creating attribute relationships is not enough to add attributes to the pool of attributes that will be considered by the aggregation designer. You must also create user-defined hierarchies.

Create user-defined hierarchies

In this procedure, you will create the Product by Category user-defined hierarchy that is a natural hierarchy and the Size by Color user-defined hierarchy that is not a natural hierarchy. You will then be able to see how these two user-defined hierarchies affect the pool of attributes that are eligible for aggregation.

1. In Dimension Designer, select the Dimension Structure tab.

2. In the Attributes pane, right-click Category and select Start New Hierarchy. A new user-defined hierarchy with Category as the top level is created in the Hierarchies pane.

3. Drag the Subcategory attribute from the Attributes pane and drop it on <new level>.

4. Drag the Product attribute from the Attributes pane and drop it on <new level>.

5. In the Hierarchy pane, right-click the new hierarchy header and select Rename.

6. In the hierarchy header, type **Product by Category** and press ENTER. Your new user-defined hierarchy should look like this.

7. In the Attributes pane, right-click Color and select Start New Hierarchy.

8. Drag the Size attribute from the Attributes pane to the new hierarchy and drop it on <new level>.

9. In the Hierarchy pane, right-click the new hierarchy header and select Rename. Type **Size by Color** and press ENTER.

    The Hierarchies pane now displays two user-defined hierarchies.

10. Select Save All from the File menu.

Now you are ready to run the Aggregation Design Wizard and view the effect of creating attribute relationships and user-defined hierarchies.

Redesign aggregations

1. In Solution Explorer, right-click AdventureWorks.cube and select View Designer. Verify that the Aggregation tab is selected.

2. On the Aggregations tab toolbar, click Standard View.

3. Right-click the Reseller Sales measure group and select Design Aggregations. On the Welcome To The Aggregation Design Wizard page, click Next.

4. On the Review Aggregation Usage page, click Next.

5. On the Specify Object Counts page, expand the Employee, Product, and Date dimensions. The Specify Object Counts page displays the attribute hierarchies that belong to the pool of eligible attributes and the attributes where the value of the *AggregationUsage* property is *Full*. Eight attributes now appear on this page—the four attributes that originally appeared, Employee, Employees, Product ID, and Date, plus Product, Color, Subcategory, and Category. Color and Category are now in the pool of eligible attributes because they are used in the top level of a user-defined hierarchy. Product is in the pool of eligible attributes because it is the source attribute ("child") for Subcategory in an attribute relationship, and Product is on a level below Subcategory in a user-defined hierarchy. Subcategory is in the pool because it is the source attribute for Category and because it is on a level below Category in a user-defined hierarchy.

   The Size attribute is not in the pool of eligible attributes even though it is on a level below Color in a user-defined hierarchy. It is not in the pool because it has no attribute relationship with Color. If you think that users will frequently query by Color and Size, you can add Size to the pool of eligible attributes by changing the value of its AggregationUsage to Unrestricted.

6. Click Back. On the Review Aggregation Usage page, set the *AggregationUsage* property for Size to *Unrestricted* by selecting Unrestricted in the Size row.

> **Important** When you change the *AggregationUsage* property on the Review Aggregation Usage page, the value of the property is changed for the attribute for the cube. If you only want to change the value of the property for the aggregation design that you are currently creating, you must change it back after you complete the wizard.

7. Click Next. On the Specify Object Counts page, expand the Employee, Product, and Date dimensions. The Size attribute now appears, indicating that it is in the pool of attributes eligible to be considered by the aggregation designer. The Estimated Count and Partition Count columns are either blank or contain a zero for the attributes that have been newly added to the pool of eligible attributes. In order to design aggregations, the wizard must know the count of members in each of these attributes.

8. On the Specify Object Counts page, click Count. Click Next.

9. On the Set Aggregation Options page, select Performance Gain Reaches and verify that the percentage value is 30. Click Start. When aggregation design is complete, the Set Aggregation Options page should look like this.

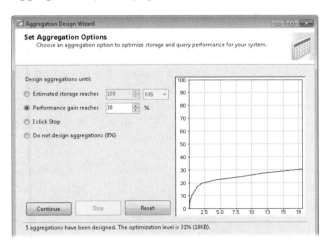

Because more attributes are eligible to be considered by the aggregation designer, more aggregations have been designed. This time five aggregations have been designed. These additional aggregations are going to require more disk space for storage when the changes are saved and the measure group partition is processed. If you find that aggregations are taking up too much disk space, you can decrease the performance gain percentage or estimated storage values on the Set Aggregation Options page to limit the number of aggregations that are created by the wizard.

10. Click Next. On the Completing The Wizard page, accept the default name, AggregationDesign 1, verify that the option Save The Aggregations But Do Not Process Them is selected, and click Finish. The Aggregations tab of the Cube Designer now displays both of the aggregation designs you have created, and the Partitions column indicates that the Fact Reseller Sales partition will use the new aggregation design. You may notice that there is a blue wavy line underneath AggregationDesign, indicating that BIDS is raising a Design Warning.

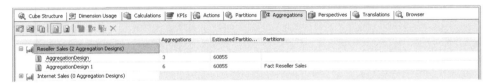

11. Point to AggregationDesign. You will see a tooltip that displays the message Remove This Aggregation Design Because It Is Not Used By Any Partitions.

12. Right-click AggregationDesign and select Delete. In the Delete Objects dialog box, click OK. You can use the Advanced View of the Aggregations tab to view the individual aggregations in the new aggregation design.

13. On the Aggregations tab toolbar, click Advanced View. Verify that Reseller Sales is selected from the Measure Group list and select AggregationDesign 1 from the Aggregation Design list.

14. Expand the Employee, Product, and Date dimensions. The Advanced View should display six columns, one for each aggregation. The order of the aggregations may vary (for example, it doesn't matter if the aggregation that contains the Color and Size attributes appears in aggregation A1 or in aggregation A4). The Advanced View should appear similar to this.

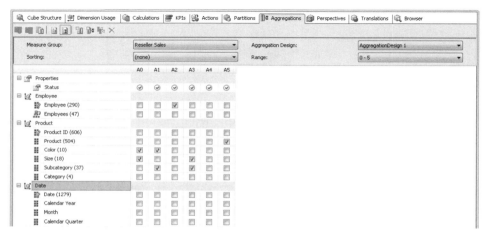

Notice that because they were added to the pool of eligible attributes, there are aggregations containing the leaf level members of the Product, Color, Size, and Subcategory attribute hierarchies. Just because an attribute is eligible for aggregation does not mean it will used. The Category attribute is in the pool of eligible attributes, but it is not used in any aggregations.

Designing an Aggregation

Because the Aggregation Design Wizard assumes that all queries are equally likely, it may not design an aggregation that you know will be frequently used. For example, you may know that users will frequently request Reseller Sales Amount by Subcategory and by Month. If, after very careful consideration, you decide you would like to add an aggregation to an aggregation design, you may do so using the Advanced View of the Aggregations tab. In the next procedure, you will add an aggregation containing the leaf level members of the Subcategory and Month attribute hierarchies.

Important When determining whether to add aggregations to your cube, you must carefully weigh the tradeoffs between query performance and the additional disk space required to store the aggregations and time it will take to process the aggregations. While it may be tempting to create aggregations that would satisfy as many query requests as possible, aggregations should be added to a cube only when deemed necessary and when the benefit of the additional query performance outweighs the cost of creating the additional aggregation or aggregations.

Design an aggregation

1. Verify that you are working with the Advanced View of the Cube Designer's Aggregations tab, that Reseller Sales is selected from the Measure Group list, and that AggregationDesign 1 is selected from the Aggregation Design list.

2. On the Aggregation tab toolbar, click New Aggregation. A new aggregation, A0, with no attribute hierarchies will be created and displayed in the first column of the designer.

3. In column A0, select the Subcategory attribute and the Month attribute. You have just designed an aggregation that should look like this.

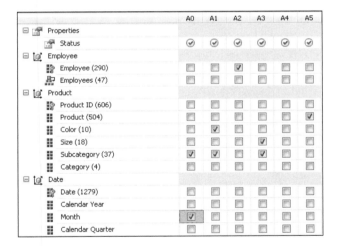

Changing Partition Counts

One of the key pieces of information that the Aggregation Design Wizard requires is the count of fact table rows as well as the count of members for all attributes that are in the pool of attributes eligible for aggregation. When you develop an Analysis Services database, you often use a development version of the source database. Because the development database might contain only a subset of the data in the source database, the count of records in the fact table and the count of members in each attribute retrieved from the development database will be different from the counts retrieved from the source database. To get an aggregation design that will be optimized for the source database while working with the development database, you can enter long-term estimates of the source database fact table record and attribute member counts. These estimates don't need to be too precise; the important thing is to get a rough approximation of the ratio of fact table records to attribute members.

In the following procedure, you will run the Aggregation Design Wizard and enter long-term estimates of the source database record counts. You will need to enter values in the Partition Count column for some of the attributes on the Specify Object Counts page. You will then be able to observe the impact of these changes on the aggregation design.

Create an aggregation design using estimated counts

1. On the Aggregations tab toolbar, click Standard View.

2. Right-click the Reseller Sales measure group and select Design Aggregations. On the Welcome To The Aggregation Design Wizard page, click Next.

3. On the Review Aggregation Usage page, click Next.

4. On the Specify Object Counts page, expand the Employee, Product, and Date dimensions.

   In Chapter 14, you will learn how to create multiple partitions. Let's assume that you will partition by year, so you will want an aggregation design based on the Date attribute having 365 members. Also, although Adventure Works has 290 employees, you know that in the long term, the sales organization only has 30 employees and five managers. Finally, you project that sales to resellers will grow to 500,000 line items per year.

5. Change the value in the Partition Count for the fact table and attributes as shown in the following table.

Cube Object	Partition Count
Reseller Sales	500,000
Employee	30
Employees	5
Date	365

   The Specify Object Counts page should look like the following image.

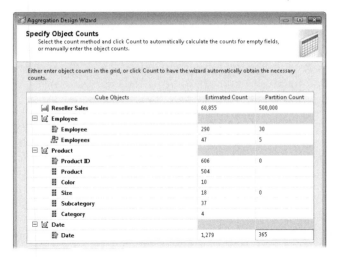

6. Click Next. On the Set Aggregation Options page, select Performance Gain Reaches and verify that the percentage value is 30. Click Start. When aggregation design is complete, the Set Aggregation Options page should look like this.

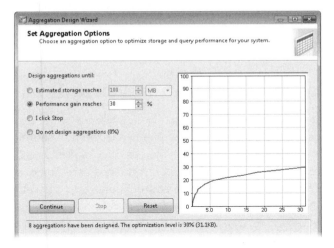

The number of aggregations has increased to eight. When you increased the count of fact records and decreased the count of attribute members, you increased the average number of fact records per attribute. The more fact records per attribute member, the greater the benefit of creating aggregates, so the aggregation designer created more aggregations.

7. Click Next. On the Completing the Wizard page, change the name to
   AggregationDesign 2, verify that the option Save The Aggregations But Do Not
   Process Them is selected, and click Finish. The Aggregations tab of the Cube Designer
   now displays the new aggregation design and indicates that the Fact Reseller Sales
   partition will use AggregationDesign 2. In the next section, you will browse the cube, so
   you need to deploy and process the Analysis Services database.

8. On the Build menu, click Deploy AdventureWorks SSAS. If the AdventureWorks SSAS
   database already exists on the server, a dialog box may appear warning that the database will be overwritten. If the warning appears, click Yes. The prior version of the database will be deleted and the current deployment will continue.

You have learned how to design aggregations using the Aggregation Design Wizard. The wizard uses a sophisticated algorithm that selects from a pool of eligible attribute hierarchies and
creates an aggregation design that may contain multiple aggregations. You then increased the
number of attributes eligible to be considered by the wizard by creating attribute relationships
and user-defined hierarchies and by changing the value of an attribute's *AggregationUsage*
property to *Unrestricted*. You also learned that it is important to provide the wizard with a
count of fact table records and attribute members based on a long-term estimate of these values in the source database. When you increased the ratio of fact records per attribute member,
the wizard designed more aggregations. If absolutely necessary, you can also design aggregations using the Advanced View of the Aggregations tab of the Cube Designer.

Using the Usage-Based Optimization Wizard

You can design aggregations using the Aggregation Design Wizard or the Usage-Based
Optimization Wizard. The main difference between the two wizards is that the Aggregation
Design Wizard considers all queries equally likely, whereas the Usage-Based Optimization
Wizard creates aggregations designed to optimize performance based on queries
selected from a log. The best strategy is to design aggregations during development with
the Aggregation Design Wizard using estimated long-term counts and a low performance
gain (20–30%). Then, if you need to improve query performance, log the queries that your
users execute and use the Usage-Based Optimization Wizard to design aggregations that can
be used to supplement or replace the aggregations designed with the Aggregation Design
Wizard.

Before you can use the Usage-Based Optimization Wizard, you must enable Analysis Services
query logging. You use SQL Server Management Studio (SSMS) to configure the connection
to the SQL Server database containing the table that will hold the log records. You will also
need to configure the proportion of queries that are logged. After you have enabled query
logging, you need to allow sufficient time for users to execute queries. When a representative sample of queries has been logged, you can then use the Usage-Based Optimization
Wizard to design aggregations. The Usage-Based Optimization Wizard will allow you to

specify which logged queries you want it to use to design aggregations. You can select queries that were executed during a date range, executed by specific users, most frequently executed, or took a long time to execute. The wizard will design aggregations that optimize the performance of these queries. You can then add these aggregations to an existing aggregation design or create a new aggregation design.

Enable query logging

In this procedure, you will enable Analysis Services query logging using SSMS.

1. On the Microsoft Windows task bar, click Start, point to All Programs, expand the Microsoft SQL Server 2008 folder, and then select SQL Server Management Studio.

2. In the Connect to Server dialog box, select Analysis Services from the Server Type list, type **localhost** in the Server Name text box, and click Connect.

3. In Object Explorer, right-click Localhost and select Properties.

4. In the Analysis Server Properties dialog box on the General page, locate the *Log \ QueryLog \ QueryLogConnectionString* property, click the cell in the Value column, and then click the button that appears in the cell.

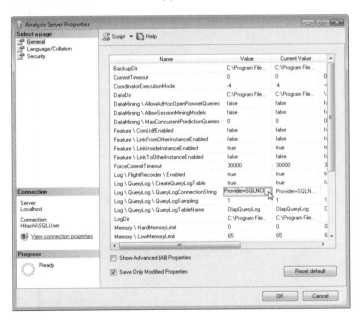

You can use the Connection Manager dialog box to specify the SQL Server database that will contain the query log table. For the sake of convenience, you will create the query log table in the SSAS2008SBS database, the same database that contains the source data. As a best practice, you will want to store this table in a separate database that is dedicated for administrative use.

5. In the Connection Manager dialog box, enter **localhost** in the Server Name text box and select SSAS2008SBS from the Select Or Enter a Database Name list. Click OK.

   The query log table will have to have a name. By default, the table is named OlapQueryLog. You can change this name if you wish, but for now accept the default value.

6. Verify that the Value column of the *Log \ QueryLog \ QueryLogTableName* property contains OlapQueryLog. You can create the query log table or use an existing table, but it is easier to let SSMS create the table for you.

7. Change the Value column of the *Log \ QueryLog \ CreateQueryLogTable* property to *True*. The table will be created at the end of this procedure when you click OK and close the Analysis Services Properties dialog box.

   Finally, you need to configure the proportion of queries that will be logged. By default, Analysis Services logs one of every ten queries.

8. Change the Value column of the *Log \ QueryLog \ QueryLogSampling* from 10 to 1. A value of 1 will cause Analysis Services to log every query. Generally, this sampling frequency would be excessive, but in the next procedure, you will want to populate the query log quickly so that you can use the Usage-Based Optimization Wizard.

   The values of the *Log \ Query Log* properties should now be configured to enable query logging.

9. Click OK.

 Important Be sure to reset the value of the *Log \ QueryLog \ QueryLogSampling* property to a more suitable value, such as the default value of 10, if you plan on using this optimization technique on your own databases. You can disable query logging by setting the value to zero.

Now that query logging is enabled, you can browse the cube and Analysis Services will create query log entries.

Populate and view the query log

In this procedure, you will browse the AdventureWorks cube using the SSMS cube browser. This browser is identical to the BIDS cube browser.

1. In Object Explorer in SQL Server Management Studio, expand the Databases folder, expand the AdventureWorks SSAS database, and expand the Cubes folder.

2. Right-click the AdventureWorks cube and select Browse.

3. In the cube browser, expand the Measures folder, expand the Reseller Sales measure group, and add Reseller Order Quantity to the Report pane totals area.

4. Add the Product dimension to the Report pane rows area. Expand the Bikes category and expand the Mountain Bikes subcategory.

5. Continue to spend a few minutes browsing the AdventureWorks cube. Add and remove hierarchies and attributes from the Date, Employee, and Product dimensions. Each time you add or remove an attribute or hierarchy from the browser, a query is executed and logged in the OLAPQueryLog table. Browse by a combination of attributes and hierarchies from multiple dimensions so that the query log contains a good variety of queries. Be sure to browse by the Date dimension Calendar Year, Calendar Quarter, and Month attributes.

   Now that you have executed some queries, you can view the records that have been entered in the query log. You will need to connect to SQL Server and then view the records in the OlapQueryLog table contained in the SSAS2008SBS database.

   You don't need to review the data in the query log before you use the Usage-Based Optimization Wizard, but it is a good idea to confirm that the log has been populated and to become familiar with the type of information stored in the table.

6. In Object Explorer, click Connect and select Database Engine.

7. In the Connect To Server dialog box, change the Server Name to **localhost** and click Connect.

8. In Object Explorer under Localhost (SQL Server...), expand the Databases folder, expand the SSAS2008SBS database, and expand the Tables folder.

9. Right-click the OlapQueryLog table and select Select Top 1000 Rows. The SSMS SQL Query Editor will open and execute a query that returns the records contained in the OlapQueryLog table. You may want to close Object Explorer and Properties windows to make it easier to view the data contained in the table.

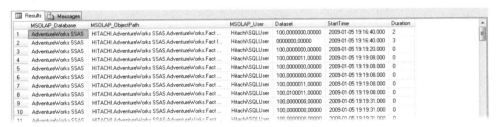

The query log table contains six columns, which are described in Table 13-2.

TABLE 13-2 **The Query Log Table Columns**

Column	Description
MSOLAP_Database	Name of the Analysis Services database.
MSOLAP_ObjectPath	Fully qualified name of the object that was queried in the format ServerName.DatabaseName.CubeName.PartitionName.
MSOLAP_User	Name of the user who executed the query.
Dataset	A string of zeros and ones indicating the level of each attribute hierarchy used to provide the query results. Don't worry about trying to interpret this string; the Usage-Based Optimization Wizard will interpret the string and display the names of the attribute hierarchies returned by a query.
StartTime	Time the query began in Coordinated Universal Time (UTC).
Duration	Length of time, in milliseconds, that it took to execute the query.

You may notice that the OlapQueryLog table seems to contain many more records than you ran queries. This occurs because Analysis Services will frequently divide a single query into multiple parts. For example, if you execute a query requesting both Category and Subcategory, Analysis Services will actually execute two queries.

 Important If you make a structural change to a cube, such as adding or removing a dimension or attribute, all of the query log entries for the cube will be deleted when the changes are deployed to the Analysis Services server.

Now that you've accumulated a set of queries in the log, you can use the Usage-Based Optimization Wizard to design aggregations.

Design aggregations using the Usage-Based Optimization Wizard

1. Switch back to BIDS. Verify that you are working on the Standard View of the Aggregations tab of the Cube Designer.

2. Right-click the Reseller Sales measure group and select Usage-Based Optimization. On the Usage-Based Optimization Wizard welcome page, click Next.

3. On the Specify Query Criteria page, there are several different filters that you can use to customize the optimization process: Beginning Date, Ending Date, Users, and Most Frequent Queries. Since the query log has only been tracking data on one day, for one user, and only for a very short period, changing the filter criteria won't make much difference right now. When you work with a database that has been placed in production, however, these filters can be quite useful. For example, you can base the optimization on the queries created by power users, so that the query performance is best for the people who use the data the most frequently. For this procedure, do not select any filter criteria options. Click Next.

4. On the Review The Queries That Will Be Optimized page, you can see the frequency with which specific attribute combinations were queried and the average duration of queries that include these combinations. You can click the Occurrences or Average Duration column headers to sort the entries, and you can clear the check box next to an entry to remove it from the optimization process. For this procedure, do not make any changes to the options on this page. Click Next.

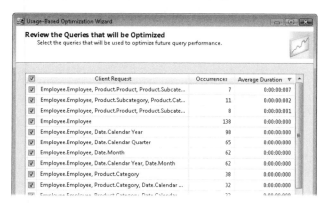

5. On the Specify Object Counts page, expand the Employee, Product, and Date dimensions. All of the attributes in the dimensions related to the measure group now appear. You will need to provide member counts for the attributes that are appearing on this page for the first time.

6. On the Specify Object Counts page, click Count. Because you want to design aggregations for this partition using long-term estimates of the source database record counts, you will need to enter values in the Partition Count column for some of the attributes.

7. Change the values in the Partition Count column for the attributes shown in the following table.

Cube Object	Partition Count
Employee	30
Employees	5
Date	365
Calendar Year	1
Month	12
Calendar Quarter	4

The Specify Object Counts page should look like the following image.

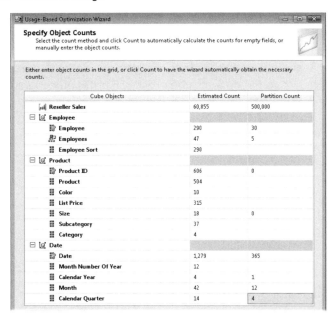

8. Click Next. On the Set Aggregation Options page, verify that Performance Gain Reaches is selected and the percentage amount is 100. When creating aggregations using the Usage-Based Optimization Wizard, you set this value to 100 so that the wizard will create aggregations for all the queries you have selected in the query log. Click Start. When your aggregation design is complete, the Set Aggregation Options page should look similar to this.

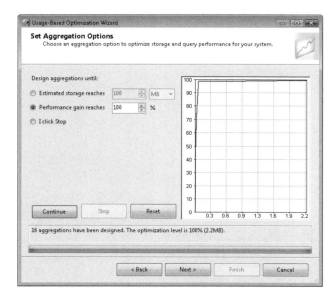

The number of aggregations the wizard created for you may differ from the number shown here, because your query log may contain different records based on how you browsed the cube.

9. Click Next. When you run the Usage-Based Optimization Wizard, the Completing The Wizard page will allow you to create a new aggregation design, or you can merge the aggregations the wizard has designed with an existing aggregation. If you have run the wizard with a representative sample of queries, then you will want to create a new aggregation design. If you selected a subset of queries from the query log, for example, you may have selected slow-running queries or queries executed by a subset of users, so you will want to merge the aggregations designed by the wizard with an existing aggregation.

10. On the Completing The Wizard page, verify that Create A New Aggregation Design is selected, change the name to **AggregationDesign 3**, and click Finish. The Aggregations tab of the Cube Designer now displays the new aggregation design and indicates that the Fact Reseller Sales partition will use AggregationDesign 3. AggregationDesign 1 and AggregationDesign 2 display Design Warnings, because they are not being used by any partitions. Delete these aggregation designs.

11. Right-click AggregationDesign 1 and select Delete. In the Delete Objects dialog box, click OK. Repeat this step for AggregationDesign 2.

12. Select Save All from the File menu and then close BIDS. Close SQL Server Management Studio.

In this chapter, you learned that aggregations enable Analysis Services to provide fast query response by precalculating summary values and storing the values on disk. You learned how to design aggregations using the Aggregation Design Wizard. The Aggregation Design Wizard assumes that all queries are equally likely, and then it designs aggregations by selecting from a pool of attributes that are eligible to be included, using the count of fact records and attribute members. You learned how to create attribute relationships that identify the natural hierarchies in a dimension and how to create user-defined hierarchies to indicate important drilldown paths. The Aggregation Design Wizard can use this information to create an improved aggregation design. You also learned how to design aggregations using the Usage-Based Optimization Wizard. The Usage-Based Optimization Wizard is similar to the Aggregation Design Wizard except that instead of considering all queries equally likely, it designs aggregations to optimize the performance of queries that have been recorded in a log.

Chapter 14
Managing Partitions and Database Processing

In this chapter, you will learn how to:

- Configure a dimension to use ROLAP or MOLAP storage.

- Configure a measure group partition to use ROLAP, HOLAP, or MOLAP storage.

- Configure rigid attribute relationships.

- Process a dimension using the Process Update processing option.

- Process a partition using the Process Incremental processing option.

- Configure proactive caching.

- Create, merge, and manage measure group partitions.

- Import an Analysis Services design into a Business Intelligence Development Studio project.

In Chapter 11, "Retrieving Data from Analysis Services," you learned how to use client tools and MDX queries to get data out of Analysis Services and into a PivotTable dynamic view or other report. In order to get data *out of* the Analysis Services database, you had to first put data *into* the Analysis Services database. In previous chapters, every time you were ready to apply your changes, you simply deployed your solution and let the Analysis Services server work its magic to determine how to go about loading the data from the relational data warehouse into the Analysis Services database. How Analysis Services actually processed and stored that data has been a conceptual black box up to this point. Knowledge is power, however, and that adage certainly holds true in the domain of Microsoft SQL Server 2008 Analysis Services. The more you know about what goes on within the black box of the Analysis Services server, the better you'll be able to troubleshoot unusual situations and find solutions to difficult problems.

This chapter explains in broad terms what goes on inside that black box. You will learn about how Analysis Services physically processes and stores data. The explanations are simplified, but they encompass some of the most complex topics in this book. If nothing else, this chapter can give you an appreciation for the sophistication and elegance of the Analysis Services server design.

Working with Storage

An Analysis Services database uses four types of information: the design of database objects (dimensions, cubes, measure groups, and so on), dimension data, detail values, and aggregated values.

Analysis Services always stores the design of database objects in XML files on the Analysis Services server, but it allows you to decide where the dimension data, details values, and aggregated values are stored. You can choose from three storage modes that correspond to different physical storage locations:

- ROLAP (relational OLAP) leaves dimension data and detail values in the relational database. If the relational database is SQL Server Database Engine, Analysis Services can also create indexed views in the relational database to store aggregated values.

- HOLAP (hybrid OLAP) leaves the detail values in the relational fact table but stores aggregated values on the Analysis Services server. HOLAP is not an option for dimension storage.

- MOLAP (multidimensional OLAP) stores dimension data, detail values, and aggregated values on the Analysis Services server.

No matter which storage mode you choose, the database design is stored on the Analysis Services server. It's the database design that makes Analysis Services data appear to be in a cube to a person running a query. That means the storage mode is invisible to client applications—that is, applications that query the cube. The client application always sees the cube. Deciding which storage option to use is primarily based on processing and query performance and has no effect on how client applications will interact with the cube.

Because a client application can't tell which storage mode you have chosen, you can change the storage mode without affecting any client applications. After you specify storage and start using the cube, you can still change your mind later and switch to a different storage type. Because a cube appears to the client application as a single, logical entity, you can use different storage modes for different portions of a cube. To avoid doing that, you must use multiple partitions. You will learn about creating partitions later in this chapter.

 Note Regardless of which storage mode you choose, Analysis Services will never allocate storage for missing values. For example, if you have a database that shows you didn't start selling products in Australia until 2010, Analysis Services will use no storage space for detail or aggregated values for Australia in 2008.

Understanding Dimension Storage Modes

You can choose to store dimension data using ROLAP or MOLAP storage mode. If you choose ROLAP storage, the dimension data will be stored in the source dimension tables. If you choose MOLAP storage, the dimension data will be stored on the Analysis Services server. You can use dimensions with ROLAP or MOLAP storage with partitions that have ROLAP, HOLAP, or MOLAP storage with one restriction: If the partition uses MOLAP storage, it must have one dimension that uses MOLAP storage. If you use a dimension with ROLAP storage with a partition that uses MOLAP storage, any time you execute a query that uses a leaf level member from an attribute in the ROLAP dimension, Analysis Services will have to retrieve the values from the relational database. For example, if Product was a ROLAP dimension and a user included the members of the Product Color attribute hierarchy in a query, Analysis Services would have to retrieve both the dimension data and the fact data directly from the relational database, and you would lose some of the query performance benefits that MOLAP storage provides. The only time you want to use the ROLAP storage mode for a dimension is when a dimension contains an extremely large number of members or when you want a measure group that uses only ROLAP storage for its dimensions and partitions.

In the next procedure you will learn how to change the storage mode to ROLAP for a dimension. Later in this chapter, you will work with cubes that contain partitions using ROLAP and MOLAP storage. You will then browse the cubes and see that to a client application, the cubes appear alike.

Modify dimension storage settings

1. Use Business Intelligence Development Studio (BIDS) to open the AdventureWorks BI solution contained in the C:\Microsoft Press\Analysis Services 2008 SBS\Chapter 14 \AdventureWorks BI folder. The AdventureWorks SSAS database contains two dimensions, Geography MOLAP and Geography ROLAP, which are identical. You will change the storage mode of the Geography ROLAP dimension to Real-time ROLAP. The other three dimensions, Date, Employee, and Product, use MOLAP storage.

2. In Solution Explorer, expand the Dimensions folder, right-click Geography ROLAP.dim, and select View Designer.

3. In the Attributes pane of the Dimension Designer, right-click the Geography ROLAP dimension and select Properties.

4. In the Properties window, select the *ProactiveCaching* property and click the ellipsis button (...) that appears on the right.

5. In the Dimension Storage Settings dialog box, drag the slider to Real-time ROLAP and click OK. The Properties window will now show that the value of the *ProactiveCaching* property is *Real-time ROLAP*, and the value of the *StorageMode* property is *Rolap*.

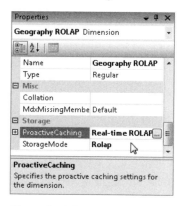

6.   Close the Dimension Designer and save the changes to the Geography ROLAP dimension.

You were able to change the storage mode of the dimension without making any other change to its design. Query performance is the only difference that a user should perceive between a dimension that uses MOLAP storage and one that uses ROLAP storage.

> **Note** In addition to query performance, there is one minor difference in the way Analysis Services will display data related to a ROLAP dimension attribute's unknown member in some special circumstances. If you are considering using ROLAP storage for a dimension that has the *UnknownMember* property enabled, refer to SQL Server 2008 Books Online for more information on this special case.

In the next section, you will learn how to change the storage mode of a measure group partition.

Understanding Partition Storage Modes

Choosing a storage mode is not as difficult as it might seem. Use ROLAP storage if your analytical solution requires real-time data or if you have insufficient disk storage or processing time to process a large volume of data into MOLAP storage. The ROLAP storage with aggregations option is rarely used because aggregations in a relational database can be bulky, and they usually only marginally improve query performance. You might choose the ROLAP storage with aggregations option if you're learning about aggregations and want to physically look at the aggregation tables, but this storage mode is rarely used in practice.

Aggregations in both MOLAP and HOLAP are identical—the only difference is where the detail-level values are stored. If you count the space required by the original warehouse as well as the space needed for the OLAP cubes, MOLAP does consume more storage space than HOLAP because the MOLAP storage option duplicates the values from the fact table. Analysis Services, however, is very efficient in how it stores data. An Analysis Services database will often use less than half of the storage space of its source database. With a very large warehouse database, you could process the data into a MOLAP cube and then archive and remove the original warehouse. By using the MOLAP storage option, you could actually end up using a fraction of the original storage space.

If you have a large, permanent warehouse—and if using aggregations can satisfy most queries—you may want to consider HOLAP storage. Queries that must retrieve detail data are slower than if the cube used MOLAP storage, but if they're infrequent, the performance gain might not be worth the incremental storage requirements. In addition, processing a MOLAP cube can take more time than processing a HOLAP cube. While developing an OLAP cube, you may want to use HOLAP storage simply to speed up processing during the time that you process frequently. When you have completed the database design, you can switch to MOLAP storage to maximize query performance.

Note Some descriptions of warehouse technology use the term ROLAP to refer to a relational data warehouse that has a fact table and dimensional tables. This is a different meaning of the term than is used within Analysis Services and corresponds most closely to a ROLAP cube with no aggregations.

The AdventureWorks SSAS database contains two cubes, ROLAP and MOLAP, that both use MOLAP storage. The cubes are identical except that the ROLAP cube contains the Geography ROLAP dimension, whereas the MOLAP cube contains the Geography MOLAP dimension. In the next procedure, you will change the storage mode of one of the partitions in the ROLAP cube. You will then browse the cubes and see that they appear to be identical.

Modify partition storage settings

1. In Solution Explorer, expand the Cubes folder, right-click ROLAP.cube, and select View Designer.

2. In the Cube Designer, click the Partitions tab. The Reseller Sales measure group contains one partition, Fact Reseller Sales. Notice that the partition's storage mode is MOLAP. In the next three steps, you will change the storage mode to ROLAP.

3. Right-click the Fact Reseller Sales partition and click Storage Settings.

Note You can also change the storage mode by clicking the Storage Settings link. However, if you click this link without first selecting a partition, the changes you make won't affect any of the existing partitions. Instead, the storage settings that you specify will become the default settings for new partitions.

4. In the Partition Storage Settings dialog box, drag the slider to Real-time ROLAP and click OK.

5. Verify that the partition's Storage Mode column displays ROLAP, like this:

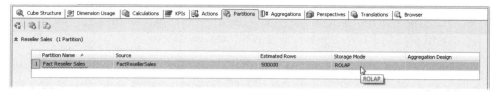

6. Close the Cube Designer and save the changes to the ROLAP cube. In the next procedure, you will browse these two cubes, so you need to deploy and process the
   AdventureWorks SSAS database.

7. On the Build menu, select Deploy AdventureWorks SSAS. If the AdventureWorks SSAS
   database already exists on the server, a dialog box may appear warning that the database will be overwritten. If the warning appears, click Yes. The prior version of the database will be deleted and the current deployment will continue.

You are now ready to browse the cubes and see that they appear identical.

In the next procedure, you will browse the cubes using SQL Server Management Studio (SSMS).

Browse the ROLAP and MOLAP cubes

1. On the Microsoft Windows task bar, click Start, point to All Programs, expand the
   Microsoft SQL Server 2008 folder, and then select SQL Server Management Studio.

2. In the Connect To Server dialog box, select Analysis Services from the Server Type list.
   In the Server Name text box, type **localhost** and click Connect.

3. In Object Explorer, expand the Databases folder, expand the AdventureWorks SSAS database, and expand the Cubes folder.

4. In Object Explorer, right-click the ROLAP cube and select Browse.

5. In the Metadata pane, expand the Measures folder, expand the Reseller Sales measure
   group, and drag the Reseller Order Quantity measure to the totals area of the Report
   pane.

6. In the Metadata pane, expand the Date dimension and drag the Calendar Year attribute
   to the columns area of the Report pane.

7. Expand the Geography ROLAP dimension and drag the Geography hierarchy to the
   rows area of the Report pane. Click the Report pane and then right-click the Area attribute and select Expand Items. The report should look like this:

8. Repeat steps 4 through 7 to create one more report that uses the MOLAP cube. In step 4, select the MOLAP cube. In step 7, use the Geography MOLAP dimension.

You should now have a window in SSMS for the ROLAP cube and a window for the MOLAP cube. The values in both of the reports should be identical. Leave these reports open—you will use them in the next procedure.

Changing Data in a Warehouse

When you process an Analysis Services database, you update the information in the dimensions and measure groups based on the data stored in the data warehouse and the design of your database. If you change the design—for example, if you add a measure or a dimension to a cube—you must process the affected portions of the database. If the data in the data warehouse changes, as it inevitably will, you will also need to process the affected portions of your Analysis Services database.

The information in a data warehouse is almost always time-dependent. That means that at the very least, you'll continually add new time periods to your data warehouse. In time, you might also add additional products or additional geographic regions. When the data warehouse changes, you need to process the database to resynchronize your Analysis Services database with the relational data warehouse.

The FactResellerSales table in the SSAS2008SBS database contains data for six countries through June 2011. In the SSAS2008SBS database, the DimSalesTerritory dimension table includes only the six countries that appear in the fact table. The DimDate dimension table, however, includes months through December 2011. It is not uncommon in a warehouse to include months in the date dimension through the end of the current quarter or year, but to add members to other dimensions only as they are needed.

Included in the C:\Microsoft Press\Analysis Services 2008 SBS\Chapter 14\SQL folder is a SQL script named Update Warehouse 1.sql. This script adds Mexico to the DimSalesTerritory table and an additional row in the fact table for a sale in Mexico for December 2011. Inserting these records into the source database for the cubes simulates, on a very small scale, the load operations that occur regularly in a production data warehouse.

In the next procedure, you'll execute queries that insert data into the warehouse and then observe the effect of changed data on the cubes. You will see that the storage mode for a dimension or measure group partition affects what data is displayed by a cube when source data is changed.

Insert source data

1. On the SSMS File menu, point to Open and select File. In the Open File dialog box, browse to the C:\Microsoft Press\Microsoft Press\Analysis Services 2008 SBS\Chapter 14\SQL folder, select Update Warehouse 1.sql, and click Open.

2. On the Query menu, point to Connection and select Connect. In the Connect To Database Engine dialog box, change the Server Name to **localhost** and click Connect.

3. On the SSMS toolbar, click Execute. After the query executes successfully, close the Update Warehouse 1.sql Query window.

4. Select the ROLAP [Browse] window and on the Browser toolbar, click Reconnect. With Real-time ROLAP storage mode, changes to the source database immediately appear in the cube, because the dimension and partition data is stored only in the source database. The newly added country, Mexico, is displayed on rows in the Geography ROLAP dimension, and the number of items in the newly added order, 122, is displayed at the intersection of Mexico and CY 2011. Aggregate values have also been updated. The total for CY 2011 has increased by 122 to 45,252 and the total for all years and all countries has increased by 122 to 214,500.

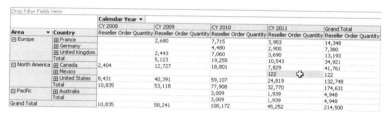

Area	Country	CY 2008 Reseller Order Quantity	CY 2009 Reseller Order Quantity	CY 2010 Reseller Order Quantity	CY 2011 Reseller Order Quantity	Grand Total Reseller Order Quantity
Europe	France		2,680	7,715	3,953	14,348
	Germany			4,480	2,900	7,380
	United Kingdom		2,443	7,060	3,690	13,193
	Total		5,123	19,255	10,543	34,921
North America	Canada	2,404	12,727	18,801	7,829	41,761
	Mexico				122	122
	United States	8,431	40,391	59,107	24,819	132,748
	Total	10,835	53,118	77,908	32,770	174,631
Pacific	Australia			3,009	1,939	4,948
	Total			3,009	1,939	4,948
Grand Total		10,835	58,241	100,172	45,252	214,500

5. Select the MOLAP [Browse] window and on the Browser toolbar, click Reconnect. The grand total for Order Quantity for all countries is still 214,378, and Mexico doesn't appear in the list of countries. All the values are unchanged from before the warehouse changed.

The MOLAP cube uses MOLAP storage, and it behaves as if you had not changed the data source. When you use MOLAP storage, with or without aggregates, the cube is completely detached from the data warehouse. You can even delete the warehouse database without affecting the Analysis Services database. With MOLAP storage, you must process a dimension or partition to resynchronize with the data warehouse.

Managing Analysis Services Processing

The easiest way to make sure that an Analysis Services database is completely consistent with the data warehouse, and with itself, is to process the entire database. When you process the database, you completely discard all the dimensions and measure group partitions within the database and create new ones. This takes place as a single transaction, which means that client applications can continue to use the existing cubes until processing is complete. It also means that if an error occurs at any point during the processing, the entire change is rolled back, again ensuring that the database is internally consistent.

Processing the entire database is the simplest option, provided that you have sufficient time and storage space available. Although processing a large database can consume a considerable amount of time, users can continue to access the existing database while data is being updated in a new version of the database. For example, suppose you have an Analysis Services database that you update every day and that requires 10 hours to fully process. Assuming you have sufficient disk space, you could still choose to process the entire database, perhaps by starting the nightly processing after 19:00 or as soon as new data is available. Users would then have access to the updated database by the next morning. You would not have to exclude users from the system or wait for them to leave for the day.

Processing a large database can also consume a considerable amount of disk space. The Analysis Services server not only creates a second copy of all the dimension and partition files created during the transaction, but it also uses additional temporary files to accumulate aggregations, particularly when creating aggregations from a large fact table.

Consequently, some databases are simply too large to process as a single transaction. Analysis Services provides several options for processing individual components of a database. These options allow you to create and manage extremely large databases, but they also require much more work to provide users continuous access to the cubes and to prevent including invalid or inconsistent values in the database.

Processing a Dimension

When you process a dimension, the server creates a map that includes the path for each member of that dimension. Every cube that includes the dimension uses that map. When you process an existing dimension, the map is destroyed and a new map is created. Destroying the dimension map invalidates all the cubes that use the dimension. When you process an entire database, the dimensions are processed first and then all the cubes are processed as well. But when you process a single dimension, you make all the cubes that use that dimension inaccessible to client applications.

Fortunately, you can make certain changes to a dimension without destroying the existing map. If you don't destroy the existing map, you don't invalidate existing cubes. Analysis Services allows you to update a dimension to make changes that don't destroy the dimension map. The most useful change you can then make is adding new members to a dimension. You can also rename, delete, or re-parent members. For example, you could re-parent the Helmets member by changing its category from Accessories to Clothing.

> **Note** If a dimension member has fact data associated with it in the cube, Analysis Services can't actually delete the member permanently during a Process Update. Instead, Analysis Services will "hide" the member in the dimension, leaving the fact data in the cube. The associated fact data will still be included in aggregated values, but it will not be displayed alongside a member in the dimension.

Unfortunately, when you update a dimension, you delete the aggregations related to that dimension. To avoid deleting aggregations when you update a dimension, you need to change the attribute relationship property *RelationshipType* from its default value of *Flexible* to *Rigid*. Changing this property allows you to update a dimension without deleting all of the related aggregations. However, if this property is set to *Rigid* and you try to update a dimension, Analysis Services will fail the operation if it detects changes in the dimension table that aren't allowed. Deleting or re-parenting members of a rigid relationship requires the dimension to be fully reprocessed, which in turn forces each cube using the dimension to be reprocessed.

The Date dimension is a good candidate for rigid attribute relationships, because you should not delete dates, and the month, quarter, and year that a date belongs to shouldn't change. A product dimension with categories and subcategories may not be a good candidate for rigid attribute relationships because products may be deleted or recategorized.

In the next procedure, you will learn how to change the value of the attribute relationship property *RelationshipType* from *Flexible* to *Rigid*.

Create rigid attribute relationships

1. Switch to BIDS. In Solution Explorer, right-click Date.dim and select View Designer.

2. In the Attributes pane of the Dimension Designer, point at the Date dimension. Design Warnings will appear, including the warning "Define attribute relationships as 'Rigid' where appropriate." You should be careful about responding to this warning. Only define attribute relationships as Rigid if you are sure that when dimension members are deleted or re-parented, you will be able to fully reprocess the dimension and all cubes that contain the dimension.

3. Switch to the Attribute Relationships tab.

4. In the Attribute Relationships pane, right-click the Date – Month attribute relationship and select Edit Attribute Relationship.

5. In the Edit Attribute Relationship dialog box, change the Relationship Type to Rigid. Click OK. The Date - Month attribute relationship is now displayed with a solid arrow indicating that it is a rigid attribute relationship.

6. Repeat steps 4 and 5 for all of the other Date dimension attribute relationships.

7. Close the Dimension Designer and save the changes to the Date dimension.

In the procedure titled "Insert Source Data" earlier in the chapter, you inserted Mexico into the DimSalesTerritory dimension table, but Mexico has not yet appeared in the Geography MOLAP dimension. In the next procedure, you will update the dimension using SQL Server Management Studio so that it will contain this new member.

Update a dimension

1. Switch to SQL Server Management Studio (SSMS). In Object Explorer, expand the Dimensions folder, right-click the Geography MOLAP dimension, and select Process. The Process Dimension dialog box is displayed.

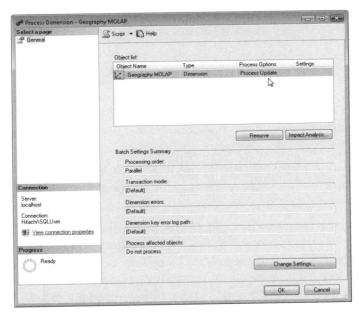

Notice that the Process Options value is *Process Update*. Analysis Services suggests the processing option with the lowest impact that synchronizes the dimension with the database design and the data warehouse. In this case, because the dimension has already been processed and no structural changes are detected in the dimension design, Analysis Services determines that full processing is not required, and suggests an update instead.

The processing option to update the dimension, Process Update, is appropriate when you make changes to the data in the dimension table. However, you will change this value to *Process Full* to observe the potential impact on other objects in the database. Notice the current setting for Process Affected Objects, visible at the bottom of the dialog box, is Do Not Process. Thus, any objects dependent on this dimension, such as partitions in the cube, will not be processed. You can review the impact of processing the Geography MOLAP dimension on other objects in the database by using the Impact Analysis feature.

2. In the Process Dimension dialog box, select Process Full from the Process Options list.

3. Click Impact Analysis. The Impact Analysis dialog box shows that the MOLAP cube and all of its measure group partitions would need to be processed if you were to perform a Process Full on the Geography MOLAP dimension. You can select objects in the Process Object column so that they will be processed immediately after the dimension is processed.

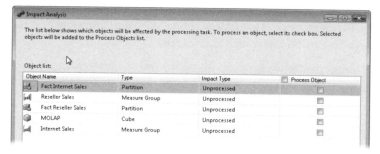

4. In the Impact Analysis dialog box, click Cancel. To avoid the need to process the MOLAP cube, change the processing options so that the dimension is updated.

5. In the Process Dimension dialog box, select Process Update from the Process Options list. Click Impact Analysis. The Impact Analysis dialog box shows that when you update a dimension, you don't need to process any other objects. You are now ready to update the dimension.

6. In the Impact Analysis dialog box, click Cancel. In the Process Dimension dialog box, click OK. The Process Progress dialog box appears, displaying the steps Analysis Services takes as it processes the dimension. When processing is complete, the Status will change to Process Succeeded. You can view additional information, including the SQL queries used to select data from the dimension table, by expanding the steps and substeps.

The "Process Cube 'MOLAP' completed" step makes it appear that the MOLAP cube was processed. However, if you expand the substeps, you will see that no SQL query was executed, meaning that no data was loaded into any of the partitions.

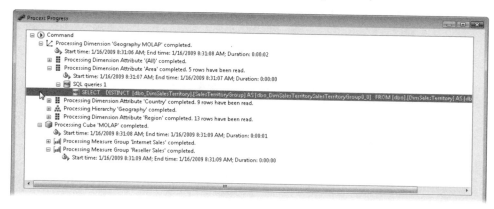

7. In the Process Progress dialog box, click Close. Now that the Geography MOLAP dimension has been updated, you should be able to see the new member, Mexico, when you browse the MOLAP cube.

8. Select the MOLAP [Browse] window. On the Browser toolbar, click Reconnect. Mexico doesn't appear. Because the MOLAP cube was not processed, no values are associated with Mexico. You will be able to see Mexico if you choose to display empty cells.

9. Right-click the Report pane and select Show Empty Cells. The report should now display Mexico as a member of the Country attribute, like this:

Area	Country	CY 2008 Reseller Order Quantity	CY 2009 Reseller Order Quantity	CY 2010 Reseller Order Quantity	CY 2011 Reseller Order Quantity	Grand Total Reseller Order Quantity
Europe	France			7,715	3,953	14,348
	Germany			4,480	2,900	7,380
	United Kingdom		2,443	7,060	3,690	13,193
	Total		5,123	19,255	10,543	34,921
NA	NA					
	Total					
North America	Canada	2,404	12,727	18,801	7,829	41,761
	Mexico					
	United States	8,431	40,391	59,107	24,819	132,748
	Total	10,835	53,118	77,908	32,648	174,509
Pacific	Australia			3,009	1,939	4,948
	Total			3,009	1,939	4,948
Grand Total		10,835	58,241	100,172	45,130	214,378

You will now learn about the options available to you when you process a cube, measure group, or partition. You will then complete a procedure that loads the Mexico sales order into the MOLAP cube.

Processing a Cube

When you click the Process command for a cube that has already been processed, the default processing option is always Process Full. When you fully process a cube, Analysis Services checks to see whether any design changes have been made to any of the dimensions used by the cube. If changes have been made, the server processes the dimensions before processing the cube. The server then generates a set of temporary files containing replacement data for the cube. As soon as processing has completed successfully, the server deletes the current files for the cube and renames the temporary files with the permanent names.

The Process Data option for a cube is virtually identical to the Full Process option. In both cases, the server generates all the files for a new cube, swapping the files into place when the processing is complete. The only real difference is that the Process Data option doesn't check to see whether you have made any changes to the dimension schema. It processes the cube using the existing dimension files.

Another option, Process Incremental, is both powerful and dangerous. The Process Incremental option allows you to process additional fact records into a cube. Analysis Services does not have the capability to identify which fact records are new. When you incrementally process a cube, you must provide Analysis Services with a SQL query that identifies the new records or identifies a table or view that contains the new records. You must be very careful to ensure that you do not include records that have already been processed into the cube and that you do not exclude any fact records. You can't use Process Incremental to delete or update records that have already been processed into the cube.

Process Incremental creates new cube files—precisely as if you were using the Process Full option. When the processing is complete, however, the server doesn't replace the old files with the new ones. Rather, it merges the two sets of files, creating a third set of cube files. Finally, it deletes all but the third set of files and renames those files to become the final cube files. One implication of this operation is that for a single cube, the Process Incremental option might actually require more disk space than the Process Full option because it creates three sets of files, rather than just two. A more important implication is that if you use the Process Incremental option using a fact table that includes values already stored in the cube, those values will be double-counted after you process the cube. An alternate option, Process Data, simply clears out the data in the cube structure and reloads data from the fact table as defined for each partition.

In the procedure titled "Insert Source Data" earlier in this chapter, you inserted a sales order from Mexico on December 31, 2011, into the FactResellerSales fact table, but this sales order has not yet appeared in the MOLAP cube. In the next procedure, you will use the Process Incremental processing option to add this record to the cube.

Incrementally process a partition

1. In the SSMS Object Explorer, expand the MOLAP cube, expand the Measure Groups folder, expand the Reseller Sales measure group, and expand the Partitions folder.

2. Right-click the Fact Reseller Sales partition and select Process.

3. In the Process Partition dialog box, select Process Incremental from the Process Options list. In the Settings column, click Configure. In the Incremental Update dialog box, you can select the table or view that contains the fact records that you want to add to the partition or you can enter a SQL query that selects the additional fact records.

 Important Analysis Services does not have the capability of identifying duplicate or missing fact records. When you perform an incremental process, you must ensure that the table, view, or SQL query that you use contains all of the additional records that should be processed into the cube and doesn't contain any fact records that have already been processed into the cube.

4. In the Incremental Update dialog box, select Query. In the Text Of The Query text box, enter the following SQL query, or you can copy the code from the file C:\Microsoft Press\Analysis Services 2008 SBS\Chapter 14\SQL\Incremental Process.txt.

```
SELECT
    *
FROM
    FactResellerSales
WHERE
    OrderDateKey = '20111231'
```

The Incremental Update dialog box should look like the following image.

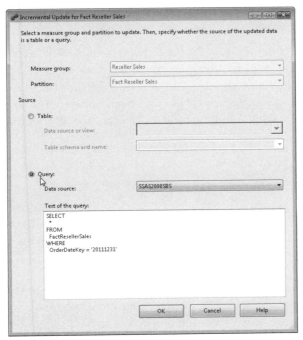

5. Click OK. In the Process Partition dialog box, click OK. The Process Progress dialog box will appear and display the steps Analysis Services takes as it processes the partition. When processing is complete, the Status will change to Process Succeeded. You can view additional information, including the SQL query used to select data from the fact table, by expanding the steps and substeps.

6. In the Process Progress dialog box, expand all of the steps and substeps and then select the substep that begins SELECT [dbo_FactResellerSales].[OrderQuantity] AS. Click View Details. The View Details dialog box displays the SQL query that Analysis Services used to select records from the fact table. The SQL query you entered in step 4 appears as a subquery.

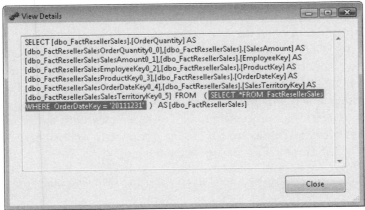

7. In the View Details dialog box, click Close, and then click Close in the Process Progress dialog box.

8. Select the MOLAP [Browse] window. On the Browser toolbar, click Reconnect. The report shows that the sales order from Mexico has been added to the MOLAP cube. The number of items in the newly added order, 122, is displayed at the intersection of Mexico and CY 2011. Aggregate values have also been updated. The total for CY 2011 has increased by 122 to 45,252 and the total for all years and all countries has increased by 122 to 214,500.

Drop Filter Fields Here

Area	Country	CY 2008 Reseller Order Quantity	CY 2009 Reseller Order Quantity	CY 2010 Reseller Order Quantity	CY 2011 Reseller Order Quantity	Grand Total Reseller Order Quantity
Europe	France		2,680	7,715	3,953	14,348
	Germany			4,480	2,900	7,380
	United Kingdom		2,443	7,060	3,690	13,193
	Total		5,123	19,255	10,543	34,921
NA	NA					
	Total					
North America	Canada	2,404	12,727	18,801	7,829	41,761
	Mexico				122	122
	United States	8,431	40,391	59,107	24,819	132,748
	Total	10,835	53,118	77,908	32,770	174,631
Pacific	Australia			3,009	1,939	4,948
	Total			3,009	1,939	4,948
Grand Total		10,835	58,241	100,172	45,252	214,500

As you've learned in this chapter, keeping an Analysis Services database up to date can be challenging. You have to consider when to process changes to database objects relative to changes in the data warehouse, how processing one object impacts other objects, and how the processing option you use affects user queries. In the next section, you will learn about proactive caching, an Analysis Services feature that simplifies database processing by managing the details for you.

Proactive Caching

The data that Analysis Services needs to respond to a query can exist in one of three storage locations, also called *caches*. Analysis Services can respond to a query most quickly if the data exists in memory. If the data is not in memory, Analysis Services can use the second-quickest option and retrieve the data from MOLAP disk storage. If the data is not available from memory or MOLAP storage, the slowest option is to retrieve the data from ROLAP storage—that is, Analysis Services has to query the source relational database.

A potential problem arises when the data in the source relational database changes. These changes cause the ROLAP cache to be out of sync with the memory and MOLAP caches. To get the three caches back in sync, you must process the dimensions and partitions that use MOLAP or HOLAP storage, and the memory cache must be cleared and repopulated. Because processing dimensions and partitions takes time and computer resources, you need to decide when you want this processing to occur and what cache(s) should be used to respond to queries while the caches are out of sync. Fortunately, Analysis Services provides proactive caching, which simplifies managing these issues.

To configure proactive caching, you need to consider the following questions:

- Should processing of the cube occur in fixed intervals of time or only when data in the underlying source has changed?

- While the cube is being processed, how should user queries be resolved—from the most recent version of the cube (which might contain old data) or from the underlying source relational database (which contains new data, but might be slower to return query results)?

- If processing will be triggered by changes to the source database, how should Analysis Services be notified of a change?

In the next procedure, you will review the available options and configure proactive caching for a partition.

Configure partition proactive caching

1. Switch to Business Intelligence Development Studio (BIDS). In Solution Explorer, right-click MOLAP.cube and select View Designer. In the Cube Designer, click the Partitions tab.

2. On the Partitions tab, expand the Internet Sales measure group, right-click the Fact Internet Sales partition, and select Storage Settings.

3. In the Partition Storage Settings dialog box, drag the slider to Scheduled MOLAP. Click Options. Notice that Proactive Caching is enabled, and the cache is configured to rebuild in one-day intervals. In this case, the MOLAP storage for this partition will automatically update once every day, unless you change the setting to a shorter interval. Unfortunately, you can change only the frequency of the rebuild, not the time of day that the rebuild takes place. The Rebuild Interval can be as often as every second or it can be set as an interval of many days.

   By using Scheduled MOLAP, you force a periodic update of the MOLAP cache, whether or not new data has appeared in the warehouse. This may result in more frequent processing of the partition than necessary if data is not regularly added to the warehouse. On the other hand, the partition may not be processed frequently enough if the intervals are too long relative to the frequency of updates to the warehouse.

4. Click Cancel. In the Partition Storage Settings dialog box, drag the slider to Automatic MOLAP. Click Options. Automatic MOLAP also enables proactive caching, but updates the cache only when the data changes, instead of on a periodic basis. The default settings start cache processing after a 10-second Silence Interval, with a Silence Override Interval of 10 minutes. The Silence Interval setting prevents processing from starting until data updates in the warehouse have completely stopped for the specified interval. This situation is analogous to waiting for rush hour traffic to end. If your warehouse is routinely updated during the first 10 minutes of every hour, that period of time is the rush period. As soon as 10 seconds (or the amount of time specified by the Silence Interval) have elapsed, the cache is processed.

But what if there are so many updates to the fact table during the rush period that processing cannot start after the expected 10-minute duration? This Silence Override Interval setting tells the Analysis server to go ahead and start processing the cache if 10 minutes have elapsed and data is still being added to the warehouse. The server uses a snapshot to isolate the records that it will include in the update process from the records that are added to the warehouse after processing has begun.

5. Click the Notifications tab. You use the notification options to specify the conditions that indicate that data has changed in the warehouse. The default value is SQL Server. Any dimension and fact tables used for the current partition are monitored for changes, but you can also specifically identify tables to be monitored. Alternatively, you can choose to have a client application send notification of changes by using the Client Initiated option, or you can choose to poll specific tables by using the Scheduled Polling option. Scheduled Polling is useful if your warehouse is stored in a relational database other than SQL Server. For more information about polling queries, refer to SQL Server Books Online.

> **Note** In order to use SQL Server notifications, either the data source or the Analysis Services service account must be configured to use an account that is either a member of the sysadmin server role or has been granted Alter trace permissions on the SQL Server database server.

6. Click Cancel. In the Partition Storage Settings dialog box, drag the slider to Medium-Latency MOLAP and click Options. The settings on this page are similar to the Automatic MOLAP settings, but now the Drop Outdated Cache option is enabled with a default value for Latency of 4 hours. With medium-latency MOLAP, the Analysis Services server will eliminate the MOLAP cache if it hasn't been processed within the past four hours (or the period that you specify if you change the default value).

When the MOLAP cache is dropped by the server, any queries will be answered from the relational data source (ROLAP cache) until a new MOLAP cache is created. Notice that the Bring Online Immediately option is enabled for medium-latency MOLAP. This option tells the Analysis server that as soon as it drops the outdated cache, queries should be resolved from the relational data source until the new MOLAP cache is available. This setting is useful when processing has started but has not completed within a desired period of time, providing users with relatively current data in response to queries. If you disable this option and you have the Drop Outdated Cache option enabled, queries cannot be answered until the new MOLAP cache is created. If you prefer to continue answering queries with the old cache while a new cache is being built, you must disable the Drop Outdated Cache option.

7. Click Cancel. In the Partition Storage Settings dialog box, drag the slider to Low-latency MOLAP. Click Options. The only difference between medium-latency MOLAP and low-latency MOLAP is that the *Latency* property changes from 4 hours to 30 minutes.

8. Click Cancel. In the Partition Storage Settings dialog box, drag the slider to Real-time HOLAP. Click Options. The storage mode has now been changed to HOLAP. In HOLAP storage, only summarized aggregations are stored in MOLAP storage. All queries that require detail data will be sent directly to the relational database.

   Because the Silence Interval value is 0, the MOLAP aggregations will be rebuilt imme-diately when Analysis Services is notified of a change to the data. The Drop Outdated Cache option causes the Analysis Services memory cache to be cleared as soon as there is a change to the data source fact table.

9. Click Cancel. In the Partition Storage Settings dialog box, drag the slider to Real-time ROLAP. Click Options. The storage mode has now changed to ROLAP. The Update The Cache When Data Changes option has been cleared, because no MOLAP cache will be created. Similar to HOLAP storage, the Drop Outdated Cache option causes the Analysis Services memory cache to be cleared as soon as there is a change to the data source fact table.

10. Click Cancel. In the Partition Storage Settings dialog box, drag the slider to Automatic MOLAP. Click OK. You have configured the partition to use Automatic MOLAP proac-tive caching to manage processing. The partition will automatically be processed start-ing 10 seconds after the last update to the source database. If 10 minutes pass since the first update to the source database and there has not been a 10-second silence interval, processing will begin.

11. Close the Cube Designer and save the changes to the MOLAP cube.

You can also configure proactive caching for dimensions. In the next procedure, you will con-figure Automatic MOLAP proactive caching for the Geography MOLAP dimension.

Configure dimension proactive caching

1. In Solution Explorer, right-click Geography MOLAP.dim and select View Designer.

2. In the Attributes pane of the Dimension Designer, right-click the Geography MOLAP dimension and select Properties.

3. In the Properties window, select the *ProactiveCaching* property and click the ellipsis button that appears on the right.

4. In the Dimension Storage Settings dialog box, drag the slider to Automatic MOLAP. Click Options. The same options are available for dimension and partition proactive caching.

5. Click OK. In the Dimension Storage Settings dialog box, click OK.

6. Close the Dimension Designer and save the changes to the Geography MOLAP dimen-sion. In the next procedure, you will have an opportunity to see proactive caching in action, so you need to deploy your changes to the Analysis Services server.

7. On the Build menu, select Deploy AdventureWorks SSAS.

In the next procedure, you will create a report using Internet sales data. You will then execute a SQL script that will insert Japan into the DimSalesTerritory table and add a record for a sale in Japan to the FactInternetSales table. You will then refresh the report and see the order for Japan, even though you haven't processed the cube.

Insert source data and browse the cubes

1. Switch to SSMS. In the MOLAP [Browse] window, click Reconnect and then remove Reseller Order Quantity from the Report pane.

2. In the Metadata pane, expand the Internet Sales measure group and drag Internet Order Quantity to the Report pane totals area. Notice that Japan is not one of the countries listed in the report.

Drop Filter Fields Here

		Calendar Year ▼				
		CY 2008	CY 2009	CY 2010	CY 2011	Grand Total
Area ▼	**Country**	Internet Order Quantity	Internet Order Quantity	Internet Order Quantity	Internet Order Quantity	Internet Order Quantity
⊟ Europe	⊞ France	59	233	2,291	2,799	5,382
	⊞ Germany	76	233	2,254	2,897	5,460
	⊞ United Kingdom	96	265	2,966	3,382	6,709
	Total	231	731	7,511	9,078	17,551
⊟ NA	⊞ NA					
	Total					
⊟ North America	⊞ Canada	47	226	3,086	3,783	7,142
	⊞ Mexico					
	⊞ United States	341	861	8,511	10,811	20,524
	Total	388	1,087	11,597	14,594	27,666
⊟ Pacific	⊞ Australia	394	859	5,335	6,384	12,972
	Total	394	859	5,335	6,384	12,972
Grand Total		1,013	2,677	24,443	30,056	58,189

3. On the SSMS File menu, point to Open and select File. In the Open File dialog box, browse to the C:\Microsoft Press\Analysis Services 2008 SBS\Chapter 14\SQL folder, select Update Warehouse 2.sql, and click Open.

4. On the Query menu, point to Connection and select Connect. In the Connect To Database Engine dialog box, change the Server Name to **localhost** and click Connect.

5. On the SSMS toolbar, click Execute. After the query executes successfully, close the query window. Proactive caching has been configured to automatically process the dimension after a 10-second quiet interval, so you may need to wait just a brief moment before refreshing the report.

6. Back in the MOLAP [Browse] window, click Reconnect on the Browser toolbar. The report shows that the sales order from the Internet order from Japan that has been added to the MOLAP cube. The number of items in the newly added order, 1, is displayed at the intersection of Japan and CY 2011. Aggregate values have also been updated. The total for CY 2011 has increased by 1 to 30,057, and the total for all years and all countries has increased by 1 to 58,190.

Drop Filter Fields Here

		Calendar Year ▼				
		CY 2008	CY 2009	CY 2010	CY 2011	Grand Total
Area ▼	**Country**	Internet Order Quantity	Internet Order Quantity	Internet Order Quantity	Internet Order Quantity	Internet Order Quantity
⊟ Europe	⊞ France	59	233	2,291	2,799	5,382
	⊞ Germany	76	233	2,254	2,897	5,460
	⊞ United Kingdom	96	265	2,966	3,382	6,709
	Total	231	731	7,511	9,078	17,551
⊟ NA	⊞ NA					
	Total					
⊟ North America	⊞ Canada	47	226	3,086	3,783	7,142
	⊞ Mexico					
	⊞ United States	341	861	8,511	10,811	20,524
	Total	388	1,087	11,597	14,594	27,666
⊟ Pacific	⊞ Australia	394	859	5,335	6,384	12,972
	⊞ Japan				1	1
	Total	394	859	5,335	6,385	12,973
Grand Total		1,013	2,677	24,443	30,057	58,190

Tip If you want to work through the procedures in this section a second time, you first need to delete the records that were inserted by the Update Warehouse 1.sql and Update Warehouse 2.sql scripts. Included in the C:\Microsoft Press\Analysis Services 2008 SBS \Chapter 14\SQL folder is a SQL script named Delete.sql that will do this for you.

Working with Partitions

Partitions make it possible for you to create extremely large cubes. You can effectively create small, medium-sized, and even remarkably large cubes without using partitions. But partitions are useful when you need to create very large, enterprise-wide applications. For that reason, the ability to manage multiple partitions is available only with Microsoft SQL Server 2008 Enterprise Edition.

Understanding Partition Strategies

Each Analysis Services measure group consists of at least one partition. You design storage modes and aggregations at the partition level. Whether a measure group contains only a single partition or many partitions, the process of designing storage is the same.

One of the benefits of creating multiple partitions is that you can design different storage for different portions of the measure group. For example, say that you have one partition that contains information for the current year and one previous year. You access this information frequently, so you specify multidimensional OLAP (MOLAP) storage with aggregations to provide a 30 percent performance gain. A second partition contains values for the third, fourth, and fifth years. These years are usually accessed only at a summary level (if at all), and the relational warehouse is also occasionally accessed, so you specify hybrid OLAP (HOLAP) storage, with aggregations that provide a 15 percent performance gain. A third partition contains several previous years. Those years are infrequently accessed and the relational warehouse is never used, so you specify MOLAP storage with aggregations to the 5 percent performance level and then archive the relational warehouse to tape.

A second major benefit of creating partitions is that you can process a partition independently of the rest of the cube. As a fairly extreme example, suppose that you have an Analysis Services cube used to monitor manufacturing activities and you want to update the information in that cube every 10 minutes. You don't have time to completely process the database every 10 minutes. By putting the current day into a separate partition, you can process that partition every 10 minutes, without having to process the rest of the cube. In effect, creating a partition for the current day is like performing an incremental update on the cube, except that you can completely replace the values in that one partition every 10 minutes, guaranteeing consistency with the relational data source.

A client application has no awareness of—let alone control over—partitions used on the server. You can modify the design of partitions without affecting any client application. The most important task when creating partitions is to make sure that each appropriate value from the fact table (or fact tables) makes it into one and only one partition.

Creating Partitions

When you're creating partitions, make sure each partition gets unique data. Otherwise, it's easy to double-count values in multiple partitions. The dangers of creating partitions are similar to the dangers of executing an incremental update on a cube. This similarity is not co-incidental. In fact, when you perform an incremental update on a cube, the Analysis Services server creates a new partition, loads values into the new partition, and then merges the two partitions. Analysis Services provides two techniques to avoid double-counting:

- Create a separate fact table for each partition.
- Specify a filter (a SQL WHERE clause) to restrict rows from the fact table.

In this section, you will create three partitions in the AdventureWorks cube Reseller Sales measure group. One partition will contain data for CY 2011, another for CY 2010, and a final partition will contain data for all prior years. In the first procedure, you will modify the existing partition so that it contains the most current data, and then in the following procedure you will create two partitions to contain data from prior years.

Modify a partition

1. Switch to BIDS. In the BIDS Solution Explorer, right-click AdventureWorks.cube and select View Designer. In the Cube Designer, click the Partitions tab.

2. In the Reseller Sales measure group, right-click the Fact Reseller Sales partition and select Properties. In the Properties window, change the name of the partition to **Fact Reseller Sales CY 2011**.

3. In the Properties window, select the *Source* property and then click the ellipsis button that appears on the right. You can ensure that the data in a partition is unique by having each partition select data from a different table or by having each partition select records using a SQL *SELECT* statement that includes a WHERE clause. The WHERE clause for each partition must filter a unique set of fact records for each partition. In the Partition Source dialog box, you choose whether the partition will be retrieving data from a table or whether it will use a SQL query.

4. In the Partition Source dialog box, select Query Binding from the Binding Type list. When you select Query Binding, the *SELECT* statement that the partition is currently using appears followed by WHERE. You need to complete the WHERE clause so that the partition selects data for CY 2011.

5. In the Query text box, change the WHERE clause to **WHERE OrderDateKey BETWEEN 20110101 AND 20111231**. The Partition Source dialog box should look like this:

6. Click Check. This will check the SQL query syntax, but it is up to you to ensure that partitions do not contain duplicated data by setting the WHERE clause appropriately. In the Partition Filter dialog box, click OK. In the Partition Source dialog box, click OK.

> **Important** Changing a partition source from table binding to query binding breaks the link between partition and the data source view. If you later make changes to the fact table in the data source view, those changes *will not* get propagated to the partition. You will need to manually update each partition.

Now that you have modified the original partition so that it only contains CY 2011 data, you can create two other partitions to contain the rest of the fact table data.

Create partitions

1. On the Partitions tab of the Cube Designer, click the New Partition link in the Reseller Sales measure group section.

2. On the Welcome page of the Partition Wizard, click Next. On the Specify Source Information page, the Measure Group value is Reseller Sales. This value defines the measure group for the new partition. The Look In value defines which data source or data source view contains the source table for the partition. Any tables that match the structure of the measure group's source table will be displayed. If multiple tables are selected from the Available Tables list, a new partition is created for each table.

3. In The Available Tables list, select FactResellerSales. Click Next.

4. On the Restrict Rows page, select Specify A Query To Restrict Rows. In the Query text box, change the SQL *SELECT* statement to **SELECT * FROM [dbo].[FactResellerSales]**

WHERE OrderDateKey BETWEEN 20100101 AND 20101231. The Restrict Rows
page of the wizard should look like this:

> **Tip** If your partition is selecting data from a single fact table and there are no named
> calculations, in the SQL query you should replace the list of column names with *. By elimi-
> nating the use of specific column names, you will not be required to modify the partition if
> you later modify the columns in the fact table.

5. Click Check. In the Partition Filter dialog box, click OK. On the Restrict Rows page of the
   wizard, click Next. If you have a very large Analysis Services database, you can allocate
   a measure group's partitions across multiple Analysis Services servers. This allows multiple servers to share the processing and query load. To learn more, see the SQL Server
   Books Online article "Creating and Managing a Remote Partition." You can also allocate
   a measure group's partitions across multiple storage locations. The Processing And
   Storage Locations page of the Partition Wizard allows you to configure these options.
   You'll accept the default options for this procedure.

6. On the Processing And Storage Locations page, click Next.

7. On the Completing The Wizard page, change the name of the partition to **Fact
   Reseller Sales CY 2010**.

   A new partition needs to have an aggregation design. You can choose to create a new
   aggregation design using the Aggregation Design Wizard, copy an aggregation design
   from an existing partition, or create or copy an aggregation design later. For this partition,
   you will copy the aggregation design used by the Fact Reseller Sales CY 2011 partition.

8. Select Copy The Aggregation Design From An Existing Partition. This will copy the aggregation design from the partition in the Copy From list. The CY 2010 partition will be
   assigned the 30 Percent AggregationDesign aggregation design, the same one used by
   the CY 2011 partition. The Completing The Wizard page should look like the following.

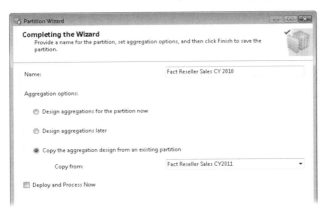

9. Click Finish. The Reseller Sales measure group now contains two partitions. Notice that both partitions are using the 30 Percent AggregationDesign. In the next step, you will create one more partition that will contain the data from all prior years. Because this historical data will be queried less frequently than the more recent data, you can choose to have fewer aggregations. With fewer aggregations, the partition can be processed more quickly and will use less storage space.

10. Repeat steps 1 through 9 to create one more partition with the properties shown in the following table.

SQL Query	SELECT * FROM [dbo].[FactResellerSales] WHERE OrderDateKey < 20100101
Name	Fact Reseller Sales History
Aggregation Option	Design Aggregations Later

11. In the Cube Designer, click the Aggregations tab.

12. On the Aggregations tab, right-click 15 Percent AggregationDesign in the Reseller Sales measure group section and select Assign Aggregation Design.

13. In the Assign Aggregation Design dialog box, select Fact Reseller Sales History from the Destination Partitions list.

14. Click OK and then click the Partitions tab. The Reseller Sales measure group should now contain three partitions. The CY 2010 and CY 2011 partitions should be using the 30 Percent AggregationDesign, and the history partition should be using the 15 Percent AggregationDesign.

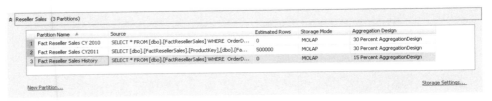

One benefit of having multiple partitions is that you can process the partitions individually, or you can take advantage of parallel processing and process several partitions at the same time. In the next procedure, you will demonstrate these capabilities.

Process partitions

1. In the Cube Designer, right-click the Fact Reseller Sales CY 2011 partition on the Partitions tab and then select Process. A dialog box may appear with the warning that the server content appears to be out of date. Click Yes and the project will be deployed to the server. When deployment is complete, the Process Partition dialog box will appear.

2. In the Process Partition dialog box, click Run. When processing is complete, the status will change to Process Succeeded.

3. In the Process Progress dialog box, click Close, and then click Close in the Process Partition dialog box.

4. Click the Browser tab of the Cube Designer.

5. In the Browser tab Metadata pane, expand the Measures folder, expand the Reseller Sales measure group, and drag Reseller Order Quantity to the Report pane totals area.

6. In the Metadata pane, expand the Date dimension and drag Calendar Year to the Report pane rows area. Right-click the Report pane and select Show Empty Cells.

   Because you processed the Fact Reseller Sales CY 2011 partition and did not process the other partitions, the report only displays CY 2011 data.

Drop Filter Fields Here	
	Drop Column Fields Here
Calendar Year ▾	Reseller Order Quantity
CY 2008	
CY 2009	
CY 2010	
CY 2011	45,252
Grand Total	45,252

   You will need to process the other two partitions in the Reseller Sales measure group so that you can see all four years of data.

7. Click the Partitions tab. Click the Fact Reseller Sales CY 2010 partition. Hold down Ctrl and click the Fact Reseller Sales History partition so that both partitions are selected. On the Partitions tab toolbar, click Process. In the Process Object(s) dialog box, click Run.

8. In the Process Progress dialog box, click Close, and then click Close in the Process Partition dialog box.

9. Click the Browser tab and click Reconnect. The report is refreshed and now displays data for four years.

Drop Filter Fields Here	
	Drop Column Fields Here
Calendar Year ▾	Reseller Order Quantity
CY 2008	10,835
CY 2009	58,241
CY 2010	100,172
CY 2011	45,252
Grand Total	214,500

Consider the situation described earlier in the section titled "Understanding Partition Strategies," where you created a new partition each day for a manufacturing cube. Each month you would create up to 31 additional partitions in the cube. Simply keeping the partitions straight would be extraordinarily confusing. One solution is to use only two partitions: one for the current day and one for all previous time. Each night, merge the current day partition with the previous time partition, and then create a new current day partition for the next day. Merged partitions don't run significantly faster than separate partitions, but they can be much easier to manage.

In the next procedure, you will learn how to merge the CY 2010 partition with the partition containing historical data.

Merge partitions

1. Switch to SSMS. Expand the AdventureWorks cube, expand the Measure Groups folder, expand the Reseller Sales measure group, and expand the Partitions folder.

2. Right-click the Fact Reseller Sales History partition and select Merge Partitions.

 Important The partition you select before opening the Merge Partition dialog box is the partition that will be retained after the merge.

3. In the Merge Partition dialog box, select Fact Reseller Sales CY 2010 from the Source Partitions list. The Merge Partitions dialog box should look like this:

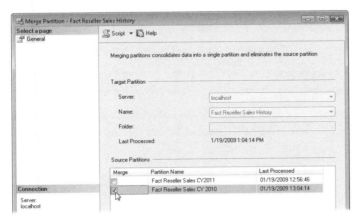

4. Click OK. Right-click the Partitions folder and select Refresh. You can see that the Fact Reseller Sales CY 2010 partition no longer appears in the list of the Reseller Sales measure group partitions. The data that was in the CY 2010 partition has been merged into the history partition.

Important Merging partitions does not update the partition query, nor does it combine fact tables. If you think you might reprocess the partition, you need to update the partition query or move the records from the fact table corresponding to the source partition into the fact table corresponding to the target partition.

You will need to modify Fact Reseller Sales History partition so that it selects all fact records dated prior to January 2011.

5. Right-click the Fact Reseller Sales History partition and select Properties.

6. On the General page of the Partition Properties dialog box, select the *Source* property and click the ellipsis button that appears on the right.

7. Change the WHERE clause of the SQL query to **WHERE OrderDateKey < 20110101**.

8. Click OK. In the Partition Properties dialog box, click OK. Close SSMS.

Because the partitions have been merged in SQL Server Management Studio, the AdventureWorks SSAS database that is deployed on the Analysis Services server is no longer synchronized with the solution that is currently open in BIDS. Whenever changes are made to an Analysis Services database in SSMS, you should import those design changes into a new project in BIDS. Then use the new project for any future design changes that will be deployed back to the Analysis Services server.

In the next procedure, you will learn how to import an Analysis Services database design into a new project in BIDS.

Import an Analysis Services database design

1. On the File menu in BIDS, point to New and select Project.

2. In the New Project dialog box, verify that the project type is Business Intelligence Projects. In the Templates pane, select Import Analysis Services 2008 Database.

3. Change the project name to **Import SSAS DB** and change the location to C:\Microsoft Press\Analysis Services 2008 SBS\Chapter 14. The New Project dialog box should look like the following image.

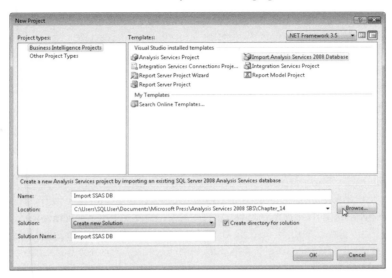

When you click OK, the AdventureWorks BI solution will be closed and the Import Analysis Services Database Wizard will start.

4. Click OK. On the Welcome page of the Import Analysis Services Database Wizard, click Next.

5. On the Source Database page, enter **localhost** in the Server text box and then select AdventureWorks SSAS from the Database list.

6. Click Next. On the Completing The Wizard page, click Finish. You should look at the partitions in the Reseller Sales measure group to confirm that the changes you made in SSMS have been imported into this new project.

7. In the Cubes folder of Solution Explorer, right-click AdventureWorks.cube and select View Designer.

8. In the Cube Designer, click the Partitions tab. The Reseller Sales measure group should contain only the Fact Reseller Sales CY 2011 and Fact Reseller Sales History partitions.

9. Close BIDS.

In this chapter, you learned that Analysis Services has three storage modes: ROLAP, HOLAP, and MOLAP. ROLAP mode leaves dimension, detail, and aggregate data in the source relational database; MOLAP stores dimension, detail, and aggregate data in proprietary data structures on the Analysis Services server; and HOLAP leaves detail data in the source relational database and stores aggregate data on the Analysis Services server. Cube data is stored in measure group partitions. A measure group can have multiple partitions. Partitions in a measure group can have different storage modes and can use different aggregation designs. You can add, delete, or merge the partitions in a measure group.

You also learned that when the data in a source database is modified, you need to reprocess MOLAP dimensions and partitions to bring those changes into an Analysis Services database. The most simple and reliable method is to fully process all affected dimensions and partitions. However, if the source database is large, time might not allow for a full process. Analysis Services allows you to update dimensions and to use incremental processing to add new source data into a measure group partition. Keeping a source database and an Analysis Services database in sync can become quite complicated. Analysis Services provides proactive caching that allows you to automate Analysis Services processing.

Chapter 15
Managing Deployment

In this chapter, you will learn how to:

- Deploy an Analysis Services database using BIDS.
- Create an XMLA script to deploy an Analysis Services database.
- Execute deployment scripts against an Analysis Services server.
- Migrate Analysis Services databases from one server to another.
- Perform backups and restores of Analysis Services databases.

This chapter examines two areas of managing an Analysis Services implementation: how code changes to an Analysis Services database are deployed to a server, and how to migrate existing databases across servers as well as how to handle disaster recovery.

Deployment Overview

When we talk about deployment, we are really focusing on the process of moving code changes in an organized manner through the different phases of the development cycle. Every organization has different environment configurations, but conceptually, a given solution has three environments: development, test, and production. Multiple physical environments may be found within these three. Examples include a user acceptance environment or preproduction.

This chapter will focus on two primary areas: moving code and moving databases. It is important to make a distinction here. In Analysis Services, when we refer to moving code, we are talking about moving the metadata structures used to create our database. These metadata structures are simply the Analysis Services files we create when building a database within Business Intelligence Development Studio. They take the form of XML files representing what the database structure should be. The second focus area, moving databases, entails movement of both the metadata and data for an Analysis Services database.

Deciding to move code or an entire database is really dependent on an organization's deployment policies and best practices. In a best-practice scenario, new code changes are promoted from Development to Test and eventually to Production through movement of code. This is commonly the case because each environment might point to a different data source and will require reprocessing when changes are made.

The next section looks at deploying code changes using three different techniques: deploying via BIDS, using the Deployment Wizard, and executing deployment scripts.

Deployment Mechanics

When you deploy an Analysis Services database, three basic steps happen before queries can be run: build, deploy, and process.

In the build step, all the source files that make up the Analysis Services database are combined into an XML file. The source files are the .ds, .dsv, .dim, .cube, .partition, and other files found in a BIDS Analysis Services project. Each file is an XML representation of an Analysis Services object. When you build an Analysis Services project, a single .asdatabase file is created to represent these files.

In the deploy step, the .asdatabase file is wrapped in an XMLA command. The XMLA command tells the Analysis Services Server what to do with the database definition. When the XMLA command is executed on the Analysis Services server, the definition is stored in the Analysis Services data directory as individual XML files. Later in this chapter, we will see how to create an XMLA script, stored in an .xmla file, using the Analysis Services Deployment Wizard.

In the final step, process, data is loaded into the Analysis Services database. At this point, the user can query the database.

The next section will take a look at how to deploy using Business Intelligence Development studio.

Deployment Using Business Intelligence Development Studio

This section will take a look at how Analysis Services databases are deployed using Business Intelligence Development Studio. It will also look at the commands sent to the Analysis Services server during the deployment process.

Explore the project's deployment properties

1. Use BIDS to open the AdventureWorks BI Solution contained in the C:\Microsoft Press \Analysis Services 2008 SBS\Chapter 15\AdventureWorks BI folder.

2. In Solution Explorer, right-click the AdventureWorks SSAS project and select Properties.

3. In the Adventure Works SSAS project Properties dialog box, click Deployment in the left navigation window. In the right pane, you will see five properties related to deployment. The first three options define how the project will be deployed. The last two define where the project will be deployed. Table 15-1 describes the properties and their related uses.

TABLE 15-1 **Deployment Properties**

Property	Description
Processing Option	Controls how the database should be processed each time it is deployed. ■ **Default** Analysis Services processes those dimensions and partitions impacted by structural design changes. ■ **Do Not Process** The database is not processed when new changes are deployed. This option can be extremely useful when deploying large databases. ■ **Full** Always does a full process of the database when it is deployed. This option could slow down deployment when dealing with long processing times.
Transactional Deployment	Transactional deployment relates to the deployment of the database changes along with processing. ■ **False** If a database is deployed but the processing fails, the new definition still resides on the server in an unprocessed state. This is the default value and is usually acceptable when deploying to development or test environments. ■ **True** Deployment of changes and processing are held in a single transaction. If the processing fails, the deployment changes are rolled back.
Deployment Mode	Determines whether only changes are deployed or the entire database is overwritten. ■ **Deploy Changes Only** Only deploys design changes to the database structure. Modified objects and objects that are dependent on the modified objects will have to be processed before they can be queried. ■ **Deploy All** Deploys the entire database. The entire database will have to be processed before any object can be queried.
Server	The name of the Analysis Services server where the project should be deployed. The server name format is *Server[\instance]*.
Database	The name that the database will be given on the Analysis Services server.

4. Change the value of the Server property to **localhost**.

5. Change the database name to **AdventureWorks SSAS Ch15**.

6. Click OK to close the Properties dialog box.

Deploy the Analysis Services database project

Now that the configuration properties are set, you can deploy the database to the Analysis Services server.

1. On the Build menu, select Deploy AdventureWorks SSAS. The Deployment Progress dialog box appears. You should see two command notifications in this dialog box. Each command notification is an XMLA statement sent to the server.

2. Double-click the first command notification. A View Details dialog box containing the command text will appear. (The dialog box might take a moment to load.) This first

command is an XMLA statement containing the database definition sent to the server. Note the Alter tag that appears after the opening Batch tag. This is the XMLA command being sent to the server. It is followed by a combination of all the files in the Analysis Services database project. Later we will see how to create the XMLA command as a file to be executed on multiple servers.

3. Close the View Details window.

4. Double-click the second command notification. A View Details dialog box containing the command text will appear. Note the Process tag that appears after the opening Batch tag. This command is an XMLA statement telling Analysis Services to process the database.

5. Close the View Details window. Note that in the Deployment window after the second command, there are status notifications generated by Analysis Services. You can examine these notifications to see exactly what Analysis Services is doing during processing, including the queries sent to the relation database.

You can now explore the deployed database. It can be accessed using SQL Server Management Studio.

Explore the deployed database

1. On the Microsoft Windows task bar, click Start, point to All Programs, expand the Microsoft SQL Server 2008 folder, and then select SQL Server Management Studio.

2. In the Connect To Server dialog box, select the Analysis Services Server type and specify **localhost** for the Server name.

3. Click Connect to connect to the server.

4. In Object Explorer, expand the Databases folder. Note that a new AdventureWorks SSAS Ch15 database has been created.

5. Right-click the AdventureWorks SSAS Ch15 database and select Properties. In the Properties dialog box, you can view information such as the last time the database was updated, the last time it was processed, and the total size on disk.

6. Click OK to close the Properties dialog box and close SQL Server Management Studio.

BIDS provides a quick mechanism for deploying to a given server. Usually this deployment method is used within a development environment; however, you can use the Configuration Manager accessible from the database properties dialog box to add information about deploying to other environments (e.g., test and production). To add more flexibility in the deployment options to environments such as test and production, SQL Server Analysis Services provides a Deployment Wizard. The next section will examine how to use the Deployment Wizard to deploy a database.

Deployment Using the Deployment Wizard

Many organizations have set policies regarding how code changes are moved from development to production environments. Additionally, Analysis Services databases are likely to be configured differently in development, test, and production. For example, data source connection strings will likely point to different servers in different environments. The Analysis Services Deployment Wizard provides the flexibility to meet these types of requirements. You can use the Deployment Wizard through the user interface (UI) or through the command line.

Deployment Wizard UI

The Deployment Wizard UI has a number of options that are not available in BIDS. Using the Deployment Wizard UI allows you to change many configuration options and deployment targets as well as allowing you to create a deployment script file. The next procedure will walk you through the UI.

Starting the Deployment Wizard

1. On the Microsoft Windows task bar, click Start, point to All Programs, expand the Microsoft SQL Server 2008 folder, expand the Analysis Services folder, and then select Deployment Wizard.

2. On the Welcome page of the Deployment Wizard, click Next.

3. Click the browse button to the right of the Database file text box.

4. Navigate to the folder C:\Microsoft Press\Analysis Services 2008 SBS\Chapter 15 \AdventureWorks BI\AdventureWorks SSAS\bin\. The bin directory contains the compiled version of an Analysis Services project. The primary file needed for deployment is the .asdatabase file. This file contains a combined definition of all the files in the BIDS project. Opening this file in Notepad will show the same XML contained in the project files.

5. Click AdventureWorks SSAS.asdatabase and then click Open.

6. Click Next to open the next page in the wizard.

7. Make sure the database name is set to AdventureWorks SSAS Ch15 and then click Next. As detailed in Tables 15-2 and 15-3, the next page specifies how deployment of partitions and security roles should be handled.

TABLE 15-2 **Partition Deployment Options**

Option	Description
Deploy Partitions	The partition definition in the .asdatabase file will be sent to the server. In some instances, this option might interfere with other processes. For example, if Analysis Services partitions are created dynamically by an ETL process, overwriting them is undesirable.
Retain Partitions	Analysis Services will keep the existing partitions on the server. Definition of partitions in the .asdatabase file that are not on the server will be deployed.

TABLE 15-3 **Role and Member Deployment Options**

Option	Description
Deploy Roles And Members	Existing security roles and membership information will be replaced with the definition in the .asdatabase file.
Deploy Roles And Retain Members	Deploys any new roles and their related members while retaining all existing roles and members.
Retain Roles And Members	Analysis Services uses the server definition and ignores the deployment script.

8. Leave the default options for partitions and security and click Next. The next dialog box allows you to update configuration properties such as database connection strings, service accounts, log files, and data storage locations.

9. Leave the default configuration settings and click Next. As detailed in Table 15-4, the Select Processing Options dialog box specifies how processing should be handled when the new definition is deployed, how writeback tables should be used, and whether processing should be handled in a transaction.

TABLE 15-4 **Processing Options**

Option	Description
Default Processing	Analysis Services determines which objects have been affected by the deployment and processes them as necessary.
Full Processing	Processes all deployed objects.
None	Does not process any objects in the database.

If any partitions allow writeback, the Writeback Table Options will be enabled. These options allow you to retain existing writeback tables and data or to delete existing writeback tables and create new ones. If you select an option that may lead to deleting existing writeback data, you need to determine if that data should be backed up prior to deployment and then inserted into the new writeback table. The check box at the bottom of the dialog box allows the deployment changes and processing steps to be handled as a single transaction. If the check box is selected and processing fails, the deployed metadata changes will be rolled back.

10. Click Next to open the confirmation dialog box, which contains the option to create a deployment script. The deployment script is an XMLA command file containing all the information set in the wizard. This XMLA command file can be saved to disk and then used on different servers. This option is very useful when dealing with a separation of deployment duties. Often the development team has no access to production servers and script files are required to promote changes.

11. Click Next to deploy the database. This dialog box will show the steps of the deployment and the status of any processing. The status text box at the bottom will display the XMLA response from Analysis Services.

12. Click Next to progress to the view the Deployment Complete page.

13. Click Finish to exit the wizard.

Running the Deployment Wizard from the Command Line

You can also run the Analysis Service Deployment Wizard from the Windows command line. This mode is useful when deployment is handled through batch scripts as part of a scheduled build process. The Deployment Wizard command line executable can be found at \Program Files\Microsoft SQLServer\100\Tools\Binn\VSShell\Common7\IDE\Microsoft.AnalysisServices. Deployment.exe.

Command-line execution uses the following syntax:

```
Microsoft.AnalysisServices.Deployment [ASdatabasefile]  {[/s[:logfile]] | [/a] |
[[/o[:output_script_file]] [/d]]}
```

The Deployment Wizard uses three primary switches, as described in Table 15-5.

TABLE 15-5 Deployment Switches

Switch	Description
/a	This switch launches the Deployment Wizard User Interface, but it will not deploy the database. It uses the answers specified in the wizard to update the .configsettings, .deploymentoptions, and .deploymenttargets files.
/s	This switch deploys to Analysis Services using the existing answer files (.configsettings, .deploymentoptions, .deploymenttargets). Additionally, a log file can be specified after the /s switch to capture the progress of the deployment.
/o	This switch uses the existing answer files to create a single deployment script. The deployment script contains XMLA that can be executed on an Analysis Server.

To help you understand the command-line deployment options, three command files are located in the C:\Microsoft Press\Analysis Services 2008 SBS\Chapter 15\Deploy Command Line folder. Table 15-6 describes the three command files. All command files use the .asdatabase and other deployment files located in the C:\Microsoft Press\Analysis Services 2008 SBS \Chapter 15\Deploy Command Line\bin directory. The files in the bin directory were created using BIDS and by selecting the Build command on the Analysis Services project.

TABLE 15-6 Deployment Command Files

File	Description
01 Command Line A Switch.cmd	Launches the Deployment Wizard UI with the /a switch. Walking through the wizard writes updated information to the deployment answer files.
02 Command Line S Switch.cmd	Deploys the .asdatabase file to the server using the bin directory deployment answer files.
03 Command Line 0 Switch.cmd	Creates an XMLA deployment script from the .asdatabase file and deployment answer files.

The Deployment Wizard gives users increased functionality over BIDS. It allows for more detailed configuration of the deployment as well as the creation of a deployment script. The next section will look at a second method of creating deployment scripts through SQL Server Management Studio.

The Deployment Wizard relies on files found in the Analysis Services project bin directory. The following procedure examines the files.

Examining Analysis Services deployment files

1. On the Microsoft Windows task bar, click Start and then click Computer.

2. In Windows Explorer, navigate to the C:\Microsoft Press\Analysis Services 2008 SBS \Chapter 15\AdventureWorks BI\AdventureWorks SSAS\bin folder. Note that there are four files in this directory. These files are created when the build process is executed from BIDS. Table 15-7 describes these four files.

TABLE 15-7 Analysis Services Deployment Files

File Extension	Description
.asdatabase	The .asdatabase file contains the combined definition of the Analysis Services database. It contains the definition of data sources, data source views, dimensions, cubes, and other database objects.
.configsettings	The .configsettings file contains configuration information such as data source connection strings and security impersonation information.
.deploymentoptions	The .deploymentoptions file contains information about how processing is handled during the deployment as well as what partition and security information is retained or updated during deployment.
.deploymenttargets	The .deploymenttargets file contains connection information about where the Analysis Services database should be deployed.

Understanding Deployment Scripts

The previous section described how you could use the Deployment Wizard to generate an XMLA file for deploying your database. You can also use SQL Server Management Studio to create XMLA deployment scripts.

Deployment scripts can be extremely useful in organizations that have a separation of duties between development and production support. In many organizations, developers are not allowed to deploy their own code into production. In these situations, it is necessary to create script files that can be executed by production support administrators. The following exercise examines how scripts can be created using SQL Server Management Studio.

Create a deployment script

1. On the Microsoft Windows task bar, click Start, point to All Programs, expand the Microsoft SQL Server 2008 folder, and then select SQL Server Management Studio.

2. In the Connect to Server dialog box from the Server Type list, select Analysis Services, and in the Server Name text box, enter **localhost**. Click Connect.

3. In Object Explorer, expand the Databases folder under the Analysis Services server and locate the AdventureWorks SSAS Ch15 database created in the previous exercises.

4. Right-click the AdventureWorks SSAS Ch15 database, point to Script Database As, point to Create To, and select New Query Editor Window.

   This script contains the entire definition of the database and can be executed on other servers to deploy the database definition.

5. Find the <ID> and <Name> XML tags located under the <Database> tag.

6. Edit the text within the <ID> and <Name> tags to read **AdventureWorks SSAS Ch15 Script**.

7. On the toolbar, click Execute to deploy the definition to the server. The Results window should show the following information if the database was successfully deployed.

8. In Object Explorer, right-click the Databases folder under the Analysis Server and select Refresh. The AdventureWorks SSAS Ch15 Script database will now appear in the databases folder.

> **Tip** You can use SQL Server Management Studio to create an XML script for any Analysis Services object—data source, data source view, dimension, cube, partition, and so forth.

The first part of this chapter demonstrated how database definitions are deployed to a server as part of a code promotion process. The second part of the chapter will look at how existing databases can be migrated across different server environments.

Migrating Databases and Disaster Recovery

The following sections will walk you through two distinct scenarios. The first is migration of databases across servers. Database migration is commonly used to move data from a staging server to a production server, to synchronize databases across multiple servers to enable load balancing, or to synchronize databases between a processing server and a reporting server. The second scenario is backup and restore. Backup and restore allows for disaster recovery and can greatly reduce downtime.

Detaching and Attaching an Analysis Services Database

The first method we'll look at is detaching and attaching databases. This process detaches the associated database files from a server instance. Those files can then be moved to a different storage location and attached to a different server. Because this process moves both the metadata and data, reprocessing on the new server is not required. Detaching and attaching a database is very useful for moving databases across servers.

Detaching and attaching an Analysis Services database

1. On the Microsoft Windows task bar, click the Start button, point to All Programs, expand the Accessories folder, and then select Windows Explorer.

2. In Windows Explorer, navigate to C:\Program Files\Microsoft SQL Server\MSAS10. MSSQLSERVER\OLAP\Data. If a User Account Control dialog box appears, click Continue. This directory is the default data directory for Analysis Services. Note that there is an AdventureWorks SSAS Ch15.0.db folder in this directory. This folder was created from deployments in the previous exercises and contains the metadata definition of the database as well as all the related MOLAP data. We will come back to this location later in the exercise.

3. Switch to SQL Server Management Studio. In Object Explorer, expand the Databases folder under the Analysis Services server and locate the AdventureWorks SSAS Ch15 database created in the previous exercises.

4. Right-click the AdventureWorks SSAS Ch15 database and select Detach. In the Detach Database dialog box, there is an option to associate a password with the database. As noted in the dialog box, specifying the password will encrypt some of the files that contain sensitive information. A password should be specified if files will be moved to different servers and file shares. Ideally, the file shares should be secured to ensure that others cannot access sensitive data.

5. Click OK to detach the database. The database is now no longer available on the server. However, the metadata and data files are still in the data directory. The database files can be viewed in Windows Explorer. To migrate the database to another server, simply copy the entire AdventureWorks SSAS Ch15.0.db folder. After the folder is moved the new server, it can be attached and is ready for use. For this exercise, you do not need to move the folder. In the next step, you will attach the database to your local computer.

6. Right-click the Databases folder in SQL Server Management Studio and select Attach.

7. In the Attach Database dialog box, click the browse button next to the Folder text box. The Browse To Remote Folder dialog box shows only those folders specified in the Analysis Services Server properties. By default, only the backup and log folders are displayed. The data files are not listed, so the path will have to be specified in the Selected Path text box.

8. In the Selected Path text box, enter the following location and click OK to exit the dialog: **C:\Program Files\Microsoft SQL Server\MSAS10.MSSQLSERVER\OLAP\Data \AdventureWorks SSAS Ch15.0.db**.

9. In the Attach Database dialog box, click OK to attach the database. Object Explorer does not refresh automatically, so the attached database will not appear.

10. Right-click the Databases folder and select Refresh. The Adventure Works SSAS Ch15 database will now appear.

Detaching and attaching is a simple way to move a database, including all data, from one server to another. The next section will look at using both the Synchronize functionality and backing up and restoring a database.

Synchronizing Databases

The Synchronize Database Wizard allows you to copy metadata and data from one server to another. This wizard is accessible via SQL Server Management Studio. Synchronizing databases can be useful when databases are spread across multiple servers for load-balancing purposes. The synchronization can be scripted and executed as part of a batch process. Additionally, the database remains available for queries during the synchronization. Because you can only synchronize databases between two different Analysis Services servers, this section does not include a step-by-step procedure. To learn more about database synchronization, see the SQL Server Books Online articles "Synchronizing Analysis Services Databases" and "How to: Synchronize an Analysis Services Database."

Backing Up and Restoring a Database

The following procedure will walk you through creating and restoring a database backup in Analysis Services.

Backing up a database

1. In Object Explorer in SQL Server Management Studio, expand the Databases folder under the Analysis Services server and locate the AdventureWorks SSAS Ch15 database.

2. Right-click AdventureWorks SSAS Ch15 database and select Back Up. The Backup Database dialog box contains the settings described in Table 15-8.

TABLE 15-8 Backup Database Options

Setting	Description
Backup File	Location where the backup file will be created. The file extension for Analysis Services backup files is .abf.
Allow File Overwrite	If selected, existing backup files can be overwritten. When cleared, if a backup file with the same name as the backup file you are trying to create already exists, the backup will fail.
Apply Compression	When selected, compresses the backup file, including data. This option can significantly reduce the size of the backup file.
Encrypt Backup File	When selected, encrypts the Analysis Services database backup and requires a password to decrypt during the restore process.
Backup Remote Partition(s)	When selected, the backup file will include remote partitions stored on a separate Analysis Server instances.
Remote Partition Backup Location	File path information for remote partitions located on a separate Analysis Server instances.

3. Clear the Encrypt Backup File check box and click OK to create the backup file.

4. Open Windows Explorer and navigate to the folder C:\Program Files\Microsoft SQL Server\MSAS10.MSSQLSERVER\OLAP\Backup. If a User Account Control dialog box appears, click Continue. This folder should contain the file AdventureWorks SSAS Ch15. abf. This file contains all of the metadata and data required to restore the Analysis Services database.

Restoring a database

1. In Object Explorer in SQL Server Management Studio, right-click the Databases folder and select Restore. Table 15-9 describes the available settings.

TABLE 15-9 Restore Database Options

Setting	Description
Backup File	Location of the Analysis Services .abf file.
Restore Database	Database that the file should be restored to.
Storage Location	Folder where the restored database files should stored. By default, it is set to the default data location for the Analysis Server.

Setting	Description
Allow Database Overwrite	■ **Selected** The existing database will be overwritten when restored. ■ **Cleared** If the database already exists, the restore process will fail, and the existing database will remain in place.
Include Security Information	■ **Selected, Copy All** Copies all security information from the backup file to the restored database. ■ **Selected, Skip Membership** Copies all database roles to the restored database but excludes all of the user or groups within those roles. ■ **Cleared** Does not restore any security information.
Password	If the database was encrypted during the backup process, the password used must be supplied to complete the restore.

2. Click the browse button next to the Backup File text box. The Locate Database Files dialog box will display two folders. The top folder is the default backup location, and the bottom folder is the default log file location.

3. In the Locate Database Files dialog box, expand the top folder, select AdventureWorks SSAS Ch15.abf file, and click OK.

4. In the Restore Database list, enter **AdventureWorks SSAS Ch15 Restore**. This will cause the restore process to create a new database. To restore to an existing database, simply select it from the list.

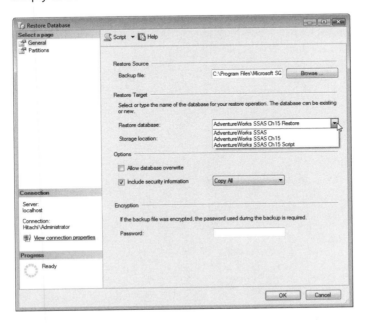

5. Click OK. The restore process will begin. Object Explorer does not refresh automatically, so the restored database will not appear.

6. Right-click the Databases folder and select Refresh. The Adventure Works SSAS Ch15 Restore database will now appear.

7. Close SQL Server Management Studio and close SQL Server Business Intelligence Development Studio.

Backups of Analysis Services databases can be extremely important for reducing recovery times. If you have not created a backup, when a disaster occurs, you will have to deploy the original database design and process the database. This takes significantly longer than restoring an Analysis Services database and also affects the source database.

This chapter covered two distinct topics. The first was deploying new code changes across development, test, and production environments. Analysis Services allows for deployment via BIDS, the Deployment Wizard, and XMLA scripts. The second topic concerned migrating databases across servers as well as disaster recovery. Databases can be migrated using detach and attach processes as well as the new Synchronize functionality. Additionally, Analysis Services provides backup and restore capabilities.

Chapter 16
Advanced Monitoring and Management Tools

In this chapter, you will learn how to:

- Monitor Analysis Services using Windows Reliability And Performance Monitor.

- Monitor Analysis Services using SQL Server Profiler.

- Retrieve Analysis Services metadata and performance information using Dynamic Management Views.

In Chapter 13, "Designing Aggregations," and in Chapter 14, "Managing Partitions and Database Processing," you learned how to take advantage of features that enable you to create large Analysis Services databases that provide fast query response. In Chapter 15, "Managing Deployment," you learned how to deploy design changes to the Analysis Services server, how to back up and restore Analysis Services databases, and how to migrate Analysis Services databases from one server to another. In these three chapters, you have gained the skills you need to design and deploy large, enterprise-scale Analysis Services databases.

The small Analysis Services databases that you create while working through the procedures in this book should have no performance problems. However, when you create large, enterprise-scale databases, you may encounter performance problems caused by poor database design or hardware limitations. When you have performance issues, it is critical to first properly diagnose the problem before you take corrective measures. SQL Server and Microsoft Windows provide tools that you can use to diagnose Analysis Services performance problems.

You have already learned about one of these tools. In Chapter 13, you learned how to use the Usage-Based Optimization Wizard to display information about slow-running queries. In this chapter, you will learn how to monitor Analysis Services performance using Windows Reliability And Performance Monitor, SQL Server Profiler, and Dynamic Management Views. You will monitor partition processing using Performance Monitor, monitor query execution using SQL Server Profiler, and execute queries using Dynamic Management Views to retrieve Analysis Services metadata and memory usage.

Windows Reliability And Performance Monitor, SQL Server Profiler, and Dynamic Management Views are complementary tools that retrieve Analysis Services performance information in different ways. Windows Reliability And Performance Monitor periodically requests performance information from Windows and from Analysis Services. SQL Server

Profiler "listens" for Analysis Services events and records information associated with those events. Dynamic Management Views retrieve metadata and the current state of the Analysis Services server.

Monitoring Analysis Services Using Windows Reliability And Performance Monitor

Windows Reliability And Performance Monitor provides tools to analyze operating system, application, and hardware performance. It consists of three components: Resource View, Reliability Monitor, and Performance Monitor. In this section, you will learn how to use Performance Monitor to analyze Analysis Services performance.

Performance Monitor periodically requests the values of a set of performance counters and displays them using a line chart, a histogram, or a report. You can also use a data collector set to log performance counter values. Performance counters are measures of system state or activity. Performance counters installed with the Windows operating system measure overall system performance such as processor utilization, memory use, and disk performance. When Analysis Services 2008 is installed, an additional collection of performance counters, organized into performance counter groups that start with the prefix MSAS 2008 for the default SQL Server instance or MSOLAP for a named instance, are also installed. These performance counters provide information specific to Analysis Services, such as the number of rows read when a partition is processed or the amount of memory being used to cache aggregations.

Many of the Analysis Services performance counters have two versions. One version will provide a total value since the Analysis Services service has been started. The other version will provide a ratio. For example, the Total Direct Hits counter displays the number of queries that have been answered from data in memory cache since the Analysis Services service was started, whereas the Direct Hit Ratio counter provides the ratio of queries answered from cache to total queries since the last request for performance counter values. In a development or test environment, you can use the performance counters that provide total values, because you can stop and restart the Analysis Services service. In a production environment where you can't stop and restart the Analysis Services service, use the performance counters that provide ratios.

In this section, you will configure Performance Monitor to display Analysis Services performance counters and create a log using a data collector set. You will then process a partition and analyze Analysis Services performance. You will also create a template that can be copied to another computer and used to quickly create a data collector set.

Configure Performance Monitor to display Analysis Services performance counters

In previous chapters, the AdventureWorks SSAS database processed very quickly because all of the dimensions and cubes are very small. The Chapter 16 version of the AdventureWorks

SSAS database contains a cube that selects more than 900,000 fact records from the source database, so that processing will take a little more time. In the following procedure, you will deploy this database and then monitor processing performance using Performance Monitor.

1. Use Business Intelligence Development Studio (BIDS) to open the AdventureWorks BI solution contained in the C: \Microsoft Press\Analysis Services 2008 SBS\Chapter 16 \AdventureWorks BI folder.

2. On the Build menu, select Deploy AdventureWorks SSAS. If the AdventureWorks SSAS database already exists on the server, a dialog box may appear warning that the database will be overwritten. If the warning appears, click Yes. The prior version of the database will be deleted and the current deployment will continue.

3. When the AdventureWorks SSAS database has been successfully deployed, close BIDS.

4. On the Microsoft Windows task bar, click Start. In the Start Search text box, enter **Reliability And Performance Monitor** and then select Reliability And Performance Monitor.

5. In the User Account Control text box, click Continue. Windows Reliability And Performance Monitor initially displays the Resource view, which provides information on CPU, disk, network, and memory resources.

6. In the Reliability And Performance Monitor console tree, select Performance Monitor. Performance Monitor initially displays % Processor Time on a line chart. You will add more performance counters than can be clearly displayed on a line chart, so you will need to change the display to a report.

7. On the Performance Monitor toolbar, select Report from the Graph Type list.

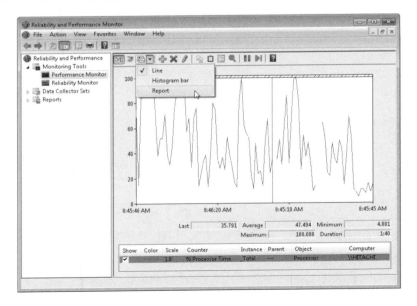

8. On the Performance Monitor toolbar, click Add. In the Add Counters dialog box, you can enter the name of the computer that you want to monitor and select the counters that you want displayed. The Processor group of performance counters is selected by default. You will need to scroll up to find the MSAS 2008 performance counters.

9. In the Add Counter dialog box, in the Available Counters list expand MSAS 2008: Proc Aggregations and select Current Partitions. You can see a brief description of a performance counter by selecting Show Description.

10. In the lower-left corner, select Show Description. The Description text box shows that the Current Partitions performance counter displays the number of partitions that are being processed. Select a few other performance counters and review their descriptions. You can add individual counters to the report or you can select a header and add all of the counters in the group at once.

11. In the Available Counters list, select MSAS 2008: Proc Aggregations and click Add.

12. Repeat step 8 to add the MSAS 2008: Proc Indexes and MSAS 2008: Processing performance counters.

The Add Counters dialog box should look like this:

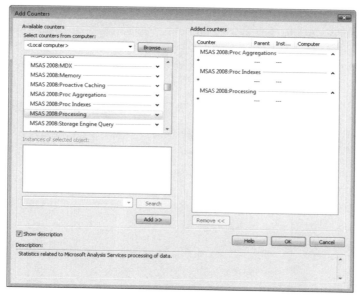

13. Click OK.

Create a Data Collector Set to log Analysis Services performance counters

In this procedure, you will create a data collector set that will log the values of the same set of performance counters that appear in the report you just created.

1. In the console tree, right-click Performance Monitor, point to New, and select Data Collector Set.

2. In the Create New Data Collector Set dialog box, change the Name to **Process SSAS** and click Next.

> **Important** The Reliability And Performance Monitor console tree contains a Reports folder that will display each log file that you create if you accept the default path in the Root Directory text box on the Where Would You Like The Data To Be Saved page. You can change this path, but instead of the log files appearing in the Reports folder, you will have to remember where they are stored and then browse to that location to open the logs in Performance Monitor.

3. On the Where Would You Like The Data To Be Saved page, click Next.

4. On the Create The Data Collector Set page, click Finish.

5. In the console tree, expand Data Collector Sets, expand User Defined, and select Process SSAS.

6. Right-click System Monitor Log and select Properties. In the Properties dialog box, you can add and remove performance counters; change the sample interval; set a maximum number of samples to retrieve; and change the log file format, name, numbering, and whether new log data will overwrite or be appended to existing log files. The Performance Counters list contains the same set of counters that appear in the Performance Monitor report. The value of 1 in the Sample Interval text box means that Performance Monitor will collect counter values every second. If you are monitoring a production environment or a long-running process, you may want to increase the length of the sample interval.

   By default, the log files are saved in a binary format, and the name of the log file is System Monitor Log. In the next steps, you will change the log file to a comma-separated values (CSV) format so that you can view the log using Microsoft Excel, and you will give the log file a more descriptive name.

7. In the System Monitor Log Properties dialog box, on the Performance Counters tab, select Comma Separated from the Log Format list.

8. Click the File tab. Change the Log File Name to **Process SSAS Log**. In the File Name Format text box, type **NNN**. Click OK. Although the name of the Data Collector, System Monitor Log, has not changed, the name of the log file will be Process SSAS Log.

You are now ready to process a partition and monitor Analysis Services using Performance Monitor.

Monitor Analysis Services processing using Performance Monitor

1. In the console tree, select Performance Monitor. The performance counters that provide total values since the Analysis Services service has been started display non-zero values. You will restart the Analysis Services service to reset these counters to zero.

2. Start SQL Server Management Studio. In the Connect To Server dialog box, select Analysis Services from the Server Type list. In the Server Name text box, type **localhost** and click Connect.

3. In Object Explorer, right-click Localhost (Microsoft Analysis Server...) and select Restart.

4. In the User Account Control dialog box, click Continue.

5. In the Microsoft SQL Server Management Studio dialog box, click Yes. A Service Control dialog box will appear and Analysis Services will stop and then start. The dialog box will close without any user input after Analysis Services has successfully restarted.

6. Switch to Reliability And Performance Monitor. Notice that all of the MSAS 2008 performance counters have been reset to zero.

7. In the console tree, right-click the Process SSAS Data Collector Set and select Start. Performance Monitor will create a log file and begin writing performance counter values to the log once every second. A small green arrow is added to the Process SSAS icon indicating that the log is running.

8. Switch to SSMS. In Object Explorer, expand Databases, expand AdventureWorks SSAS, expand Cubes, expand Big, expand Measure Groups, expand Reseller Sales, and expand Partitions.

   In steps 9 and 10, you are going to process the Fact Reseller Sales BIG partition and then watch the performance counters change while the partition is being processed. You should be prepared to quickly switch from SSMS to the Reliability And Performance Monitor. While the partition is processing, you will first see the Processing performance counters change as Analysis Services selects data from the fact table and writes detail data to the partition, and then the Proc Aggregations and Proc Indexes counters will change as Analysis Services creates indexes and aggregations.

9. Right-click the Fact Reseller Sales BIG partition and select Process. In the Process Partition dialog box, click OK.

10. Switch to Reliability And Performance Monitor. You will know when processing is completed because the performance counters will quit changing.

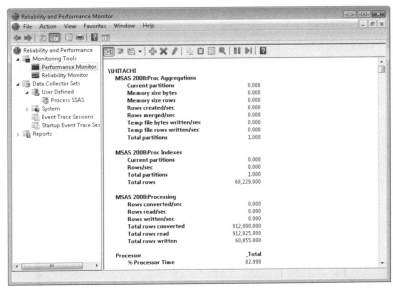

The MSAS 2008:Processing Total Rows Read counter shows that 912,825 fact records were processed into the partition, and the Total Rows Written counter shows that these fact records were consolidated into 60,855 detail level cube records. The MSAS 2008:Proc Indexes Total Rows counter shows that 68,229 index records were created. The MSAS 2008:Proc Aggregations Total Partitions counter shows that aggregations were created for one partition.

You need to turn off Performance Monitor logging so that the log file does not get too large.

11. Right-click Process SSAS and select Stop. The log file is stored in the C:\PerfLogs \Admin\Process SSAS folder. You can open this file and use Microsoft Excel's charting and data analysis features to further analyze Analysis Services processing performance.

An open Process Progress dialog box in SSMS needs to be closed.

12. Switch to SSMS. In the Process Progress dialog box, click Close.

You can use the Process SSAS Data Collector Set to create a template that can be copied to another computer or used to quickly create a data collector set.

Create a Data Collector Set template

1. Switch to the Reliability And Performance Monitor. Right-click Process SSAS and select Save Template.

2. In the Save As dialog box, browse to the C:\Microsoft Press\Analysis Services 2008 SBS\ Chapter 16 folder. In the File Name text box, type **Monitor SSAS Processing** and click Save. To create a new data collector set from the template, you will use the Create New Data Collector Set Wizard.

3. In the console tree, right-click User Defined, point to New, and select Data Collector Set. This launches the Create New Data Collector Set Wizard.

4. On the How Would You Like To Create This New Data Collector Set page, in the Name text box, enter **Process SSAS 2** and click Next.

5. On the Which Template Would You Like To Use page, click Browse. Select Monitor SSAS Processing.xml and click Open. Click Next.

6. On the Where Would You Like The Data To Be Saved page, click Next.

7. On the Create The Data Collector Set page, click Finish. The Process SSAS 2 data collector set appears in the Performance Monitor. You will now verify that the new data collector set contains the same performance counters and file information as the original.

8. In the console tree, select Process SSAS 2.

9. Right-click System Monitor Log and select Properties. View the selected performance counters and file information to verify that it matches the original information you saved in the template. Click OK.

10. Exit the Reliability And Performance Monitor.

In this section, you learned how to configure Performance Monitor to display Analysis Services performance counters and you learned how to create a log of performance counters using a data collector set. The procedures in this section used a limited set of performance counters to monitor Analysis Services partition processing. You can also use Performance Monitor to analyze other Analysis Services activities. There are many performance counters that were not included in the procedures in this section. You should view the description of these counters, add them to the Performance Monitor display, and view the information that they provide. In this section, you also learned how to create a Data Collector Set template. You can copy this template to another computer and use it to quickly create a new Data Collector Set.

In the next section, you will learn how to use SQL Server Profiler to monitor Analysis Services performance.

Monitoring Analysis Services Using SQL Server Profiler

SQL Server Profiler can capture events from Analysis Services to help you monitor and troubleshoot performance. Not only can you spot operations that are running slowly, but you can also view the actual Analysis Services Scripting Language (ASSL), Multidimensional

Expressions (MDX), and Structured Query Language (SQL) statements that are executed. You can view the events as they occur and you can also create a record of the events, called a *trace*, in a SQL Server table or a file for later review or playback.

When you create a SQL Server Profiler trace, you give the trace a name, select an Analysis Services server that you want to monitor, and designate the file or SQL Server table where you want to save the trace. You then select the events that you want to record. For example, you can record Discover events that occur when a client application queries Analysis Services for dimension and cube metadata, record Command events that occur when an Analysis Services database is deployed or processed, or record Query events that occur when a user executes a query. You can learn more details about the events that you can record in the SQL Server Books Online article "Analysis Services Event Classes."

When you use SQL Server Profiler, you should only monitor those events that you are most interested in. Monitoring too many events makes it hard to interpret the results, impacts performance, and causes the trace to become very large. You can also filter events so that you only record events generated by a particular user, client application, or Analysis Services database. After you have created a trace, you can save it as a template so that you can easily execute a trace with the same settings at a later date or on a different server.

In this section, you will create a SQL Server Profiler trace and monitor Analysis Services while you execute a series of MDX queries. You will then create a template from the trace and export the template to a file that can be copied to another computer.

In the following procedure, you will create a new Profiler trace and monitor a few of the query-related events. In the next procedure, you will execute a series of MDX queries and review the information provided in the Profiler trace.

Create a SQL Server Profiler trace to monitor MDX queries

1. On the Microsoft Windows task bar, click Start, point to All Programs, expand the Microsoft SQL Server 2008 folder, expand the Performance Tools folder, and then select SQL Server Profiler. SQL Server Profiler appears with a blank work area. You will need to configure and start a new Profiler trace.

2. On the File menu, select New Trace.

3. In the Connect To Server dialog box, select Analysis Services from the Server Type list. In the Server Name text box, type **localhost** and click Connect.

4. On the General tab in the Trace Properties dialog box, change the Trace Name to **Profile SSAS Queries**.

5. Select Save To File. In the Save As dialog box, browse to the C:\Microsoft Press\Analysis Services 2008 SBS\Chapter 16 folder. In the File Name text box, verify that the file name is Profile SSAS Queries.trc and click Save.

The General tab of the Trace Properties dialog box should look like this:

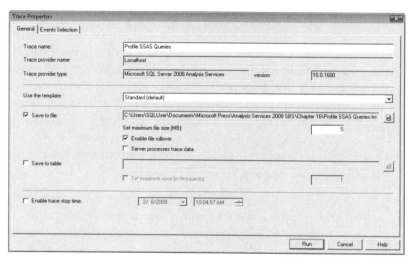

You now need to select the events that will be included in the trace.

6. In the Trace Properties dialog box, click the Events Selection tab. Clear all of the events except the following.

Category	Event
Errors and Warnings	Error
Progress Reports	Progress Report Begin
	Progress Report End
Query Events	Query Begin
	Query End
Query Processing	Query Subcube

By default, the Events Selection tab does not show you all of the events that can be included in a trace. In particular, some of the events that you will want to use to monitor MDX queries are hidden.

7. In the lower-right corner of the Events Selection tab, select Show All Events. Select the following events.

Category	Event
Query Processing	Get Data From Aggregation
	Get Data From Cache
	Query Cube Begin
	Query Cube End
	Query Subcube Verbose

8. Click Run. The Trace Properties dialog box will close, and the new trace window will appear. The top pane of the window will display a line for each event. The bottom pane of the window will display the text data associated with the event.

You will now use SQL Server Management Studio (SSMS) to execute a series of MDX queries and Profiler to view the events that occur when a query is executed.

Monitor queries using SQL Server Profiler

1. Switch to SSMS. On the File menu, point to Open and select File. In the Open File dialog box, browse to the C:\Microsoft Press\Analysis Services 2008 SBS\Chapter 16\MDX folder, select Query.mdx, and click Open.

2. Select the entire text of Query 1, and on the SSMS toolbar, click Execute. This query requests Internet Order Quantity By Month. Because this is the first time a query has been executed since the cube was processed, the results have to be retrieved from disk, not from memory cache. Also, the cube has no aggregations containing the members of the Month attribute, so the query will have to retrieve detail level data and summarize to the month level when the query is executed.

3. Switch to SQL Server Profiler. SQL Server Profiler displays the events that occurred during the execution of Query 1.

4. Select the row with Query Subcube in the EventClass column and 2 – Non-cache data in the EventSubclass column. The non-cache data event subclass indicates that Analysis Services had to retrieve data from disk. The text data associated with the event is a series of zeros and ones that indicate the level of each attribute hierarchy that was requested by the query. This is the same notation used to populate the Dataset column of the query log table that you learned about in Chapter 13.

5. Select the row with Query Subcube Verbose in the EventClass column and 22 – Non-cached data in the EventSubclass column.

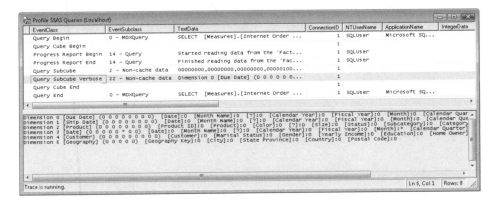

The text data associated with this event displays the level of each attribute hierarchy that was requested by the query in a more readable format. It first lists the name of a dimension and then a list of the attribute hierarchies in the dimension. In some instances, the name of an attribute hierarchy is replaced by a question mark. This indicates that the value of the attribute's *AttributeHierarchyEnabled* property is *False*. In the TextData column for this event, each attribute hierarchy can be followed by a member name, a zero, a plus sign (+), or an asterisk (*). The following table explains the meaning of the data associated with each attribute.

Member name	The query requested a single member from the leaf level of the hierarchy.
0	The query requested the All member for the hierarchy.
+	The query requested multiple members from the leaf level of the hierarchy.
*	The query requested all leaf level members of the hierarchy.

6. Select the row with Query End in the EventClass column and 0 – MDXQuery in the Event Subclass column. This event is particularly useful if you are using a cube browser or other application that does not display the MDX queries that it submits to Analysis Services. The text data associated with this row shows the MDX query that was executed. If you want, you can copy this query, paste it into a SSMS MDX query window, and execute it. The row also displays the duration (in milliseconds) that it took to execute the query. You do not have to clear the trace window between executing queries, but it does make it easier to identify the events associated with each query.

7. On the toolbar, click Clear Trace Window.

8. Switch to SSMS. Select the entire text of Query 2, and on the SSMS toolbar, click Execute. This query requests Internet Order Quantity by Calendar Quarter. Because the cube has several aggregations containing the Calendar Quarter attribute, Analysis Services should access one of these aggregates and not need to summarize detail data when it responds to the query.

9. Switch to SQL Server Profiler. Select the row with Get Data From Aggregation in the EventClass column. Drag the divider between the TextData and ConnectionID column headers to the right until the column is wide enough to display all of the data in the TextData column for this row.

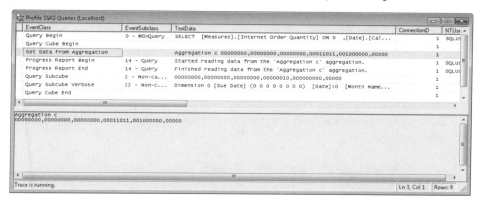

The Get Data From Aggregation event class indicates that Analysis Services was able to retrieve data from an aggregation when it responded to the query. The TextData column contains several ones, indicating that the aggregation used to respond to the query includes several attributes, not just the Calendar Quarter attribute.

10. Select the row with Query Subcube in the EventClass column and 2 – Non-cache data in the EventSubclass column. The 2 – Non-cache event subclass indicates that Analysis Services had to retrieve the aggregation data from disk. The TextData column contains a single one. The query requested the All member from every attribute hierarchy except for the Calendar Quarter hierarchy. When you compare the value in the TextData column in this row to the value of the same column in the Get Data From Aggregation row, you can see that the aggregation Analysis Services used to respond to the query contains more detail than the query results. The aggregation contains summary values for the leaf level members of some of the attribute hierarchies other than Calendar Quarter, but only the All level was required to satisfy the query. Analysis Services was able to summarize these aggregated values to obtain the All member more efficiently than it could have without the aggregation. Knowing which aggregation was used to satisfy the query can provide valuable information, because this tells you how Analysis Services is using the aggregations that are stored on disk. If an aggregation is rarely used but takes up a lot of disk space, you can consider removing that aggregation from your database.

11. On the toolbar, click Clear Trace Window.

12. Switch to SSMS. Select the entire text of Query 3, and on the SSMS toolbar, click Execute. This query requests Internet Order Quantity by Calendar Quarter for CY 2009. Because you have already executed a query that requested all calendar quarters, Analysis Services should be able to use data from memory cache to respond to this query.

13. Switch to SQL Server Profiler. The row with Get Data From Cache in the EventClass column indicates that Analysis Services was able to use data from memory cache to respond to the query.

14. On the toolbar, click Stop Selected Trace. On the File menu, select Close.

You can use SQL Server Profiler to open and view the trace that you saved to a file. You can also create a template from the trace and export the template so that you can copy it to other computers.

Create and export a SQL Server Profiler template

1. In SQL Server Profiler, on the File menu, point to Open and select Trace File. In the Open File dialog box, browse to the C:\Microsoft Press\Analysis Services 2008 SBS\ Chapter 16 folder, select Profile SSAS Queries.trc, and click Open. The trace file contains all of the events that you recorded in the previous procedure.

2. On the File Menu, point to Save As and select Trace Template. In the Select Template Name dialog box, type **SSAS Queries**. Click OK. In the SQL Server Profiler dialog box, click OK.

3. On the File menu, point to Templates and select Export Template. In the Select Template Name dialog box, select SSAS Queries (user) from the Template Name list.

4. Click OK. In the Save As dialog box, browse to the C:\Microsoft Press\Analysis Services 2008 SBS\Chapter 16 folder. In the File Name text box, type **SSAS Queries** and click Save. In the SQL Server Profiler dialog box, click OK. The Profiler trace template is now stored as the file SSAS Queries.tdf in the Chapter 16 folder.

5. On the File menu, select Exit.

In this section, you have learned to use SQL Server Profiler to monitor Analysis Services MDX queries. The procedures in the section used a limited set of events to make it easier to interpret the results. You can also use Profiler to monitor other activities such as database deployment, dimension and cube processing, and metadata requests. Several event classes and events were not included in the procedures in this section. You should create a Profile trace that includes these events and view the information that they provide.

In this section, you also learned how to create a Profiler trace template and how to export the template to a file. You can import a trace template into Profiler on another computer using the Import Template command found within Templates on the Profiler File menu.

In the next section, you will learn how to retrieve information from Analysis Services using Dynamic Management Views.

Analysis Services Dynamic Management Views

Dynamic Management Views (DMV) allow you to retrieve Analysis Services server state and metadata using the Transact SQL language. These views expose information that in prior versions of Analysis Services was only available using XML for Analysis Services. The new capability to query Dynamic Management Views using SQL means that you can document Analysis Services design, resource utilization, and performance using a reporting tool like SQL Server Reporting Services.

In this section, you will learn to query DMVs using SQL Server Management Studio. You connect to Analysis Services and then open an MDX Query window. In the MDX query window, you execute a Transact SQL statement that selects columns from one of the DMVs. The DMVs are exposed in the $SYSTEM schema. So, for example, if you wanted to retrieve information about all of the dimensions that exist in an instance of Analysis Services, you would execute the following SQL query:

```
SELECT * FROM $SYSTEM.MDSCHEMA_DIMENSIONS
```

The most important DMV is the DISCOVER_SCHEMA_ROWSETS view. This DMV lists all of the other DMVs and the columns that you can use to filter the rows returned by the DMVs. You can then search for a particular DMV in SQL Server Books Online to get a description of the columns returned by the DMV. Some of the DMVs require that you filter by one or multiple columns. Unfortunately, the required restrictions are not documented, so you must use a trial-and-error method to discover which column restrictions are required and which are optional.

In the following procedure, you will select the list of all DMVs from the DISCOVER_ SCHEMA_ROWSETS view. You will then retrieve dimension metadata from the MDSCHEMA_ DIMENSIONS and MDSCHEMA_HIERARCHIES views and learn how to restrict the rows from a DMV using the DISCOVER_DIMENSION_STAT view. Finally, you will retrieve Analysis Services resource utilization information from the DISCOVER_OBJECT_MEMORY_USAGE view.

Explore Dynamic Management Views

1. Switch to SSMS. On the File menu, point to Open and select File. In the Open File dialog box, browse to the \Microsoft Press\Analysis Services 2008 SBS\Chapter 16\MDX folder, select DMV.mdx, and click Open. The key to understanding Analysis Services DMVs is the DISCOVER_SCHEMA_ROWSETS view. This view contains a list of all of the other DMVs and the restriction columns that you can use as filters to limit the number of rows returned by the view.

2. In the DMV.mdx query window, select the Key To The Universe query. On the SSMS toolbar, click Execute.

3. In the Results pane, expand the width of the SchemaName column. In the DBSCHEMA_
COLUMNS row, click the plus sign (+) in the Restrictions column. The list of DMVs
should look like this:

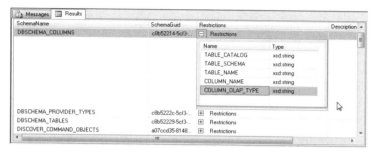

You can see that there are five columns that you can use to restrict the rows returned
by the DBSCHEMA_COLUMNS view.

4. In the DMV.mdx query window, select the All Date Dimensions query, and on the SSMS
toolbar, click Execute. This query shows that you can use a *WHERE* clause to filter rows
and an *ORDER BY* clause to sort rows. Unfortunately, you can include only one column
in the *ORDER BY* clause.

The DIMENSION_NAME column contains the name of a cube dimension and the
DIMENSION_MASTER_NAME column contains the name of the corresponding database
dimension. The All Date Dimensions query returns all of the cube dimensions created
using the Date database dimension. For example, you can see that the AdventureWorks
cube contains Date, Due Date, and Ship Date role-playing cube dimensions created using the Date dimension.

5. In the DMV.mdx query window, select the Date Dimension Hierarchies query, and on
the SSMS toolbar, click Execute. The Date Dimension Hierarchies query returns a list of
all of the attribute and user-defined hierarchies in the Date database dimension. Notice
that when the value in the CUBE_NAME column is preceded by a dollar symbol ($), the
row is referring to a database dimension.

> **Tip** You may need to enclose a column name in square brackets. For example, in the Date
> Dimension Hierarchies query *WHERE* clause, the DIMENSION_UNIQUE_NAME column
> name must be enclosed in square brackets. This is because DIMENSION_UNIQUE_NAME is
> the name of an intrinsic member property in MDX and must be enclosed in brackets when
> used in the DMV query.

In addition to specifying column values in the *WHERE* clause, you can also use restrictions to filter the data that is returned by the DMV. Restrictions use a different syntax
than the *WHERE* clause and can either be optional or required. If a required restriction
is not specified in the query, an error message will be returned. The next three steps

give an example of using the trial-and-error method to discover how to query a DMV that has required restrictions.

6. In the DMV.mdx query window, select the Date Dimension Stats #1 query, and on the SSMS toolbar, click Execute. The results window displays the error "The 'DIMENSION_NAME' restriction is required but is missing from the request. Consider using SYSTEMRISTRICTSCHEMA to provide restrictions." This error message indicates that you must select from the *SYSTEMRESTRICTSCHEMA* function. Instead of using the DISCOVER_DIMENSION_STAT DMV in the *FROM* clause of your query, you will instead call the *SYSTEMRESTRICTSCHEMA* function and include the DMV name DISCOVER_DIMENSION_STAT as the first parameter and a DIMENSION_NAME column filter as the second parameter.

7. In the DMV.mdx query window, select the Date Dimension Stats #2 query, and on the SSMS toolbar, click Execute. The results window displays the error "The 'DATABASE_NAME' restriction is required but is missing from the request..." The DISCOVER_DIMENSION_STAT view must also be restricted by a filter on the DATABASE_NAME column.

8. In the DMV.mdx query window, select the Date Dimension Stats #3 query, and on the SSMS toolbar, click Execute. The query executes successfully, indicating that the DISCOVER_DIMENSION_STAT view has two required restrictions. The view displays the names of all the non-key attributes and lists the number of members in each attribute.

   The queries you have executed in steps 1 through 8 all return metadata. In the next step, you will execute a query that displays the amount of memory consumed by hierarchies in the Date dimension.

9. In the DMV.mdx query window, select the Date Dimension Memory Usage query, and on the SSMS toolbar, click Execute.

   In this procedure, you have selected data from just of few of the available Analysis Services DMVs. You should take a moment to review the information provided by some of the other views. First execute the Key To The Universe query, review the list of DMVs returned by the query, and then write and execute a few SQL *SELECT* statements to retrieve data from some of the other DMVs.

10. Exit SSMS.

In this chapter, you learned to monitor Analysis Services performance using Windows Reliability And Performance Monitor and SQL Server Profiler. You also learned to retrieve Analysis Services metadata and status using Dynamic Management Views. This chapter has only presented an introduction to performance monitoring; a thorough discussion of the subject would fill an entire book. You should take some time to further familiarize yourself with the tools and experiment with all of the events, performance counters, and DMVs that these tools make available to you.

Index

actions tab of, 234
aggregation design and, 317
Analysis Services project created in, 38–39
attribute relationship setting and, 350
Count aggregate function and, 142
cubes and, 102–104, 113
currency conversion and, 218
database administrative access and, 298
dimensional storage settings and, 343
dimensions added to cubes in, 179
for deployment, 372–374
language translations and, 227
partitions and, 362, 368
performance counters and, 387
perspectives and, 258
proactive caching and, 357
SQL Server Database Engine, 34
SQL Server Management Studio (SSMS), 36, 52
    See also Object Explorer
    Analysis Services project deployment and, 374
    backing up databases and, 382
    data source insertion and, 348, 360
    database migration and, 380
    dimension updating and, 351
    MDX Query Editor in, 262
    MDX query execution by, 395
    MDX statements executed by, 254–256
    partition incremental processing and, 354
    partition merging and, 367, 368
    Performance Monitor and, 390
    Query Editor of, 335
    query logging and, 332
    restoring databases and, 382
    ROLAP and MOLAP cube browsing with, 346
    server role membership and, 295–297
    SQL Server Profiler and, 396, 397
SQL Server Profiler, 392–398
    queries monitored by, 395–398
    template for, 398
    trace creation in, 393–395
standard actions, in cubes, 234–237
standard dimensions
    deployed to Analysis Services, 65–68
    deploying and browsing, 76–77
    Design Warnings in
        dismissing, 77–78
        rules of, 78–79
        viewing, 71–72
    Dimension Wizard to create, 62–65

hiding attribute hierarchies of, 74
NameColumn property in, 69–71
time dimensions as, 91
user-defined hierarchies in, 72–74
star schema, 19–20
Status value, for KPIs, 171
storage
    dimension modes for, 343–344
    partition modes for, 344–347
    retrieval layer and, 2, 21, 34
    warehouse for, 347–348
subcubes, 115, 170
subject area diagrams, 47–49
Sum aggregate function, 141, 142, 146, 208
summary values, aggregate values versus, 17, 29
surrogate keys, 17–18
surveys, analysis of, 3
switches, deployment, 377
synchronizing databases, 381
System Monitor log, 389
SYSTEMRESTRICTIONSSCHEMA, 401

T

tables. See also cubes; See also fact tables
    alternative structures for, 18–21
    data source view and, 42
    dimension, 15–17, 62–63
    in currency conversion, 218–219
    OlapQueryLog, 334, 335
    pivot, 2, 58, 169, 267–271, 274–275, 279
    redundant values in, 19
    Tables list of, 50
    time dimension created from, 80, 81
    viewer for, 60–61
    writeback, 376
target currency, 216 See also currency conversion
target, action, 234, 238, 247
Templates pane, 284
Teradata, 39
textual attributes, 186
THEN expression, 172
time dimensions, 79–91
    attribute relationships modified in, 86–87
    Calendar Date user-defined hierarchy in, 85
    chronological sorting and, 88–90
    creating, 80–83
    deploying and browsing, 87–88, 90–91

For C# Developers

Microsoft® Visual C#® 2008 Express Edition: Build a Program Now!
Patrice Pelland
ISBN 9780735625426

Build your own Web browser or other cool application—no programming experience required! Featuring learn-by-doing projects and plenty of examples, this full-color guide is your quick start to creating your first applications for Windows®. DVD includes Express Edition software plus code samples.

Microsoft Visual C# 2008 Step by Step
John Sharp
ISBN 9780735624306

Teach yourself Visual C# 2008—one step at a time. Ideal for developers with fundamental programming skills, this practical tutorial delivers hands-on guidance for creating C# components and Windows–based applications. CD features practice exercises, code samples, and a fully searchable eBook.

Learn Programming Now! Microsoft XNA® Game Studio 2.0
Rob Miles
ISBN 9780735625228

Now you can create your own games for Xbox 360® and Windows—as you learn the underlying skills and concepts for computer programming. Dive right into your first project, adding new tools and tricks to your arsenal as you go. Master the fundamentals of XNA Game Studio and Visual C#—no experience required!

Programming Microsoft Visual C# 2008: The Language
Donis Marshall
ISBN 9780735625402

Get the in-depth reference, best practices, and code you need to master the core language capabilities in Visual C# 2008. Fully updated for Microsoft .NET Framework 3.5, including a detailed exploration of LINQ, this book examines language features in detail—and across the product life cycle.

Windows via C/C++,
Fifth Edition
Jeffrey Richter, Christophe Nasarre
ISBN 9780735624245

Jeffrey Richter's classic guide to C++ programming—now fully revised for Windows XP, Windows Vista®, and Windows Server® 2008. Learn to develop more-robust applications with unmanaged C++ code—and apply advanced techniques—with comprehensive guidance and code samples from the experts.

CLR via C#,
Second Edition
Jeffrey Richter
ISBN 9780735621633

Dig deep and master the intricacies of the common language runtime (CLR) and the .NET Framework. Written by programming expert Jeffrey Richter, this guide is ideal for developers building any kind of application—ASP.NET, Windows Forms, Microsoft SQL Server®, Web services, console apps—and features extensive C# code samples.

ALSO SEE

Microsoft Visual C# 2005 Step by Step
ISBN 9780735621299

Programming Microsoft Visual C# 2005: The Language
ISBN 9780735621817

Debugging Microsoft .NET 2.0 Applications
ISBN 9780735622029

For Visual Basic Developers

Microsoft® Visual Basic® 2008 Express Edition: Build a Program Now!

Patrice Pelland

ISBN 9780735625419

Build your own Web browser or other cool application—no programming experience required! Featuring learn-by-doing projects and plenty of examples, this full-color guide is your quick start to creating your first applications for Windows®. DVD includes Express Edition software plus code samples.

Microsoft Visual Basic 2008 Step by Step

Michael Halvorson

ISBN 9780735625372

Teach yourself the essential tools and techniques for Visual Basic 2008—one step at a time. No matter what your skill level, you'll find the practical guidance and examples you need to start building applications for Windows and the Web. CD features practice exercises, code samples, and a fully searchable eBook.

Programming Microsoft Visual Basic 2005: The Language

Francesco Balena

ISBN 9780735621831

Master the core capabilities in Visual Basic 2005 with guidance from well-known programming expert Francesco Balena. Focusing on language features and the Microsoft .NET Framework 2.0 base class library, this book provides pragmatic instruction and examples useful to both new and experienced developers.

Programming Windows Services with Microsoft Visual Basic 2008

Michael Gernaey

ISBN 9780735624337

The essential guide for developing powerful, customized Windows services with Visual Basic 2008. Whether you're looking to perform network monitoring or design a complex enterprise solution, this guide delivers the right combination of expert advice and practical examples to accelerate your productivity.

ALSO SEE

Microsoft Visual Basic 2005 Express Edition: Build a Program Now!

Patrice Pelland
ISBN 9780735622135

Microsoft Visual Basic 2005 Step by Step

Michael Halvorson
ISBN 9780735621312

Microsoft ADO.NET 2.0 Step by Step

Rebecca Riordan
ISBN 9780735621640

Microsoft ASP.NET 3.5 Step by Step

George Shepherd
ISBN 9780735624269

Programming Microsoft ASP.NET 3.5

Dino Esposito
ISBN 9780735625273

Debugging Microsoft .NET 2.0 Applications

John Robbins
ISBN 9780735622029

Microsoft® *Press*

microsoft.com/mspress

Resources for SQL Server 2008

Microsoft® SQL Server® 2008 Administrator's Pocket Consultant
William R. Stanek
ISBN 9780735625891

Programming Microsoft SQL Server 2008
Leonard Lobel, Andrew J. Brust, Stephen Forte
ISBN 9780735625990

Microsoft SQL Server 2008 Step by Step
Mike Hotek
ISBN 9780735626041

Microsoft SQL Server 2008 T-SQL Fundamentals
Itzik Ben-Gan
ISBN 9780735626010

MCTS Self-Paced Training Kit (Exam 70-432) Microsoft SQL Server 2008 Implementation and Maintenance
Mike Hotek
ISBN 9780735626058

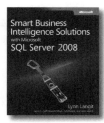

Smart Business Intelligence Solutions with Microsoft SQL Server 2008
Lynn Langit, Kevin S. Goff, Davide Mauri, Sahil Malik, and John Welch
ISBN 9780735625808

COMING SOON

Microsoft SQL Server 2008 Internals
Kalen Delaney *et al.*
ISBN 9780735626249

Inside Microsoft SQL Server 2008: T-SQL Querying
Itzik Ben-Gan, Lubor Kollar, Dejan Sarka
ISBN 9780735626034

Microsoft SQL Server 2008 Best Practices
Saleem Hakani and Ward Pond
with the Microsoft SQL Server Team
ISBN 9780735626225

Microsoft SQL Server 2008 MDX Step by Step
Bryan C. Smith, C. Ryan Clay, Hitachi Consulting
ISBN 9780735626188

Microsoft SQL Server 2008 Reporting Services Step by Step
Stacia Misner
ISBN 9780735626478

Microsoft SQL Server 2008 Analysis Services Step by Step
Scott Cameron, Hitachi Consulting
ISBN 9780735626201

microsoft.com/mspress

About the Author

Scott Cameron is a Senior Manager of Specialized Services with Hitachi Consulting's Business Intelligence practice. Scott has been developing BI solutions for 12 years and has been performing data analysis for more than 20 years. Scott's experience includes implementing Microsoft Analysis Services at large corporations, working with independent software vendors to integrate Analysis Services into their products, and teaching Microsoft SQL Server BI courses in the United States and Europe. He has worked in the healthcare, software, retail, insurance, legal, vocational rehabilitation, travel, and mining industries. Scott has a B.A. in Economics and Asian Studies from Brigham Young University; his M.A. in Economics is from the University of Washington. He is a coauthor of *Microsoft SQL Server 2005 Integration Services Step by Step* and a contributing author of *Microsoft SQL Server 2005 Analysis Services Step by Step*. Scott lives in the Seattle area with his wife, Tarya, and beagles, Hunter and Si.

Contributing Authors

Dave DuVarney is a Senior Manager for Hitachi Consulting's national Microsoft practice. He has broad technical knowledge stemming from his experiences as a software developer, a certified public accountant, and a technology trainer. Dave has been involved in multiple software development projects ranging from contract management systems to human rights auditing. He is proficient in numerous development languages as well as Microsoft Business Intelligence technologies. Most recently he has been consulting and delivering on SQL Server 2008 Analysis Services, Reporting Services and Integration Services. Dave is the coauthor of *Professional SQL Server Reporting Services 2000* and *Professional SQL Server Reporting Services 2005*.

Joe Kasprzak is a Senior Manager at Hitachi Consulting with over 17 years of comprehensive business and technical experience providing business intelligence consulting services for clients worldwide. Joe has worked with business and government organizations providing consulting services for the design and development of full life cycle implementations of strategic Business Intelligence and Performance Management (BIPM) analytical solutions. With experience from over 50 projects, Joe has specialized to provide clients with Microsoft Business Intelligence technology expertise and mentoring. His BIPM projects include Retail Marketing Analytics, Labor Analytics, Corporate Performance Management and Reporting, and multidimensional Financial Analytics. Joe has provided formal SQL Server mentoring sessions (both public and private), and is a contributing author and coauthor of other Microsoft Press Step-by-Step technical instruction books and educational courseware, including *Microsoft SQL Server 2005 Analysis Services Step-by-Step*, *Microsoft SQL Server 2005 Reporting Services Step-by-Step*, and *Microsoft SQL Server 2005 Integration Services Step-by-Step*.

Bryan C. Smith is a Senior Manager of Specialized Services with Hitachi Consulting's Microsoft Database Technologies team. As a member of this team, he designs and implements BI solutions for clients in a variety of industries using the products in the SQL Server suite. Bryan has degrees from Texas A&M and Duke Universities, holds a number of Microsoft certifications, and has more than 10 years of experience developing solutions supporting data analysis. Bryan lives in the Dallas area with his wife, Haruka, and their two children, Aki and Umi.